THE HISPANIC WORLD

THE HISPANIC WORLD

CIVILIZATION AND EMPIRE
EUROPE AND THE AMERICAS
PAST AND PRESENT

EDITED BY
J.H. ELLIOTT
TEXTS BY
ANGUS MACKAY
J.H. ELLIOTT
PETER BAKEWELL
J. JORGE KLOR DE ALVA
JUAN PABLO FUSI AIZPURUA
W.J. CALLAHAN
JONATHAN BROWN
JAMES CASEY
B.W. IFE
J.W. BUTT
AND OTHERS

320 illustrations
100 in colour

THAMES AND HUDSON

Page 1: Torero from Picasso's *Toros y Toreros*, 1961
Page 3: St James of Compostela, from a screen in Burgos Cathedral

Editor and publisher wish to acknowledge the generous advice
given by all the authors on the selection of the illustrations
and the wording of the captions; it must be made clear,
however, that final responsibility for the picture sections
remains entirely with the publisher.

Translations from the Spanish by Alan Berson,
Marigold Best and Nigel Gallop.

Maps by Hanni Bailey

Picture research by Georgina Bruckner

Printed in Singapore

CONTENTS

2 THE SPANISH CHARACTER AND HERITAGE

3 CREATIVE DIVERSITY

Man as master of the world:
a detail from Velázquez's
painting *Democritus* (or 'The
Geographer'), 1628.

INTRODUCTION

J.H. ELLIOTT

SPAIN, THE MYTH AND THE REALITY

The first copies of a new French encyclopaedia reached Madrid in 1783. Royal officials, and then the king himself, turned to the entry on Spain, written by Nicolas Masson de Morvilliers, and were outraged by what they read. 'What', asked Masson, 'do we owe to Spain? What has it done for Europe in the last two centuries, in the last four, or ten?' The Spanish ambassador in Paris demanded, and eventually received, an official apology, but the damage was done. In asking his scandalous question, Masson was voicing the assumptions and the prejudices of a Europe that had turned its back on Spain – on the very country that, little more than a century earlier, had not only been the dominant military and political power on the continent, but had also exercised a profound influence on European civilization and manners.

For Masson, as for many Europeans of his generation, Spain's image was that of a backward country, destroyed by bad government, fanaticism, and sloth. This image, which was primarily inspired by Spain's vicissitudes in the seventeenth century and was nurtured by persistent religious hostility, proved to be remarkably long-lasting. An Englishman still alive today remembers his mother telling him how in her childhood her governess, running through the characteristics of different peoples, had the following to say about the Spaniards: 'The Spaniards are a proud and haughty nation possessing exaggerated notions of honour. They are, however, indolent and revengeful. Their religion is the Roman Catholic and none other is tolerated.' This unflattering image penetrated deeply into Anglo-American folk consciousness, and in many ways still informs popular attitudes to the Hispanic world. Moreover, at quite a different level, Masson's question of two centuries ago still lingers in the air, to judge from the exclusion of Spain from Kenneth Clark's enormously influential survey, *Civilisation*, first published in 1969. 'If I had been talking about the history of art', he writes, 'it would not have been possible to leave out Spain; but when one asks what Spain has done to enlarge the human mind and pull mankind a few steps up the hill, the answer is less clear.'

While images persist, however, countries themselves change, and there is little resemblance now between the dynamic and democratic Spain currently celebrating the fifth centenary of its discovery of America, and the backward and ignorant Spain denounced by Masson. The past, however, cannot be summarily abolished. It intrudes at many points, not only in the images of Spain current in the non-Hispanic world, but also in those still prevalent in Spain itself. For the response of Spaniards to their long period of relegation to the sidelines of history following their great imperial age of the sixteenth and seventeenth centuries has often been to picture their national history in terms of national failure. While it is true that the history of Spain is marked, perhaps more than that of many countries, by dark and painful episodes, it also contains many moments of brilliance, which tend too easily to be overlooked or forgotten. The present volume, while not passing over the darker passages of the Spanish past, aims to recover for a Hispanic and non-Hispanic public alike something of that brilliance.

The quincentennial of Spain's first encounter with an America which it did so much to destroy and then to build anew is a particularly appropriate moment to attempt a reassessment of the Spanish past and of the Spanish contribution to the modern world. There are over 320 million Spanish speakers in the world today. Spanish values and traditions – in religious and family life, in political and social organization – have made a deep and lasting imprint on large portions of the globe. In the visual arts, in literature, in ways of perceiving and thinking about the world, the Spanish heritage explored in this book has been distinctive, influential, and often controversial.

The very fact that it has been, and still is, contested, not least by those who are themselves of Hispanic origin, suggests that it is a heritage that remains very much alive. It also suggests why it needs to be discussed and analysed, rather than embalmed. We still need to explore why Spanish civilization evolved as it did, why certain possibilities were developed, while others were ignored. We need, too, to understand better those springs of creativity which periodically seem to well up in Spanish life after long periods of relative quiescence.

These are important questions which this book can only touch upon; but if it is too soon to provide firm answers, at least it can suggest a few clues. In particular, it seeks to get away from an interpretation of the Spanish past and Spanish civilization which identifies them almost exclusively with Castile, the central, and for so long the dominant, region of the Iberian peninsula. Spain, as this book seeks to show, is a land of enormous regional diversity – a diversity officially, and belatedly, recognized in the 1978 constitution of the new, united and democratic Spain, with its acceptance of 'the right to autonomy of the nationalities and regions' of which it is composed.

The tension between unity and diversity has in fact been a constant in the history of Spanish society and Spanish civilization. Often seen as destructive, it has also been creative. It is the interplay of Castilians and Andalusians, of Basques and Catalans, of Galicians, Aragonese, and the inhabitants of the other regions and 'autonomies', that has made Spain what it is. These nationalities and regions, having recently acquired their autonomous status, are now busily rediscovering their distinctive pasts. Something of this rediscovery is reflected in the collective chapter of this book on 'creative diversity', which seeks to indicate their distinctive characteristics and their contribution to the life of Spain as a whole.

The Hispanic world, then, which this book aims to illuminate and explore, is a world which – however monolithic it may seem to outsiders – is rooted in diversity. That diversity, often denied in the structure of the Spanish state, has in reality been a source of enormous cultural enrichment. A pluralist society has possibilities of self-renewal absent from monolithic structures, and contemporary Spain has shown a capacity for self-renewal which has seized the imagination of the world. The Habsburg monarchs styled themselves kings, not of Spain, but of 'the Spains'. The pages that follow trace the vicissitudes, the failures, and the achievements, of 'the Spains' – of a Hispanic world at once various, and one.

Is there a Spanish face? To the non-Spaniard it irresistibly seems so, yet what is particularly Spanish in these examples is more a matter of expression than of physiognomy, a quality of dark, brooding inner life.

Top row: an unknown man by El Greco, late sixteenth century; a *torero*, Valencia, 1950s; S. Juan de Dios by Alonso Cano, seventeenth century; Picasso's Harlequin, 1923.

Lower row: the actress Antonia Zárate by Goya, about 1805; and Picasso's Mother and Child, from his series of acrobats' families, 1905.

FRANCE

Finisterre

Gijón
Santander Guernica San Sebastián
Oviedo Cañgas de Onís
ASTURIAS Covadonga CANTABRIA Bilbao
Santiago BASQUE PROVS. PYRENEES ANDORRA
de Compostela Pajares PROVS.
NAVARRE
León Vitoria Pamplona
GALICIA Estella
Astorga Burgos LA RIOJA Olite Sangüesa Gerona
CASTILE AND LEÓN Calahorra
Ebro Tudela Huesca CATALONIA
Medina de Rioseco Soria Tarazona
Zamora Valladolid Saragossa
Duero ARAGON Barcelona
Medina del Campo Calatayud Tarragona
Coca
Salamanca Segovia
Avila Guadalajara MENORCA
El Escorial Alcala de Teruel MALLORCA
Madrid Henares
Yuste Toledo VALENCIA IBIZA BALEARIC ISLANDS
Tagus Aranjuez
Trujillo Belmonte Valencia
Cáceres Guadalupe CASTILE AND
EXTREMADURA LA MANCHA Alcoy
Badajoz Ciudad Real Alicante

ATLANTIC OCEAN

PORTUGAL

Fuenteovejuna MURCIA
Ubeda
Cordoba Jaén
Guadalquivir
Seville ANDALUSIA
Palos Granada
Sanlúcar
Jerez de la MEDITERRANEAN SEA
Cadiz Frontera Malaga

Algeciras

0   100 Mls
0   160 Km

1 A NATION OF NATIONALITIES

The cloister of Gerona Cathedral, north of Barcelona, is still powerfully evocative of twelfth-century Spain. Its carved capitals combine biblical scenes with motifs that must be derived from Muslim sources. Gerona figured early in the Reconquista – the campaign to free the peninsula from Islam. It was taken by Charlemagne in 785 but recaptured by the Moors and not secured permanently for Christendom until 1015.

A PLURALIST SOCIETY: MEDIEVAL SPAIN

ANGUS MACKAY

What people believe, even if their beliefs take the form of myths and legends, often becomes of greater importance than objective fact. This was particularly true of medieval Spaniards, and so this chapter begins by considering how a well-informed fifteenth-century Spaniard would have viewed the momentous events of the preceding seven centuries in Spain, in short the Middle Ages.

Lost paradise

What had happened would have seemed to him fairly obvious. In 711 the Muslims invaded the Iberian peninsula and brought about 'the destruction of Spain'. The fundamental reason for their success was that the Christian Visigothic kings were plunged in sin, and this corruption had spread to the rest of society so that the Christians were in no position to cope with the invaders. King Witiza (698–710) began his reign well, but subsequently he gave himself up to lechery to such an extent that his example contaminated the great nobles and, eventually, the humbler members of society. He even compelled the clergy to take wives. In addition he put out the eyes of the son of a previous king, exiled a noble named Pelayo, and forcibly installed his brother Oppa as archbishop of Toledo while the previous incumbent was still alive. Thus 'just as he polluted himself in carnal adultery, so he polluted his brother in spiritual adultery'. Witiza was succeeded by the last of the Visigothic kings, Roderic, who ravished the beautiful daughter of the powerful Count Julian, governor of Ceuta. In revenge Count Julian helped the Muslims to invade Spain, and at the battle of the Guadalete river King Roderic and his army were defeated.

The destruction of Spain, therefore, was a divine punishment for the sins committed by the Christians. Indeed later Spaniards would write about these events almost as if they constituted another 'Fall' in the Garden of Eden. Immediately after narrating the Christian defeat at the Guadalete river, for example, King Alfonso X of Castile (1252–84) in his *Primera crónica general* describes the Spain that had been lost as an earthly paradise, a land flowing with milk and honey, a country which God endowed, above all others, with everything that man could want. In presenting Spain as a kind of Garden of Eden, King Alfonso was here following a tradition of writing such 'praises' or *laudes* which stretched back at least as far as St Isidore of Seville (d. 636). 'Oh Spain! There is no tongue or wit that can describe your goodness.' But all this had been lost, and immediately after his 'praise' of Spain, King Alfonso launched into the other traditional theme associated with these events, namely the 'lament' or 'grief' over the loss and destruction that had taken place.

Nevertheless, all had not been lost. Sent into exile, Pelayo had taken refuge in the Asturian mountains, and it was there that he rallied his forces and defeated a Muslim army at Covadonga in 718 or 722. This was probably little more than a skirmish, but it was later to be built up as the starting point of the reconquest of Spain by the Christians, a process which was not to be fully achieved until 1492. Pelayo had taken refuge in the cave at Covadonga and, despite being urged to submit by the treacherous Archbishop Oppa, who accompanied the Muslim army, Pelayo defiantly proclaimed: 'Christ is our hope that from this little hill Spain may be saved and the army of the people of the Goths restored.' And when battle was joined a decisive Christian victory was ensured by divine intervention: miraculously, the enemy arrows turned round in full flight and killed the Muslims, while those who managed to escape were subsequently destroyed by a collapsing mountain. Inevitably, the wooden cross which had accompanied the Christians into battle became a sacred relic which King Alfonso III of Asturias (866–910) lovingly encased in gold and precious stones.

The destruction of Spain, therefore, was counterbalanced by the centuries-long task of the recovery or reconquest by the Christians of all that had been lost, and this makes it possible to tell a coherent story. Yet it must also be emphasized that there was an extraordinary degree of religious, ethnic and political diversity. When the Muslims invaded in 711, for example, Spain already had a relatively large population of Jews, as well as Christians. But even to stress that the country was a land of three religions tends to simplify matters. Amongst the Muslims, for example, Arabs from different tribes and clans constituted an ethnic minority; the Berber majority was reinforced by the political and military interventions in Spanish affairs of the North African Almoravids and Almohads in the eleventh and twelfth centuries respectively: and former slaves from other societies could play an important socio-political role. As for the Christians, they were made up of different ethnic and regional groups with their own characteristics, traditions, and in some cases even languages: for example, the Basques, Galicians, Aragonese, Asturians, Castilians, Catalans and Valencians. Then, too, there were those who were to come to Spain from other countries. It is true that not all of these stayed. Some, like Italian merchants from the thirteenth century onwards, engaged in trade and banking, and then usually returned home. Others came to fight for a while, for there was something peculiarly attractive and spiritually rewarding in doing battle against the infidel in Spain. In 1330 Sir James Douglas and many of his Scottish knights, the bearers of a casket enclosing the heart of Robert the Bruce, perished in the battle of Teba de Ardales, while Chaucer's perfect knight took part in the campaign of Algeciras in 1344, and then went on to fight the Marinids in North Africa. But many French, Italians, and others came and remained in Spain, even if they did not stay in the one

place. For if the ethnic diversity was marked, matters were further confused by the way in which colonists travelled long distances to settle in areas which the Christians had reconquered from the Muslims. For example, when in the far south the town of Jerez de la Frontera was definitively taken in 1264, the Spanish Christian settlers who moved in came from as far north as Galicia, Asturias, the Basque country, Navarre and Catalonia, and this is without mentioning those who came from Portugal, France and Italy, as well as a solitary Englishman named Robert.

Foundation of the Christian Kingdoms

Politically, the existence of several Spanish kingdoms or polities also emphasizes a diversity which cannot be examined here in detail. Broadly speaking, they can be divided into three groupings. The Muslims called the lands they conquered al-Andalus. In 756 al-Andalus became a politically independent emirate, although it still recognized the religious supremacy of the caliphate at Baghdad; but in 929 its ruler, Abd al-Rahman III, assumed the title of caliph and, becoming fully independent, al-Andalus entered its golden age which was to last till the early eleventh century. Thereafter al-Andalus disintegrated: by 1031 the caliphate officially ceased to exist and was replaced by well over a dozen petty kingdoms. From 1086 the Almoravids of North Africa restored unity in al-Andalus, as did the Almohads who had succeeded them by the mid-twelfth century. But by 1236 Muslim power began to crumble rapidly, and the Christians in effect reconquered all of Muslim Spain, apart from the small Nasrid kingdom of Granada, which survived till 1492.

In the western part of Christian Spain Pelayo was the first ruler of the kingdom of Asturias which was centred on Oviedo; when the court moved to León in the tenth century, however, this polity became the kingdom of León. The county of Castile became an independent kingdom in 1035 and eventually dominated all the central and western part of Spain as well as spearheading the reconquest of Muslim-held territories. North-eastern Spain included the kingdom of Navarre, the county of Aragon (which became a kingdom in 1035), and various counties which quickly began to develop into a Catalan entity centred on Barcelona. In 1137 the kingdom of Aragon and Catalonia were united to form the Crown of Aragon, which later also included the kingdoms of Mallorca and Valencia, which were annexed by conquest.

All this political fragmentation may appear bewildering. Moreover, there were plenty of wars between Christian kings, and there were even many occasions when Christian rulers allied with Muslim infidels against other Christians. But while noting these complexities and confusions, it is evident that the long-term trend was different. In this land of three religions the

In the work of scribes and artisans, we can see how the medieval Spaniards perceived themselves. Their peninsula was the setting for a ceaseless crusade against the Muslim Moors. *Above*: two illustrations from Beatus of Liébana's commentary on the *Apocalypse*. An infantryman (late tenth/eleventh century), clad from head to foot in mail, holds a sturdy spear. A Christian knight (tenth century), his dress and equipment modelled on those of the Muslims, defeats a serpent, symbol of evil. A marble relief (*right*, eleventh century) shows a warrior capturing a town, a scene that must have been common as the Christians forced their way south. A more peaceful aspect of medieval Spain (*opposite above*): two scribes preparing parchment sheets in the *scriptorium* of the monastery of San Salvador de Tábara. It would have been in just such a room that this tenth-century manuscript would have been written.

Christians and Muslims were locked in an armed struggle which would never cease until one side had been completely defeated. Medieval Christian Spaniards, for example, knew that history had a special meaning and that it was moving in a definite direction. History began with the Creation of the World; then there came the Fall and the Expulsion of Adam and Eve from the Garden of Eden, a disaster which was redeemed by the Crucifixion and Resurrection. And just as certain as these events were those which were foretold in the *Apocalypse*, or *Book of Revelation*, about the Anti-Christ, the Second Coming and the end of the world. Within this global context the history of Spain had its own rather similar meaning. The Christian Visigoths had enjoyed the Garden of Eden for, as Alfonso X put it, 'this Spain that we are talking about is like God's paradise'. But because of their sins the Christians had been expelled from paradise by the forces of the Anti-Christ. Perhaps no text gripped the imagination of medieval Spaniards as much as the *Apocalypse*. As early as the eighth century the Asturian monk Beatus of Liébana wrote a commentary on it, and in the following centuries illustrated manuscripts of his commentary were produced by skilled illuminators working in *scriptoria*, or special rooms in monasteries which were set aside for the writing or copying out of such texts. In these illustrations the apocalyptic visions of St John vividly portray the triumph of God's people over his satanic enemies, especially the Muslims, who as early as the ninth century were being compared to the Beast of Ten Horns who appears in both the book of *Daniel* and *Revelation*.

History, then, had a meaning and was moving towards an ultimate purpose designed by God. But history did not proceed in a straight line; it sometimes tended to repeat itself, although each new cycle was not an exact repetition but marked a progression towards the end. The reconquest, therefore, went forward in stages. For both the Christians and the Muslims permanent or long-lasting peace treaties, such as those that were agreed to between Christian rulers, were inconceivable; only short-term truces were acceptable, because the natural and proper relationship between the two sides was that of war. Moreover, as far as the Christians were concerned, the ideology of the reconquest also implied the 'restoration' of Spain as it had existed before the 'destruction', and that Spain had been a single *Hispania*, not a confused assortment of different kingdoms. Hence throughout the medieval centuries writers, chroniclers, and historians tended to think of Spain and its peoples as being in some sense one entity, as if the Muslim presence was an aberration. Even in those cases where chroniclers concentrated mainly on one region or kingdom, the narrative and the events described were still seen as forming part of a larger 'Spanish' picture. Certainly there were tensions and even wars between the Christian kingdoms, but in the last resort these were envisaged as being temporary quarrels between relations and as such they were totally different from the state of permanent hostility towards the infidel.

Despite Pelayo's early victory at Covadonga, it was some considerable time before the reconquest began in earnest. True, during the ninth century the Christians advanced from Asturias down to the river Duero and, eastwards, the counts of Barcelona were already free from Muslim domination. For the most part, however, the Christian settlers were moving into free land, the Duero wilderness which the Muslims were not really interested in contesting. But matters changed dramatically when the caliphate of Cordoba disintegrated in the early eleventh century: the Christians advanced from the Duero to the Tagus, and Toledo, the old Visigothic capital, was captured in 1085. Above all, however, this was the age of Castile's epic hero Rodrigo Díaz de Vivar, otherwise known as El Cid, this latter title deriving from the Arabic sīd, meaning 'lord'. His exploits, part fact and part fiction, are celebrated in the famous *Cantar de Mio Cid*, which is one of the greatest epics of medieval European literature. In its present written form it was probably composed around 1207, although it may well have existed in earlier oral traditions.

El Cid

The Cid was born round about 1040 in Vivar, near Burgos. In 1079 he was sent by Alfonso VI to collect tribute money from the Muslim ruler of Seville, but shortly after he fell foul of the king and was sent into exile. Exiled, the Cid nevertheless not only managed to survive but also captured Valencia from the Muslims in 1094 and became its independent ruler until his death in 1099, after which the city and its region once more fell under Muslim domination. Although the *Cantar de Mio Cid* contains much that is fiction, this does not detract from its usefulness as a guide to the characteristics, attitudes and beliefs of its times.

On a first reading, the quality of the poem most likely to strike one is its down-to-earth nature, one might almost say 'realism', particularly if it is compared to other European epics such as *Beowulf* or the *Chanson de Roland*. Much of what is related in the poem is historically accurate, and even the fictional episodes are believable; indeed at times it is so difficult to distinguish fact from fiction that even today scholars are liable to become involved in heated arguments over such matters. As for the Cid himself, he is portrayed in a manner which already reveals the preoccupations and characteristics of many Spaniards over the ensuing centuries. Fighting for him is not so much glamorous as a way of making a living: in exile, for example, he advises his retinue that they must keep moving because they live by their swords and lances and the land is too lean for them to remain in the one spot. Written records are kept about the booty and spoils which are accumulated, and all profits are shared out according to well-established rules. Yet although the Cid is hard-headed about the economic problems of making a living, he is also intensely preoccupied with honour, both his own and that of his family. Honour requires that wrongs must be put right, and this the Cid is determined to achieve and does achieve. But he does not do this in an impulsive or hot-blooded way; on the contrary, his outstanding characteristic in this respect is *mesura*, the ability to ponder matters seriously before taking action.

Above all the *Cantar* is important because it reveals changes in values which had taken place or were about to take place. The Cid is born into the lesser nobility, yet by his military exploits he becomes the greatest hero of his age; his enemies, the evil princes of Carrión, are born into the highest social status, yet by their cowardice and scheming at the royal court they are revealed as being completely without honour. Honour, therefore, depends not on one's birth but on one's actions; not on enjoying the life at court but on fighting out there on the frontier. Honour also requires that a man should stay steadfastly loyal to his natural lord, the king, however unjustly he may feel that he has been treated by him.

Finally the poem contains two important pointers for the future. The first concerns the way in which the Cid obtains his revenge. We might expect this epic hero to kill his enemies personally and very bloodily. Instead the Cid has his wrongs put right in a court of law and according to the principles of Roman law. Society is in transition; previously based on the vendetta and blood feuds, it is now beginning to operate according to what we today would recognize as law and order. Not without reason, many modern scholars suspect that the poem, as we know it, was composed into its present form by a lawyer. The second pointer concerns attitudes towards the Muslims and the reconquest. The reconquest had gathered pace, but it was not yet quite a crusade. It is true that the Christians in the poem invoke Santiago (St James) before going into battle and that this adds a notable religious dimension. Legend had it that St James, the brother of St John, had preached in Spain, and indeed that after his death in Jerusalem his body was brought back and buried in Galicia, where in the ninth century his tomb was supposedly discovered and subsequently became the focus for the famous pilgrimage to Santiago de Compostela. More to the point Santiago 'Matamoros' (Moor-slayer) was not infrequently to make his appearance on the Christian side in crucial battles against the Muslims. In contrast to this, the poem portrays the Cid's Muslim friend Abengalbón as being nobler and morally superior to the Christian princes of Carrión, although it prudently says nothing about the fact that the historical Cid had not been averse to serving the Muslim ruler of Saragossa for five years. Yet a nascent crusading zeal can be detected in the poem in the person of Bishop Jerome, a Cluniac monk from France who became bishop of Valencia shortly after the Cid captured it. He openly declares that he has come to Spain because he wants to kill Muslims; before battle he celebrates mass, absolves the soldiers, and promises them paradise should they be killed; and he demands the honour of striking the first blows in battle. Bishop Jerome, not the Cid, points to the future.

The crusade against Islam

In the event 'crusading' fervour was imported from both North Africa and Europe from the late eleventh century onwards. On the Muslim side the fanatical North African Almoravids and Almohads successively preached Holy War against the Christians. But the latter too were heavily influenced by crusading zeal. Although Pope Urban II appealed at the Council of Clermont (1095) for volunteers to fight in a crusade in the Holy Land, the infidel could also be fought in Spain. This can be clearly seen during the reign of Alfonso I, 'the Battler', king of Aragon and Navarre (1104–34), when, with the help of many French knights whose crusading impulse was deflected into Spain, most of the Ebro valley was taken and towns such as Saragossa (1118) and Calatayud (1120) fell to the Christians. But Alfonso I went much further than this: he dreamed of mounting an expedition to Jerusalem itself, and in his will he even attempted to bequeath his kingdoms to the great crusading orders, such as the Hospitallers and the Templars.

Further west, the crusading impulse was just as strong, if more practical. During the second half of the twelfth century the famous indigenous military orders of Alcántara, Calatrava, and Santiago were founded. These military orders fully expressed the crusading ideal of the reconquest by integrating the religious and military factors that made up that ideal. Influenced above all by Cistercian monasticism, the knights of these orders were in a sense monks who were licensed to kill, who had embraced the Cross and vowed to avoid fighting other Christians, devoting all their religious and military efforts to defeating the infidels. Moreover crusading fervour did not take long to produce startling results. Between them Alfonso VIII of Castile (1158–1214), the archbishop of Toledo, and Pope Innocent III (1198–1216) organized a special crusade in Spain which terminated in a brilliant Christian victory at the battle of Las Navas de Tolosa in 1212. Even more significant, perhaps, was the fact that men from all the Christian kingdoms participated in the crusade and fought in the battle.

The Christians were now not slow to take advantage of their opportunities, and between them James I of Aragon (1213–76) and Ferdinand III of Castile and León (1217/30–52) almost completed the reconquest, James I taking Mallorca (1229), followed by Menorca and Ibiza, and then Valencia (1238), while Ferdinand III gained Cordoba (1236), Jaén (1246), and Seville (1248). Virtually all Spain had now been recovered by the Christians apart from the small Muslim kingdom of Granada. To many all these successes seemed miraculous, and indeed people were quick to attribute them to the Virgin Mary, who appeared to help the Christians at every crucial battle and siege. And as the cathedral or chief church in every reconquered town was dedicated to the Virgin, Santiago now had to take second place. For the Muslims it was a disaster, prompting the poet ar-Rundī to write an elegy lamenting the loss of flourishing cities, the humiliation of their inhabitants, and the tyranny of Christian barbarians who converted mosques into churches by installing crosses and bells in them.

Yet the reconquest was still not complete, and the kingdom of Granada was to survive until 1492. Why did it take the Christians so long to complete the task they had set themselves? Part of the answer had to do with problems of manpower. After each successful phase of reconquest the lands that were taken had to be resettled with colonists, and within a few years the thirteenth-century Christians had been so successful that they had doubled the territory under their control. Landed resources had easily outstripped the supply of population, and this situation was further aggravated by the consequences of the Black Death of 1348. But in addition the fourteenth and fifteenth centuries witnessed an endless series of internal dynastic crises, civil wars, and ugly episodes of anti-Semitism. If we take the case of Castile, for example, not one of the nine reigns from 1296 to 1504 escaped either the dangers posed by a minority or those associated with a disputed succession. In addition the Castilian kings had to try and cope with military and political intervention in their affairs by France, England, Aragon, Portugal and contingents of free-lance foreign mercenaries, a situation which was worsened by the constant tendency of Castilian noble factions to seek foreign help during the civil wars. The Castilian kings, therefore, tended to try and promote stability on the Moorish frontier by entering into a series of truces with the Muslims of Granada, in order to prevent the opening up of yet another military front in times of crises.

Despite the anarchy and despite the truces with Granada, however, the ideology of reconquest not only survived but was augmented to incorporate new elements. For centuries European apocalyptic legends had foretold that at the end of days there would be a king who would completely defeat Islam, conquer Jerusalem, become emperor of the whole world, and then renounce his empire directly to God. In the Spanish version of this legend, the Anti-Christ would appear in Seville, but he would be defeated by the messianic king, identified as

Two scenes from one of Alfonso X's *Cantigas de Santa María*. After a dispute with a learned Jew, Merlin asked the Virgin that the Jew's son should be born with his head back to front as a divine sign. Merlin then took the deformed baby from his father, who wished to kill him. Later (*far left*), he converted the Jews by showing them the boy and they were baptized (*left*) under the gaze of the Virgin's statue.

'the hidden one' or 'the bat', who would then go on to conquer Granada, Jerusalem, and the rest of the world. The long-desired conquest of the kingdom of Granada, therefore, was now only one element in a much larger apocalyptic picture. Moreover, although it was certainly the case that the Anti-Christ was sometimes envisaged as a specific individual (it was frequently asserted that the Messiah awaited by the Jews would in fact be the Anti-Christ), Spaniards also tended to assert that the Anti-Christ was generic, encompassing not only Muslims, but Jews and 'bad Christians' as well.

The fate of the Jews

During the later medieval period the situation of the Jewish communities in Spain deteriorated rapidly. Even at the best of times the Jews enjoyed only a relative tolerance, as the poems and magnificent illustrations of the thirteenth-century *Cantigas de Santa María* illustrate. The *Cantigas* treat several of the standard medieval themes about Jews: Jews as disciples of the Devil, as traitors, and as child murderers. But in comparison to later attitudes these thirteenth-century views can be seen as 'optimistic'. The Jews are not presented as irremediably wicked and satanic; on the contrary, as potential converts they can become just like Christians by accepting baptism. By peaceful persuasion, friendly disputation, and good example, therefore, the Jews would be converted. Yet although there were isolated cases of conversion, in general terms peaceful persuasion failed for the simple reason that Jews did not want to convert and regarded Christian arguments that Christ was the Messiah and that the New Testament was the fulfilment of the Old as illogical and absurd. Peaceful persuasion, therefore, gave way to attempts at conversion under pressure, a change that mirrored the intransigent zeal of the Franciscans and Dominicans as well as the apocalyptic belief that all infidels would be converted to Christianity before the last days. But the rising tide of intolerance and hate was due to other reasons as well: when faced with inflation and rapidly rising prices, increasing taxation, bad harvests, or plague, the urban population tended to turn on the Jews, and the nobility were not averse to using anti-Semitic propaganda during times of civil war. During the second half of the fourteenth century the situation deteriorated rapidly and culminated in the savage pogroms which, starting in Seville in June 1391, spread to most of the major towns of Spain during the remainder of June, July, and August. Amid the killings, thousands of terrified Jews converted to Christianity.

But were the New Christians, who were known as *conversos*, genuine converts, or were they crypto-Jews? Many Old Christians regarded them with the utmost suspicion, and matters were not helped either by the way in which many *conversos*

rapidly established themselves in key posts in urban government and the royal administration or by the serious economic dislocations which took place from the 1440s onwards. More pogroms occurred, but now they were directed at the *conversos*: in Toledo in 1449 and again in 1467, and in some of the major towns of Andalusia in 1473.

One man knew the solution to the problem of the *conversos*, the Franciscan friar Alonso de Espina who completed his book, the *Fortalitium Fidei*, in 1460. The book contains a gruesome catalogue of the blood libels, host desecrations, and other satanic misdeeds supposedly committed by Jews and *conversos*. Although Espina was convinced that *conversos* were crypto-Jews, the fact that they had been baptized meant that they were technically Christians, which in turn meant that they were 'bad Christians' or heretics, and hence subject to the Inquisition. But no Inquisition existed in Spain, and the whole point of Espina's book was to demand that one should be set up. If Alfonso X had described Spain as God's paradise, Espina regarded Castile as a miserable kingdom located at the ends of the earth, where all the filth and excrement of Christ's enemies had been piled up. Espina found little support for his ideas at the court of Henry IV of Castile (1454–74), a king depicted by his enemies with some justification as a kind of Anti-Christ who contaminated the very air he breathed, a useless ruler with a penchant for *conversos*, Muslim habits, foul smells and sodomitical lovers. Espina did not live to see his Inquisition, and indeed it was widely believed that he was poisoned by the king's Jewish physician, Master Semaya.

The end of the Reconquest

Then everything changed. Later, men would declare that it was a miracle, brought about by a divinely guided queen and king, 'the Catholic Monarchs', Isabella of Castile (1474–1504) and Ferdinand of Aragon (1479–1516). Isabella and Ferdinand married in 1469; Isabella claimed the throne of Castile in 1474, and Ferdinand became king of the Crown of Aragon in 1479. Castile and Aragon were 'united' in the sense that dynastically they would from now on have the same monarchs, although they would in almost all other ways retain their separate and markedly different institutions. In 1478 the Spanish Inquisition was set up in Castile and shortly after began its search for heretic *conversos*; subsequently Ferdinand extended the Inquisition into the Crown of Aragon, thus providing 'Spain' with a common political and religious institution, the only one apart from the monarchy itself. Then in 1482 the Catholic Monarchs systematically set out to conquer the Moorish kingdom of Granada, laying siege to one town after another. And as their successes multiplied, so there was an explosion of exuberance and a multiplication of prophetic texts, commentaries and even

ballads which identified Ferdinand as 'the hidden one' or 'the bat' who would conquer Granada, destroy all the Moors of Spain and all renegades to the Faith, subdue all Africa, conquer Jerusalem, and become emperor of all the world.

On 2 January 1492 Granada finally surrendered and a man named Christopher Columbus watched as the crucifix and royal standards of the Catholic Monarchs were raised above the towers of the Alhambra. Shortly after on 30 March the Catholic Monarchs, who were still in Granada, signed the edict of expulsion of all Jews from their kingdoms within the next four months. After an initial period of tolerance this policy of forcing a choice between conversion or expulsion was extended in 1502 to the defeated Moors of the kingdom of Granada. Henceforth everybody would in theory be Christian. The reconquest had been triumphantly completed, religious unity had been achieved, and the Spanish Inquisition was at hand to root out heretics and suspect Christians.

But what would happen next? Columbus had been in Granada busy peddling what he called his 'Enterprise of the Indies'. What he proposed to do was to go to the East, to India and Asia, and there establish contact in Cathay with the pro-Christian Grand Khan of the Mongols, who wished to be instructed in the Faith, in order to secure an alliance between the forces of Eastern and Western Christendom which would defeat the Muslims and recover Jerusalem. At the moment of their triumphant conquest of Granada, this enterprise was one of great interest both to the crusade-minded Isabella and to 'the hidden one' or 'bat'. On 17 April 1492 agreement was reached on the nature and terms of the 'Enterprise of the Indies', and in August Columbus set off for the East, not by travelling overland, but by sailing west. A more curious, thoroughly medieval, and Spanish background to the discovery of America could not have been imagined. But Ferdinand the Catholic would continue to affirm, even after Isabella's death in 1504, that the conquest of the Holy City belonged to him, and the title of 'King of Jerusalem' was added to the other titles held by the monarchs of Spain.

One chronicler who reflected on all these miraculous events – the reconquest of Granada, the expulsion of the Jews, the forcible conversion of Moors, the investigations of the Inquisition and the discovery of America – clearly saw God's hand at work. His name was Andrés Bernáldez, and he was the priest of Los Palacios, a place near Seville. For him Isabella was no ordinary queen, and when her death drew near God arranged visible cosmic portents and signs of the impending demise of 'such a Catholic and necessary queen', in the same way as he had done hundreds of years before for the Holy Roman Emperor, the glorious and saintly Charlemagne.

The reconquest, religious unity, and a measure of political unity had taken almost eight hundred years to achieve. The

The Catholic Monarchs aspired to convert the whole world to Christianity. *Left*: in a printer's device from a historical account in verse of Ferdinand and Isabella's reign, the Cross is advanced to the three continents (1518). In Spain itself, their entry into Granada (*centre*) was followed by the attempted conversion of its Moors; in 1502 they were presented with a choice between baptism (*below*) or exile.

existence of a frontier, or a succession of frontiers, during the long period of reconquest had left indelible marks on Spain, particularly in the kingdom of Castile. In a society perpetually at war, or perpetually under the threat of war, the priorities had to be military ones. Already by the end of the eighth century Castile was a land of castles which the Muslim chroniclers called *al-Qila*, 'the castles', and when town life began to develop from the eleventh century onwards, frontier towns, such as Avila, took the form of defensive fortresses. Moreover, since the Muslims could and did attack at any point across the frontier, it followed that all sections of society had to make a military contribution of some sort and that speed and mobility were essential in both defence and attack. Hence the importance of the horse in warfare, and the fact that in addition to the nobility, who were traditionally associated with a military function, there came into existence large numbers of *caballeros villanos*, or 'commoner knights', who were granted some noble privileges as long as they maintained a horse and armour and fought as knights. These 'villein knights' made their greatest military contribution in the late eleventh and twelfth centuries in the lands between the Duero and the Tagus, where they soon came to dominate the towns on which the frontier defence of these regions depended. Furthermore, since one of their privileges was the all-important noble right of tax exemption, families of 'villein knights' who managed to provide knightly service over two or three generations were easily assimilated into the ranks of those Castilians who were noble by birth, the *hidalgos*.

All this was to have important consequences for the future. By the end of the medieval period Castilian society had a higher percentage of nobles than the other countries of Western Europe: 10 per cent in Castile, for example, as compared to only 1 per cent in France. Among these nobles, however, there were enormous discrepancies in power and wealth by the later medieval period. Some fifteen families with enormous wealth and power produced the grandees or *grandes*, so often regarded as being archetypally Spanish. Below them there were a large number of nobles who maintained the socially prestigious life-style appropriate to knights. But there were also very many nobles who were desperately poor, *hidalgos* who had no property or possessions, did not have the horses which were essential to a knightly style of life, and yet who clung on grimly to their privileges. Their plight, which would be described in the literature of the early modern period, was already the subject of proverbs which are best conveyed in English as question and answer riddles.

    Q. Why are poor *hidalgos* lucky?

    A. Because they go through purgatory before death.

    Q. What has a shoe on one foot but not on the other?

    A. The *hidalgo*'s son.

Agriculture and trade

Despite the military priorities, however, the reconquest would not have succeeded if, at each stage, the lands which had been taken were not colonized by Christian settlers who would contribute to economic and military stability. Down to the eleventh century much of this colonization was carried out informally by free men who established small estates on their own account. Thereafter, however, the rulers of Castile, Aragon, and Catalonia began to play an active role by granting lordships and charters which provided guidelines and conditions for the resettlement of the towns and countryside, while at the same time offering exemptions and privileges which would attract settlers to the frontier regions. Royal intervention reached its peak in the thirteenth century when kings commissioned officials to share out reconquered lands in Andalusia, Murcia, Mallorca, and parts of Valencia in a detailed manner among colonists, and to record the results in special 'registers of repartitions'. Despite this detailed system of land allocation, the results were transitory. Almost immediately an active land-market sprang up as some colonists gave up and returned north or emigrated to the towns, while others accumulated land at cheap prices. When the reconquered lands of Andalusia had been originally allocated in the thirteenth century, large numbers of small and medium-sized estates had been created; over the next two centuries, however, the great landed estates or *latifundios*, which were to be so typical of the south, came into existence in a variety of ways ranging from legal purchase to downright usurpation.

If colonization followed in the wake of the reconquest, so too did the organization of economic life, and already by 1300 the fundamental features which were to typify the economy of Spain in the following centuries were either in place or developing. The existence of the frontier had naturally stimulated pastoralism and ranching, because any alert of an impending attack often made it possible to move livestock out of danger and into safety. But when the Castilians won the rich grasslands of La Mancha and Extremadura, pastoralism boomed and the vast seasonal movements of transhumant sheep between the northern and southern pastures came into being, with the interests of the stockmen being upheld and organized by the famous *Real Concejo de la Mesta* which was created by the crown in the 1260s. In marked contrast to this, and to the dry-farming agriculture which prevailed in most of Spain, the *huerta* (irrigated) regions of Valencia were characterized by sophisticated systems of irrigation which distributed water on a co-operative basis over large areas.

Spain also played an important role in international trade. The merchants of Burgos and other Castilian towns exported wool to the Low Countries, and a Castilian commercial colony came into existence at Bruges. The Basques exported iron and shipped Gascon wine to England. After the thirteenth-century reconquest, the Straits of Gibraltar were opened up to link the Mediterranean and Atlantic economies, and Andalusia, which had much to offer for export in the form of olive oil, tunny fish, soap, wine, sherry and dried fruit, quickly attracted the attention of Italian entrepreneurs. Well before the discovery of America, Seville was a rapidly expanding and prosperous city in which the Genoese, Piacentine, and Catalan merchants established their *lonjas*, or trading and banking centres, near the cathedral. As for the Catalans, and more especially the merchants of the great city of Barcelona, they were to be found all over the Mediterranean, in North Africa, and to a lesser extent in the Atlantic, trading in spices, grain and textiles. And from these far-flung commercial activities of the Spaniards there derived other benefits. Already by 1272 Mallorcan sailors navigated by compass and increasing use was being made of *portolani* charts, while *mappae mundi*, such as the famous world atlas of Charles V drawn by the Mallorcan Jew Abraham Cresques round about 1375, revealed just how much had been learned about such things as the West African kingdom of Mali, the gold trade across the Sahara, the Great Khan of the Mongols, and the cities of central Asia and China, such as Peking and Canton. In addition both the Crown of Aragon and the kingdom of Castile were formidable naval powers, with the latter on occasion playing a spectacular role in support of the French during the Hundred Years' War between France and England.

Cultural cross-currents

By 1504 Spain was already a major European power which in theory enjoyed religious and political unity. Yet during the preceding centuries and even after 1504 the outstanding feature of Spain's history was its diversity. Spain had been a land of three religions, and not only had each one of these made its own contribution to Spanish and European civilization, but cultural developments had also been affected by processes of 'borrowing' or accommodation which took place between Christians, Muslims and Jews. Some of these processes represented deliberate attempts at 'borrowing' because, for example, down to the thirteenth century the Christians recognized that much was to be admired in the cultural and technological achievements of the Muslims. But in many other areas the processes of acculturation can almost be regarded as unconscious or accidental.

Deliberate 'borrowing' is best illustrated by the example of the translators of the twelfth and thirteenth centuries who provided Western Europe with texts and knowledge which had long been unavailable. Indeed scholars from other European countries came to Spain in search of these texts, men like

In medieval Spain, Jews and Christians borrowed, both deliberately and unconsciously, the best elements of the culture of their Moorish neighbours.

The intricate interlacing of a pattern from an Islamic Koran (*above*) is mirrored in a Jewish Haggadah (*opposite below*) and in the stone ribs of the rose window of the monastery of Guadalupe, which became fabulously wealthy with gifts from the New World. The geometric ornamentation in the brickwork of the Mudejar church tower (*far right*) of San Andrés, Calatayud, also shows strong Islamic influence.

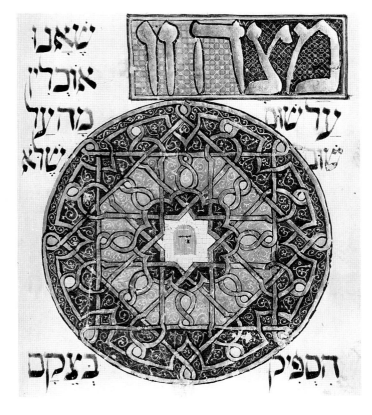

27

Gerard of Cremona, Rudolph of Bruges, and the Englishmen Adelard of Bath, Robert of Chester, and Daniel of Morley. These men were principally interested in works of Greek philosophy and science which had been translated, and in some cases enriched and improved, by the scholars of Islam. Accordingly important works of philosophy, mathematics and astronomy were translated in such centres as Toledo, Barcelona, Tarazona and Segovia. The task was complicated and demanded cooperation from scholars of different faiths. For example, we know from one of the translations of a work by the great Persian Avicenna, the philosopher and physician who so profoundly influenced European scholasticism and the study of medicine, that a Jewish scholar first of all translated the Arabic text into Castilian, and that then a Christian translated the Castilian into Latin. Similarly we know that other translations were carried out with the help of Muslims and Mozarabs, that is Christians who lived or had lived in Muslim Spain. In the final phase of translation Alfonso X of Castile actively patronized the task of cultural transmission, directing his attention particularly towards the astronomical heritage of Muslim Spain, as is evidenced by such works as the *Books of Astronomical Knowledge* or the *Alfonsine Tables*.

While the translators of the twelfth and thirteenth centuries on the whole directed their efforts at the philosophical and scientific texts of Arabic-Greek learning, it should not be supposed that 'borrowing' was confined to these centuries, these topics, or the Greek heritage. Alfonso X, for example, was also interested in history and chess; from 1422 to 1433 Rabbi Mosse Arragel of Guadalajara devoted his efforts to producing what is now known as the Alba Bible, an elaborately illustrated and new Castilian translation of the Old Testament which had been requested by the Master of the Military Order of Calatrava, Luis de Guzmán, and in 1455 the *imām* of Segovia, Içe de Gebir, set off for the abbey of Aiton in Savoy in order to provide his fellow townsman, the scholar John of Segovia, with an Arabic text of the Koran, which he wrote out from memory, as well as to collaborate on a literal translation of it.

Examples of startling processes of acculturation which seem almost accidental are best illustrated by appealing to the visual senses. Muslims who lived within the Christian states were known as Mudejars, and many of them made a living as skilled architectural artisans, working as bricklayers, carpenters, and plasterers. Even today the visitor to Aragon cannot help but be astonished by thirteenth-century brick parish churches, the belfries of which are so obviously nothing more or less than Muslim minarets. In Muslim Spain there was the extraordinary case of the paintings executed in the Alhambra palace in Granada. Islam was hostile to the depiction of living beings in art, and yet well before the reconquest of Granada these paintings portrayed scenes from Christian chivalric tales, and were probably executed by Mudejar artists from Castile who were used to providing their patrons with works which dealt with 'Christian' chivalric themes. Indeed the Mudejars were so indispensible to crafts relating to building and ornamentation that their legacy can be detected in the most unlikely places, such as the synagogue of *El Tránsito* in Toledo or the famous Jeronymite monastery of Guadalupe.

Language and literature provide other examples of interesting processes of diversity and acculturation. Arabic provided the Castilian language with more words than any other language apart from Latin, and above all it did so in those areas of economic life where the Muslims for so long had been more sophisticated than the Christians, activities such as building, irrigation, and agriculture. But by the fourteenth century there were already signs that some Jews and Muslims were losing their ability to understand Hebrew and Arabic respectively, as was evidenced by the development of *aljamiado* literature, that is works in Spanish but written in Hebrew or Arabic letters. A poem about the life of the biblical Joseph, for example, was composed in Spanish using the Hebrew alphabet, and seems to have been aimed at Jews who no longer understood Hebrew; and when the representatives of the Jewish communities of Castile drew up a set of ordinances in 1432, they did so in a mixture of Hebrew and Castilian. This development was much more pronounced as far as the Muslims or Moriscos were concerned. The spoken Arabic of Granada was a dialect far removed from the language of the Koran, and in these circumstances a good deal of the *aljamiado* literature was devoted to explaining matters of faith in Spanish but using an Arabic script, such as Içe de Gebir's short treatise on the thirteen fundamental articles of the Islamic faith which all Muslims had to believe. But in addition to such devotional treatises, *aljamiado* literature also included juridical texts and works on such legendary heroes as the companions of Muhammad.

The fact that so much *aljamiado* literature was concerned with religious matters helps to emphasize another important aspect about the diversity which lurked behind the façade of unity. When the Christians reconquered Granada in 1492, the centuries-old medieval frontier in Spain was doomed to disappear, but mental and religious frontiers remained inside the hearts and minds of many of those who were supposedly Christians. Crypto-Jews and crypto-Muslims were to cling tenaciously to the beliefs and rituals of their religions, religions which no longer officially existed in Spain. Forced to behave like Christians, *conversos* and Moriscos developed subtle strategies to cope with their predicaments. They could hardly avoid having their children baptized in Christian churches, but safe within their own houses they celebrated an anti-ritual which was

designed to efface the Christian sacrament. In church the *conversos* would say 'in the name of the Father' but they would not say 'in the name of the Son', and they would make a semblance of making the sign of the cross while taking care not to do it properly. The Moriscos for their part adopted the Muslim doctrine of *taqiyya* which allowed them to pretend to convert to Christianity while remaining Muslims in secret, because in times of danger what really counted was the inner intention of the believer rather than outward appearances. Like the *conversos* they too found practical ways of dealing with their dilemmas. Thousands of copies of the Koran may have been burned by the Christian authorities, but Moriscos secretly passed on Muslim devotional works from generation to generation or held group readings of Arabic books translated into Spanish; forced to go to confession, they discovered that they had nothing to confess or they would even seek out a deaf confessor; forced to observe Christian holy days, they developed a particular attachment to St John's day because it coincided with the Muslim festival of *'ansara*, which they continued to celebrate with an early morning ritual wash. The Inquisition tried to root out this diversity, playing a grim game of 'hide and seek' with their adversaries.

King and Cortes

Diversity was not confined to religious matters. The Crown of Aragon and the kingdom of Castile, theoretically united after 1479, retained radically different systems of central and local government, taxation and constitutional principles. The differences had emerged over the medieval centuries, and they were so varied in detail that it would be impossible to deal with all of them properly here. But one outstanding feature demands attention, and that is Spain's contribution to the theories and practices concerning political authority, and the way in which Castile and the Crown of Aragon came up with such contrasting views on these matters.

To begin with, it would be as well to attempt to dispel the anglo-centric myth that England was 'the mother of parliaments' and that Magna Carta in some way provided the first and crucial step towards what we today understand as democracy. The first parliament in European history was held in Spain when King Alfonso IX summoned the *Cortes* (parliament) of León in 1188, and the eight-hundredth anniversary of this 'mother of parliaments' was fittingly celebrated in Spain by a series of conferences between 1986 and 1988 which were inaugurated by King Juan Carlos and Queen Sofia. Yet it would be idle to pretend that this promising start of 1188 led to the emergence of a strong medieval tradition of representative Castilian Cortes capable of redressing subjects' grievances and of controlling the monarchy, legislation and taxation. On the contrary by the

mid-fifteenth century only seventeen royal towns sent representatives to the Cortes, the clergy and nobility took little interest in its proceedings, and entire regions such as the Basque provinces, Galicia, Asturias and Extremadura enjoyed no 'parliamentary' representation. Summoned and dissolved as the king wished, the Cortes dutifully voted taxation and then presented petitions which the king usually answered in an evasive manner.

Although the Castilian Cortes seemed to be a vulnerable institution, it could occasionally resist royal claims to increasing powers. For Spain offered the two most radical alternatives concerning political and constitutional authority to be found anywhere in Western Europe. If the kingdom of Castile failed to develop a strong 'parliamentary' tradition, emerging theories about royal power eventually produced exalted pretensions of absolutism. Already in the great law code known as the *Siete Partidas*, which was completed in the 1260s, Alfonso X of Castile had discussed such key problems as who had the power to make law, where power was located, and what was the justification for sovereign kingship. According to the *Siete Partidas*, the king received his power directly from God, whose vicar he was in his own kingdom, and not from the people or the Church. The king, therefore, governed society and created the laws. By the reign of John II (1406–54) these claims about royal power were being elaborated into a full-blown theory of absolutism. So great was the king's power, it was asserted, that all the laws and all rights were beneath his feet. The king could justify his actions and policies by claiming that he was using his 'absolute royal power', for the king was accountable to God alone. Time and again the doctrine of the divine right of the king and his absolute authority above the law was asserted.

These claims to absolute royal power were not universally accepted and they were at times challenged. The Cortes of Valladolid of 1442, for example, seized the opportunity presented to them when John II fell into the hands of his noble opponents in order to secure substantial concessions from the king. These included the establishment of a solemn pact (*pacto*), contract (*contracto*) and law (*ley*) between the king and his subjects which prohibited the alienation of royal towns to the nobility. If John II or any of his successors failed to observe the contract, then those subjects who were affected by any such alienation had the right to organize armed resistance. This is precisely what the people of Fuenteovejuna did in 1476. Following a traditional form of organization which had characterized many other similar episodes in medieval Castile, and which would be highly influential in the revolt of the Comuneros of 1520, they had entered into a sworn association or *comunidad*, and on the night of 22 September they rose up and killed the tyrannous Fernán Gómez de Guzmán who illegally held the

Spain's vast array of castles, now such evocative
and picturesque features of the landscape, in fact
represent the history of a people permanently at
war. For centuries the threat of violent conflict
was never far from Spanish life.

Upper row, left to right: the Alcázar of Segovia
and ruins at Clavijo. It was at Clavijo that Santiago appeared in battle against the Arabs.
Lower row: the castles of Coca, built for the
Fonseca family, and Belmonte (New Castile).

Dynastic union is the key to Spanish history up to the end of the fifteenth century, and that is why heraldry is so conspicuous throughout Spanish art. The marriage of Isabella of Castile and Ferdinand of Aragon in 1469 was the culmination of these unions and it made Spain a single nation for the first time. They reigned as equal monarchs and were buried together in the cathedral that was built in the last city to be won back from the Moors, Granada. The splendid grille to their tomb, made in 1518 by Bartolomé de Jaén, shows their united coat of arms: the castles and lions of Castile and León quartered with the vertical stripes of Aragon.

town. The rising was to be immortalized by Lope de Vega's play *Fuenteovejuna*, but it was by no means exceptional. A *comunidad* would come into existence when grave abuses were perceived to exist or when royal and urban authorities were failing in their duties. In such cases a *comunidad* regarded its violence as being justified, acted as it felt the authorities should have been doing, and usually made a point of focusing its activities openly and 'lawfully' on the main square of the town. Despite the development of absolutist theories about royal power, the towns of Castile still retained strong constitutionalist and communal traditions.

In contrast to the absolutism of Castile, the Crown of Aragon developed an extreme form of constitutionalism which is best described as 'pactism'. The powers of the king were derived not from God but from a contractual relationship or 'pact' between the king and his people. In fact in the kingdom of Aragon proper it was believed that these contractual arrangements were enshrined in the *fueros* or customary laws of the legendary kingdom of Sobrarbe, and that their essence was contained in the Aragonese oath of allegiance to the king:

> We who are as good as you and together are more powerful than you, make you our king and lord, provided that you observe our *fueros* and liberties, and if not, not.

Similarly in Catalonia political authority was envisaged as having been originally created by free and equal men for their own convenience and on the basis of contractual agreements. 'Never', wrote the Catalan Francesc Eiximenis (*c.* 1340–1409), 'did people grant absolute authority to anyone save on the basis of certain pacts and laws.' It followed, therefore, that any system of government that involved the use of absolute power and was not based on pactism was tyrannous.

What is remarkable about such theories concerning the nature and origins of political authority is that they were backed up by institutions which made constitutionalism feasible in practice. The Cortes of each of the states which made up the Crown of Aragon emerged during the thirteenth century, and they quickly established effective limitations on royal power. In these Cortes, for example, the grievances of subjects had to be redressed before the king was voted any taxation, and since the rulers had to swear to observe the laws, the Cortes also had a great deal of legislative power. Indeed by the end of the thirteenth century the Cortes shared sovereignty with the monarchy, and shortly after they established the principle of regular meetings irrespective of whether the ruler wished to hold them or not, with triennial meetings being stipulated for the Cortes of Catalonia and Valencia, and biennial ones for Aragon. But the truly unique feature about the powers of these Cortes was the emergence of a powerful standing committee, known as the *Generalitat* or *Diputació*, which was created to ensure a continuity of 'parliamentary' control. The Catalan *Generalitat*, for example, had already emerged by the end of the thirteenth century on a temporary basis, but it became permanent after 1359, and from 1365 onwards it established its headquarters in Barcelona. What this meant in practice was that between meetings of the Cortes the monarch and royal officials were subject to the strict control of the *Generalitat*, which by the mid-fifteenth century virtually collected and controlled royal taxation, acted as the treasury of Catalonia, and had vast legal and bureaucratic powers. In no other state of Western Europe did 'parliamentary constitutionalism' develop in such a sophisticated and powerful way. By the end of the Middle Ages, therefore, 'united' Spain contained the uneasy combination of the constitutionalism of the Crown of Aragon and the absolutism of the kingdom of Castile.

This combination, however, proved fruitful to historical and political thought, and perhaps no better example of Spain's contribution in these fields can be chosen than the outstanding intervention of the Spaniards in the debates at the great General Council of Basle (1431–49). Fairly early in its proceedings the Council was plunged into a bitter dispute over a matter of protocol, namely which of the two 'nations' of Spain and England should enjoy precedence in the seating arrangements. It fell to Alonso García de Santa María, bishop of Burgos and son of the ex-rabbi Pablo de Santa María, to state the Spanish case. His famous speech was very much in the tradition of the *laudes Hispaniae*. Spain, he argued, clearly deserved precedence over England because its people were noble and ancient, being the direct descendants of the Visigoths and, through them, the heirs to the Roman empire. Moreover Spain had a magnificent record in the defence of Christendom and the Church, being the birthplace of martyrs and *reconquistadores*. This speech by a Castilian *converso* bishop in praise of 'the Spanish nation' nicely illustrates the theme of unity and diversity. But so too do the debates about conciliar and papal power which followed. For the leading exponent of those who argued that the council was sovereign and the pope merely its minister was John of Segovia who, by claiming that power resided in the community and not with individuals, was putting forward ideas about constitutional monarchy which anticipated Locke and Rousseau. Opposed to this view were the supporters of papal monarchy led by another Spaniard, the *converso* Dominican Juan de Torquemada, whose arguments about the absolute sovereignty of the monarch anticipated the ideas of Jean Bodin. The fact that the leading political thinkers were Spaniards, that one of them was a *converso*, and that they argued such diametrically opposed views, demonstrates that 'the Spanish nation' at Basle had much to offer in terms of sophistication, unity, and diversity.

u bun gelus udpsehendia
draconem & ligauia eum
In abissum . Id est
diabolum

The myth of Spain's destiny

Throughout the Middle Ages, Christian Spain was at war with the Moors, an alien people identified with the enemies of Christ. As the Christians gradually, over hundreds of years, succeeded in pushing back the frontiers and reconquering the peninsula, they saw themselves as fulfilling God's purpose and regaining a paradise that had been lost through the sins of their ancestors. It was not an ordinary war, but a cosmic drama.

Apocalyptic writings foretelling the triumph of Good over Evil were significantly popular in Spain. A commentary by the eighth-century monk Beatus of Liébana on the Book of Revelation was illustrated many times, its vision of the victory of angelic light over satanic darkness giving visible form to the faith that sustained Christian Spain. *Opposite*: a page from a manuscript made in the eleventh century. The Angel with the key binds the Dragon and shuts him in the bottomless pit. *Above*: St Isidore, a detail from the miraculous banner of Baeza, thirteenth century. *Left*: miniature from Alfonso X's *Cantigas de Santa María* showing the Christian army.

The three cultures of medieval Spain

The co-existence in Spain of the three religions – Christianity, Islam and Judaism – produced unprecedented tensions but also brought unprecedented rewards. Nowhere else in Europe was the cultural mix so rich or the intellectual horizons so wide, and it was the Christians who were the main beneficiaries.

For the Jewish community in Toledo Moorish craftsmen built the synagogue of El Tránsito in 1366 (*far left*). It represents a moment of harmony between the three religions: the inscriptions, in Hebrew and Arabic using Hebrew script, praise God, King Pedro, the ruler of Toledo, and Samuel Levi, his treasurer, who paid for it. The harmony did not last; Levi was later executed by King Pedro.

An Old Testament commissioned in 1422 by Don Luis de Guzmán – the Alba Bible – represents an even closer co-operation. Don Luis called upon Jewish scholars to provide a rabbinical commentary on the text and to advise on the illustrations. These were made by Christians but reflect Jewish interpretations. Here (*above left*), in the miniature of Moses bringing the Tablets of the Law from Mt Sinai, the Commandments seem to have been written (in Hebrew) by a Jewish scribe and then combined rather awkwardly with the figure of Moses by a Christian artist.

A tale of chivalry or romance clearly derived from Christian prototypes appears unexpectedly on a ceiling in the Hall of the Kings in the last great Moorish palace of Spain, the Alhambra in Granada. The artists, probably of the late fourteenth century, seem to have been Moors from Castile who had worked for Christian patrons. How these pictures were reconciled with the Islamic ban on figural art is unknown.

The terrain

The Spanish landscape, with its harsh contrasts of parched desert and lush farmland, has been vital to Spanish history. Large parts of the country consist of sierra – bare hills, barren and difficult of access. The mountain barrier of the Pyrenees effectively isolated the peninsula from the rest of Europe for long periods.

In the sierras rainfall is low (less than 20 cm a year) and the soil unsuitable for either crops or pastures. This area (*left*) is part of the old kingdom of Granada. By contrast, the fertile regions, often more fertile in the past than they are now, have tempted invaders and provoked jealousies between local rulers. At La Hiruela, in the province of Jaén (*below*), the valleys can be terraced and planted with olives and other crops.

When Ferdinand and Isabella were married in 1469, it prepared the way for the union in 1479 of two of the major power blocs into which Christian Iberia was divided, the Crown of Aragon and the kingdom of Castile (the third was the kingdom of Portugal). It was a marriage of the most far-reaching consequences for Spain, for the church and for the world. For Spain because they completed the reconquest and began the process of making Spain a single state; for the church because they made religious unity a condition of political unity, vowing to suppress not only Judaism and Islam but Christian unorthodoxy as well; and for the world because it was under their auspices that Columbus sailed to the New World. Their portraits (*right*) appear on the façade of Salamanca University; the encircling inscription in Greek reads: 'The monarchs to the university and the university to the monarchs.'

UNITY AND EMPIRE, 1500–1800: SPAIN AND EUROPE J.H. ELLIOTT

For about three hundred years, from the early sixteenth to the early nineteenth century, Spain was a major European power; and for perhaps one hundred of those three hundred years, between the mid-sixteenth and the mid-seventeenth centuries, it was the greatest power in the Western world. The experience of power – of power gained and then of power diminished and lost – had a profound impact not only on the way in which Spanish society and civilization developed during the course of those centuries, but also on the way in which Spaniards continued to think about themselves and their place in the world in the two centuries that followed. The questions pressed in upon Spaniards of the post-imperial era. What had made Spain great? Why had its greatness come to an end? Why did the country which once believed itself entrusted with the destiny of Europe now find itself apparently excluded from that same European destiny?

These questions, once the source of such anguished introspection, have lost something of their urgency as a changing Spain assumes its place within the new European community of the late twentieth century. But they remain significant, not least because the suggested answers helped to create the self-image of generations of Spaniards, leaving them with the sense that the very qualities and characteristics that had enabled them to win and govern an empire left them somehow ineligible for full participation in the life of modern Europe. By interpreting the achievements and the failures of the past in terms of a presumed Spanish national character, which became fixed at some given moment in the course of Spanish history, a succession of nineteenth and twentieth-century Spanish philosophers and historians contributed to the creation of a collective consciousness which took as its starting-point the belief that Spain was somehow *different*.

'The Pyrenees', wrote one of the most influential of these authors, Angel Ganivet, in his *Idearium Español* of 1897, 'are both an isthmus and a wall; they do not prevent invasions, but they isolate us and allow us to preserve our independent character. In reality, we have always thought ourselves islanders, and perhaps this error may explain many anomalies in our history.' This sense of Spain's difference, based on the preservation of its 'independent character', was to some Spaniards, and most recently to the propagandists of the regime of General Franco, a source of national pride. To others it was a source of profound concern, and even of national shame. But both groups saw the difference of Spain as some kind of magic key for unlocking the mysteries of the Spanish past, and neither appreciated its inadequacies as an instrument of historical explanation.

All peoples possess a certain idea of themselves and of the community which they constitute, and in the course of time this sense fosters the development of certain shared characteristics. These in turn shape the peoples' response to specific historical situations, but those situations will tend to reinforce some characteristics at the expense of others, and so change the composition of the 'national character'. As a result, 'national character' itself is as much a variable as any other historical phenomenon, dominant at some moments, less dominant at others, and subject to the transforming effects of time and events. This is what happened with Spain. Its acquisition and subsequent loss of empire were the product of a multitude of forces, some of them intrinsic to the peninsula itself, and others common to the wider European world of the sixteenth and seventeenth centuries. The interplay of those various forces gave 'Spain' – the new Spanish entity created by the dynastic union of Castile and Aragon at the end of the fifteenth century – its moments of triumph and defeat, shaping the structure of Spanish government and society, and with them the whole collective experience that went towards the making of modern Spanish identity.

Nationhood and Empire

When Granada fell to the forces of Christian Spain in 1492, and Columbus brought back to the Spanish sovereigns the news of strange islands and peoples far away to the west, there was little to indicate that, within two generations, Spain would have become the greatest power in Europe. Indeed, there was no guarantee that 'Spain', as such, would continue to exist. The union of Castile and Aragon was purely dynastic, and correspondingly fragile, since it depended on the unpredictable life prospects of a handful of royal personages. Its fragility was exposed for the first time in 1497 when Prince John, the only son of Ferdinand and Isabella, died at the age of nineteen. When Isabella herself died in 1504, the throne of Castile passed to her eldest surviving daughter, Joanna, married to the Burgundian Archduke Philip, who was heir to the Austrian House of Habsburg. Ferdinand, who outlived his wife by twelve years, remained king of Aragon. Disturbed at the prospect of his inheritance passing to a foreign dynasty, Ferdinand promptly remarried, this time a French princess. It was only the blighting of his hopes of succession by this second marriage that ended the possibility of a dissolution of the union of Castile and Aragon and of a new fragmentation of the 'Spain' that he and his first wife had worked so hard to create.

It was this Spain – a Spain as yet without Portugal, in spite of repeated dynastic marriages between the Castilian and Portuguese royal houses – that was to be inherited on the death of Ferdinand in 1516 by his fifteen-year-old Habsburg grandson, Charles of Ghent. In 1517 Charles arrived in Spain from the Netherlands, where he had spent his youth, to assume direct

41

The revolt of the Comuneros (so-called because they set up communes of their own) was motivated by Castilian resentment of the wider national and international policies of Charles V, which seemed to ignore Castilian interests. It ended with defeat at Villalar in April 1521, when their leaders, including Juan Bravo, the Segovia captain, were captured and executed. As an expression of local patriotism, however, the Comuneros continued to strike a chord in Castilian hearts. This monument to Bravo was erected in Segovia in the nineteenth century.

control of his new inheritance from his mother, Joanna, who had lost her reason after the premature death of her husband and was deemed unfit to govern. Two years later, Charles was elected Holy Roman Emperor in succession to his paternal grandfather, the Emperor Maximilian. As a result, for the best part of the next forty years, until the Emperor Charles V abdicated as king of Spain in 1556, the Spanish realms formed part of a wider grouping, a supranational European community, whose constituent parts all owed allegiance to the man who claimed the titular leadership of Christendom by virtue of his position as Holy Roman Emperor. The community over which he presided consisted of his Burgundian inheritance of the Netherlands, his Habsburg patrimonial inheritance of the Austrian lands, and his Castilian-Aragonese inheritance of the Iberian peninsula itself, together with Aragon's possessions in Italy, and Castile's new transatlantic dominions, at this very moment being dramatically extended by Cortés' conquest of an empire in Mexico.

During the years in which it was subsumed into this supranational empire of Charles V, Spain acquired a mission, or more accurately, had a mission thrust upon it. Under Ferdinand and Isabella it had already pursued expansionist policies in Italy, where its defeat of the French laid the foundations for a Spanish-Italian empire embracing Sicily and Naples, and also in North Africa, to which Castile had carried the victorious war of reconquest against Islam after capturing Granada. Now, however, as a result of Charles' dynastic and imperial interests, Spain faced the prospect of an open-ended commitment of its manpower and money to the support of its ruler's interests and ambitions in central and northern Europe.

The commitment was expressed by the emperor's advisers in terms of a historic mission. At a meeting of the Cortes of Castile held in Santiago de Compostela in 1520, just before Charles left the peninsula for northern Europe to assume his new inheritance as Holy Roman Emperor, the deputies were told that 'Spain's glory, long asleep, has now returned. Those who have sung its praises tell us that when other nations sent tributes to Rome, Spain sent emperors . . . Now the empire has come to Spain in search of an emperor and our King of Spain has, by God's grace, become King of the Romans and emperor of the world.'

Tensions in Castile

In the short run, this appeal to Spaniards, and in the first instance to Castilians, to identify themselves with a divinely ordained imperial mission, fell on deaf ears. Its audience heard in the appeal not so much a historic call to arms, as the jangling of coins in purses. By the time Charles was embarking for northern Europe in May 1520, Castile was in a state of rebellion. The

revolt of the Comuneros – the communes of Castile – was to cast a long shadow over the future of Spain, creating a set of popular heroes, who, in the more propitious climate of the nineteenth century, would be commemorated by statues in town *plazas* like that of Juan Bravo erected in Segovia by a liberal city council.

Their rebellion, at least in its opening stages, represented a remarkably coherent movement of protest by the cities of the central Castilian tableland, like Toledo, Segovia, Avila and Valladolid, in defence of an endangered community of the realm. But if in the first instance it was a movement of protest against foreign rulers, foreign involvements, and foreign-inspired taxes, it was also a movement designed to save and restore a system of government rooted in the historical traditions of medieval Castile – a system founded on the belief that the king had certain contractual obligations towards the community he governed, and that if he ignored those obligations the community had the right to rise against a tyrannical ruler in the name of the common good.

As the revolt of the Comuneros swept through the cities of Castile, it began to develop radical tendencies that frightened members of the upper classes whose support was essential to its prospects of success. With the nobility turning against the rebels and rallying to the crown, the Comunero cause began to crumble; and in April 1521 the rebel army was defeated by royalist forces on the field of Villalar. This was to be the last great insurrection in Castile until the early nineteenth century, when once again the people would take up arms, this time against the invading armies of Napoleon.

By the standard of most European countries, Castile in the nearly three centuries between the defeat of the Comuneros and the Napoleonic Wars displayed a remarkable degree of public order and political stability. But the order and stability were achieved at a price. The defeat at Villalar represented the defeat of what had until then been a vigorous Castilian tradition of communal rights against authoritarian government – a tradition of which the cities were the proud guardians, and which was institutionalized, however inadequately, in the parliamentary body of the Cortes of Castile.

The Castilian Cortes, which soon came to consist exclusively of the representatives of eighteen principal cities, still remained capable on occasions of vigorous opposition to the fiscal demands of the crown, and would continue to be summoned with frequency until 1665. But the suppression of the Comunero revolt effectively stunted the possibilities for securing some wider participation of the community in the political process. Since other sixteenth-century European states were also moving in a more authoritarian direction, the Castilian experience was by no means unique. But the defeat of the

Ceiling of the ballroom of the palace of the Buen
Retiro, painted by Luca Giordano with an allegory glorifying the Spanish monarchy. At the top
sits Jupiter surrounded by the Olympian gods;
beneath him the celestial globe with the constel-
lations; then Spain as a crowned and throned
female figure; and at the bottom Charles II's
ancestor, Philip the Good, Duke of Burgundy,
receiving the Golden Fleece from Jason.

rebels, by weakening the rich communal and libertarian traditions of medieval and Renaissance Castile, reduced the
possible range of future options for creative response when
problems multiplied. It also sharpened the constitutional differences between political life in Castile and other regions of the
peninsula, particularly the Crown of Aragon (the kingdoms of
Aragon and Valencia and the Principality of Catalonia), whose
representative institutions served as a valuable shield against
the arbitrary exercise of power by the crown.

If, in the short run, Charles V's appeal to his Castilian subjects
to assist him in his imperial mission was rejected, in the longer
run he won the support of a political and religious establishment which had nowhere else to turn. Although for much of his
reign Charles' imperial obligations kept him away from the
Iberian peninsula, he managed with the passage of the years to
identify increasingly with his Spanish kingdoms – so much so
that, on handing over power to his son Philip II in 1556, he chose
Spain for his retirement, settling down with his little court in a
small palace adjoining the remote monastery of Yuste, in
Extremadura. For his part, Philip II, born and brought up in
Castile, but subjected as a young man to the cultural influences
of Italy and the Netherlands, would be a purely Spanish king.

As if in compensation for this gradual hispanicization of the
dynasty, the Castilian elite moved closer towards identifying
itself with the dynasty's aims. For the sons of many of the noble
and *hidalgo* (gentry) families of Castile, prospects at home
were limited, and Charles' imperial commitments created new
possibilities for office, honour, and military command. Charles,
for his part, increasingly needed the soldiers and the money
that Castile, of all his dominions, could best provide.

'One monarch, one empire and one sword'

But there were other, less tangible, reasons why Spain, and
particularly Castile, should have assumed the role of standard-
bearer of the Habsburg imperial mission – a mission graphi-
cally expressed in Charles' emblem of the Pillars of Hercules
with its motto of *Plus Ultra* suggesting unlimited possibilities far
beyond Europe's traditional boundaries. Habsburg universa-
lism gave the Castilian elite an ideology and a cause. At a time of
military expansion and the acquisition of a great new empire in
America, the sense of participation in a divinely ordained
mission conferred a valuable legitimacy on the triumphs of
Spanish arms. As the victories multiplied, the Castilians came to
think of themselves as a people chosen by God for His special
purposes. Contemplating the great and growing expanse of
their monarch's dominions on both sides of the Atlantic, they
also saw themselves as the heirs, and even the superiors, of the
Romans in the magnitude of their conquests and the heroism of
their deeds.

The young Charles V, aged 20, looking more like his Habsburg father than his Spanish mother. Charles was born and grew up in the Netherlands, not visiting Spain until 1517, when he came in order to be recognized as king, first by Castile and then by Aragon.

But what was the divinely ordained purpose of empire, and what were the special obligations that it conferred upon Castile? In a famous sonnet addressed to Charles V, the Spanish poet Hernando de Acuña looked forward to the day when there would be one shepherd and one flock in the world, and 'one monarch, one empire and one sword'. Charles, as Holy Roman Emperor, saw himself as the Christian knight on horseback, charged with the holy task of saving Christendom from foreign enemies and its own internal feuds – an image which in due course would be immortalized on canvas by the genius of Titian. The enemy battering at the gates of Christendom were the Ottoman Turks, the warriors of Islam. The internal feuds sprang from the rivalries of Christian princes and, more ominously still, from the spread of Protestant heresy in the wake of Luther's challenge to the papacy. It became Charles' life mission, therefore, to throw back the Turks and bring back a divided Christendom to allegiance to the Roman church. Although, on his abdication, the title of Holy Roman Emperor passed along with the Habsburg patrimonial lands to the junior, Austrian, branch of the family, his mission was transmitted to his Spanish Habsburg successors in their capacity as kings of Spain and as heads of the so-called Spanish Monarchy, the *monarquía española*.

The Spanish Monarchy, then, under Castilian leadership, was to be the champion of Christian values and the guardian of stability, hierarchy and order in a storm-tossed world. This was the image constantly purveyed by the poets and playwrights who sang its praises, and by the artists who celebrated its triumphs in peace and war. In 1697, three years before the extinction of the male line of the Spanish Habsburgs, and at a moment when the princes of Europe were hovering around what appeared to be the deathbed of the Spanish Monarchy, the Italian artist Luca Giordano painted an allegorical ceiling for the Casón of the Buen Retiro palace on the outskirts of Madrid. Seated between two sinister figures symbolizing respectively the Age of Bronze and the Age of Iron, the radiant figure of the Monarchy presides beneficently over her peoples, while her enemies lie subjugated at her feet. In 1764 a greater Italian artist, Tiepolo, decorated the throne room of the new royal palace in Madrid with another allegorical painting depicting a similar theme – the figure of Spain surrounded by images of imperial grandeur, while her peoples enjoyed the fruits of peace and prosperity, and the royal standard floated over the defeated Moors. Times might change, but over three centuries the message remained the same. Oblivious of time's ravages, Spain continued to fulfil its mission, upholding the Christian virtues and bringing peace and prosperity to its peoples.

The peace, unfortunately, was only relative and by no means universal. For most of the time during its three imperial centuries, Spain was at war, although, except during the worst years of the seventeenth and early eighteenth centuries, the fighting was in large part conducted outside the peninsula. But Spain, while it might enjoy peace at home, was regarded by much of the rest of Europe as harbouring dangerous aspirations after universal monarchy. The silver flowing in from its American dominions created an image of boundless wealth enabling it to pursue its sinister designs; its treatment of the Indian population of the New World, widely reported through sixteenth-century Europe, fostered a Black Legend of Spanish atrocities; and although Europeans might laugh at the swagger and bravado of the Castilian infantrymen who manned the famous *tercios*, they also feared them as the all too effective agents of an arrogant world power.

For the rulers of Spain in the sixteenth and seventeenth centuries, however, the picture of the world was a very different one. Naturally they greeted the triumphs of Spanish arms – the victory of Charles V over the German Protestant princes at Mühlberg (1547), the defeat of the Turks at the great naval battle of Lepanto (1571) – as clear evidence of God's favour for His chosen people. By the same token, they acknowledged with gratitude the extension of Spanish dominion through the world. The conquest of the Philippines in the 1560s provided new opportunities for the propagation of the faith. The extinction of Portugal's native ruling house and Philip II's subsequent acquisition of Portugal and its overseas empire in 1580 made it possible to realize at last the old dream of uniting the peninsula beneath a single ruler. Yet even as Spain appeared to the rest of the world to be moving implacably towards universal empire, Philip and his ministers felt the heavy burdens upon them – the need to hold the Turks at bay in the Mediterranean and North Africa, and to check the spread of heresy through central and northern Europe, where it was contaminating even Philip's own subjects in the Netherlands. Each new acquisition of territory brought fresh responsibilities, extending the area of Spain's vital interests, and requiring fresh sacrifices of its peoples.

Government by paper

All these extensive territories in Europe and America had somehow to be governed and defended, and it was in the reign of Philip II (1556–98) that the great bureaucratic and military apparatus required for the maintenance of empire was finally consolidated. During the reign of Charles V, power had travelled with the emperor, who was always on the move, and although effective institutional structures existed for the government of the Spanish realms, there was no capital city in Spain to serve as a fixed centre of empire or as a residence for the court. It was only in 1561 that Philip settled on the small town of Madrid, in the very centre of Castile, as the seat of his court

Charles V as the champion of Catholicism at the battle of Mühlberg (1547), where his armies defeated the Protestant princes of Germany. The painting by Titian is a powerful image of imperial authority, though Charles did in fact take part in the battle wielding a lance. More typically Spanish is Antonio de Pereda's 'Memento Mori' (*right*), painted in the next century; a winged angel points to Charles's immense empire on the globe, surmounted by a portrait medallion, as an allegory of the vanity of human ambition.

With Philip II the modern age of 'government by paper' was born. Like a meticulous civil servant, the king (*below*, portrayed by Pantoja de la Cruz) ruled his diverse territories from his office in Madrid or in the Escorial.

and administration, setting aside the superior claims of the more famous cities of Toledo and Valladolid. The old royal castle, the Alcázar, overlooking the unimpressive River Manzanares, became at once his principal royal residence and the bureaucratic centre of empire. Two years later, the king began work on the construction, thirty miles north-west of Madrid, of the great granite monastery-palace of the Escorial, which would not be completed until 1584. Here, on the southern slopes of the Guadarrama mountains, he could escape the intense heat of the Madrid summers, while continuing to govern his empire from his desk.

In the following decades, Madrid's 20,000 inhabitants would increase dramatically in number, to reach perhaps 100,000 by the end of the century. A city of bureaucrats and courtiers, and of an expanding service population to cater to their needs, it would become the parasitic centre of a world-wide empire, draining life away from the proud cities of the region which a generation earlier had been in the forefront of the Comunero revolt. Toledo retained its cultural and intellectual vigour into the early seventeenth century; and, away to the south, Seville, nourished by the constant flow of silver from the Indies, and with a population of some 150,000 by 1600, was a world unto itself. But from the early seventeenth century civic culture began to retreat before the court culture of Madrid. As a contemporary refrain put it: *sólo Madrid es corte* – Madrid alone is the court.

The growing dominance of Madrid was the dominance of an essentially artificial capital city, designed to meet the functional requirements of empire. The administration, housed in the Alcázar palace on the floor beneath the royal apartments, consisted of a series of councils, largely staffed by professional bureaucrats. There were councils for the government of the different territories of the crown – Castile, Aragon, the Indies, Italy, Portugal and Flanders – as well as councils with specialist concerns, such as finance, war, and the Inquisition. A Council of State, consisting largely of nobles and a sprinkling of clerics, advised the monarch on matters of high policy. At the centre of this system sat the supreme source of authority and patronage, the king. Philip II, that most conscientious of monarchs, took his governmental duties with extreme seriousness, seeing them as a divinely imposed obligation, for God and the king of Spain were always close allies, or so at least each king of Spain was brought up to believe. He would spend long hours at his desk poring over his correspondence and the *consultas*, the minutes of the councils, which he would meticulously annotate in his spidery hand. One day alone he read and signed four hundred documents. No wonder his eyes grew red with the strain, or that his face acquired the parchment colour of a man who had come to live among, and for, his papers.

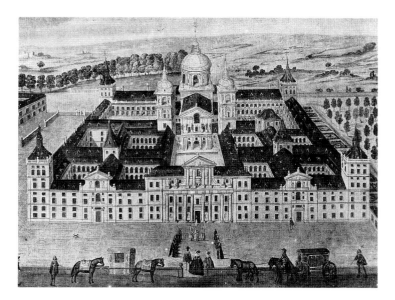

The Escorial itself (*left*) was the perfect expression of Philip's character: a Jeronymite monastery dedicated to St Lawrence (and reputedly taking the grid-iron of the saint's martyrdom as the model for the plan) was also the centre of government and the mausoleum of his dynasty. From here Philip issued his instructions in the form of written memoranda, a vast number of which survive. This example (*centre left*) is a letter from the pope annotated in his own hand. The same Spanish bureaucracy was transferred virtually unchanged to the empire in America. *Bottom*: a drawing by the Peruvian Guaman Poma de Ayala showing an administrative official.

The steady stream of information flowing in from all parts of the world to Madrid, to be duly scrutinized, discussed and summarized by the councils and the secretaries before being transmitted upwards for decision by the king, was critical for the administration of Spain's vast and dispersed global empire. Without all this documentation, and the officials who generated and sifted it, and saw that it was eventually deposited in the royal archive established for the purpose by Charles V at Simancas on the outskirts of Valladolid, the Spanish Monarchy and empire could never have survived for three centuries.

Government by paper, on a scale hitherto unprecedented in Western societies, was to be one of the most enduring, if ambiguous, legacies of Spain to the modern world. It brought with it many important benefits. Carefully compiled questionnaires provided the crown with large quantities of detailed information about the lands and peoples that it ruled; and every act by a royal official was carefully scrutinized and reported to Madrid. As a result, it was possible to establish and maintain orderly administrative procedures over vast areas of territory. The subjects of the king of Spain were, by the standards of the time, a much governed people, and they grew accustomed to turning to government and the law for the redress of grievances. The discontented and aggrieved, whether they were Neapolitan nobles or Indian villagers in Mexico, soon learned how to use the system, how to lobby at different levels of the bureaucratic hierarchy, and how to pursue their claims all the way, if necessary, to the highest levels in Madrid. The king, supreme but remote, was seen as the final figure of resort, always ready – it was assumed – to restore justice when it was abused by ignorant or corrupt officials lower down the scale.

Many of the officials who manned the vast bureaucracy fulfilled their duties conscientiously and devoted their professional lives to upholding the royal authority they had been called upon to serve. Indeed it was for this that they had been trained. The crown needed responsible and informed officials, and its rapidly expanding bureaucratic requirements during the sixteenth century had important, and in many ways beneficial, educational consequences within the Spanish peninsula. From 1493 a university training in the law became an essential requirement for those aspiring to serve in the royal administration, and this led to a dramatic expansion in the number of universities in Spain – from 11 at the beginning of the sixteenth century to 33 by the end of it. The expansion of the universities was accompanied by a parallel rise in the number of primary and secondary schools in Castile, extending to small towns and even villages. As a result, literacy rates in Castile by the late sixteenth century, at least among the male population, were very respectable by contemporary European standards, reaching 60 per cent or more. This was a society which could, and did, read books – many of them books of devotion, but also books of chivalry, which were enormously popular – and a vast mass of ephemera, of broadsheets and chapbooks.

The price of bureaucracy

Against these beneficial consequences of Spanish pioneering in bureaucratic government, however, must be set the more negative consequences – the chicanery and corruption, the narrowness of vision of excessively legalistic officials, and, above all, the interminable delays. 'If', remarked one of Philip II's viceroys, 'death came from Madrid, we should all live to a very old age.' Yet the Spanish bureaucratic apparatus could be highly effective, and nowhere more so than in mobilizing armies and equipping fleets. The preparation of the great Spanish Armada sent against England in 1588 was a formidable piece of organization on a scale which no other contemporary European state could have begun to contemplate, and if organization by itself were enough to win battles, the Invincible Armada would indeed have been invincible. But if, when roused to action, the king of Spain's officials were capable of spectacular achievements, the large and cumbersome bureaucracy to which they belonged had the natural tendency of all bureaucracies to inertia. Philip II himself was almost overwhelmed by the machine, and his less conscientious or less able Habsburg successors, Philip III (1598–1621), Philip IV (1621–65) and Charles II (1665–1700), were in effect its prisoners, forever putting their signature to orders which were all too liable to become trapped somewhere in the system, and which met with a greater or lesser degree of compliance depending on the nature of their contents and the willingness of subordinates to see them carried out.

Bureaucracy was to leave a deep imprint on the Hispanic world, giving official documents, duly notarized and certified, a heavy symbolic and practical importance in the lives of individuals and communities far beyond the days of the Habsburgs and their eighteenth-century Bourbon successors. This generalized need for documents inevitably gave officials countless opportunities for the exercise of influence. As a result, the legitimacy that adhered to authority in the societies of the Hispanic world was not necessarily accompanied by any high degree of respect. Yet given the enormous logistical problems involved in running a world-wide empire from Madrid, the heavy weight of bureaucracy, however unfortunate, would have been difficult to avoid. In this, as in many other areas, imperial Spain and its territories were to pay a heavy price for its pioneering enterprise.

By the later sixteenth century something of this price was already becoming clear. The maintenance of empire, and the unflagging pursuit by the dynasty of its global mission, were making demands on Spanish society which would profoundly affect its long-term development, and its image of itself. In particular, Spain's European mission could only be realized – or so it seemed – through discipline and unity. A country engaged in unceasing struggle with the forces of Islam and heresy had no hope of victory unless it remained unswerving in its own single-minded devotion to the faith. But Spain, in spite of the events of 1492, was still in essence a pluralistic society, consisting of considerable Moorish (Morisco) minorities, heavily concentrated in the south and the east, and also of many families of Jewish origin, which had formally converted to Christianity during the fifteenth century. Morisco communities, although forced to renounce their faith, still clung to their old traditions and ways of life, while the genuineness of many of the Jewish conversions remained open to doubt. In such circumstances, how could there be true unity and purity of the faith?

The price of unity

The Inquisition was active from the first in pursuing any hints of deviation, and Moorish and Jewish converts were obvious targets of suspicion. The rise of heresy in northern Europe, and the fear that it would infiltrate into the peninsula, merely added to the doubts about the reliability of these minority groups. Royal and ecclesiastical preoccupation with the preservation of religious orthodoxy on the one hand, and the popular hostility of Old Christians to the ethnic minorities on the other, combined to produce a society that became obsessed in the sixteenth century with the idea of *limpieza*, of purity and cleanliness. In the desire to cleanse the community of all its impure elements, regulations were introduced to exclude those 'tainted' with Jewish and Moorish blood from holding office in secular and ecclesiastical corporations, and in the service of the crown. These *limpieza* statutes, even if often evaded, spread fear and distrust through society, creating opportunities for denunciation which added immeasurably to the tensions within it, and blighting many lives.

In effect, the obsession with purity, whether of the faith or of blood, increasingly narrowed the range within which sixteenth-century Spaniards operated, constricting their cultural world and reducing the formerly rich diversity of their civilization. Many of the converted Jews – the *conversos* – learnt to manoeuvre around the rocks and shoals that now loomed up before them, but the Moriscos, as concentrated communities consisting largely of labourers and artisans, were particularly vulnerable to the growing pressures for greater orthodoxy. In 1568 the Granada Moriscos of the Alpujarras rose up in a rebellion which was only suppressed after a long and bloody struggle; and in 1609 the crown 'solved' its Morisco problem by ordering the expulsion of all the Moriscos from Spain. The

The last act of the Reconquest took place in 1609, when the Moors were finally expelled, all attempts at conversion having failed. For a thousand years Spain had been their home. As late as the sixteenth century (*bottom*), they were a familiar part of the scene in Granada. A vivid near-contemporary drawing (*below*) shows them embarking – 300,000 of them – under the eyes of Spanish soldiers on to the boats that would take them to North Africa.

solution was in effect an admission of failure. Christian Spain had failed to secure the genuine conversion and assimilation of its Moorish minority, and the long, pathetic lines of Moriscos – some 300,000 all told – struggling along the roads to the ports of embarkation bore vivid witness to the completenes of the failure.

The *conversos* presented a still more formidable problem, because Jewish blood flowed through the veins of so many members of the urban patriciate and the Castilian nobility. The pernicious assumption that Jewish blood created a predisposition to religious deviancy – in the words of Philip II, 'all the heresies in Germany, France and Spain have been sown by descendants of Jews' – poisoned sixteenth-century Castilian society, and filled the authorities and people alike with irrational fears. The result was an increasingly shrill insistence on the most rigorous orthodoxy, expressed not only in the persecuting activities of the Inquisition, but also in strict measures of censorship, and in a systematic attempt to seal off the peninsula from dangerous foreign influences. In response to the discovery of alleged 'Protestant' cells in Seville and Valladolid, a new and severe Index of prohibited books was introduced in 1559, and Spanish students were forbidden to study in foreign colleges, other than those in Rome, Naples, Bologna and Coimbra.

As Spain entered the age of the Counter-Reformation, therefore, it sought to buttress its own orthodoxy by withdrawing behind a *cordon sanitaire*. In this it was not unique – other European societies were similarly engaging in persecution and strict censorship, in an effort to save themselves from religious division, which was everywhere seen as a sure invitation to political instability. Nor was the process of exclusion ever complete, or completely applied. Spain, after all, was a European power, with important territorial possessions in Italy and the Netherlands, and the constant and continuing contacts with these territories meant a steady inflow into the Iberian peninsula of cultural and intellectual influences from Italy and the north. But at the same time, the intensity of the Spanish response to the perceived threat of contamination by religious heresy – an intensity encouraged by its self-appointed role as the champion of Catholic Christendom, and by the racial diversity of peninsular society – helped to create a fortress mentality with profound implications for Spain's cultural and political development.

A fortress mentality is the mentality of an embattled society, and Spain's image of itself as an embattled society was to survive for many generations, instilling an innate caution in intellectuals and creating in many sections of Spanish society a distrust, amounting at times to paranoia, of new-fangled 'foreign' ideas. This distrust was one reason, although not the only

Increasingly under Philip II, Spain assumed the position of champion of Catholicism and chief opponent of the Reformation. This terracotta figure represents the Duke of Alba subduing a hydra whose heads, symbolizing the enemies of the king, include the Elector of Saxony and Elizabeth I of England.

one, for the relative weakness – by no means foreordained – of Spain's contribution to the rise of modern science. Renaissance Spain shared in the scientific movements of the early sixteenth century. Salamanca was unique among European universities in allowing a place for Copernican astronomy in its curriculum in 1561; and Spaniards made valuable contributions to cosmography and the art of navigation. The sheer insistence on the practical application of scientific inquiry to meet the needs of the state may indeed in the long run have prejudiced its development in Spain by discouraging theoretical speculation with less utilitarian ends. Scientific inquiry suffered, too, from the attempt to drive to the margins of national life men of Jewish origin, who in earlier times had made such a distinctive contribution to Spanish science and medicine. But the turning in of Counter-Reformation Spain upon itself, and the consequent reinforcement of scholastic orthodoxy in Spanish universities, was to shut off the peninsula from vigorous new currents of thought which were to renovate and transform European science in the seventeenth century. As a result, the age of the scientific revolution was to be an age on which Spain turned its back.

But the implications of the new isolationism of the later sixteenth century extended beyond the realms of science and philosophy to affect the whole character of the society and the way it thought about itself. By rejecting Europe, or what it thought of as Europe – a world of dangerous heresies and political disorder – it rejected part of itself, reinforcing certain innate tendencies in peninsular society at the expense of others of which it stood in need. In a society where diversity had once been accepted as a part of life, intolerance, traditionalism, and conformity became the order of the day; and if all European societies of the period were profoundly suspicious of innovation, this one seems to have endorsed with particular fervour the sentiments expressed by the character who appears in one of the vignettes of the seventeenth-century writer, Francisco de Quevedo: 'If we are to survive, let us cling fast to the aphorism which says: "Let what always was done, always be done" (*lo que siempre se hizo, siempre se haga*), because, if it is observed, it will save us from novelties.'

Crisis point

To save oneself from novelties is to run the risk of stagnation, and it was to stagnation that Spain succumbed in the century following the death of Philip II in 1598. Towards the end of his reign, the high price of empire, and of Spain's anti-Protestant crusade in northern Europe, was becoming painfully evident. His long years of power had seen important successes, not least against the Ottoman Turks. But it had also seen major failures, of which the most devastating was its inability to crush heresy and suppress revolt in Spain's northern outpost of the Netherlands. The revolt of the Netherlands in 1566 opened a running sore in the side of the Spanish body politic. The army which the Duke of Alba led northwards from Italy in 1567 to stamp out rebellion failed in its mission; and for the following eighty years, until the formal recognition of Dutch independence by Spain in 1648, the provisioning of the army of Flanders, and the struggle to preserve the integrity of the loyal and Catholic southern provinces of the Netherlands, constituted an enormous and continuing drain on Spanish manpower and resources.

Still worse, the problem of the Dutch became a general northern problem, as Protestantism consolidated itself not only in the rebellious provinces of the northern Netherlands, but also in the British Isles and in large regions of France, including regions adjoining the frontier with Spain. The Atlantic sea-routes linking Spain to its American possessions now became dangerously vulnerable to attack by northern privateers, and this in turn pushed up the costs of imperial defence. Philip II's 'enterprise of England' of 1588 constituted a bold attempt to deal with this problem at source, and the defeat of the Spanish Armada represented a major setback to his policy of turning the tide of heresy in northern Europe and bringing back his rebellious Dutch subjects into the Spanish fold.

Although Spain still remained the dominant power in Europe for the first forty years of the seventeenth century, many contemporaries, not least in Spain itself, felt that the colossus was tiring. The continuous burden of warfare and high taxation had begun to take its toll, especially of Castile, which had borne the brunt of the crown's fiscal and military demands. There was a crisis in the Castilian countryside as heavily taxed peasants deserted their villages, and harvest failure and plague in the closing years of the sixteenth century wiped out some half a million of Castile's population of around 6.5 million. Continuous deficit spending had played havoc with the royal finances, which were dangerously dependent on the regular arrival of large sums of silver from the mines of Mexico and Peru; and the crown's reliance on borrowing had led to the establishment of a system of funding through government bonds which diverted private resources away from more socially productive investments and turned Castile into a *rentier* society living on its annual returns. In Castile, great wealth and great poverty existed side by side, as they did in all European societies of the period. But, in contrast to the vigorous societies of the Protestant north, it was not by the seventeenth century a productive society that was generating significant sources of new wealth.

Many Castilians by the early seventeenth century were aware of the acute difficulties facing their society, and some of them, surveying its earlier achievements, began to think of their country's history in terms of *decline*. This perception of

The Count-Duke of Olivares took over the reins of government from the weak hands of Philip IV. A dynamic and charismatic leader, Olivares laboured to unify and centralize the power of the monarchy and undermine regional independence. This splendid portrait by Velázquez makes him the epitome of Baroque panache.

Charles III was a shrewd and experienced ruler who initiated a period of reform in Spanish economic and political life, choosing enlightened ministers such as Gaspar Melchor de Jovellanos (*far right*), the author of a treatise on Spanish agriculture. A far less appealing character was Manuel Godoy (*bottom*), who rose to power through the queen's favours. All three portraits are by Goya.

decline, which was also taken up by foreign observers and commentators, did not necessarily correspond at all points to reality. Spanish military power in the early seventeenth century was still extremely formidable and Spain's cultural influence in Europe was never greater than in the first four or five decades of the century, when the writers of Spain's Golden Age were widely read and admired, and lesser foreign princes imitated the grave ceremonial of the Spanish Habsburg court. Moreover, many of the economic and social difficulties experienced by seventeenth-century Spain were also being experienced by other European societies of the period. But there was enough truth to the perception of Spain as a great power in decline to establish in the European consciousness an association between Spain and decadence which is only now in the late twentieth century being finally dispelled.

The retreat from empire

Much of the history of Spain in the seventeenth and eighteenth centuries can indeed be interpreted as a commentary on, and response to, the theme of perceived decline. Of all the possible responses to decline, the most obvious, but also the most difficult to implement, was for Spain to retreat from the more isolated and vulnerable outposts of empire, and cut its coat according to its cloth. The crown, after all, was regularly spending far more than its annual income. The costs of imperial defence were rising, and, from around the second decade of the seventeenth century, changing circumstances in the Indies were beginning to reduce drastically the amount of American silver it could expect to receive in any one year.

But retreat from empire is always a delicate enterprise. An imperial elite living on the profits of empire has an obvious interest in the preservation of the status quo, and the Castilian elite, which had for long enjoyed the lucrative pickings of the viceroyalties of Italy and America, was no exception to the rule. In addition, any abandonment of a territory like the southern Netherlands meant placing the Catholic cause in jeopardy, and hence betraying the Habsburg mission. Strategic interests were at stake, too, since it could be argued with some plausibility that to abandon one outpost of empire was to leave the next dangerously exposed to attack. The persistent tendency among the rulers of the Spanish Monarchy in the seventeenth century was therefore to hang on, in the hope that God would once again smile upon His people of Castile.

In the long run, this policy failed in the sense that, in spite of a vast military effort, Spain's Monarchy in Europe suffered a gradual diminution between 1640 and 1714. In 1640, Portugal was to break loose and proclaim itself once again an independent kingdom, after sixty years of 'Babylonian captivity' to Spain. In 1659, under the terms of the Treaty of the Pyrenees,

which ended in France's favour a war for hegemony in Europe that had begun in 1635, the Catalan boundary areas of Roussillon and Cerdagne on the northern side of the mountain range were surrendered to the French. During the reign of Charles II (1665–1700), Spain saw the boundaries of its loyal provinces in the Netherlands eroded, and lost the old Burgundian county of the Franche-Comté, once so dear to the heart of Charles V. Finally, the War of the Spanish Succession of 1701–13, which saw the installation in Madrid of the French Bourbons in succession to the extinct male line of the Habsburgs, ended with the loss to the Emperor in Vienna of the Spanish Netherlands and the Spanish possessions in mainland Italy, of Sicily to the Duke of Savoy, and of Gibraltar and Menorca to England.

Spain fought hard to prevent this slow dismemberment of its European empire. Particularly in the 1620s and 1630s, an enormous effort was made to restore Spanish power and reinvigorate the Castilian economy in the hope of reversing the process of decline. The figure most identified with this effort was the Count-Duke of Olivares, the favourite and principal minister of the young king Philip IV. The ministry of Olivares from 1621 to 1643 was a critical moment for the development of modern Spain because it set the reform agenda for the best part of two centuries, while it simultaneously saw the consolidation of the forces in Spanish society resistant to reform.

Towards unitary government

Olivares appreciated, as his ministerial successors of the eighteenth century were to appreciate, that success in foreign wars was dependent on drastic change at home. A major part of his effort was directed towards strengthening the power and authority of the crown; and for him this meant attempting to establish unified principles of government and taxation throughout the Iberian peninsula, in place of the constitutional and administrative diversity which had distinguished it since the union of Castile and Aragon under Ferdinand and Isabella. This scheme for a unitary Spain, in which all the peoples of the peninsula shared equally in the burdens, and the benefits, of empire, seemed eminently rational to the ministers in Madrid. But to the Basques, the Catalans, the Portuguese and the Valencians it had all the appearance of a sinister design to deprive them of their cherished laws and liberties and to reduce them to subjection to Castile. They therefore resisted to the best of their ability the encroachments of royal power, and in 1640, at a time when the balance of forces in Europe was beginning to tilt against Spain, both Catalonia and Portugal revolted against the government in Madrid.

While Portugal succeeded in retaining its independence, Catalonia, exhausted by war and plague, returned to allegiance to Philip IV in 1652. But the return to allegiance was

Eighteenth-century crafts represented on
Catalan tiles: blacksmith and weaver.

conditional on the king's promise to respect Catalonia's traditional laws and privileges; and during the second half of the seventeenth century the Spanish crown, defeated in its foreign wars, was in no position to resume Olivares' offensive against provincial liberties. But sooner or later the question of a unitary state was bound to return to the top of the royal agenda, if only because, in the Europe of the seventeenth and eighteenth centuries, kings and ministers tended to regard centralization and unity as essential to the enhancement of the power of their states.

Madrid's opportunity came with the change of dynasty on the death of Charles II in 1700. In the disputed succession that followed, the kingdoms of the Crown of Aragon sided with varying degrees of commitment with the Austrian Habsburg claimant against Spain's first Bourbon monarch, Philip V, Charles' chosen successor to his throne. Philip's victory in the War of Succession gave him and his ministers the opportunity to achieve what Olivares had failed to achieve. Using the rebellion of the Crown of Aragon as their pretext, they introduced into Aragon and Valencia, and finally, in 1716, into a defeated Catalonia, the so-called *Nueva Planta* – a new form of government which involved the abolition of their Cortes and traditional constitutional systems, the imposition of new laws, new officials and new taxes, and a ban on the use of the Catalan language for all official business.

With the exception, therefore, of the Basque provinces and Navarre, which maintained their semi-autonomous status until the 1870s, Spain became after 1716, in theory, if not always in practice, a unitary state governed from Madrid. This represented a fundamental change in the equilibrium of forces within the Iberian peninsula, and although the Crown of Aragon in the eighteenth century accommodated itself to the new system with considerable success, the imposition of the heavy hand of Madrid on provincial life was in due course to generate a new set of domestic tensions, and nourish deep springs of resentment against Castile for presuming to identify all Spain with itself.

From the point of view of the dynasty, however, the imposition of the *Nueva Planta* completed a significant piece of business on Madrid's long-standing agenda of reform and constituted an essential precondition for the recovery of Spain as a great European power. But other parts of the agenda proved much harder to realize. In the 1620s Olivares, drawing on the reformist ideas that had surfaced during the reign of Philip III (1598–1621), had put forward ambitious plans for the regeneration of Castilian society and the Castilian economy. 'We must devote all our efforts', wrote Olivares, 'to turning Spaniards into merchants.' These words were written under the impact of the economic successes of the Dutch, and it was in

the first instance to the Dutch – with their trading companies, their technological skills and their industriousness – that he turned for the formulas that could bring salvation to Spain. In other words, Spanish reformers, conscious of their country's declining power and prosperity in relation to former days, were beginning to measure their own against other European societies, and, in the process, to look outside Spain for answers to their problems. Modernization conceived in terms of Europeanization was to be an increasingly insistent theme of Spanish reformers in the coming centuries as they despairingly contrasted the apparently growing backwardness of their own country with the scientific and technological progress being registered by other parts of Europe.

But to turn 'Spaniards into merchants' involved a profound transformation of values in a society in which the aristocratic-religious ethos was deeply entrenched. The same held true of other borrowings from Europe – a Europe against which the Spain of the later sixteenth century had sought to close its doors. The whole programme of reform, therefore, ran up against the engrained resistance to change of a society that had been taught to see resistance to change as essential for the preservation of traditional Spanish values which were everywhere under attack.

If the church and the Inquisition played a leading part in resisting innovations like the liberalization of attitudes to the *conversos*, such resistance was at least tacitly supported by powerful sections of society which feared the impact of reform on their own vested interests. Such people were known from the seventeenth century as the *poderosos* – the powerful ones. As members of the aristocratic, the ecclesiastical and the bureaucratic establishment, the *poderosos* exploited the crown's financial weakness during the seventeenth century to consolidate oligarchical control over the towns and large areas of the countryside, especially in the south. Their pervasive influence was to present a major obstacle to the movement of reform from above, which, after its spectacular failure in the age of Olivares, sprang once again to life with the advent of the Bourbons.

The aim of the Bourbons, as of Olivares before them, was to restore Spanish power through a more rational exploitation of the resources of the Monarchy. The transformation of Spain into a more or less unitary state under Philip V represented an important stage in this process. So, too, did major administrative reforms under Philip and his equally unprepossessing successor, Ferdinand VI (1746–59). The old class of grandees, which had reasserted its influence in the second half of the seventeenth century and controlled large areas of power and patronage through its domination of the Council of State, was once again relegated to the sidelines, as in the reign of Philip II,

For Godoy's palace in Madrid Goya painted roundels symbolizing Industry, Agriculture and Commerce. There was a fourth, Science, which has not survived.

and the Council of State itself was reduced to insignificance. The Bourbons' administrative reforms effectively undercut the traditional Habsburg system of conciliar government by the device of deploying ministers and secretaries directly dependent on the king. Spain, in other words, was adopting a more 'modern' form of government, closely modelled on that of Bourbon France – a form which included the introduction of French-style intendants to strengthen royal administration at the local level.

An agenda of reform

As a result, a new administrative class began to emerge in eighteenth-century Spain, in spite of dogged resistance from the old bureaucracy and its supporters in the universities. It was to this new administrative elite, many of its members drawn from families of the provincial nobility and trained in the law, that the most reform-minded of the eighteenth-century Bourbons, Charles III (1759–88), turned for support. The ministers and civil servants of Charles III – such men as Floridablanca, Jovellanos and Campomanes – had a high sense of royal authority and of the role of the state in promoting reform. In the tradition of Philip II and Olivares, they were strong regalists, determined to reassert the powers of the crown against the encroachments of the church. They saw Spain's possessions in America as the key to its revival in Europe, and embarked on an ambitious reform programme in the Indies, designed to maximize its revenues, while at the same time liberalizing commercial regulations in an effort to recover control of Spain's transatlantic trade from the hands of foreign merchants. Above all, they were almost obsessively interested in the cause of agrarian reform, idealizing the small private-freeholder in line with eighteenth-century fashion.

Although these reforming ministers clothed their reforms in the fashionable language of the European Enlightenment, many of their ideas closely resembled those first advanced in the Spain of the early seventeenth century. In other words, they belonged to an indigenous reform tradition, which in spite of the vicissitudes of the later seventeenth century had never been extinguished. But in the eighteenth century, as in the seventeenth, the obstacles to reform were numerous, and the success even of Charles III's dedicated ministers was limited.

The eighteenth century in Spain was, admittedly, a century of growth – growth, in particular, of population, which stood at 8.2 million in 1717 and at 11.5 million by the end of the century. There was growth, too, in the manufacturing industries, especially in the peripheral regions, like Catalonia, where the textile industry was to lay the foundations of an industrial revolution in the nineteenth century. Agriculture became more buoyant, and foreign trade increased. Recovery, however, was

already beginning under the last of the Habsburgs in the 1680s, as the great recession of the seventeenth century drew to a close, and the reforms of the middle and later years of the eighteenth century can be seen, at least in part, as an attempt to grapple with the social and administrative problems generated by this process of recovery.

As such, their results were in many respects disappointing, and perhaps the most enduring legacy of the Bourbon reform programme was the professionalization of the state apparatus – a process which inevitably made the crown still more remote from the people and began to erode the respect in which it had traditionally been held. The new administrative professionalism was accompanied by a comparable process of professionalization in the armed forces, as Spain tried to equip itself with an army and navy worthy of a great imperial power. By the late eighteenth century the military had emerged for the first time as a distinctive social class, set off from the rest of society by its corporate legal privileges – the so-called *fuero militar*. This development was to have ominous consequences for the political life of nineteenth and twentieth-century Spain.

In professionalizing its bureaucratic and military apparatus Spain was only following a pattern common to eighteenth-century European states; and if this was the area of most effective reform, this tended to be true also of attempts at reform from above in other eighteenth-century states. Everywhere, privilege and hierarchy complicated the task of the reformers, and in this respect Spain proved no exception to the rule. But its partial isolation from Europe for a century or more meant that reforming ideas were especially tender plants in the eighteenth-century Spanish environment. New scientific and medical ideas from Europe had begun to percolate into the peninsula in the last years of the seventeenth century, but the assumptions and practices of the European Enlightenment remained confined to small groups in Spanish society, and were very thinly spread. The reformers, therefore, even when enjoying the support of the crown, remained an embattled group, always vulnerable to the forces of reaction. Enlightened Europe, for example, watched with amazement as Pablo de Olavide, the reforming intendant of Seville, disappeared into the cells of the Inquisition in 1776.

At every turn, therefore, would-be reformers confronted a heavy legacy from Spain's imperial past – an imperial past that the dynasty remained determined to restore. The preoccupation of the Spanish Bourbons with their international standing and the defence of their imperial possessions in the Indies involved Spain in constant wars throughout the eighteenth century, especially with Great Britain. These wars, and the heavy costs they imposed, helped to channel the reform movement in certain directions, many of them of more benefit to the state than to society at large. In this respect the Bourbon reforms resembled those of Olivares, but by the eighteenth century the weight of the imperial past was even heavier than it had been a hundred years before, and the forces of oligarchy, dominating the commanding heights of the agrarian economy, were correspondingly more effective in their resistance to change.

Against the combined forces of the oligarchy the reform movement was already losing momentum by the time of Charles III's death in 1788, and he bequeathed to his dim and indolent successor, Charles IV (1788–1808), a state well on the road to bankruptcy thanks to heavy war expenditure. Manuel Godoy, a young officer spectacularly raised from the ranks of the household guard to become the royal favourite and the effective ruler of Spain, was ill-equipped to handle the great national and international crisis now looming over the peninsula. The outbreak of revolution in France in 1789 had thrown the reform circles into disarray and played into the hands of the conservatives by reviving many of the old phobias about the contamination of Spain by dangerous foreign ideas. Godoy, while doing something to keep alive the flickering flame of enlightenment, was now faced with the massive power of a revolutionary France which had killed its Bourbon king.

Once again Spain and Europe stood in that ambivalent relationship which had characterized their mutual histories ever since Charles V had appealed to Spaniards to identify themselves with his mission. For over two centuries the European and imperial ambitions of the Habsburgs and Bourbons had offered Spain opportunities to find its identity in some wider cause; and for one of those centuries, from around 1540 to 1640, Spain had come close to imprinting its identity on Europe. But its rulers had also demanded of it enormous sacrifices which had crushed it beneath the weight of an irresponsible fiscalism, and had favoured the consolidation in Spanish society of those forces most resistant to progressive change. Now, at the end of the eighteenth century, the crown, which had sought to direct change from above, stood exposed as financially and morally bankrupt. The consequence was to leave it further removed from the people than at any time since the troubles of the fifteenth century. It was therefore not surprising that the forces of radical change unleashed on the continent by the French Revolution should have evoked diametrically different responses from different sections of Spanish society. Developing their own distinctive visions of the extraordinary process of Spain's rise and decline, the liberals and conservatives of the nineteenth century would struggle to determine the future of a divided nation in the light of their reading, and misreading, of its imperial past.

Power and duty

Both Charles V and his son Philip II were dedicated to their royal responsibilities. Charles V carried those responsibilities for forty years, abdicating in 1556. Philip reigned for another forty-two years until his death in 1598. During their combined lives it seemed that Spain had inherited another God-given mission – to save not simply the peninsula for Catholicism, but the whole world.

Under Charles V Spain became for the first time a great European power, and for much of his reign Charles's own energies were occupied more with issues outside than inside the Iberian peninsula. In some sense he was a foreigner in his own land. Castile, the centre of his patrimony, felt its traditional position being betrayed in the interests of his other possessions, and rose in revolt. But Charles's gifts of diplomacy, his willingness to compromise and his vast practical experience in 'the art of the possible' in the long run achieved a remarkable record of strong, peaceful government. He was buried in the church of the Escorial, beneath a magnificent effigy in bronze-gilt by Pompeo Leoni (*left*). Charles kneels with his wife Isabella, his daughter Maria and his two sisters.

Philip II had as a prince travelled extensively in Italy and northern Europe, but as king he identified himself strongly with Spain, and particularly with Castile, where he chose Madrid as his capital. Here, or in his vast palace-monastery of the Escorial, he spent most of his working life, governing through written orders distributed by a huge network of civil servants. Motivated by a deep Catholicism, convinced of his duty and unsparing of his own labours, he tried to impose a uniformity of conduct and belief that eventually lost him the northern provinces of the Netherlands. El Greco's portrait (*right*) catches his devout sense of mission and the dark melancholy of his character.

Philip IV (reigned 1621–65) is now more famous as the subject of Velázquez's superb portraits than for any talents of his own, but he was not lacking in intelligence and was a great patron of the arts.

The Count-Duke of Olivares, Philip IV's favourite and principal minister, directed the policy of Spain between 1626 and 1643, when he was forced to resign after revolts in Catalonia and Portugal.

A meeting of kings: in 1659 Philip IV's daughter Maria Teresa married Louis XIV of France, a union that symbolized the ending of twenty-four years of war between France and Spain. Under the terms of the Peace of the Pyrenees, Louis renounced all claims by his wife's descendants to the Spanish throne. Here (*right*), the two kings greet each other with ceremonial courtesy.

Spain's Golden Age

Charles V and Philip II created Spain's greatness; their successors enjoyed it. The seventeenth century, corresponding almost exactly to the reigns of only three kings – Philip III, Philip IV and Charles II – was a Golden Age of the arts but a time of flagging economic fortunes. The bureaucracy built up by Philip still ruled, but effective power was often exercised by a royal favourite rather than the king. As the century progressed the demands of Spain's empire and of her position as the leading Catholic power in Europe began to outstrip the benefits that they conferred.

The glittering façade

The eighteenth century was an age of continuing internal conflict for Spain. It was also an age of administrative reform and of modest economic revival after the troubles of the seventeenth century. It began with a change of dynasty. Charles II, the last of the Habsburgs, died childless, bequeathing his throne to his Bourbon great-nephew Philip, grandson of Maria Teresa and Louis XIV, in spite of the terms of the Peace of the Pyrenees. Other European powers objected and the War of the Spanish Succession broke out, ending in 1713 with the Bourbons installed on the Spanish throne.

Ferdinand VI enters Seville with his wife Barbara of Braganza. Ferdinand was the son of Philip V and reigned from 1746 to 1759. The city of Seville, made rich in earlier times by the silver of the Indies, had a rooted sense of its own worth, and could still put on a dazzling show for occasions such as this.

Charles III invited Tiepolo to Madrid in 1762 to work on the Royal Palace. He was to remain there for eight years until his death in 1770, but he was old and his star was waning. His main work for the king was the vast ceiling of the Throne Room, eleven by twenty-six metres, illustrating the glory of Spain and its dominion over the world. For a smaller room, the *saleta*, he did another painting of the same theme, of which this is the preliminary sketch, *The Triumph of the Spanish Monarchy*. Spain, a beautiful and richly dressed woman, sits amidst Olympian gods and allegorical figures who pay her homage.

SPANISH AMERICA: EMPIRE AND ITS OUTCOME PETER BAKEWELL

Columbus's four voyages between 1492 and 1504 were without doubt remarkable feats of navigation and discovery. But the deeds of exploration, conquest and settlement by Spaniards for which those voyages opened the way on the American continent are more impressive still. After a breathing space of some fifteen years on the island of Hispaniola (now shared between Haiti and the Dominican Republic), during which the early settlers accustomed themselves to living an ocean's span from home, from 1508 onwards the Spaniards fanned rapidly out into the other large islands of the Caribbean, to the isthmus of Panama, and, after 1517, to Mexico. From Panama, after 1520, expeditions reconnoitred the west coast of South America. Everywhere, major and minor native cultures were rapidly dominated, at least in the miltary sense. The Aztecs succumbed to Hernan Cortés in 1521, and the Incas had fallen before Francisco Pizarro and his men by 1536. By 1540, less than fifty years after Columbus first set sail to the west, substantial Spanish settlements stood in place from Guadalajara in western Mexico, to Santiago in central Chile – a distance over land, as the crow flies, of some 5,000 miles, almost ten times the north-south extent of Spain, and two and a half times that of Europe, from the North Cape to the southern tip of Greece.

Transplanting the Spanish bureaucracy

The Spanish had explored, conquered, occupied and settled these immense American tracts in the face of the opposition not only of their native inhabitants but also of nature itself. They tramped, dogged and apparently unstoppable, across rain forests, swamps, sand deserts and vertiginous mountain ranges, taking in their stride natural obstacles far more daunting than anything Europe had to offer. In this sense, José Clemente Orozco's depiction of the conquistador as a man of steel is close to the mark. But toughness was not a quality of conquerors alone: it was a rare Spanish bureaucrat of the sixteenth century, who, travelling for example from Lima on the Pacific shore to occupy some judgeship in the central Andes, would report more of the mountain road he followed than that it was 'unpleasant' or 'cold' in places. The same spirit of dedication would leave him completely unaware of the dramatic beauty of these new landscapes. The land was simply there to be taken and organized.

Organization proceeded apace in the wake of discoveries and conquests, founded upon an ever expanding bureaucratic base. Indeed, officers of the royal treasury generally accompanied expeditions of conquest to supervise the collection of the king's share of whatever booty might be taken. They also served to relay information about new lands and peoples back to Spain. Soon Spanish administrative institutions began to be transferred to America. Key among these was the *audiencia*. In

Spain this was a high court of justice. In America this function continued, but added to it was another of equal and, in many cases, greater importance, as these courts became administrative tribunals with executive powers over great areas of the empire. The first American *audiencia* was created in Santo Domingo in 1511, and oversaw colonial expansion in the Caribbean, and, over the following decade, into Panama and Mexico. By the end of the sixteenth century eight *audiencias* had been established between western Mexico and Charcas (the region corresponding to present-day Bolivia); and a ninth was added in Chile in 1609. In some cases, their territories became, in due course, the basis of nation states existing today. The modern frontiers of Colombia, Ecuador, Peru and Bolivia, for example, descend directly from the jurisdictions of the *audiencias* erected in the mid-sixteenth century in the cities of Santa Fe de Bogotá, Quito, Lima and La Plata (now Sucre).

As the extent and the potential wealth of the mainland colonies became clear, a yet more imposing institution of government was implanted in America: the viceroyalty. The first viceroy in and of the Spanish Indies was, legally speaking, Christopher Columbus. But he proved an inept and uninterested administrator, so that the viceregal office in the New World to all intents and purposes came into being in 1535 with the appointment of the first viceroy of New Spain (that is, Mexico). A second viceroyalty was set up in 1544 with its capital in Lima. For almost two hundred years thereafter these were the two great divisions of the Spanish American empire. The viceroy of New Spain had final responsibility for the government and defence of Mexico, Central America, the Spanish Caribbean and, once they were effectively brought into the Spanish world in the 1570s, the Philippines; while his counterpart in Lima, the deceptively titled viceroy of Peru, had dominion in fact over almost the entire area of South America, with the exception of Venezuela and the territories in the east of the sub-continent falling to Portugal under the terms of the Treaty of Tordesillas (1494), which split the New World into Spanish and Portuguese spheres of influence. Not until 1739 was this vast jurisdiction subdivided, with the insertion of the viceroyalty of New Granada, centred on Bogotá, in the north-west of South America. And finally in 1776 the south-east was gathered together under the control of a new viceroy of the River Plate.

The viceroyalty, like the *audiencia*, was an import from Spanish administration in Europe. So too were many of the lesser components of the governing machine built in the sixteenth century. The office of *corregidor*, for instance, employed by Isabella in the years before Columbus's voyages to reinforce royal power in the cities of Castile, was used in the new American towns for the same end. But if the offices had their roots in Spain, they were inevitably reshaped to some

The conquistadors have been seen throughout history as men of iron, forging an empire through brutal force and determination – as indeed they were. *Right*: two images, one of 1549, a figure on the Casa de Montejo, Merida, Yucatan; the other of 1938 by José Clemente Orozco in the Hospicio Cabañas, Guadalajara, Mexico.

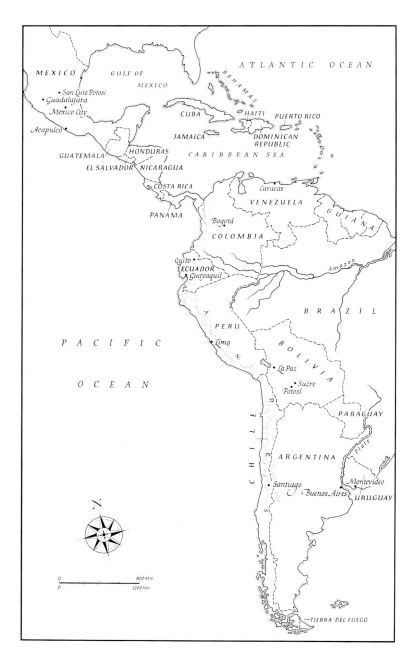

The Spanish empire in Central and South America.

extent by the new demands made on them in America. Viceroys necessarily became even more autonomous agents than their counterparts in Spanish European territories because their lines of communication with the home government were tenuous. Judges in *audiencias* based hundreds, if not thousands, of miles from the viceregal capitals inevitably came to make, as well as to apply, local laws. In addition, the office of *corregidor* proved adaptable to the administration of Indians in rural districts as well as of Spanish-dominated towns, so that the *corregidor de indios* became a common figure in many parts of the empire.

An impressive governing apparatus had grown up by the middle of the sixteenth century. The declared main purpose of the machinery, emerging as it did from the medieval tradition of Spanish monarchy, was to provide access to legal recourse for all the king's subjects. In 1554 the Council of the Indies (the Spanish council of state responsible for running the American empire) advised the Emperor Charles V that his chief obligation was to provide 'an excess of justice' for his people. Governors in Peru two decades or so later might well have held that this was precisely what had been done, since, in their view, Indians were spending altogether too much time and money in litigation in the *audiencias*. It is certainly true that the native people often enough made skilful and energetic use of the conquerors' legal system to defend their lands or rights from attacks either by Europeans or by other Indians; but it must be granted that, ultimately, courts at all levels were loaded in the invaders' favour.

The conquest of the conquistadors: 1540–1600

In matters of executive control, several decades passed before the machinery of government gained a good purchase on the colonial terrain. Simply not enough prepared officials were available for some time to cope with vast and still expanding regions. And, in any case, until silver mining in New Spain and the central Andes began to produce abundantly, which did not happen until the 1560s and 1570s, the crown had too little American income to pay for a fully adequate machinery of executive government. Consequently, in the first half of the century, much local authority was allowed to remain in the hands of other figures. Notable among these were minor Indian leaders who had survived the conquests, and missionary friars of the Franciscan, Dominican and Augustinian orders. The most serious obstacle of all to the solidifying of royal powers in the Indies was, however, the continued presence of conquistadors in the new lands. To ensure the permanent settlement of conquered regions, the crown had made grants of the labour service and tributes of native people to the men who had taken part in the fighting. The practical purpose of these grants,

Three drawings from a manuscript written by the Peruvian *mestizo* Guaman Poma de Ayala about 1600, which illustrate the transference of Spanish bureaucracy to America. *Top*: Don Luis de Velasco, viceroy of Peru from 1595 to 1603. *Centre*: the *audiencia* (high court of justice) of Lima. *Bottom*: the *corregidor de indios*, a royal official, with his scribe.

known as *encomiendas*, was to give restless Spaniards a stake in the new lands and to encourage them to settle down to economic activities that would produce both private and public profit. In promoting the accumulation of private wealth, the scheme was only too successful, so that before 1540 the crown found itself confronted in the Indies by what suddenly appeared to be a new colonial nobility, consisting of *encomenderos* (holders of *encomiendas*) who asserted lordship over large numbers of native people, had assembled large landed estates, controlled the councils of Spanish towns, both large and small, and in every way posed a growing political and economic threat to the royal interest. Since a major political success of Isabella's reign in Castile during the final quarter of the previous century had been to reassert royal power over the nobility, the rise of the *encomenderos* in America, even though they never numbered above two thousand in the whole empire, was an especially unwelcome prospect. How much more difficult it would be, at a distance of several thousand miles, to cut these regional power groups down to size than it had been to bring the peninsular nobles into line. By the late 1530s, with *encomenderos* ensconcing themselves in Peru to add to the problem posed by those already well entrenched in Mexico, some action to reconquer the conquerors was urgently needed. Fortunately, the requirements of politics coincided nicely with another necessity that the Spanish crown, at least intermittently, took seriously: that of protecting the native peoples from ill-treatment by the colonists. So, from 1542 onwards, salvos of laws were fired off at the colonies by the home authorities, restricting the *encomenderos'* right to use as labourers the Indians granted to them and, most serious of all for the colonists, the heritability of *encomiendas*. This curbing of the *encomenderos* provoked a revolt in Peru in the mid-1540s, during which the first viceroy of the colony was killed in a battle with the rebels – the only such incident in the entire colonial history of Spanish America. But ultimately, through politic concessions and skilful playing upon the underlying psychological orientation of the settlers towards Spain, the crown succeeded in imposing its will, and in doing so fatally undermined the social position, wealth and political footing of the *encomenderos*.

In the 1550s and 1560s similar campaigns of attrition by law were launched against the power of local native leaders and the missionary clergy; aided, in the latter case, by the strong inclination of the church at the time, expressed in the decisions of the Council of Trent, to concentrate power in the episcopal hierarchy with a consequent reduction of the autonomy of the orders. So it was that by the early 1570s the weight of the Spanish state was felt as never before in the New World colonies, represented by a burgeoning bureaucracy of, on the whole, remarkably able and dedicated colonial administrators. The centralizing of power that had begun almost a century before with Isabella's accession to the Castilian throne had been successfully carried to America, despite the vast distances and natural obstacles that intervened. Not until the final decades of the eighteenth century did Spain again hold the colonies in so tight a grip as she did between 1570 and 1600.

The tragedy of the native peoples

Time-consuming and urgent as the problem of subduing the conquerors was in the first half of the sixteenth century, it paled before the far more complex and many-sided challenge of dealing with the defeated native peoples of Middle and South America. The first and fundamental problem was that of placing the American peoples within the general framework of humanity. This was an intellectual question, eagerly tackled by Spanish theologians, lawyers and thinkers, but one that had vast practical, political and moral connotations. By 1550 or so, after extensive appeal to both classical philosophers and the authorities of the church, and after long and sometimes virulent debate, the broad conclusion reached was that American Indians were indeed full human beings, but not yet wholly mature in their intellectual and moral faculties. Indians were thus regarded in Spanish colonial law as minors, incapable of taking on anything more than simple legal obligations. Their assignment to this child-like level of responsibility removed them from the purview of the Inquisition. It also served to emphasize the obligation to protect and evangelize the American native people that the Pope had laid on the Spanish monarchy at the outset of New World settlement. At the same time, though, this lowly legal ranking could only serve to reinforce the settlers' ever more common assumption in practice that Indians were a naturally inferior kind of people who could properly be treated in a manner that at best could be termed authoritarian.

The state's dealing with the Indians was both complicated and simplified by the enormous losses in numbers that they suffered during the century after first contact with Europeans. The native population of the Bahamas and the Greater Antilles disappeared completely during the sixteenth century. Nowhere on the mainland was this experience repeated, but declines of 90 per cent or more seem to have taken place in most regions. The true size of the pre-conquest populations will probably never be known. But it is possible that Peru (within its present boundaries) held as many as 9 million people in the early 1520s; by 1620 the number had fallen to 600,000. Mexico suffered an equal loss. The population of central and southern Mexico was probably over 10 million in the early years of the sixteenth century. The post-conquest demographic low point in Indian

numbers, reached around 1620 to 1625, was some 730,000. Rare were the areas that escaped these disastrous slumps, which were mainly the outcome of diseases imported, unintentionally but inevitably, from the Old World. Because the American peoples, long isolated from the rest of humanity and its germs, had no resistance to them, smallpox, plague, measles and other ailments scythed their way through the native populations – their virulence intensified by the adverse effects, both physical and psychological, of conquest and subjugation. The labour demands of *encomenderos* and other early settlers, for instance, often weakened and even killed many forced workers. The depopulation of the islands resulted almost wholly from ill-treatment of that sort.

The dramatic decline in numbers certainly simplified organization and control of the native people in some respects for the colonizing state. Local government could shrink in proportion to the losses, and the need for continued reliance on surviving native leaders, with the risk which such dependence brought, declined. But the problems caused by depopulation were still greater. Foremost among them was labour. At first it had seemed that there would be more than enough native workers to satisfy the demands of the crown and of triumphant conquistadors for tribute. But as the epidemics wrought their havoc, it soon enough grew clear that shortage rather than abundance of native labour would be the rule. By the 1550s the colonial government was beginning to take charge of labour supply, organizing drafts so that at least the most productive activities pursued by colonists (agriculture and mining of precious metals, for example) should have a reliable supply of hands. The drafts were hedged about with regulations on wages and treatment in an honest attempt to protect workers from exploitation.

But inevitably, with labour growing ever scarcer, the danger of exploitation increased. And when the drafts failed to meet the settlers' needs, as happened widely in the 1570s and 1580s, employers started to hire Indians individually as wage labourers. The salaries paid were generally much higher than what native people had received in the drafts. But the change to wage labour weakened the state's control over conditions of work, which in some cases exposed Indians to new abuses.

In a broader sense than labour alone, the sixteenth-century collapse of the native population changed the economic nature of the Spanish Indies. At first it had seemed that a tribute-based empire could be built in America, with settlers being supported by a part of the surplus product of vast numbers of natives, while the state took much of the rest of that surplus. But that was not to be. And by mid-century it was obvious that economic enterprise on an Old World model would be needed, particularly in the form of capital substituting for labour. So, in

The conquistadors and their descendants had access to the labour of the Indians. *Opposite, centre* and *far right*: Indians weave cloth in eighteenth-century Peru. Another part of the workforce, and one destined to have important effects on the ethnic character of the population, was the black slaves brought to America by the Spaniards, seen here engaged in the making of pitch (*right*). Although the Spaniards introduced some new technological processes, for instance to improve the refinement of silver, many have remained virtually unchanged: a modern pottery vendor in Guatemala (*opposite, below right*).

varying degrees in different times and places, mules and ox-carts came to replace human carriers; extensive agriculture, using animal-drawn ploughs, prevailed over the Indians' traditional, intensive methods; water wheels and new high-volume methods of refining, employing mercury, pushed aside the comparatively small-scale native methods of producing silver. By 1600 the number of Spaniards actively working with these imported technologies would have astonished and dismayed the conquistador generation, with its hopes for, if not a life of leisure, at its most energetic one of lordly disposition of the labour of countless minions.

Even more profound and enduring than the economic effects of depopulation were its cultural consequences. Total disappearance of the native people, as happened in the Greater Antilles, obviously removed forever a way of life, except for whatever aspects of native material culture – the use of particular foods such as manioc, for example – the Spaniards and their black slaves might already have adopted. In most regions, some natives survived. But their culture was inevitably weakened by their numerical losses; and today's Spanish America is indisputably less Indian than it would have been if the germs so devastatingly introduced in the sixteenth century had not taken their toll. Some regions heavily struck by the epidemics, it is true, did remain remarkably Indian in nature: southern Mexico, for instance, or much of the Andean highland. These were areas where heavy concentrations of Spaniards did not develop, so that even the shrunken Indian populations were able to stay culturally intact. But in general, the smaller the remaining native group in a given region, the more rapidly miscegenation tended to proceed. With racial mixture came cultural mixture, and the development of the *mestizo* lifestyle so common in Spanish America, with its blending of native and Spanish ways. And in the post-conquest decades, the growing number of African slaves and servants brought by the Spaniards began to add their genes and their customs to the blend. The great depopulation of the sixteenth century, therefore, contributed much to making Spanish America the largest world area of recent ethnic and cultural mixing. That mingling is still very much in progress, and has some way to go before it produces homogeneity.

The sixteenth century, then, saw much achieved and to a degree fixed in Spanish America: rapid occupation of the land; a pattern of towns built; an activist bureaucracy put in place; economic adjustments made to compensate for the vast loss of native people (resulting in an economic structure that combined native and imported elements); and racial and cultural fusion set in motion.

The rise of the criollos: 1600–1750

During the century and a half extending roughly from 1600 to 1750, after which the tide of Bourbon reformism began to rise on American shores, most of these accomplishments and processes persisted and gathered strength. But new developments in various aspects of colonial life also began to assert themselves and to work profound changes in parts of the sixteenth-century legacy. Chief among these was the growth of an American-born white population, the inevitable outcome of the encouragement that the Spanish crown had given to settlement and occupation of the land. By 1600, great-grandchildren of the mainland conquistadors were on the scene; and however desirable their physical presence might be for securing Spain's claim to America, they posed a growing problem to the home government. For these *criollos*, as they came to be known, had an inevitable orientation to the lands in which they had been born and raised. This inclination had some ethnic component, too; for although *criollos* were in name and in law white, few of the old families lacked a modicum of Indian genes, acquired in the early days when conquistadors of lowly origins had been pleased to take mistresses and even wives from conquered native nobilities. By 1600 *criollos* in all likelihood outnumbered Spanish-born immigrants; and though thoughts of parting from Spain can rarely and barely have crossed their minds, they certainly made clear their resentment over ill-treatment allegedly received from the Spanish crown and from peninsular Spaniards as a whole: removal of their *encomienda* Indians, preference denied in the awarding of powerful and lucrative offices in the colonies, and their constant displacement in private economic activities by newcomers to the Indies. Their resentments were in part a reaction to the forced economic changes of the sixteenth century already outlined. Among the *criollos* there lived on a measure of the old seigneurial aspirations of the conquistadors. And some of them could not or would not adjust to the new entrepreneurial spirit that was called for in an age of scarce Indian labour.

Revolutionaries the *criollos* were not, nor were they to be until the early nineteenth century. But in the seventeenth and early eighteenth centuries they found ways to assert their interests and inclinations that sapped the strength of the Spanish hold on America. The sale of offices of state, to which the crown was driven by fiscal needs, gave them access to the positions of formal power from which they had been excluded during the construction of a bureaucracy manned by peninsular Spaniards after 1550. As the 1600s wore on, ever higher offices in administration, treasury and judiciary were put up for sale; before the seventeenth century was out, even the office of viceroy in both New Spain and Peru had been sold, though not to *criollos*. But having installed themselves during the seventeenth century in

The *criollos* were Spaniards born in America, often with some Indian blood in their veins. In the century following the conquest they became the most powerful class, their loyalty being to their own birthplace rather than to Spain. *Right*: a *criollo* nobleman of the seventeenth century, hardly inferior to his counterpart at home. *Below right*: an Inca princess of about the same date. In her right hand she holds a sacred flower called *nakshu*; in her left a spindle, a blend of Inca and Christian symbolism.

the highest posts of the colonial treasury, *criollos* proceeded between 1701 and 1750 to buy eighty or more positions of judge or crown prosecutor in American *audiencias* (about a quarter of such appointments made). They also received, without payment, some fifty other *audiencia* positions. The result was that by the mid-eighteenth century the important *audiencias* of New Spain, Lima and Santiago de Chile had majorities of *criollo* judges. Naturally not all *criollo* office holders were corrupt. But their rising presence in government contributed to a palpable decline after 1600 in the keenness and efficacy of colonial administration. That decline had other roots as well – though they too are connected with the *criollo* advance. One, which is immediately evident from a comparative reading of sixteenth and seventeenth-century government correspondence, was a growing sense of familiarity and routine in imperial affairs. For the most part, seventeenth-century officials simply did not have the active interest in their jobs that their predecessors had shown; they were content to report without suggesting innovation. Another change, far deeper and more enduring, was the growth of wide family networks in the Spanish colonies. This process, entirely typical of the whole Spanish world, had begun in America almost with the conquest. But after 1600 it flourished, giving private interests powerful connections in, say, local and central government and in the church in the form of well-placed brothers, cousins and relatives by marriage. Marriage, indeed, drew peninsular officials inextricably into *criollo* circles, however fiercely the law might prohibit such links. Here again, the pattern set in middle colonial times has changed little over the subsequent centuries.

Trade, legal and contraband

Criollos who retained something of the enterprising spirit of immigrants – and such people were not rare – could also find opportunities to exercise it in the seventeenth century that had rarely offered themselves before. One possibility was participation in a growing contraband trade. From the start of the century, and notably after 1620, the French, Dutch and English discovered that the decline of Spain's relative strength at sea gave them the chance to create settlements in the Caribbean. And these communities, in such places as Saint Domingue (later Haiti), Curaçao and Jamaica, quickly became bases for contraband. *Criollos* participated eagerly, since the European goods available through this channel were cheaper than those shipped through the cumbersome official trade between Spain and America. The *criollos'* gains in lower prices were, of course, losses to Spanish shippers; and also loss to the Spanish treasury through reduced customs duties.

Spain's export trade to the Indies also suffered after 1600 as increased American production of items previously imported

Peru was rich in silver and the mine-owners made enormous profits. The most successful of them in the seventeenth century was López de Quiroga. The 'silver mountain' of Potosí rises behind him on the right. *Below left:* Sister Juana Inés de la Cruz. Offspring of Spanish parents (one Basque), born in 1648, and entering a Jeronymite nunnery in Mexico City at the age of 21, she became prominent as a writer and intellectual. Here she stands in her library (the three volumes lying next to the inkwell are her own works), wearing a framed vellum painting of the Annunciation round her neck.

cut into the market for European wares. Whereas in the early days almost all the settlers' desires for familiar goods had had to be met through imports, even down to wheat and wine, by 1600 all except luxury articles were being produced in the colonies. Emigrant Spanish craftsmen had brought over the common trades. Journeymen from Spain could set up as masters in the Indies and proceeded to train Indians, Blacks and, increasingly, *mestizos* in their skills. Native expertise from pre-conquest times was absorbed into this small-scale manufacture, run by immigrants and *criollos*. In this way serviceable American textiles, pottery, metalwork, tools, furniture, and so on, were readily available in colonial markets by 1600. The only demand that this sort of production could not meet resulted from the penchant of the rich for the cachet and elegance of Old World goods. And these were as likely in the seventeenth century to cross the Atlantic in a contraband vessel as in a Spanish galleon.

Furthermore, there is a great deal of evidence suggesting that by the early 1600s American products were beginning to circulate in an inter-colonial trading network, run by *criollos* and immigrants, from such centres as Mexico City, Lima, Guayaquil and even distant Manila, capital of the Philippines. Silver from the mines of the central Andes provided one powerful motor for this system, stimulating the southward movement of Mexican goods such as textiles and sugar, and also the re-export to South America of the oriental silks and spices that entered Acapulco in the trans-Pacific galleons returning from Manila. Similarly, cacao from Guayaquil and Venezuela passed to Mexico and Central America, as did wine from irrigated valleys in the desert coast of southern Peru. What in general was happening by the turn of the sixteenth century was that the Spanish American colonies were starting to develop regional specialization in production, in line with their resources, climate, soils and possibilities of communication. As these regional natural advantages became apparent, and costs of production fell, long-distance exchange of goods among the colonies became profitable. *Criollos* were those who gained most from these transactions, and in pursuing them weakened the economic tie between colonies and mother country. In the early decades of the seventeenth century *criollos* also began to take an active part in the diminishing official trade between Spain and America, displacing to a degree the Seville-based merchants and their American agents who had until then assumed that they had a monopoly over such commerce. By the 1630s and 1640s, feelings ran high in Seville against these upstart colonials.

Taken together, the assorted administrative, political and economic changes in the Indies whose origins can be traced to the early years of the seventeenth century amount to a rising autonomy of the Spanish Indies in the middle colonial period.

The more energetic, imaginative and ambitious *criollos*, frequently in alliance with new immigrants from Spain, were able to combine the new ease of access to office holding with a growing appreciation of the colonies' economic possibilities, to secure for themselves and their families an expanding share of the empire's product. Aiding them in this was the dwindling authority of Spain herself, sapped by decades of over-extension in Europe in the sixteenth century, by external debts, by enervation of industry, and by the rise of other economic, political and military rivals in north-western Europe. Spain could not stop the French, English and Dutch from planting new colonies in the Caribbean in the seventeenth century, and by the end of the century had had to recognize through formal treaties their permanent presence there. Spain could not afford, once the century of conquest had passed, to expand her administrative bureaucracy in America to keep pace with the growth of the *criollo* population; and much less to pay her officials salaries high enough to turn them from the temptations of business and family associations with *criollos*, or even from direct participation in contraband. Rising foreign presence on the fringes of the empire meant that more income from American taxes than before had to be spent on fortresses, ships and men to defend America. So the amount available for maintaining a sufficient and honest imperial bureaucracy was even smaller. Weakness generated further weakness in a descending spiral. But Spain's loss was the *criollos*' gain. An unusually dedicated, and ultimately frustrated, Spanish administrator, sent in 1648 to clear up adulteration of the coins being struck at Potosí in the central Andes, the greatest of Spanish American mints, reported to the king: 'There is no difficulty, sire, in being a judge in Spain, for there the river knows the rock that guides it; but here rivers are not happy unless they run free.' For a loyal servant of the king, it was a bitter truth to recognize: colonial society, dominated by *criollo* interests, was now taking its own course far more often than before, and Spain could do little to stop or divert it. It had been possible to 'reconquer' conquistadors and *encomenderos* in the mid-sixteenth century. A century later, their descendants, far more numerous, and with much attenuated affective ties to Spain, were altogether a tougher proposition.

The racial balance changes

If the middle colonial period was the domain of the *criollos*, it was also a time in which other levels of Spanish American society saw their fortunes improve. At different moments in the seventeenth century, in almost all areas of the empire, native populations stopped shrinking as immunity to the bacteria and viruses introduced with the conquest increased. First to rebound was the Quito district in the northern Andes (modern highland Ecuador), where recovery began with the start of the century. In much of Mexico, the lowest point was passed in the 1630s. In the central Andes and elsewhere, decline persisted almost until 1700, or even into the new century. But it was now a slow drift downwards, rather than the succession of precipitous collapses that had followed the conquest. An improved living standard for many of the surviving native people probably helped to bolster immunities. As their numbers had dropped, their value as workers had increased; and there is good reason to think that the real wages they could command in the seventeenth century were a distinct improvement on what they had received in the sixteenth. Besides this, farming could now be concentrated on a smaller area of high quality land, since the total demand for food was so much lower than before. This tended to improve the productivity of farm work, and thus the general standard of living, even for most of those near the bottom of the social and economic scale. It is likely that for most peasant farmers life in the seventeenth century was better in the colonies than in Spain itself.

The middle colonial period was still more notable for the uninterrupted growth, both absolute and relative, of segments of the population other than the native peoples. Dependable figures are hard to find because of lack of records and difficulty in their interpretation. But for central Mexico there are well-considered estimates. There, in 1568 to 1570, in a total population of some 2,350,000, Spaniards (either immigrants or *criollos*) constituted 2 per cent of the total, *mestizos* 0.1 per cent, and *pardos* (people wholly or partly black) 0.8 per cent. The balance of 97.1 per cent (in absolute numbers, some 2,284,000) was Indian. By 1646, the population of the same area had dropped to about 1,230,000, entirely as the result of the decline of the Indian portion to 1,073,000. This number of natives now amounted to only 87.2 per cent of the whole; while the proportion of all three of the other groups had grown. Spaniards now were 8 per cent of the total, *mestizos* 1.1 per cent, and *pardos* 3.7 per cent. The *mestizos*, some 14,000 in number, were still the smallest segment of the population; but they had shown by far the largest proportional increase, by a factor of eleven, since 1570. The same pattern continued over the next hundred years. In the mid-1740s, central Mexico was about 74 per cent Indian, with each of the other three groups forming a roughly equal part of the balance (about 9 per cent). The *mestizo* component had, then, grown about eight times since 1646; while the *pardos* had rather more than doubled, and the Spanish-*criollo* group remained much the same, proportionally speaking. Absolute figures for the Mexican population in the 1740s are not easily available. But the population of the complete Mexican territory in 1810 has been estimated at about 6,121,000: 3,676,000 Indians, 15,000 Spaniards, 1,092,000 *criol-*

los, 704,000 *mestizos* and 634,000 *pardos*. This total, it should be noted, is considerably less than conservative estimates of the Mexican native population just before the Spanish conquest.

It seems likely that the *mestizo* part of the population of other regions of the Spanish empire – certainly of those regions, such as the Peruvian coast and the Andean mining districts, where large numbers of Spaniards and *criollos* lived – would have multiplied between the mid-sixteenth and the mid-eighteenth centuries much as it did in Mexico. Furthermore, the *mestizo* figures given here for central Mexico certainly underrepresent the true rate of ethnic mixing between natives and newcomers, since the Spanish category contained many individuals with some Indian blood who passed as Europeans; and among the *pardos* there soon came to be many blends of native and Black, and of native, Black and European.

'Pigmentocracy': race, colour and status

As mixing of races proceeded and the number of recognized mixtures increased, social ranking in Spanish America grew more complex and subtle. In the sixteenth century, colonial society divided broadly into Indians and Europeans. Blacks were in general associated with the European side, being regarded by both Indians and Europeans as servants and agents of the colonists. For several decades after the military conquests, pre-existing native social distinctions persisted to a surprising degree. But in the middle decades of the sixteenth century, with the rise of Spanish bureaucracy and a consequent and intentional reduction of the political role played up to then by local native rulers, native society suffered a downward levelling. At the same time, settler society began to acquire a more defined and permanent set of stratifications as immigrants arrived who lacked the status assumed by conquerors and first settlers, but who proved more willing than those early families to apply enterprise to the economic opportunities offered by the New World. So, by 1600, a Spaniard's or *criollo's* standing might vary considerably according to whether he was the owner, at one end of the scale, of a large cattle-raising hacienda, or, at the other, of a small smithy. Nonetheless, both shared the social advantage of belonging to the once-conquering, still-controlling segment of the colonial population. Indians remained forever the conquered.

Between the extremes of controllers and conquered, evergrowing numbers of mixed-blooded people, neither one nor the other in historical identity, entered society in the middle colonial period. At first, standing was ascribed to them above all according to the degree of their physical resemblance to Europeans or Indians. *Mestizos* whose appearance was almost Spanish would find themselves regarded and treated almost as Spaniards. Conversely those who could barely be dis-

tinguished from Indians might find themselves counted as such, and in danger of having the Indians' obligations of tribute and draft labour thrust on them. The more European a person's appearance, the wider became the range of economic opportunities generally available to him. Similarly, *pardos* of mixed blood who closely resembled Blacks might well find themselves being regarded and treated very much as if slaves. This system of ascription of social standing existing in Spanish America after 1600 has sometimes been called a 'pigmentocracy'; and indeed, skin colour (or rather, the degree to which an individual's physical appearance approached the ideal of 'Whiteness', 'Indianness' or 'Blackness') does seem to have set status and put limits on that person's economic and social possibilities.

The gradations of colour and appearance produced by ethnic mixing sat well with the Spanish predilection, deriving from Catholic medieval sources, to view society as a natural hierarchy. Each member had his or her place and function in the structure, from which it was difficult, and even to some extent wrong, to move. Inequality, furthermore, was implicit in such a hierarchy. These conceptions were implanted in Spanish America in the sixteenth century and have persisted there to a greater or lesser degree to the present.

Nonetheless, there was a limit to which 'pigmentocracy' could ultimately serve the purposes of such a scheme. As the increase of mixed-blooded people accelerated in the seventeenth century and the number of combinations of Indian, Black and White grew, ever more discriminating descriptive terms were coined to categorize them. For example, the child of a Spaniard and *mulatto* was termed a *morisco* (Moor); that of a Spaniard and a *morisco*, an *albino*; that of an *albino* and a Spaniard, a *tornatrás* ('turn back'); that of a Spaniard and a *tornatrás*, *tente en el aire* ('stay up in the air'); and so on, through dozens of finely divided categories. But the practical difficulty was that given the variable workings of genetics, it was impossible to deduce someone's parenthood from his or her appearance with this degree of precision. The children of, say, a *mestizo* (a person of mixed Spanish and Indian blood) and *mulatto* (a person of mixed Spanish and African blood) might range in appearance anywhere within the boundaries of pure Indian, pure Black, and pure White; and would probably differ significantly in pigment and features one from another. The attempt to form a precise hierarchy based on fine differences of genetic origin, as judged by appearance, was therefore doomed; and it seems, in fact, more of a rearguard neo-scholastic exercise than anything else. In practice, the quainter terms of genetic description were little, if ever, used. Most people came simply to be placed in the broad categories of Spaniard, *criollo*, Indian, Black, *mestizo* and *mulatto*.

Another change in the criteria of social ranking accompanied the inevitable decline of fine gradation measured by ethnic appearance. This was the increase of the importance of wealth as a determinant of rank. In truth, wealth had from the start probably been more powerful in this respect than it was in Spain. After crossing the Atlantic (itself considered a feat admirable enough to bring a gain in status), immigrants, whether of high or low position in Spain, found the standing ascribed to them at home falling away, growing less confining, as if a skin were being shed. In comparison with Spain, then, the power of wealth, or of its lack, to modify social standing was increased in America. Similarly, once maintaining a social hierarchy according to ethnic appearance became problematical, an individual's wealth contributed more than before to defining his status. At the same time, however, ethnicity still had much to do with access to economic opportunity. Someone clearly Indian or Black was unlikely in the extreme to become a merchant operating in the intercontinental or intercolonial trade, or the owner of large silver mines, or of a large hacienda; whereas a *mestizo*, especially one distinctly European in appearance, might possibly aspire to such occupations. Much the same is still true today of those parts of modern Spanish America that have an Indian or Black component in their populations (as do all the major countries to a significant extent except Argentina, Chile and Uruguay). Wealth, if he can get it, may carry a person up the social scale; but getting it may be an insuperable problem in the first place.

The empire draws apart
It was not only in matters of society and its ranking that the years 1600 to 1750 produced significant changes in colonial Spanish America, but also in still broader questions of political and administrative conduct. The conquest had begun in the late fifteenth century in an age of political centralization in Spain: in what was, indeed, possibly the period of most rapid and powerful centralization in the entire history of the country – the reign of the Catholic Monarchs, Isabella of Castile and Ferdinand of Aragon. Columbus made his first voyage immediately after the reconquest of Granada, an event that brought territorial and religious unity to Spain for the first time since the Moorish invasion in 711 AD. In Castile, Isabella is renowned for having brought the power of church, towns and nobility into alignment with that of the crown, and in so doing greatly increasing the authority of the monarchy (in part by undermining the potential for growth or reassertion of regional power). The conquest and settlement of America then proceeded, in the sixteenth century, in a continuation of that centralizing momentum. Her grandson and successor, the Habsburg Emperor Charles V, despite multiple preoccupations with his realms in

other parts of Europe, kept a firm grip on the peninsular territories, and was instrumental in extending the power of the Spanish state across the Atlantic. It was largely in the latter years of his reign (1516–56) that the 'reconquest' of the conquistadors was accomplished. This was concluded during the reign of Philip II (1556–98), who also oversaw, from the 1560s on, the full assembling of the bureaucracy that was to represent the Spanish state in the Indies, without much formal alteration, until well into the eighteenth century.

The application of centralizing state power to the Indies in the sixteenth century was reinforced and complemented by another drive, both psychological and ideological, present in Spanish rulers and their advisers in the sixteenth century. This was the conviction that Spain had a divinely appointed task, as the leading secular power of Catholicism, to extend true religion over the globe, and to bring newly discovered peoples into the universal community of the church. The term 'incorporation' was often used, indeed, instead of 'conquest' to describe Spain's domination of the New World peoples and territories. This underlying urge to include, to gather in, to work toward the completion of a Catholic world family, has much to do with the notable keenness displayed by Spaniards in the colonies, both officials and private citizens, to explore and settle the land. That was not merely the result of pursuit of wealth in its various forms; though the wealth yielded by America was seen, by both state and individuals, as a divinely granted reward for the effort and sacrifices of incorporation.

By 1600 or so, incorporation had been achieved to a considerable extent: the land explored, its more welcoming regions settled, the native people to a degree persuaded to adopt both the conquerors' faith and various aspects of their secular life, from pigs to municipal administration. By that time, though, disillusion had firmly set in about the possibility of full hispanicization of native Americans. They were still, despite the efforts of missionaries and administrators, profoundly alien; and seemed likely to remain so. Furthermore, the *criollo* view of Indians, one bred of lifetime familiarity, was both more practical and more jaundiced than that held in the early colonial decades by both missionaries and many administrators. The impulse for incorporation, then, faded in the seventeenth century. Its decline severely weakened one important link between Indies and mother country; and in doing so, attenuated the presence of the Spanish state in America, as governors at all levels felt ever less obliged to reach out from their mainly urban bases to come to grips with the largely rural native people.

The link between Spain and America was also weakened in the seventeenth century by the consequences of the Habsburg conception of monarchy. This held that the separate realms and

The conversion of the Indians to Christianity was a main preoccupation of the conquistadors, an extension of the policy that had been applied to the Jews and Moors at home. In this seventeenth-century portrait, a member of the Inca royal family is shown in a Christian context, but wearing the headdress of Atahuallpa and with the Sun symbol blazoned across his breast.

provinces at home and overseas which made up the Spanish empire (Castile, Aragon, Sicily, New Spain and Peru, for example) had no unifying political ties below the monarch. He or she was ruler of each of them, and only in that authority were they united. This pluralistic conception of monarchy had distinct pros and cons. It meant that a strong ruler, assisted by a vigorous and able staff, could be an immense force for the integration of the entire structure. Conversely, an incompetent monarch with incompetent or divided ministers might contribute mightily to imperial dissolution. The first situation characterized the sixteenth century; the second, the seventeenth (with the outstanding exception of the regime of the Count-Duke of Olivares between 1621 and 1643 under Philip IV). In the sixteenth century a Spanish empire came together, extending from the Netherlands and Italy, via those parts of America lying between New Mexico and Tierra del Fuego, to the Philippines. In the seventeenth and early eighteenth centuries, various components fell away completely, and the edifice in general developed perilous saggings and swayings. The rising autonomy of the American realms that has already been described was part and parcel of this process. It was the outcome both of ever more apparent degeneration at the imperial centre, and of the kinds of developmental changes taking place at the periphery mentioned before: maturation of the colonial economies, growth of trade among them, the rise (through contraband) of essentially free trade with Europe, and above all the growth of a locally oriented *criollo* population. The Spanish-staffed bureaucracy which after 1550 had so impressively subdued and organized unruly colonists now in increasing measure became the domain of the *criollo* descendants of those dispossessed conquistadors and *encomenderos*. Some of them used it to gather illicit wealth; for others of lesser ambition it provided a safe haven in which to spend a respectable, if unproductive, life. In this respect the seventeenth century left a deadening legacy that modern Spanish America would do well to discard.

A pattern of Spanish history: autonomy v. authority

The history of the Hispanic world has shown a remarkable pattern of alternating centralism and regionalism over the past several centuries. The concentration of monarchical power achieved by Isabella and Ferdinand put an end to regional dispersion of power in the peninsula that had begun in the fourteenth century. The sixteenth century administrations in this respect continued what the Catholic Monarchs had begun, even managing to bind to the centre vast and distant areas of the New World. The following century brought a new breakdown and a return to regionalism – signally marked in the peninsula by the revolts of Catalonia and Portugal in 1640. Overseas, not only did the Indies loosen their ties with Madrid, but individual regions within the empire became remarkably self-sufficient and self-determining. After 1700, with a new Bourbon dynasty on the Spanish throne, a renewed drive for concentration of power was begun. America was little touched by it before 1750; but after this date a remarkable, though short-lived, reassertion of imperial authority took place there. The subsequent independence of almost all the American colonies between 1810 and 1825 was, of course, the ultimate manifestation of collapse of imperial power in Spain. But within the new countries, too, crumbling of the centre continued after independence until the final third of the nineteenth century; and the same can be said of Spain itself. The present century has continued the oscillations: dictatorship in Spain itself yielding in the past fifteen years to the assertion of regional *autonomías*; and many Spanish American states veering to and fro between attempts at democratic localism and dictatorship. It long seemed that Mexico, with its single-party political structure of the PRI (Party of the Institutionalized Revolution), had found a workable compromise between the deeply rooted centrifugal and centripetal impulses; but now strong stirrings of regionalism are again evident there, and it remains to be seen whether the system that has operated tolerably well for the past sixty years can adjust to accommodate them.

Tension between centre and region is far from unique to the Spanish world. But there the excursions seem too violent, too wide for the good of the state. It is as if the bouts of centralism overcompress the political structure, until they culminate each time in a sort of 'Big Bang'; in its aftermath, the regions fly out in all directions until the underlying gravity of centralism again pulls them together. It has been suggested that the toleration of diversity that is implicit in regionalism is, indeed, fundamentally alien to the Spanish world; that Spain's, and hence Spanish America's, medieval and Catholic political heritage, drawing from Augustine and Aquinas, has as its fundamental tenet the pursuit of the common good of society; that the self-interest of individuals, which pluralistic democracy seeks to promote, is seen as a lesser goal than the common good; and that the common good is best achieved through securing political, social and economic unity, which implies suppression of diversity. Clearly, if all this is so, centralism is the true bedrock of Hispanic political culture; and with such a foundation, neither regionalism nor liberal, pluralistic democracy can ultimately be expected to last. This may be too severe a judgment. But the history of the Hispanic territories over the past five centuries suggests that it should not be dismissed out of hand.

The second reconquest: 1750–1808
Certainly, the history of Spanish America in the eighteenth century, or more precisely in its second half, shows how quickly central administrative control could be restored in an empire that had been drifting away from it for 150 years. The Bourbon line that was established on the Spanish throne by the War of the Spanish Succession (1700–13) brought with it from France the authoritarian and centralizing inclinations that marked the regime of Louis XIV, together with certain specific techniques of government that had served those inclinations well in France. So, for example, the unwieldy Council of the Indies, which since 1524 had been, bar the monarch, the ultimate source of executive, legislative and judicial authority over the empire, was replaced in 1714 by a single minister responsible to the king for the administration of both the Indies and navigation to and from them. But the first two Bourbon kings, Philip V (1700–46) and Ferdinand VI (1746–59), found themselves fully occupied with the restoration of Spain itself. And in the first half of the century the only major administrative change made in America was the creation in 1739 of a third viceroyalty, centred on Santa Fe de Bogotá, with authority over much of north-west South America. True, this had the effect of cutting into regional autonomy, since the territory of the *audiencia* of Santa Fe (roughly present-day Colombia) had long been outside the effective control of the viceroy in Lima. But the main reasons for the innovation were the rising wealth that a boom in gold mining was creating in the region, a consequent growth in population, and a developing threat from foreign shipping on the Caribbean coast of the region. These together provided reason enough for a new viceroyalty.

It was mainly in the reign of Charles III (1759–88) that Bourbon reformism reached the Indies. Underlying the various political, administrative, fiscal and economic reforms that were applied was a new, rational approach to the colonies that reflected the aims of Bourbon centralism. It was developed by Spanish political economists working in the technocratic and problem-solving spirit of the Enlightenment. The central intent was that the Indies should become the economic servant of the home country. This meant that their illegal commercial ties with the non-Spanish world should be cut; that the system of trade between Spain and America should be revamped with an eye to efficiency and cost reduction; that active governmental measures should be taken to increase output of American goods useful to Spain; that the operation of the royal treasury in the colonies should be improved to ensure fuller collection of taxes; and that tariff structures should be changed to promote exports of American raw materials to Spain, and export from Spain to the colonies of manufactured goods. As far as possible, the American empire was to be made dependent on Spain for its supply of manufactures; and this commercial dependence was explicitly conceived as a guarantee of political dependence. Historians have often proposed that it was only with the Bourbons' application of these and other measures that Spain's American territories became true colonies in a modern sense of the term: overseas possessions whose own interests were subservient to those of the metropolis. Gone now was the notion of equality among the royal domains, at home and overseas, that had been implicit in the Habsburg theory of unity in the monarch. America, as colony, was now to serve Spain, as state.

Or such was the intent. It was partially achieved through a series of practical reforms implemented from the 1750s until the end of the century. Single merchantmen were now allowed to sail from ports all around the coast of Spain directly to a variety of American ports, delivering their goods more cheaply than had been possible with the traditional system of large convoys departing only from Seville or Cadiz, and docking at only a few points of entry in America. Scientific expeditions were dispatched to gather information on American resources, with a view to their more effective exploitation. Silver production was boosted by an ingenious mix of measures, ranging from rewarding successful mine owners with titles of nobility to cutting the price of mercury, the basic reagent needed for refining. In administration, lawyers were replaced by men of more practical training, often former military officers. Determined efforts were made to oust *criollos* from government and replace them with peninsular Spaniards. A fourth, and final, viceroyalty was created in 1776, based on Buenos Aires, and embracing the territory now covered by Argentina, Uruguay, Paraguay and Bolivia. Its purpose was to resist Portuguese expansionism from Brazil, oversee the rising, export-based prosperity of the River Plate region, and strengthen defence of Spanish territories in South America on the Atlantic side. These, and many other measures brought some of the results that the reformers sought: the foreign share of the Indies trade, though not eliminated, certainly shrank, while that of Spanish shippers and manufacturers rose; colonial production of basic materials grew impressively, especially in Mexico; Spain's administrative grip on the empire tightened; simple knowledge of what America held in the way of human and natural resources was vastly expanded. The effect of Bourbon reforms, and particularly of those applied in the reign of Charles III, could perhaps be termed a second reconquest of Spanish America. It was a recuperation comparable to what had been managed in the middle decades of the sixteenth century, with the addition of that far more explicit and authoritarian aim; subordination of the colonies' interests to those of Spain.

Liberation: 1808–1825

Particularly because of that addition, the second reconquest could be made no more lasting than the first had been. The sixteenth-century recuperation had been undone by, among other things, the growth of the *criollo* population. Now, however, *criollos* did not need to wait for their numbers to increase. They already vastly outnumbered the peninsular Spaniards in America. In Mexico, by 1810, 15,000 Spaniards faced over a million *criollos*. If such a majority resolved to rise and shoulder off the newly imposed weight of an exploitive colonialism, it would be irresistible. The *criollo* reaction was delayed for some years for a variety of reasons: inertia, conservatism, a certain fear of mass movement in the lower levels of society if the status quo were changed, some sharing in the economic growth of the colonies in the late 1700s, and a cultural orientation among elite *criollos* towards Europe. But eventually the reaction came.

It was triggered by the collapse of Spanish authority that resulted from Napoleon's invasion of Spain in 1808, and from his subsequent imposition of his brother Joseph as king. Radical *criollos* seized on this turmoil in the imperial centre to make a bid for self-determination, and eventually for outright independence. The most powerful and enduring movements began in two parts of the empire that had only recently been fully integrated into its structure, Venezuela and the Río de la Plata. Both were outward-looking areas facing the Atlantic, with a potential for vast exports to the industrializing nations bordering on that ocean: cacao, tobacco and cotton from Venezuela, and hides and salt beef from the Río de la Plata. Both had thrived in the late decades of the eighteenth century, but stood to gain much more through wider freedom of trade than Bourbon commercial reforms were ever likely to allow. That commercial aim sustained the drive for self-determination in both regions, but was far from being its sole inspiration. Outright political radicalism had its part too. Manuel Belgrano, a leading insurgent in Buenos Aires, recalled that he had been in Spain training as a lawyer 'in 1789 at a time when the French Revolution was causing a change in ideas . . . [and] the ideas of liberty, equality, security and property took a firm hold on me, and I saw only tyrants in those who would prevent a man . . . from enjoying the rights with which God and Nature had endowed him . . .' Simón Bolívar, chief among independence leaders in South America, traced his thinking to Locke, Condillac, Buffon, D'Alembert, Helvetius, Montesquieu, Rousseau and Voltaire, among others. And even where the Enlightenment did not provide precise political and social prescriptions, the challenge that it embodied to the status quo worked to open paths to change in the mental vistas of many *criollos*.

In the original heartlands of Spanish America, notably central Mexico and the central Andes, these commercial and ideological influences weighed less heavily. Here economies were less export-driven and the ambition for free trade weaker. The *criollo* mentality here was indeed generally more inwardly

Simón Bolívar, the reality and the myth. *Left:* drawn from life in 1830, a few weeks before his death at the age of 47. *Below left:* 'the Liberator' transformed into a heroic warrior in the equestrian statue commemorating him in Quito, Ecuador. In 1822 Ecuador had joined an alliance with Venezuela and Colombia, but that only lasted until 1829.

turned, and resistance to the influx of foreign liberal notions consequently greater (though by no means universal). These old central regions also possessed the largest native and mixed-blooded populations, and *criollo* conservative elements were reinforced by fears of popular risings if the Spanish presence were to disappear. Alarming Indian and *mestizo* revolts over rising taxation had in fact taken place in New Granada, southern Peru, and northern Charcas (soon to become Bolivia) in 1780–81, memories of which faded only slowly, inhibiting many a *criollo* aspiration for greater autonomy. In Mexico, the experience of a quickly improvised and clearly premature bid to oust Spain, led by the radical priest Miguel Hidalgo y Costilla over a few months in late 1810 and early 1811, had the same outcome. Though Hidalgo tried to make his largely *mestizo* followers distinguish between Spaniards and *criollos*, in practice both 'white' groups saw their property destroyed by a rampaging mob army, which was overcome by organized Spanish military effort. And so almost all Mexican *criollos* retreated for a decade into alliance with the colonial government, or at least into acquiescence in its continued presence.

In South America, then, the two originating points of permanently successful movement towards independence were Caracas, the capital of Venezuela, and Buenos Aires. From them extended the movements that ultimately freed the other South American colonies. In both cases the initiating actions came early in 1810 in reaction to news of the almost complete French occupation of Spain, and of the dissolution of the central junta that had been formed to resist the foreign incursion. Now there seemed no 'Spain' left to command an empire, and radical *criollos* in Caracas and Buenos Aires struck out for self-government. For Buenos Aires and its surroundings, the basis of the future Argentina, the initial blow proved enough to oust Spanish authority permanently. But Venezuela was much fought over before Spain was finally ejected in 1821.

The insurgent leader in most of that fighting was Simón Bolívar, son of a Venezuelan *criollo* family of rich cacao growers. The immense energy, daring, strategical imagination and political intelligence of this dashing, charismatic 'Liberator' of the Spanish empire are indisputable. After finally clearing Venezuela of Spanish troops by mid-1821, he went on over the next four years to direct the freeing of the lands that would become Colombia, Ecuador, Peru and Bolivia. It was a hard struggle, becoming ever more challenging as he approached the core of Spanish strength and *criollo* conservatism lying in Peru itself. Peru was to a degree prepared for his efforts on its behalf by the earlier arrival there of the other monumental figure of South American independence, José de San Martín, the leading general of the Río de la Plata. San Martín, a plodding

campaigner in comparison with Bolívar, had nevertheless earlier shown much strategic verve in leading an Argentine army over the Andes in 1817 to defeat the Spanish in Chile (where an earlier local bid for autonomy had faltered). From there he took his force by sea to Peru, in the hope of encouraging an insurrection of native *criollos*. But the Peruvians still held back. It was only after Bolívar's army arrived from the north in 1823, under his brilliant lieutenant Antonio José de Sucre, another Venezuelan, and then in 1824 succeeded in inflicting two defeats upon the remaining Spanish forces, that independence finally came to Peru.

The Mexican independence movement had minimal contact, except for the broad one of circumstance, with the struggles in South America. After Hidalgo's defeat early in 1811 by well-organized and well-led Spanish militia, his insurrectionary effort was continued by another radical priest, the *mestizo* José María Morelos. But despite Morelos's notable qualities as a military leader and political theorist, he was unable to win over enough *criollo* support to offset Spanish strength in arms. Spanish resistance stiffened, as it did also in South America, once the French were driven from Spain and the Bourbon line was restored in the peninsula in March 1814. And Morelos, captured after various defeats, was finally executed in December 1815. For five or more years thereafter the Mexican effort was reduced to isolated guerrilla action. Then in 1820 an unexpected eruption of liberalism in Spain, leading to the constitutionalizing of the monarchy, presented Mexico with a set of proposed reforms of church and society that many *criollos* could not stomach. An ensuing complex political and military manoeuvre, under the leadership of Agustín de Iturbide, managed to combine prevailing *criollo* conservatism with the remnants of radicalism in an alliance which was brief, but endured long enough for its purpose; and together these sufficed to dislodge the Spanish colonial regime – Mexico declared its independence in September 1821. The provinces of Central America, previously part of the viceroyalty of New Spain, in due course took the same path.

So by 1825 all the mainland colonies were free, Spain retaining until 1898 Cuba and Puerto Rico as the sole residuum of the previously vast American empire. Although, as with any large change in history, a multitude of specific motives can be found for the Spanish American independence movements – and a different balance of those motives in different regions – the collapse of the empire can broadly be seen as a further example of that recurring process in Spanish history: excessive pressure of centralism resulting in an explosive reaction. This time, however, the reaction blew the American components of the Spanish world well beyond the recuperative powers of the home country, and into a different political universe.

Spanish America since 1825: some reflections

A different universe it was indeed, but many of its features were little changed. The land was still exactly as before, tantalizing its inhabitants with prospects of immense mineral and agricultural wealth, but shutting many of those resources away among mountains and impenetrable vegetation. Like North America, South America had and has a vast central plain; but it is an area of tropical forest, poor soils and excessive rain, rather than one of workaday timber and fertile prairie. Railways, foundations of industrialization and growth in nineteenth-century Europe and North America, were, except in the Pampas of the Río de la Plata and the high plains of northern Mexico, an altogether tougher proposition in Spanish America. Built they could be, and built they were in the Andean countries; but only with inordinate effort and cost. To this day, Spanish America, especially Spanish South America, remains topographically, climatically, and hence economically fragmented. Vast areas are too dry or too wet; too cold or too hot; too high or too low for utility and comfort.

Having divided themselves from the Spanish empire, the new countries then proceeded for much of the nineteenth century to divide themselves internally, repeating the pattern of resurgent localism that had followed the Spanish destruction of the native empires three hundred years before. Centralism and federalism (if not outright regional autonomy) became political poles between which various nations lurched for several decades. The clearest case of this was Argentina. Mexico suffered the same instability, and here tensions were sharpened as federalists adopted the imported ideology of liberalism, while centralists were strongly conservative. In the Andes, Bolívar had hoped to unite the lands he had liberated in a new Greater Colombia. By the time he died, however, in 1830, this assemblage of Venezuela, Colombia, Ecuador, Peru and Bolivia had fallen apart; and he ended his days lamenting that those who had struggled for the freedom of Spanish America had 'ploughed the sea'. The component parts then proceeded to fracture themselves internally.

For most countries, a semblance of national unity did not reappear until some time in the second half of the nineteenth century. Before then, the nearest approach to coherence came when from time to time strong militaristic rulers emerged to rope errant provinces into submission. But these episodes were for decades transitory. Militarism, nonetheless, established itself as a permanent feature of Spanish American life in the aftermath of independence. This was a most striking reversal of the colonial state of affairs, since until the late eighteenth century military forces had scarcely existed in the empire, and armed conflict all but disappeared once the conquests were over. The militias that were organized after 1750 by Bourbon reformers served as training grounds for many *criollos* who went on to fight for their regions' liberty from Spain. But the independence wars also gave opportunities for personal distinction, power and gain to men lower down the social scale; and this incidental function of militarism has doubtless contributed to keeping it a prominent part of Spanish American political culture from independence to the present.

Sometimes the filtering and tempering of lower-class ambition provided by the military has yielded remarkable results. One such case was Porfirio Díaz, president and increasingly dictatorial ruler of Mexico from 1876 to 1880 (at which point he organized the election of a protégé to replace him), and then (no longer bothering with such niceties) from 1884 to 1910. Díaz conducted Mexico through a period in which increased political stability and striking economic growth reinforced one another, as foreign capital was attracted for the first time in large amounts by the safe opportunities for investment that Mexico now offered.

This same mutual bolstering of stability and growth took place in other Spanish American countries in the late nineteenth century. The process, of course, had external stimuli as well, notably the growing demand from the now many industrializing countries for Spanish American primary products: wheat, wool, and beef from Argentina and Uruguay, nitrates from Peru and Chile, tin from Bolivia, cacao from Ecuador, metals (silver, copper, lead), cotton, sisal and, towards the end of Díaz's period, oil from Mexico – to mention only a few. Foreigners provided not only demand, but in many cases technical advances that made the exploitation of such products more possible and profitable than before: barbed wire and refrigerator ships boosted production and export of good-quality meat from Argentina; cyanide processing stimulated production of silver and gold in Mexico from about 1880; and almost everywhere foreign capital and engineering were largely responsible for the building of the railways that made possible the carriage of bulky prime products to ports or points of exit.

In a few countries, the rise of export-based prosperity in the second half of the nineteenth century accompanied more than a simple increase in political calm. It actually seems to have favoured a movement toward constitutional and elected civilian government. The dominant ideological note was the imported one of liberalism, both political and economic. Some degree of democracy in the creation of government was found desirable; religious toleration was pursued, along with attacks on the influence and economic power (largely in landholding) of the Catholic church; and economic life was seen as a matter of open competition, from the level of individuals up to that of nations. Maximizing freedom of trade was therefore seen as the best way of increasing national prosperity. The prime example of many of these tendencies is again Argentina, where in the wake of the liberal constitution of 1853, modelled on that of the United States, there came universal male suffrage, freedom of religion, a wide extension of public education, openness to immigration from Europe and, above all, a series of civilian heads of government. Free trade, along with abundant immigrant labour, promoted Argentina's agricultural exports to such good effect that from 1880 to 1914 the country averaged 5 per cent in annual economic growth, and its per capita income reached half that of the United States.

Economic liberalism had, though, adverse as well as positive effects in many countries. The free trade and encouragement of foreign investment typical of Spanish America after 1850 or so led to a condition that some have called 'informal empire', in which foreign financial power, first mainly British and then, later in the century, North American, gained a large degree of control over the economic affairs of the states in which it invested. Powerful native groups, the owners of land and capital, often found alliance with foreign interests irresistible, collaborating with them in the exploitation of national assets – a practice labelled *entreguismo*, or 'surrenderism', by its critics. The dedication to tariff-free trading by those primary producers who stood to gain from it most also prevented protection of nascent industry in the small markets that most Spanish American states offered, so that foreign manufactures flooded in and national industrialization stood very little chance of success. Then again, economic liberalism, as another of its tenets, and for the sake of efficient competition, opposed the granting of economic privileges to any group or corporation in society. This was one of its main objections to property holding by the church, and the cause of loss of church lands in many Spanish American states in the nineteenth century. But equal objection was raised to landholding by Indian communities in, for example, Mexico and the central Andean countries, so that native villagers whose common lands had been protected by Spanish law in colonial times now found governments taking their holdings and putting them up for sale. This generally contributed both to the growth of private estates and to the rise of a landless peasantry. Indians, as individuals, were hardly equipped to compete in an economic free-for-all with their more westernized countrymen, as economic liberals would have had them do.

So, in countries with large traditional peasant populations (which was all of them except for Argentina, Uruguay and Chile), the dominant economic policies of the late nineteenth century led to growing inequalities of wealth and income. The new century began, therefore, with economic and social tensions running high in many places, and being increased, moreover, by the penetration of new currents of socialist and

Independence was won by 1825, but political stability proved harder to achieve. In most countries, populist governments have alternated with dictatorships and military rule. Porfirio Díaz was a man of the people and a reformer, but also an autocrat. In 1957 (*above*) David Siqueiros portrayed him as the stereotype decadent ruler, flanked by a general and a capitalist and relaxing with his courtesans. Fernando Botero's *Presidential Family* of 1967 makes the same satirical point, the 'family' including the church and the army.

anarchist thought from the industrial world. These conditions have generally persisted in the present century, and have led to various disturbances of greater or lesser violence.

The first of these, and the most striking both in its ferocity and in its effects, was the Mexican Revolution of 1910 to 1917. Repression and impoverishment of the peasantry was certainly one of its roots. But the Revolution was, again, a more general reaction to over-centralization of power, achieved this time by the Díaz regime in its apparently endless tenure. Among the notable outcomes of the conflict, in the long term, were wide redistribution of land and nationalization of various Mexican resources, including minerals and oil. Indeed, the Revolution marks a broad emergence of nationalism in Mexico that still persists. Many other countries soon followed Mexico down the nationalist road, perhaps partly in reaction to foreign economic domination in the nineteenth century.

Only two other revolutions in twentieth-century Spanish America have had results comparable in scope and permanence to those of the Mexican civil war: the Bolivian episode of 1952 and the Cuban of 1959. Most of the other political coups that have taken place have been little more than that: small-scale conflicts permitting the circulation of power among limited groups in the population, when no firmly embedded traditions existed to allow this to happen by orderly and constitutional means. One of the disappointments of twentieth-century Spanish America is that countries that appeared well on the way to securing such traditions, such as Chile, Argentina and Uruguay, have swerved off course, finding themselves in recent decades under posturing military regimes of severely limited vision. Though militarism has retreated in the past few years, it is far from defeated.

The general prospect offered by Spanish America in this century, indeed, is not a cheerful one. In economics and politics, at least, the future seemed on balance promising in 1900. That much has soured since then is the result of both internal failures and adverse external trends. One damaging failure has been negligence in correcting the inequalities of income and wealth already visible early in the century. Even in Mexico, where redistribution of land and other revolutionary reforms should have brought greater evenness, this did not happen in the longer term. In the early 1970s the top 10 per cent of earners in Mexico received 49.9 per cent of all wages – a slightly higher proportion than in Peru and Colombia (49.2 and 48.0 per cent respectively). In 44 other developing countries the corresponding figure was only 44 per cent. A persisting sense of natural hierarchy in Spanish American society, still reinforced in many countries by ethnically based ranking, doubtless contributes to this lasting inequality; which in turn has helped to provoke episodes of conflict, especially in rural areas, such as the *Violencia* of Colombia in the 1950s and the Shining Path of present-day Peru.

Failure to slow population growth has certainly hindered both an increase in general prosperity and a reduction of inequalities in many countries. Three times as many people – some 18 million – now live in Mexico City alone as inhabited the entire colony in 1800. Elsewhere the increase has been less fast, but still marked. Colombia grew from 3.9 million inhabitants in 1900 to 25.6 million in 1980; Peru in the same period from 3 to 16.8 million. Resources ranging from farmland to education have been strained by such changes.

Externally, Spanish America, as a producer of prime materials, has suffered broadly over the past century or more from a deterioration in its terms of trade. The quantity of manufactured goods obtainable through exchange of a fixed amount of raw materials dropped by almost a third between 1880 and the end of the Second World War; and the deterioration has continued since then.

Despite the nationalism so apparent in many Spanish American countries for much of this century, vestiges of a colonial mentality are still present. The First World is still a natural reference point for many members of Spanish America's upper classes – not only as somewhere to bank and invest, but for education, fashion, entertainment, medicine and lifestyle broadly speaking, not to mention science and technology. Buenos Aires until quite recently prided itself on being the 'Paris of South America'. There is a common (though not universally shared) suspicion that many of life's more complex or subtle activities cannot be learned or practised as well in Mexico City, or Bogotá, or Lima, or Santiago de Chile, as they can in the great cities of Europe or North America. To the degree that this feeling has a real foundation, it derives from Spanish American nations' still incomplete maturity, from what in another context might be termed the imperfectly rounded identity of the adolescent. And this in turn follows, in many countries, from the fact that the ethnic and cultural blending that started with the Spanish conquest has still not run its full course. But in many regions it is nearing completion; and that it is doing so is shown by the emergence here and there in the past several decades of what are recognized as genuinely Spanish American voices, fully worthy of being heard on a world stage: the work, for example, of the Mexican muralist painters; or, even more conspicuously, that of many Spanish American writers: the poetry and essays of Octavio Paz and the novels of Carlos Fuentes, from Mexico; the alternately sombre and wry fiction of Mario Vargas Llosa, from Peru; and from Colombia, perhaps most truly Spanish American of all, the magic realism of Gabriel García Márquez. All indications are that the best of Spanish America is still to come.

THE HISPANIC WORLD IN THE UNITED STATES J. JORGE KLOR DE ALVA

As early as 2015 Hispanics may well become the biggest 'ethnic' subgroup in the United States. Although the arguments supporting this projection are compelling – the nation is already almost 10 per cent Hispanic – and Latinos have been a leading force shaping the economic foundations of the nation, they are rarely present in the mainstream arts or the popular media, in national or state governments, or in the world of letters and science. Until recently, Hispanics had remained, as the New Mexican educator George I. Sánchez stated in 1940, a 'forgotten people'. While many reasons can be given for their limited role in the cultural and political life of the country, one has stood out above the others from the beginning.

The search for the excluded middle

Anglo-Americans in the US, following the logic of the way slavery operated in their society, never developed an intermediate category in which to locate half-castes, or mulattos. A cultural concern with racial purity and related problems of ambiguity, coupled with the desire to distinguish slaves physically and link civil status to 'race', gave birth to a rigorous social calculus founded on the law of the 'excluded middle'. This fundamental principle disregarded actual genetic combinations and instead assumed that, from a biological perspective, each group could remain 'pure': any degree of blackness ('black blood') would make one completely black, while whites always remained white. In the absence of an accepted hybrid type, no space was left in the popular or official imagination for 'mixed' groups or cultures; instead, the English colonists classified everyone as either white or black and, ultimately, as American or alien.

Because Indians in Anglo-America were systematically marginalized, they were never able to transcend their otherness and be acknowledged as a third type of American. Consequently, in the early nineteenth century, when extensive contact was first made with the Mexicans residing in what was then Mexico's northern half, no cultural pattern of ethnic inclusion existed outside the polar categories of white or black. Whether as 'Spanish' aristocrats or as labouring 'greasers', Hispanics – a complex mixture of *mestizos* and *mulattos* – had to conform to known cultural types or risk being ignored or conceived as foreigners.

How Mexicans in the US have responded to this difficult situation has depended on their number, their socioeconomic status and the sociopolitical climate of the country. Throughout the nineteenth century their primary desire was to be left alone, but as Euro-American migration to the Southwest increased, especially in the last decades of the nineteenth century and the first half of the twentieth, many in the middle class, painfully aware of the racial logic behind Anglo-American interethnic relations, struggled to be included as Caucasians. However, their 'success' at being reclassified backfired when, after a 1954 desegregation case, they were used to integrate impoverished 'Negro' schools. In effect, until the 1960s, when they were first recognized by the courts and the public as a distinct 'minority', Mexicans and other Hispanics were generally considered to be either whites or blacks, depending on their socioeconomic condition and the effect being sought by those who could impose their judgment of status.

The Hispanization of the United States

Before the English set foot on the American seaboard, Spaniards were already exploring North America from coast to coast. They established St Augustine (Florida) forty-two years before the founding of Jamestown in 1607, and settled Santa Fe (New Mexico) only three years later. In what was to become the US Southwest, for hundreds of years *mestizos* – bearers of creative mixtures that began as European, Indian and African genetic and cultural traits – settled among, fought against and bred with both Native Americans, whose territory and labour they sought to appropriate, and later with westbound Euro-Americans. By sheer force or through accommodation, the Hispanics patched together a cultural quilt in the Southwest that reflected their many regional *mestizo* styles. This was even more the case in the second half of the nineteenth century when thousands of Mexicans trekked north to make possible the new agricultural, ranching and mining enterprises, and to maintain the Chinese-built railroads.

But the march north by Mexicans was quickly surpassed by the Anglo-Americans' relentless drive west. The latter thrust led to and was stimulated by the Texas revolt of 1836, the Mexican-American War of 1846–48 – when Mexico lost almost half of its territory – and the California gold rush of 1849; in addition, the move west was facilitated by the growing railroad networks and ubiquitous land grabbing and promotion schemes. The violent meeting of cultures and economic interests soon began to unravel the *mestizo* patterns so that by the century's end new 'gringo' politicians, social practices and cultural forms had generally replaced or transformed the old Hispanic ones. By the First World War, only in New Mexico did Latinos maintain significant command over important towns and major tracts of land, and even there control continued to slip away despite the fact that more Hispanics than ever were migrating to the US.

With the Spanish-Cuban-American War of 1898, which ended with Puerto Rico becoming a colony of the US, a small but steady stream of Puerto Ricans journeyed to New York, joining the thousands of Cubans already residing there and in southern Florida. Although extremely important in the context of the East

Coast, this migration was dwarfed by the simultaneous large-scale movement of Mexicans into the Southwest, resulting from both the economic development they helped to drive in southern California and the Mexican Revolution of 1910–17. By the 1930s more than 655,000 Mexicans had already entered and the Puerto Rican and Cuban communities numbered approximately 53,000 and 19,000, respectively. These population flows did not end until the Depression, when a reversal took place as many Mexicans, including some who were US citizens, were forcibly deported. But following the Second World War, Mexican and Puerto Rican migrants began to reach the US once more, this time in record numbers of hundreds of thousands. Only during later periods of economic contraction in the US would Puerto Rican and Mexican migrations slow down or reverse (as has sometimes been the case with Puerto Ricans). Thus by 1988 there were more than 2.5 million Puerto Ricans and well over 12.1 million Mexicans in the country.

As is well known, Cubans began to immigrate in great numbers after Fidel Castro's rise to power in 1959. Three large migrations, each followed by small but constant trickles, brought the total number of Cubans to over one million by 1987. Meanwhile, the number of Dominican immigrants in New York City alone was estimated in 1981 to be between 300,000 and 500,000. In addition, the political and social conflicts in Central America and Colombia during the 1970s and '80s drove the number of people in the US from these areas to over 2.2 million by 1988. Consequently, by 1990 legal and undocumented Latinos had already surpassed the 20 million mark and could be found in significant numbers in every major state of the Union. By this recent date they had transformed the country into the fifth largest Hispanic nation and, as was already noted, were projected to become the largest ethnic subgroup within twenty-five years.

These population figures refer to more than demographic possibilities. In the US these numbers and projections are symbols loaded with ambivalent meanings and sociopolitical implications. Most important of all, they are staggering paradoxes for a nation which, given its East Coast focus and immigrant roots, has built its social and cultural world around the ideal of a supposedly unitary American version of English culture. For most Euro-Americans, the expectation that Latinos, Asians and African Americans together will constitute over 50 per cent of the population by 2080 cannot but signal the end of the principles behind the nation-building project that has defined the nation for two centuries. In short, while 'Americans all' continues to be a unifying ideal, the parameters of the word 'American' are inescapably being put in question by the cultural and social demands of the Hispanic residents and others of non-European origin.

The first Spanish speakers in what is now the USA were colonists who had migrated north from their newly settled country. Until the mid-nineteenth century the south-west states of the USA were part of Mexico, though there was little direct administrative control. Los Angeles, founded in 1781, was taken over by the US in 1846 but for long remained Spanish in character. A photograph of a fiesta parade of 'vaqueros' (cowboys) in Main Street (*top*) must be of the 1880s or '90s, and the bearded pair in formal costume about the same date. *Right*: an inscription on the rock of El Morro, New Mexico, where explorers and travellers from 1605 onwards recorded their names.

Ramon García with his family celebrates the first communion of his daughter at Santa Fe, New Mexico, about 1890. *Right*: Antonio Coronel, former 'alcalde' (mayor) of Los Angeles in 1853.

Diversity and identity

The distinct histories of each of the Latin American nations have helped to shape the diverse ways of being Latino in the US. As Octavio Paz and other writers have noted, since the nineteenth century Mexicans have defined a significant part of their collective self in opposition to the US. In addition, inspired by the Mexican Revolution's (1910–17) emphasis on Mexico's Indian heritage, it has once more become fashionable to be anti-Spanish too. There were two telling symptoms of the rejection of things Spanish among Mexicans in the US during the 1960s and '70s; first, the extensive display of Aztec, rather than Ibero-Mexican, symbols and the use of the term 'Chicano' by young activists, especially when they made a point of identifying themselves as *mestizos* (mixtures of Indian and Spanish) to the exclusion of any traces of Anglo-American; and secondly, the middle-class Mexican's resistance to the label 'Hispanic' and insistence on the use of 'Latino'. In contrast to this distancing from Spanish and US cultures, island Puerto Ricans have been under the direct influence of the US for almost a century, have been US citizens since 1917, and many, if not most, are expecting to vote in favour of statehood in the early 1990s status plebiscite. Furthermore, except for the small *Independentista* (pro-independence) sector, Puerto Ricans generally identify their historical origins as Spanish and, therefore, have no difficulty honouring the conqueror Ponce de León as a national hero, whereas Cortés is emphatically rejected as a hero in Mexico.

Dominicans identify themselves as Afro-Hispanic. Unlike island Puerto Ricans, they have not had an implicit government and educational policy aimed at eradicating the memory of their African past – for instance, by commonly identifying 'salsa' music as 'black' rather than Puerto Rican – but, like the Puerto Ricans, they too suffered the loss of their native Indian populations within decades of the Spanish conquests. Thus they share many of the key social and cultural elements common among Spanish-speaking Caribbeans, including relaxed gender relations and tropical musical tastes, but, in opposition to Puerto Ricans, US Dominicans share with other Hispanic but non-Caribbean groups the effects of immigrant experiences, greater distance from US culture and less urbanized lifestyles. Like Mexicans and Central Americans, Dominicans are more rural in orientation even if they hail from urban centres. This implies special, though difficult to describe, relations to the land, plants and animals; and modes of social interaction that are circumscribed by attention to loyalties and honour common in small social units. While more openly expressive than the typically guarded Mexicans, recent Dominican immigrants do not equal the Puerto Rican flexibility in communication across cultures. Of course, the more acculturated future generations

will change all this, as is already becoming evident with the Cubans, who are quickly becoming a Latino (US Hispanic) ethnic group as they shed their refugee status and 'foreign' customs.

However, the great range of Latino cultural styles, social configurations and political attitudes are the result of more than the presence of distinct national groups. The contrasting reasons why they migrated, their diverse 'racial' (physical) features, class statuses, generations and geographic locations have likewise contributed to the great variety of ways of being Hispanic. For instance, Mexicans long resident in the US and even some recent immigrants look upon the Southwest USA as a lost homeland and their relation to it is intimate and proprietary. Little wonder, then, that they have clashed fiercely with Anglo-Americans for the last two centuries. Meanwhile, Puerto Ricans, emigrating from a US colony, are also fully conscious of a special link that transcends any found among other Hispanic or Old World immigrants.

Most Hispanics have immigrated as a result of politically threatening or weak economic circumstances at home and the expectation of employment in the US. They have generally been both optimistic about their economic future and cautious about the effects of US culture on their own and their family's lives. However, since the great majority have arrived with only agricultural or low-level, semi-industrial skills, the first and frequently the second or later generations have shared many of the experiences and institutions common among other lower working-class immigrants. These include segregated settlement patterns and great social distance from middle-class Euro-Americans, reliance on mutual aid societies and ethnic organizations, ethnic stores and services, inadequate education and low-status occupations, closely knit extended family networks, internally defined markers of prestige and status, and the stresses and stigmas associated with a precarious economic condition.

Cubans, unlike most of the poor Central American immigrants who had been persecuted in their countries, entered the US as political refugees. This status made available to them the public assistance needed to overcome the worst hardships they faced in the new land. In addition, the initial waves of Cuban refugees (especially the first) included many successful businessmen and professionals who escaped in possession of critical human resources and some financial wealth. In Florida and to a lesser extent in the New Jersey-New York area, where most were relocated, they immediately organized enclave communities with their own financial, service, recreational and manufacturing centres. As a consequence, when more refugees arrived in later waves, these could be employed in large numbers by Cuban concerns which had already been estab-

lished. After an initial drop in status, therefore, Cuban immigrants collectively are economically located today just below the Euro-American community and far ahead of other Latino groups.

The few affluent non-Cuban Hispanics who have immigrated usually do not reside in segregated communities, do not depend on ethnic organizations for support, identity or recreation, and tend to interact little with their own kind. Instead, they socialize and commonly intermarry with Euro-Americans and thereby tend to become assimilated with relative ease. In contrast, although much intermarriage with Euro-Americans takes place even within the clearly defined and consciously identified middle-class Cuban, Colombian and Central American communities, they are not disappearing; indeed, to the extent that they stop conceiving of themselves as foreigners they are actually becoming more visible as 'ethnic' Latinos. That is, as the second generation and the immigrants educated in the US put aside their desire to return to their homeland, they become more committed to life in the US and their place in it as Americans. This is reflected in their high naturalization rates and the facility with which their attention has turned to what are considered ethnic concerns: collective economic advancement, political power and cultural survival.

The millions of undocumented Hispanic immigrants, most of whom are Mexican or, in smaller numbers, Dominican and Central American, occupy a number of migratory statuses. Some take advantage of the best economic circumstances of both sides of the border and enter only for short stays; others, without documents or with lapsed visas, as is frequently the case with Dominicans and Central Americans, stay for many years or remain permanently. The immigrants who enter for a brief sojourn have the least cultural impact on their communities, but they provide a constant Hispanicizing effect. Their presence, like that of first-generation migrants in general, produces a cultural counterforce to the ubiquitous pressures to acculturate. The presence of immigrants, along with frequent trips to their parents' homelands, makes it possible for second and subsequent generations to continue to understand Spanish and to identify with their ancestral origins. Furthermore, although most desire to do so, the majority of older immigrants do not return to their homeland, remaining instead as a critical source of support for the customs and beliefs of the old country, often in opposition to their English-speaking children and grandchildren. Together, these factors help to produce communities that are culturally bifurcated, with a first generation sector continually at hand providing a culturally conservative base on which second and later generations create their more Americanized cultural styles. Hence, in contrast to the Europeans who immigrated earlier in the century, most Latinos are

Arriving in the USA can be a very different experience according to the immigrants' place of origin. Early Cuban refugees (*below*), most of them middle-class, prosperous and politically motivated, were able to adapt to US life comparatively painlessly. Among Mexicans, on the other hand (*bottom*), many are poor and uneducated, cross the border illegally and are subject to humiliating searches for drugs and guns.

still attached to their cultural roots and are constantly being nourished by them. As a group, therefore, they seem more resistant to acculturation than were their European counterparts.

Racism and ethnocentrism on the part of Euro-Americans also contribute to the maintenance of traditional cultural traits by promoting the segregation of the less affluent Latinos. As was already discussed, those who are very dark-skinned or who are considered blacks by non-Latinos suffer from the types of social isolation, discrimination and oppression (sometimes violent) commonly practised against African Americans. And in addition to having to struggle with the effects of having a low socioeconomic status and being a 'person of colour', poor unacculturated Mexicans and Puerto Ricans, like other Hispanics similarly situated, suffer from the stigmas attached to having a poor command of English, believing in (the 'superstitions' of) Roman Catholicism, practising folk medicine and holding social and cultural values opposed to those prevalent among middle-class Euro-Americans. For many Latinos the inevitable results of such segregation are inferior housing, health, employment, work environments and educational facilities, and, until very recently, political powerlessness.

On the positive side, the oppression and exclusion faced by many Latinos have led to the maintenance of many homeland survival strategies and the development of new adaptive manoeuvres and institutions. These range from the promotion of empathetic herbal curers to the establishment of culture-affirming ethnic parades. Furthermore, on top of the resources provided by local and federal governments, community networks of family and friends everywhere provide a significant share of the 'social insurance' needed against unemployment, disability, widowhood or old age. And voluntary associations such as rotating credit groups, mutual aid societies, political and hometown clubs, and some trade unions continue to provide, as they have in the past, sources of capital, means for labour advocacy, social and political forums, and nuclei for public entertainment and for organizing on behalf of urgent needs.

Light-skinned Hispanics, facing fewer obstacles than their darker working-class compatriots, are less likely to suffer from or be conscious of discrimination, and are therefore more likely to look favourably upon American society. If they migrated as children or are beyond the first generation, their problems of self-identity tend to be focused on the competing demands of ethnic loyalties and cultural preferences. On the other hand, for 'black' Caribbeans the problem becomes one of finding their own place in a society that tends to divide between Anglo-Americans and African Americans. That is, Latinos who are considered 'black' are regularly treated as American

For Mexicans in the USA the question of cultural identity is doubly difficult. They are Spanish in that they speak that language, but many prefer to seek their roots in pre-Columbian Mexico and to be known as 'Chicanos'. At the same time most are US citizens and proud of it.

blacks by both African and Euro-Americans, leaving them far less space than other Hispanics to negotiate their identity.

Mestizo or *trigueño* (swarthy) looking Puerto Ricans, who cannot readily pass for white but lack salient black features, have resisted attempts to acculturate into either community by emphasizing their Puertoricanness. In the past, however, before the massive migrations of the 1950s brought almost half a million of them to the mainland, especially New York City, a more generalized 'Hispanicity' shaped the identity of Puerto Ricans surrounded by many other Hispanic and non-Hispanic ethnic groups. Today, Dominicans, Colombians, Panamanians and others, who live close to each other in New York, have sufficient mass to maintain collectively some degree of national identity. But scattered individuals or smaller national communities embedded in a sea of Cubans, Puerto Ricans or Mexicans frequently lose their public and at times their personal ethnic identities. Thus it happens, for instance, that Puerto Ricans in small Californian communities may come to see themselves and be seen as Mexicans, while young Hondurans in New York may experience their identity as Puerto Rican, especially if there are socioeconomic, legal (migratory status) or cultural advantages to this substitution.

Cultural stereotypes and social realities

It is often claimed that 'Hispanic' culture – defined as a fixed set of practices and beliefs – is deficient. For instance, it is described as anti-intellectual, anti-capitalist and anti-work. These failures, it is argued, are compounded by both an absence of a future orientation (an unwillingness to plan for the future or delay gratification) and the presence of a noncompetitive, nonprogressive and easily satisfied psychological makeup, conditioned by a family-oriented, fatalistic world-view. Together these factors are said to stand as obstacles to the development of the hard-working, forward-looking and self-sacrificing individualism believed to characterize the successful white, Anglo-Saxon, Protestant middle class.

This cultural deficiency model springs from a series of stereotypes, whose pedigree can be traced to the early days of the anti-Spanish Black Legend that flourished in Britain and its New World colonies. At its most extreme, the model characterizes Latinos as violent, but they are more commonly seen as over dependent, prone to welfare fraud and drug and alcohol addiction; irresponsible, irrational, and likely to abuse their spouses and children, to abandon or neglect them, and to disregard family planning. In short, they are seen as immature and improvident, incapable of holding a serious job or of adequately providing for themselves or their families.

These negative stereotypes are symptomatic of the continuing sad state of Anglo-Latino relations. Latino scholars and

politicians point out that when translated into public policy, they are merely justifications for doing nothing on behalf of Hispanics or for limiting the support given to them. They are responsible for keeping Latinos as an undereducated, powerless mass, forced to perform the many necessary but menial services that more privileged groups naturally shun. Many middle-class Latinos agree that the stereotypes contain some truth – but only when applied to the desperately poor. It does seem to be the case that poorer Mexicans, regardless of generational status, are more affirmative about the family than are those in the middle class. But most Hispanics, like Euro-Americans, seem to put efficiency and economic considerations (including individual advancement) above a loyalty to family that would limit employment opportunities.

Nonetheless, it is true that a very significant percentage of Latinos are poor, and became poorer in the 1980s, when there was an annual influx of approximately 250,000 much needed, but mostly impoverished and low-skilled Hispanic immigrants. By 1987 40 per cent of all Latino children were living in poverty and the percentage of poor families had risen to 25.8, from the 23.5 per cent recorded in 1981. One symptom of poverty was female-headed households. Meanwhile, the median family income had declined to $20,306 in 1987 from $20,631 in 1981. In educational attainment, Latinos were at the bottom. The situation is so critical that, unless there are dramatic changes, half the Hispanic population is expected to be functionally illiterate by the early 1990s.

While all discussions both inside and outside the Hispanic communities on stereotypes and their supposed effects are polemical, the following figures suggest the extent to which Latinos must be seen as more than an oppressed, impoverished 'ethnic minority'. As early as 1978 more than 100 Latino-owned businesses each had sales of over 3 million dollars per year; by 1982 there were over 248,000 Hispanic-owned enterprises; and in 1989 the Latino consumer market reached a phenomenal 171 billion dollars. By 1990 over 2.6 million Hispanics (approximately 13 per cent) had household incomes of over $50,000.

Culture, the family and religion

The truth is that there is no such thing as 'the Hispanic culture', 'the Latino family', or 'the dominant trait'; indeed, even the use of Spanish is far from universal. Whatever the ideals might be, Latino families, kinship patterns and gender roles are extremely diverse. For instance, in 1985 Mexican families were the largest with 4.15 members, while Cubans had only 3.13. The number of households headed by women also varied dramatically from 44 per cent of Puerto Rican families to only 18.6 per cent for Mexicans. At the same time, the median age of the latter was 23.3 years compared to 39.1 for Cubans. Most of these

The consumer market follows Hispanic needs and Hispanic tastes. 'Spraycan art', used by some as a means of making public, semi-political statements, is also a popular form of self-assertion, and cars (*left*) are a medium for its display. *Left and centre*: advertisements aimed at Hispanic customers and (*bottom*) an announcement advertising a typical combination of herbal and spiritual remedies.

empirical differences can be accounted for by studying the class and geographical context of the diverse communities, but the more subtle cultural distinctions are obviously less amenable to quantitative assessment.

For example, the importance of the family, the degree of patriarchism and the extent to which it is centred on the mother are dependent not only on generational, residential and class patterns, but also on employment opportunities and related cultural assumptions. Thus, while it is typical for the first generation to bring with it a stronger family orientation than is common in the US, if employment for the women is the main source of support or is away from the family setting, the power reversals established and influences from outside are very likely to set off cultural conflicts at home. After all, for many women, employment had been culturally restricted to informal forms of labour and what can be done at home, in the company of family members, or in otherwise supervised contexts. This ideal of women's dependence on men, which entails discouraging their employment outside the home, is seriously challenged when both men and women must work to make ends meet, or when men have to rely on child benefits (paid to the mother) to support their families. These situations place great strains upon the traditional roles of the sexes.

In such cases, if the male head of the household is deprived of the prestigious role of economic provider, because he is consistently unemployed or is relegated to labour considered demeaning, the women will tend to take charge of domestic responsibilities and the man's status suffer. When the woman is the consistent provider, whether through welfare or employment, female-based families tend to emerge in which the central bond is between mother and children, with the men (husbands or lovers) coming and going, but the children – half-siblings or not related at all – remaining with the mother. This situation is found particularly in impoverished Dominican and Puerto Rican families, many of whom bring with them mother-based patterns that are the continuing result of their past experiences of slavery and current poverty.

Latino life-cycle rituals and beliefs also vary widely, but some features are commonly shared and others are conditioned by the way non-Latinos typically respond. For instance, working-class households make much of babies even when born out of wedlock, but the male-centred bias dictates that fathers prefer a son as the firstborn. Acculturated parents logically prefer to christen their offspring with English names, and even those who do not will nevertheless see them translated by the schools. Last names, customarily made up of both parents' surnames, are usually reduced by bureaucrats and teachers to the father's patronymic and, if it survives at all, the mother's frequently becomes a middle name. And regardless of the depth of spiritual conviction, naming ceremonies usually take place during religious baptisms. Among the more acculturated, however, this ceremony focuses on the parents and the baby, while working-class parents use the occasion to strengthen their support system through the recruitment of reliable godparents, who may even be called upon to take care of the child in their absence. Nevertheless, beyond the first generation these potential responsibilities tend to lose their meaning as the ties of *compadrazgo* ('godparenthood') come to represent little more than a sign of friendship.

When the need arises among, say, poor Puerto Rican or Dominican mothers, these are much more likely to place their children in the hands of trusted *comadres* ('godmothers') than are their Mexican counterparts, who usually find childcare outside the immediate family unacceptable. Older siblings are expected to care for the younger ones and this, in part, helps to establish the ideal age and gender hierarchy of authority and respect common in Latino households. At the same time, a heightened gender-consciousness among Hispanics results from and in turn leads to boys and girls being raised even more dissimilarly than is the case in most Euro-American homes. Children's playmates are separated more by sex than age, and they learn early on that there is a female world focused on the home, the moral centre of the family, and a male world negotiated in the streets, where personal and family reputations are made, safeguarded and lost.

As with all immigrants, the widespread conflicts between Latino generations represent cultural clashes. Children, who are typically the first to learn English and become familiar with the world beyond the home, often become the mediators and interpreters between the cultures. But by the time they are teenagers they are anxious for their privacy and independence. Frequently, as they become more insistent on asserting the antithetical cultures of the school and streets, those raised in tradition-bound Hispanic households quickly exhaust their parents' capacity to understand and cope with change. The contradictions in values, the opposing demands of peers and the burdens of familial expectations can precipitate problems that can lead to delinquent behaviour, involvement with illicit drugs and participation in warring gangs.

The extensive interaction between different Latino groups and with others living in close proximity has led to high rates of intermarriage. Many factors affect these rates, but except among Puerto Ricans in the 1980s, the first generation intermarries less than the second, working-class Latinos tend to marry each other, women intermarry more frequently than men, and small Latino subgroups and those with highly skewed sex ratios (like the Cubans and Puerto Ricans) intermarry extensively. Mexicans, whose intermarriage rates ranged in the 1970s from

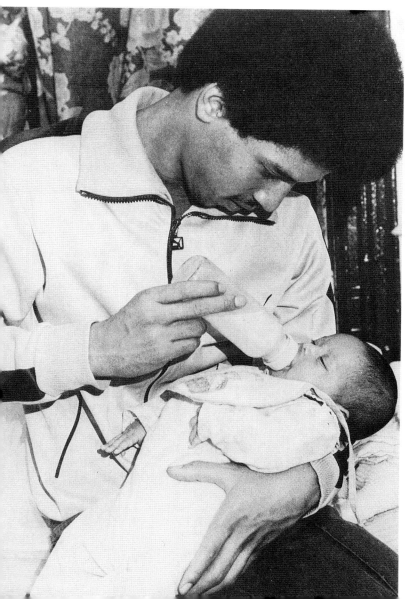

over 50 per cent in California to 9 per cent in southern Texas, often marry whites, but Latino exogamous marriages among non-Mexicans are usually to members of other Hispanic groups or, to a much smaller extent, to African Americans.

Although most Latinos are Catholic, each national group has its distinct beliefs and forms of worship reflecting the unique history of the church in the homeland. The perennial shortage of trained clergy and the Indians' or African slaves' insistence on the maintenance of their traditional faiths, however transformed, resulted almost everywhere in the development of sometimes highly unorthodox folk Christianities. In the Southwest, the lack of Spanish-speaking clergy and the dominance of Protestantism served to distance the church from the faithful, who were neither understood nor fully accepted. A similar separation resulted from the American takeover of Puerto Rico. The Indo-Afro-Christian religion of the peasants, already alienated from the more European Catholicism of the urban elite, was denigrated or disregarded by the English-speaking priests. In both cases an austere, formal orthodoxy, associated with the foreigners, confronted a vital, personal religion born out of the local needs and experiences of the faithful. The church's solution to this problem has been to build parochial schools and to integrate parishioners by means of Spanish-language services – primarily in response to the extensive inroads made by Protestant missionaries since the 1950s and to the pressures felt by the church following the civil rights movements.

Since the 1960s Protestant sects have been much more involved in social action projects to support Latinos than has the Catholic church. A substantial percentage of the Puerto Rican population is Protestant and the number of Mexican and Cuban converts has grown significantly in the last two decades. Protestantism, especially Pentecostalism, has been successful because the communities of worshippers are small, personal and actively engaged in creating an everyday religious environment that addresses the actual physical, social and emotional needs of its members. In addition, most of the ministers are Hispanic, making it possible for them to act as mediators between their congregation and the dominant community, and helping them to preserve their link to the homeland and to cope with life in the US. Finally, Pentecostalism makes room for the folk-based spiritual and healing beliefs of the congregation, neither challenging nor ignoring them.

While most Latinos rarely draw on them to the exclusion of modern medicine, the Indian-Spanish herbal and faith healing practices of *curanderismo* ('folk curing'), and the beliefs and rituals of *santería* and *espiritismo* are extremely popular. The first is widespread among Mexicans, *santería* is particularly popular among Dominicans and Cubans, who are deeply influenced by Afro-Christian religious and medical practices, and *espiritismo* is more common among Puerto Ricans, who mixed its beliefs, introduced from Europe in the nineteenth century, with their own brand of Afro-Christianity. All three forms of healing blend folk spiritual beliefs with knowledge of curing herbs and patent medicines in an attempt to effect the cure of culturally defined mental health problems and diseases.

By way of a conclusion

The United States, as the meeting place of every Hispanic type in the world, is the site of the last and perhaps most complex moment of the Spanish diaspora set in motion in 1492. On that emblematic date the world-wide dispersal, forced or voluntary, of Spanish Jews, Muslims and Christians set off a chain reaction of imposed migrations, lethal epidemics and cultural permutations that was to transform the genes and the behavioural patterns of Iberians into countless new ways of looking, acting and being Hispanic. More than ever before, after the fifteenth century no set of isolated physical or social characteristics could be used to define all Hispanics.

All the major Hispanic types in existence today can be found in the US. Furthermore, contemporary relations in the US both among them and between them and others are more varied and potentially more momentous than those experienced anywhere else in the world. On the one hand, their phenomenal demographic growth, especially in the last decade, their concentration at the younger end of the age-scale, and the recent development of a substantial third generation of Puerto Ricans and Cubans portends a dramatic shift in US politics, culture and society. While most Latinos back the Democrats, Cubans have been overwhelmingly Republican, but as the latter become 'ethnics' their affiliation may shift. A Democratic party strongly supported by Latinos may lead to significant transformations not only in domestic policies, but also in US-Latin American and US-Spanish relations. On the other hand, the inevitable appearance of a non-Euro-American majority in the near future may also signal the beginning of substantial constitutional crises, as the Euro-American minority reconsiders its commitment to democratic principles. The recent successful efforts of the 'English Only' movements to limit the use of Spanish by state governments in sixteen states (including California and Florida) is a sign of the growing 'nativist' backlash and the political crises that may lie ahead. Yet the changing demography and the need for Hispanic labour, to counter the shrinking numbers of Euro-American workers, will force the continued Hispanization of the nation.

Lastly, second and subsequent generations of Latinos are already defining a new pan-Latino identity in those communities where no one national group dominates demographically.

In Chicago, Puerto Ricans and Mexicans have joined forces on many occasions as a result of the need to band together to promote their interests. These cooperative efforts force each national group to set aside its individual agendas in favour of unexpected alliances, cultural compromises and expressions of communal sentiment. Together these collective affirmations promise to shape a new 'Latino ethnic consciousness'. The same might be said for San Francisco, where the nationalist priorities of Central Americans, South Americans and Mexicans have been checked wherever possible by the collective Latino initiatives and conviction that are being defined under the rubric of 'La Raza'. And in New York, where the massive migration of Dominicans and Central and South Americans during the 1970s and '80s has forced the proportion of Puerto Ricans to decline steadily, a state of transition is afoot that may bring the city closer to the model of pan-Latinoism. If this were to happen, and non-Mexican Hispanic immigration continues into the Southwest, the world may experience the rise of a totally new Hispanic ethnicity that would draw as deeply from Anglo-American culture as Spanish civilization has previously drawn from the Muslim, American Indian, or African cultures.

The new leadership. As Latinos (Hispanics) establish themselves in American society, they are inevitably rising to political office. Henry Cisneros was elected mayor of San Antonio, Texas, in 1981.

Modern Spain was born amid the horrors of the revolution provoked by Napoleon's invasion. On 2 May 1808, the people of Madrid, more patriotic than their king, rose against the French. The savage repression of that revolt was immorta-lized by Goya's *The Third of May*. But the spirit of nationalism grew, nourished by the ideals of the French Revolution, and when Napoleon was finally defeated, the Spanish people were not content to submit tamely to Bourbon despotism. A new constitution envisaged the return of power to the Cortes and the transformation of Spain into a constitutional monarchy. Promul-gated in Cadiz in 1812, this was only gradually and with many setbacks made a political reality.

ADJUSTMENT TO MODERNITY:1800–1992 JUAN PABLO FUSI AIZPURUA

In the nineteenth century, Spain lost its great overseas empire. Between 1810 and 1825, after several years of war, it relinquished almost all its possessions in America; in 1898, after a brief war with the United States, it gave up Cuba, Puerto Rico and the Philippines. As the twentieth century dawned, the once powerful Catholic monarchy of the Habsburgs was a modest nation, with virtually no influence on world affairs, which retained a few minor possessions in Africa as a pale reflection of its formidable colonial past. Spain took no significant part in modern imperialism: it just exercised, jointly with France, the protectorate over Morocco after 1912 and acquired, shortly afterwards, some territories on the Atlantic coast of the Sahara.

Nobody, except a few fascist ideologues in the 1940s, ever again seriously considered Spain capable of recovering a new and vigorous imperial mission. There were, of course, occasions on which Spanish governments, for reasons of prestige or strategic purposes, embarked on new overseas action, as for instance during the 1860s, or later, in the twentieth century, in Morocco. But there was no redefinition of a possible new role for Spain in the world. On the contrary, for a long time Spain lacked any real foreign policy. It found itself excluded from the reconstruction of post-Napoleonic Europe, in spite of the decisive part played by the Peninsular War in the defeat of Napoleon. Subsequently, its foreign relations were subordinated to those of France and Great Britain. From the last third of the nineteenth century up to the Franco era (1939–75), Spain engaged in a policy of isolation and withdrawal whose principal theorist was Antonio Cánovas del Castillo (1828–97). It is no coincidence that he was also the historian of Spain's decline in the seventeenth century, which convinced him that Spain lacked the economic basis to sustain neo-imperialist adventures.

Spain had become a minor power. It did not take part in either of the world wars, a fact which certainly weakened even more its much-diminished international standing. The establishment of Franco's regime made things even worse. Its initial alignment with the fascist Axis powers and its antidemocratic nature meant the exclusion of Spain from the United Nations from 1945 to 1955. Franco later sought, and achieved, the support of the United States and the Vatican, of the right-wing regimes of Latin America and the Arab world, and, in time, established normal relations with almost every country in the world. But the weakness of his international position was obvious. In 1956 he had hastily to give independence to Morocco, to which he subsequently ceded Ifni and, later, the Sahara. In 1968 it was the turn of Equatorial Guinea, the tiny colony he had retained in West Africa. Worse still, Spain was left out of the European Economic Community, created in 1958.

All this was highly significant from the Spanish point of view, since, even before the loss of its empire, Spain had been searching for a new collective identity. An intense intellectual debate had taken place throughout the nineteenth and early twentieth centuries. The question of Spain as a nation and its relation to European culture had absorbed intellectuals, from Cadalso and Jovellanos to Unamuno, Ortega y Gasset and Azaña. The diplomat and writer Juan Valera (1825–1905) summarized it all around 1890: '. . . in the eighteenth century', he wrote, 'we awoke from our dreams of ambition and found ourselves far behind cultivated Europe, unable to catch up, forced to tag along in the rear.' The europeanization of Spain was, then, a long-standing and vague demand which intellectuals had been pursuing since at least the end of the eighteenth century, when Montesquieu and Masson de Morvilliers questioned Spain's contribution to the civilized world. After the 1898 defeat by the United States, which was a catalyst for a deep crisis of the national consciousness, europeanization became almost a political programme, at least for men like Joaquín Costa (1844–1911), the energetic Aragonese intellectual, and José Ortega y Gasset (1883–1955), the brilliant leader of the twentieth-century liberal intelligentsia. It is quite clear what lay behind this. Europe, from the Spanish perspective, meant parliamentary democracy and industrialization, precisely the double challenge which modernity had posed for Spain since 1800, the key to understanding its history in the nineteenth and twentieth centuries. Spain's answer to that challenge had little to do with Spanish national character: it had to do with political, social and economic problems, complex and difficult, which, moreover, could have taken a different form.

The old regime restored

Many of these problems had profound historical roots. Spain entered the nineteenth century with a national culture deeply imbued with the spirit of the Counter-Reformation and without a recent, modern tradition of representative institutions. And, for geographical reasons, it would long remain in a peripheral position with relation to the global economy and modern capitalism. Such a historical legacy was bound to condition the fate of the liberal and industrial revolutions in the peninsula. The transition from ancien régime to liberal state (1808–40) constituted an undefined, incomplete and discontinuous revolution which culminated in a compromise between liberalism and the army. The origin of the Spanish revolution did not result either from ideas or from the conflict between power and society. It was unleashed by the Napoleonic invasion and the war of independence waged by popular forces and Wellington's troops between 1808 and 1814. For that reason, the Spanish revolution bore within it an irreconcilable contradic-

Civil war broke out in 1833, when Ferdinand VII (restored to the throne in 1814) died leaving a disputed succession, between his brother Don Carlos and his infant daughter Isabella. In simplified terms, the Carlists represented conservatism, regionalism and the church; Isabella's party (however unwillingly, under the regency of her mother), liberalism. *Right*: a revolutionary scene in the Ramblas, Barcelona, during an uprising in 1835. *Below*: Queen Isabella II, who was declared of age in 1843, when she was thirteen, seen here with her husband, a Bourbon cousin, whom she married in 1846. But by 1868 her increasingly repressive rule provoked a new revolution and she fled to France.

tion: the divorce between, on the one hand, the liberal minority which, taking advantage of the power vacuum created by the war, managed to call together the Cortes and to approve in 1812 a democratic constitution – valid, however, only in the city of Cadiz – and, on the other hand, the vast majority of the country, who had fought in the war under the spiritual leadership of the clergy, in the name of King Ferdinand VII (a prisoner of Napoleon) and of the Catholic religion.

The approval of the Constitution of 1812 was, then, a mere illusion. Absolute monarchy was restored without opposition in 1814 by the immensely popular Ferdinand VII. Lacking significant social support, liberalism was forced to resort to clandestine conspiracy and to place all its hopes in the hands of discontented military officers. Its future lay not in its own strength but in the double weakness of Ferdinand's absolutism: first, the lack of any minimally effective apparatus to run the state, the military and the police, the ancien régime having been practically destroyed by the war of 1808–14; and secondly, the incapacity of Ferdinand VII's governments to face up to the formidable problems of the nation's finances. Liberalism was restored to power by a lucky military coup in 1820, but, after a disappointing four years' experience, was again overthrown in 1823 by the combined effect of internal divisions and the destructive action of extremist radicals, popular counter-revolution and the intervention of the French army in support of the king.

Carlist wars and the army in politics

Liberalism triumphed, finally, in 1833, on the death of Ferdinand VII, basically for two reasons: first, because the succession to the throne of Isabella II had been challenged by the partisans of Ferdinand's brother Don Carlos, and her regent, the widowed Queen María Cristina, was therefore forced to summon the liberals to power; and secondly, because the army supported Isabella's lawful succession against the Carlist insurrection, a predominantly rural movement with strong clerical support which emerged in 1833 in defence of Catholic unity and the 'legitimate' king. The civil war, which raged from 1833 to 1839, therefore sealed the compact between the liberals and the army. The war gave prestige to the military and led them into politics. It made evident the enormous weakness of civil power and spread the conviction that the constitutional regime – which received a new constitution in 1837 – needed, somehow, the protection of the army. Five generals, the progressives Espartero and Prim, the centrists Serrano and O'Donnell and the conservative Narváez, were the protagonists of political life between 1839 and 1868. The army, not the electoral and parliamentary mechanisms, became the instrument of political change. It was still a constitutional army, which acted at the

Juan Prim (*below left*), the successful general with liberal sympathies who had been one of the engineers of Isabella's fall, is symptomatic of the growing influence of the army in politics. In 1869 he became prime minister and led the search for a new dynasty that would free Spain from the Bourbons altogether. The choice fell on Amadeus of Savoy, but on the day he set foot in Spain, 27 December 1870, Prim was assassinated. Five years later the Bourbons were back on the throne, where they were to remain until 1931.

service of the political parties within a non-militarist and liberal concept of power and politics. This became clear later, both in 1868, when the army overthrew Isabella and inaugurated a six-year democratic experiment, and in 1875, when General Martínez Campos restored the monarchy and ushered in a long period of liberalism which lasted for nearly fifty years. But the preponderance of the military gave legitimacy to army interventionism and crystallized into a national-military theory which made the armed forces the fundamental institution of the state and of the nation and the ultimate guarantors of the unity of the country; it was precisely this theory which inspired the conservative and reactionary coups of Generals Primo de Rivera and Franco in 1923 and 1936 respectively.

Military power was strong in Spain because civil power was weak, as Jaime Balmes (1810–48), the Catholic writer, noted around 1840. The parliamentary institutions were born with no historical legitimacy. The liberal political parties which emerged in the 1830s reflected the ideas and aspirations of a small elite of eminent personalities. Political parties did not represent the opinion of the country and, dominated by personal factionalism and political 'clientelism', proved to be feeble and ineffective bodies. The great majority of Spaniards abstained from participation in public life. Rural Spain, 80 per cent of the country, remained sunk in silence and age-old routine. Madrid, the capital, was described by the best journalist of his time, Mariano José de Larra (1809–37), as a society of 'idle chatterers', dedicated to malicious gossip, gaming and social gatherings – visits, *tertulias* (regular social circles), theatre, opera, cafes – where being a civil servant and having a salary were the highest social aspirations.

Spain was, moreover, a Catholic country, despite the serious conflicts between the liberal regime and the church that took place from 1833 to 1850. The ethics and values of Catholicism had a profound influence on the perceptions of Spaniards: the Carlist Wars were seen as a Catholic and counter-revolutionary crusade against liberalism. Indeed, Catholicism seemed to be an essential element in the Spanish national character. It impregnated the mentality of the majority with ideas of solidarity and social protection, but it did so to the detriment of the individualistic conscience which constituted the fundamental basis of liberalism. Catholic Spain, and the church – whose work in the fields of education, religion and welfare was immense – always maintained, with a few isolated exceptions, considerable reservations, if not open hostility, with regard to the liberal regime and to secular and modern thinking. This would become apparent from 1931 to 1936 and in the very wide Catholic support given to Franco's uprising in 1936.

Long before, in the years from 1845 to 1868, the Moderate Party, the right wing of historical liberalism, encouraged a conservative and even neo-Catholic deviation of the Spanish liberal revolution. Thus the Constitution of 1845, inspired by French doctrinarianism, went so far as to deny the principle of national sovereignty, to reinforce the power of the crown and to make Catholicism the official religion of Spain. In 1851, a concordat signed with the Vatican restored the church's central role in society which had been taken away by the radical legislation of 1836–37. Finally, the Progressive Party remained virtually excluded from power and from the regime during all those years except for 1854–56.

The regime of the Moderates laid the foundations for the construction of the modern Spanish state and created the conditions for the transformation of the country and the affirmation of the bourgeoisie as a class and as a social force. Beneath the governmental and political instability which characterized the whole reign of Isabella II (1833–68), there took place a quiet and slow revolution which transformed Spain. A uniform and centralized system of provincial and local administration was developed. The state was endowed with an effective and powerful paramilitary organ of repression, the Civil Guard, created in 1844. A national system of secondary and higher education was established. The administration of justice was regularized and homogenized, penal law was codified and numerous provisions were enacted to regulate the various judicial procedures. The disorder and arbitrariness which had governed entry into the different categories of the civil service began to change in the 1850s, with the creation, or reform, of professional bodies for the different departments of the state (such as the postal service, health, prisons, accountancy and state treasury, customs, education or tax inspection). The navy, non-existent since Trafalgar, was rebuilt and the army restructured and modernized. Finally, in 1845, the Moderates reformed the financial system and created the system of taxation which was to prevail, practically unaltered, until 1900 and to condition all subsequent reforms. The chaotic and inefficient conglomerate of taxes of the ancien régime was now converted into a simple scheme of direct and indirect contributions.

The beginnings of prosperity

The writer Valera, who was also an elegant and intelligent historian, observed that, especially after 1843, a notable enrichment of the country had occurred, based principally on the sale of disentailed church lands – a process initiated by the liberal left in 1836 and extended in 1855 to include communal village property – and on the building of railways, which began in 1848. Both operations led to the transfer of millions of pesetas. About 25 million acres of land were sold in the course of the nineteenth century, when Spain passed from importing wheat to exporting it. Almost 4,000 miles of railway were built between 1855 and

1874. Nor were these the only manifestations of change. Sizable investments of foreign capital, which played a decisive part in the construction of the railway, stimulated the first upsurge of Spanish mining. The vinegrowing area increased significantly during the century. Wine and sherry became basic Spanish export products. The growth of the cities activated local economies. Between 1850 and 1880 alone, sixteen provincial capitals doubled their population; from 1840 onwards Madrid experienced considerable development. Starting in the 1830s, Catalonia underwent a real industrial revolution based on the cotton industry. Between 1856 and 1866 numerous banks were founded. Speculation on the Stock Exchange and investment in state bonds mobilized large quantities of capital.

The limits of this development were evident. The fiscal system, even after the reforms of 1845, was conservative and inefficient. Agriculture, in spite of disentailment and the population growth, remained backward and traditional, carried on with very primitive techniques. Production per acre was very low and great areas of land were occupied by *latifundios* (large landed estates), especially in the southern regions. The process of urbanization was slow and not until well into the twentieth century did a real network of urban cultures emerge. Industry was over-dependent on foreign capital and tariff protection. There was no modern iron and steel industry until the 1880s brought the industrialization of the Basque Country. The banking sector was still very fragile and weak and experienced spectacular crises before 1868.

Spain was, then, a comparatively backward country. It was growing, certainly: the population rose from 13.3 million inhabitants in 1834 to 15.6 million in 1860 and 18.5 million in 1900. But it was growing at a slower pace than other countries in Europe. The Spain of Isabella II was essentially a dual economy, to use the expression of the historian Nicolás Sánchez Albornoz. A poor, traditional, stagnant subsistence economy – which was to be idealized by the romantic imagination – coexisted with a modern, urban and capitalist economy in which cities (Madrid and Barcelona above all) were 'islands of modernity', as Ortega y Gasset termed them. Cities were the sphere of the social life of the most dynamic classes of nineteenth-century Spain. The aristocracy lost all its legal privileges, though not its lands, after 1833 and, although it retained part of its formal presence, it became gradually diluted within a new upper class of bankers and businessmen, the upper echelons of the army and the administration and successful professionals who together formed that nucleus of 6,000 to 8,000 people who, according to Valera, constituted the power elite of Spain in the 1870s. The cities were also the sphere of activity of the middle classes and the urban petite bourgeoisie so splendidly portrayed in the novels of Benito Pérez Galdós (1843–1920).

Spain did not have a strong bourgeoisie. The modern Spanish state was built over a country which was unevenly developed, geographically badly integrated in spite of the railways, and where local life remained exceptionally strong. From 1840 onwards, there was a certain administrative order and numerous instruments for the exercise of state functions. But the state was poor and weak. Services were limited and the central government's size remained small until well into the twentieth century, a fact which encouraged the usurpation of state functions by 'clientelism' and patronage. The cities might be islands of modernity, but rural Spain was languishing, deprived of mobility and ideological ferment, burdened by the weight of custom and the authority of the local notables and, frequently, the church. The emergence of an independent and responsible electorate was slow and relative, and was not completed until the 1930s. Wide sectors of opinion remained until that date on the margin of politics. All these factors combined to make the consolidation of a constitutional and parliamentary liberal regime problematic and difficult.

Republic and restoration

This would become evident when the democratic revolution which, under the leadership of General Prim (1814–70), overthrew Isabella II in 1868 found itself unable to create a political consensus and to consolidate a stable party system. The revolutionary bloc split irreversibly as soon as the establishment of a democratic monarchy in the person of Amadeus of Savoy was decided, a solution which, to put it briefly, served only to resuscitate Carlism and revitalize the Republican party. From 1872 civil war again plunged the country into bloodshed, especially the Basque Country; in addition, insurrection broke out in colonial Cuba. In 1873, after the abdication of the honest and disappointed Amadeus, the Republic was proclaimed, an extraordinary occurrence in a country where the monarchic principle, along with religion, always seemed one of the pillars of national identity. The First Republic, overwhelmed by the wars and by revolutionary insurrections in Murcia and in the south, saw the almost total collapse of the authority of the state. A military coup put an end to the situation in 1874 and after a year of interim government the monarchy was restored, in the person of Alfonso XII (1876–85).

The Restoration was, above all, the work of the historian of Spain's decline, Antonio Cánovas del Castillo (1828–97), a liberal-conservative politician of singular talent, learned, caustic, impatient and resourceful, whose pragmatism and scepticism had given him an exceptional sense of the state and politics. Cánovas's idea was to create a regime of liberty and concord, a stable system based on a prestigious civilian power, supported by solid, strong political parties capable of alternat-

ing harmoniously in government, with a reduced electorate and an open constitution – sovereignty being shared by the crown and the Cortes – where the defence of traditional values such as family, religion and property would be compatible with a certain degree of state intervention in favour of the needy classes and for the protection of national industry. The country was pacified after the defeat of Carlism in 1876 and the end of the colonial war two years later. The 1876 Constitution, in force until 1931, reflected Cánovas's conservative ideas, but it was sufficiently flexible to incorporate, in time, many of the democratic principles of the revolution of 1868: universal male suffrage was approved in 1890. The Constitution recognized Catholicism as the official state religion and gave the church control of education. But it authorized the private exercise of other religions and coexisted with cultural liberalism, to the extent that liberal, not Catholic, culture was dominant in Spain – in the press, in the theatre, in literature, in art – until 1936.

Cánovas managed to create a two-party system. The regular rotation between conservative and liberal parties defined Spanish politics from 1876 to 1913 and, despite difficulties, up to 1923. The punctiliously constitutional behaviour of Alfonso XII and of his widow, María Cristina of Habsburg (regent from 1885 to 1902), gave the monarchy a prestige it had not enjoyed since Charles III. This meant a significant contrast with the experience of the years 1833 to 1868, particularly in one respect: the withdrawal of the army from politics (which lasted until 1917). The generals continued to form a very strong pressure group and the army remained very sensitive to all external criticism. But political stability meant that the military ceased to be the essential instrument of political action and change.

Entering the twentieth century

Thus, the monarchy of 1876 managed to create the conditions which made possible the beginning of a not insignificant process of modernization and economic and industrial development which, in spite of serious deficiencies and recurrent crises, was maintained until the end of the 1920s. The Catalan textile industry, which employed 70,000 workers, had its golden age between 1876 and 1884. Under the leadership of a dynamic industrial and commercial bourgeoisie, Catalonia later diversified its production. The electrical and engineering industries – including the production of motor cars, which began in 1904 – and the chemical industry allowed the region to retain its economic dynamism. In 1930 more than 70 per cent of its labour force worked in the industrial and service sectors. Barcelona was a city of one million inhabitants (the whole of Catalonia had three million).

Railways and mines – iron, copper, lead, coal, mercury – experienced a huge new development after 1876. In the Basque

Country the export of iron-ore, estimated at some 170 million tons between 1876 and 1920, brought about a rapid and powerful process of industrialization. Between 1886 and 1899 alone, nearly 650 enterprises were set up in Vizcaya. The small province became the centre of the iron and steel industry, naval production, banking capital and the country's merchant navy. Bilbao became Spain's main port and one of the most important in Europe. This had enormous repercussions, because the Basque economy, unlike the Catalan, would eventually have a decisive weight on the national economy. Basque capital, represented above all by the Banks of Bilbao (1857) and Vizcaya (1901), was, thus, essential in the process of electrification initiated in 1900. Moreover, important industrial foci – such as coalmines – were created in Asturias. Madrid itself was transformed between 1875 and 1900 into a commercial and banking city: in 1900 it had somewhat over half a million inhabitants (Spain had 18.6 million); in 1930, nearly one million (Spain had 23.3 million). Agriculture remained a negative burden for the development of Spain. But even so, wine exports, favoured by the crisis in the French vineyards, reached a remarkably high level between 1876 and 1886. Even if this could not be maintained, a new export agriculture, citrus fruits, transformed the economy of the eastern part of the country.

The fact was that after the great prosperity brought about by neutrality in the First World War, Spain ceased to be a predominantly agrarian country. In 1930 more than 50 per cent of the population worked in either the industrial or the service sectors. 42 per cent lived in medium-sized towns and 15 per cent lived in towns of more than 100,000 inhabitants which offered, to a greater or lesser degree, most of the services and improvements of other European cities (electricity, trams, gas, motor cars – the Madrid Metro was built in 1919). Only 34 per cent of the population lived in centres with less than 5,000 inhabitants. The aristocracy had lost even that formal presence which it had preserved in the nineteenth century. Ways of life, the predominant mentality, customs, clothes, leisure activities, values, all reflected the tastes and aspirations of the middle classes, 'the nerves and marrow of the country', as Unamuno, the Basque writer, put it in 1933. Culturally, Spain was going through a second golden age which found its expression in what became known as the 'Generation of 1898' (the writers Unamuno, Baroja, Azorín, Valle-Inclán, Machado, the painter Zuloaga) and the 'Generation of 1914' (Ortega y Gasset, Dr Marañón, the poet Juan Ramón Jiménez, Salvador de Madariaga and many others), which would later be prolonged, in the years of the Second Republic, by the young men of the generation of García Lorca, Buñuel and Dalí. Mass entertainment like cinema and football arrived in the 1920s to democratize leisure time and give it a degree of cosmopolitanism which traditional bull-

The last thirty years of the nineteenth century saw a vigorous industrial and economic development in Spain. Railway building, an essential preliminary, had begun in 1848. This splendid locomotive (*far left*), photographed with its personnel in 1867, is at Cordoba station. The two most heavily industrialized areas were the Basque Country, where iron was found, and Barcelona, centre of textile manufacture. *Left*: two images of Barcelona – a panorama of smoking chimneys painted in 1920 and a machine factory in 1874.

Two giant engineering projects separated by fifty years. *Below*: construction of the Canal de Isabella II in 1855, bringing water to the parched plains of central Spain. *Right*: the Biscay Transporter Bridge, which spans the river mouth below Bilbao, an outstanding work of the engineer Palacios in 1893.

fighting (which, in spite of all the changes, also experienced a golden age in the first third of the twentieth century) obviously lacked.

Dualism

From the beginning of the century the industrial working class already constituted a social reality of increasing importance and weight in economic and political life. In 1879, the Socialist Party was founded and shortly afterwards, in 1888, the socialist trade union organization, the U.G.T., soon to become highly powerful in Vizcaya, Madrid and Asturias. In 1911, the anarcho-syndicalists founded the National Workers' Federation (*Confederación Nacional de Trabajo*), influential in Catalonia and Andalusia; and the church promoted, without much success, the creation of Catholic trade unions and agrarian organizations. Spanish society became familiar from the end of the nineteenth century with class conflict and class terminology. Labour legislation – accident and health insurance, Sunday rest, the regulation of women's labour – began to take shape from 1900 onwards. In 1919 the eight-hour day was introduced. After the First World War, Spain also saw the gradual formation of a professional society: experts and professionals in increasing numbers began taking up relevant posts in the state bureaucracy and the economic management of industries, businesses and banks.

Admittedly, the Spain of the first third of the twentieth century still remained a rural country. In comparison with the more developed parts of Europe, Spain's backwardness was evident. Regional imbalances had even worsened after the industrial take-off of some provinces. Dualism still defined the Spanish economy. 'Spanish society', wrote Manuel Azaña, principal leader of the Second Republic, in 1939, referring to the situation which he inherited on coming to power in 1931, 'presented the most violent contrasts. In certain urban centres, a high standard of living, adapted to all the usages of contemporary civilization, and, a few kilometres away, villages which seem trapped in the fifteenth century.' In Madrid, magnificent palaces next to miserable shacks; tiny smallholdings in the north-east and vast *latifundios* in the south; great cities, manufacturing centres and the industrial proletariat on the one hand, and, on the other, the hunger and destitution of the landless proletariat of Extremadura and Andalusia. Everything was just as Azaña described it. But nonetheless the transformation which had been effected since 1876 had been extraordinary. The flourishing Spain of 1927 which brought to a victorious conclusion the Moroccan war was not the backward Spain which had been defeated in 1898.

It was precisely the contradiction between that changing society and the limitations of the political regime of 1876 which,

to a great extent, gave rise to the political problems of Spain in the twentieth century. The regime was defined by Costa as one of 'oligarchy and caciquism'. Indeed, the monarchist politicians who governed until 1923 were in fact simply a liberal oligarchy. Conservatives and Liberals belonged to the same social group: the wealthy and prestigious upper bourgeoisie and the well-off professional middle class. The system set up by Cánovas did not allow any true opposition: the Liberal party was the 'tame' alternative which the political game demanded. Political parties were mere cliques of notables and alliances of parliamentarians – not mass parties with programmes, ideas, militants and regular voters. Caciquism was the essential element in the system. By means of agreements with local bosses and recourse to fraudulent practices, the buying of votes and the falsification of voting registers and returns, governments 'fabricated' elections and achieved the parliamentary majorities which suited them. Caciquism was almost a natural process in a country where the state was still poor and weak and where, for that reason, local bosses usurped its functions – in exchange for securing electoral support for the government in their district – and where patronage had deep roots derived from the intensity of the links of family and friendship. In the short term, caciquism guaranteed the stability of the system. But it was an artificial and very fragile structure which could not withstand the slightest shift in public opinion, as was first seen in Barcelona where Catalan nationalism and the Radical Republican party displaced the monarchist parties after 1901. So, in the long term, caciquism left the 1876 monarchy, headed between 1902 and 1931 by King Alfonso XIII, with no support except for a narrow oligarchy of notables. In the final analysis, that was to be the reason for its failure in 1923 and 1931.

Cánovas's system survived the defeat of 1898 remarkably well, but its response to the demand for the regeneration of the country which then became the popular cry – and which had in Costa its principal theoretician – was inadequate. The conservative leader Antonio Maura (1853–1925) propounded the theory of a revolution from above, that is to say, the creation of a strong state capable of governing which, by reforming the administration, would eradicate caciquism. He wanted a system based on modern parties: a conservative party which would have the electoral support of the conservative classes and Catholic opinion – and of the Catalan and Basque nationalists – and a liberal party supported by the middle and working classes who were being attracted by the Republican and Socialist parties. Maura governed with exceptional energy between 1907 and 1909, but his own dynamism contributed to the breakdown of the two-party system and the polarization of political life. In 1913 he refused to alternate in power with the Liberals because they had collaborated from 1907 to 1909 with

Outside the industrial areas, Spain remained a largely agricultural country, and the contrast between urban wealth and rural poverty remained striking. *Above*: a fashionable salon of 1895, a society still dominated by the landed nobility. *Left*: village pump in the countryside near Almeria, Andalusia, photographed in the 1950s.

the non-monarchist parties and shared in the furore unleashed by the execution by firing-squad of the anarchist teacher Francisco Ferrer (accused of being responsible for the revolutionary agitation stirred up in Barcelona in 1909). As a result, the system was left almost in ruins. After 1914 the fragmentation of the party system was total; government instability became endemic. The governments of the monarchy, which between 1913 and 1923 had an average life-span of five months, were incapable of solving the problems of the country. They could neither hold back the astronomical inflation engendered by the First World War, nor deal with the labour unrest it gave rise to, nor meet the demands for autonomy of Catalan and Basque nationalism which sprang up in the last years of the nineteenth century and which had acquired significant electoral and social support in their respective regions. Worse still, they failed to satisfy an army which was increasingly discontented with its economic situation, concerned about the emergence of peripheral nationalisms and the deterioration of public order, and inspired by the Moroccan war with a new and aggressive nationalistic mentality. The political stability and consensus which had been achieved in 1876 collapsed. An unsuccessful revolutionary attempt took place in 1917. Later, the grave social and labour problems experienced by Barcelona after 1919 and the devastating defeat suffered by the army in Morocco in 1921 – which caused serious tensions between the civil and military powers – finally finished off the system. Alfonso XIII, deprived of instruments of government and disgusted by his politicians, accepted the coup d'état carried out in 1923 by General Primo de Rivera (1870–1930), with the support of a large part of the country.

The first dictatorship and the Second Republic

The dictatorship of Primo de Rivera (1923–30) was, in its own way, a regenerating dictatorship, which drew up an ambitious programme of public works, gave a notable impetus to communications and electrification and brought about important economic reforms. However, it ended by confirming that the social evolution which Spain had experienced since 1876 required profound political transformations to make possible at the very least the integration into public life of the urban population (42 per cent of the whole by 1930). Primo de Rivera failed precisely because he was unable to create a political system of his own. His fall in 1930 implied the fall of the monarchy: in April 1931 a Republic was proclaimed for the second time in the history of Spain. After the June elections, the most democratic thus far in Spanish history, a Republican-Socialist coalition emerged. It was led by Manuel Azaña (1880–1940), a previously little-known intellectual, of a disdainful and bitter temperament, a marked and complicated sensitivity, but possessed of a deep sense of

patriotism and a conviction that only a democratic reform which would change the politics and even the collective consciousness of the Spaniards would make a national regeneration possible.

The Second Republic – defined by the left-wing, progressive constitution of 1931 – brought new hopes for the transformation of Spain. Azaña's coalition government set about solving what he believed to be the great problems which had conditioned and impeded Spain's difficult evolution towards modernity: the agrarian, military, religious and regional problems. Azaña and his government wanted to expropriate the *latifundios* and distribute the land among the peasants; to create a professional, democratic army obedient to the civil authorities; to limit the influence of the church, secularize social life and promote a liberal and secular education; and to rectify state centralism by granting autonomy first to Catalonia and eventually to the Basque Country, and perhaps to Galicia and other regions.

The government's plans polarized political life, partly because of the resistance which the reforms provoked in the sectors affected by them – the church and Catholic Spain, the landowners and part of the army – but also because of technical difficulties (as in the case of agrarian reform) and because of the aggressiveness and sectarianism which lay behind such measures as the dissolution of the Jesuits or banning the religious orders from teaching. The government thus alienated large sectors of the urban and rural middle classes who, after 1932 to 1933, lost confidence in the Republic as a regime. The Azaña coalition also failed to fulfil the expectations of the peasants – agrarian reform was slow and did not resolve the great problem of Spanish agriculture, which was not so much the *latifundios* as the lack of capital – and of important sectors of the working class; the anarcho-syndicalists had unleashed a revolutionary offensive against the government from the summer of 1931 which greatly helped to alarm capital and entrepreneurs and to discredit the Republic.

The rejection of the Second Republic by conservative Spain became evident when the 1933 elections radically changed the political balance. The centre-right governments which ruled between 1934 and 1935 carried out a systematic reversal of the 1931–33 legislation, which amounted to a virtual redefinition of the Republic from within. This, and the maximalist tendency adopted after 1933 by the country's two principal parties, the Socialist Party and the CEDA (Spanish Confederation of the Autonomous Right), influenced by the international rise of fascism, made the republican experiment unviable.

The Civil War and Franco

The revolution launched by the Socialist Party in October 1934 against the entry of the CEDA into the government seriously damaged the legitimacy of the regime. When the left, united in the Popular Front led by Azaña, won the elections in February 1936, the right-wing military moved directly into a conspiracy leading to a coup d'état which finally took place on 18 July of that year. Under the leadership of Generals Mola, Franco, Sanjurjo and Queipo de Llano part of the army rose up. They revolted for a variety of reasons: they believed that the Republic had no historical legitimacy and that the army was the ultimate instrument of national salvation; they saw in the autonomy movements the break-up of national unity; they identified laicization as an attack on the Catholic essence of Spain and attributed the disorders and strikes to the democratic system's lack of authority. The right idealized the civil war which followed the military uprising as a crusade against communism, while the left idealized it as the resistance of the people and the proletariat against fascism. Azaña saw it as a 'collective delusion'.

The war lasted three years. It cost 300,000 lives, devastated 183 urban centres and some 250,000 buildings, destroyed 50 per cent of the railway's rolling stock, a third of the country's cattle and a third of the merchant navy. Victory, achieved on 1 April 1939, opened the way for the personal dictatorship of General Franco (1893–1975), a soldier forged in the Moroccan war, conservative and Catholic, a man of small stature, dour, suspicious, prudent, obsessed by communism and freemasonry, who believed that liberalism and political parties were the cause of Spain's ills.

Franco's regime, which lasted until his death on 20 November 1975, was not just a parenthesis in the history of Spain: it represented a decisive turning point and created a new economic and social order. Based on the nationalistic and fascist ideas of the Falange – created in 1933 by José Antonio Primo de Rivera (1903–36), son of the earlier dictator – on the social thought of the church and on the principles of order, authority and unity of the military, Franco's regime was initially totalitarian, openly aligned with Hitler's Germany and Mussolini's Italy. After 1939 Spain saw the creation of a broad corporatist state, the inclusion of fascist rituals into official life, the intensification of religious life and the adoption of economic policies based on autarchy and state control. After the defeat of the Axis in 1945, Franco's regime gradually came to define itself as a social and Catholic monarchy – although the king was not restored – and as an organic democracy. The representative body of the regime, the Cortes, was undemocratic. Most of its members, who represented the family, the state trade unions and the municipalities, lacked any legislative power; this was retained by Franco. The dictatorship was always a repressive regime – although the years of most intense repression were 1939 to 1945 – which, unlike other similar regimes, sought to depoliticize Spanish society and which, by appealing to the

The establishment of a new republic in 1931 did not heal the deep rift in Spanish society, and in 1936 General Francisco Franco attempted to repeat Primo de Rivera's coup and establish a military dictatorship. This time the forces of the left were stronger, and three years of civil war had to elapse before he could claim success. *Left*: Republicans beneath the banner that became their watchword: 'They Shall Not Pass.' *Below left*: Franco at the victory parade in Madrid in May 1939. Note behind him the ancient coat of arms of Charles V, with the motto 'Plus Ultra', and the by-now-familiar heraldry of Castile, León, Aragon and Navarre.

Franco's right-wing dictatorship lasted thirty-five years. When he died, in 1975, Spain (under a restored constitutional monarchy) regained freedom of expression and with it the clash of political ideologies. *Below*: Basque radicals (who go further than any other Spanish group in demanding autonomy) burn an effigy of Franco. *Right*: a poster of the Spanish Workers' Socialist Party. *Centre right*: Dolores Ibarruri ('La Passionaria', a heroine of the Civil War) returns in triumph after Franco's death. *Bottom*: the young leader of the Workers' Socialist Party, Felipe González.

Spain today is still a balance of opposing forces, but has harmonized those forces so that they are fruitful rather than destructive. Past and present are reconciled with the establishment of a constitutional monarchy under Juan Carlos (grandson of the king exiled in 1931) presiding over a democratic parliament. The provinces enjoy substantial autonomy while (with varying degrees of commitment) endorsing and submitting to central government. Economically Spain flourishes, as the new architecture of Madrid (*below right*) and other cities testifies. And for the first time she is truly a part of Europe in every sense, joining the EEC in 1986 and in 1992 preparing to host the next great International Exhibition and the Olympic Games (*right*).

most traditional values of that society, achieved stronger social support than its enemies ever recognized. There was, at least, a gradual accommodation of Spanish society to Francoism, although the system, like every authoritarian regime based on personal power, always lacked any trace of democratic legitimacy.

By subordinating the whole economy to politics and by imposing state control on numerous sectors – railways, mines, petroleum, air transport – Franco's regime encouraged an extraordinary growth in the size and extent of the machinery of the state. A strong public sector was created after the setting up in 1941 of the National Industrial Institute (I.N.I.) to promote the industrialization of the country. In fifteen years, the I.N.I. built a considerable number of aluminium and nitrate factories, chemical and pharmaceutical industries, shipyards, large iron and steel works, oil refineries and lorry and car factories. The regime promoted public works: dams, reservoirs, power stations. Rigid controls on prices and salaries were established. Imports were restricted. Workers and management were forced to join fascist trade unions – which became a vast Falangist bureaucracy – and a complex system of social security was created. Never before had the state taken on so many responsibilities for regulating the economic and social life of the country; never had its bureaucracy been so large, nor had it penetrated so deeply into society.

And yet the results were negative and counter-productive. Autarchic industrialization was inordinately costly and produced extremely high inflation. The equipment of the new enterprises was totally insufficient and the materials they used were of very poor quality. Wages always lagged behind prices. The years from 1939 to 1942 were years of hunger. Production, in spite of the state's efforts to invest, stagnated until 1959. During the 1950s, when Franco received the support of the United States and his regime was admitted to the United Nations, things improved, once the government had been forced to liberalize external trade and prices (which provoked fresh outbreaks of inflation). Even so, after twenty years of the new regime, Spain was in 1960, together with Portugal, the poorest country in Western Europe.

The turn of the tide

Spain changed during the 1960s, after the government, which now included a considerable number of technocrats from Opus Dei, abandoned between 1957 and 1961 the economic ideals of the Falange and the early Franco period and, following a painful period of stabilization, embarked on a neo-capitalist liberalization of the Spanish economy. The years of development (1961–73) amounted to a real revolution which turned Spain into an industrial and urban country. Great internal and external migrations transformed its demographic structure. An exceptional upsurge in tourism changed the economy of many coastal zones and the habits and behaviour of the Spaniards. The modernization and secularization of society was accelerated. The purchase of motor cars and domestic electrical equipment increased dramatically. Industrial production grew between 1960 and 1973 at an annual rate of 10 per cent, double the European average. In 1970 three quarters of the working population was employed in industry and services and only 25 per cent in agriculture. In 1975, about 75 per cent of the population lived in towns of more than 10,000 inhabitants. In 1960 only 4 per cent of Spanish households had a car and only 1 per cent owned a television, but in 1975 the figures were 40 per cent and 85 per cent respectively. In 1960 there were six million tourists; in 1975 thirty million. Income per capita, which in 1960 was $300, reached $2,486 in 1975.

Nevertheless, development brought with it grave negative consequences and heavy social costs. Regional imbalances within the country were further accentuated. The neglect of agriculture condemned more than two million Spaniards to emigration. The growth of the cities was disorderly and improvised. A huge, shabby industrial belt grew up in the periphery of Madrid, where the population increased from 2,260,000 in 1960 to nearly 3,000,000 in 1975. Most cities were victims of catastrophic urban development, and nearly all of them saw the mass of industrial workers huddled into poor slum districts, deprived of most essential services. Development demanded an extraordinary effort from the middle and working classes: the Francoist fiscal system, based on indirect taxes, was crushingly regressive.

The development decade also saw the reappearance of internal conflict in Spain, which put an end to one of the great myths of Francoism: that of Franco's peace. Students and intellectuals rebelled in demand of democratic rights and freedoms; the workers sought trade union freedom and freedom to negotiate collective agreements. ETA, the Basque terrorist organization created in 1959, revived nationalist claims in the Basque Country. Finally, the church increasingly divorced itself from Franco's regime, especially after the Second Vatican Council, held in 1964: its opposition began to delegitimize the theory of a crusade used by Franco's regime to justify its origins and the Civil War of 1936–39. The conflicts of the '60s and '70s revealed the growing contradiction between a modern, industrial, urban society, which Spain had already become, and an authoritarian and undemocratic political regime. There were tensions within the regime itself from the '60s on (as indeed there had always been). And after 1969 – when Franco, on completing the institutional development of his system, named Prince Juan Carlos, grandson of Alfonso XIII,

The discovery of the New World, a discovery whose true scope and significance only gradually dawned upon the West, gave Spain peculiar advantages, but also peculiar problems and responsibilities. The very wealth which made her the envy of Europe had the long-term effect of destabilizing her economy, while the task of governing and living with the native peoples once they had been conquered raised issues – moral, theological and social – that no country had ever faced before. To devout Christians, the thought that God had laid these duties upon Spain for good reasons was unavoidable. A painting by Alejo Fernández made for a chapel in Seville about 1535, during the lifetime of Cortés and Pizarro, expresses this sense of divine mission. 'The Virgin of the Navigators' spreads her protective arms over the conquistadors and their ships. The man on the left is probably Columbus. In the background kneel the shadowy figures of Indians to whom the blessings of Christianity have been brought.

as his successor – an open crisis developed when Francoism was torn between liberalization (or *aperturismo*, 'opening up') and continuity (*inmovilismo*), a controversy which dominated Spanish politics until 1975. By 1975, the year of Franco's death, Franco's men were aware that the regime lacked democratic legitimacy; that it was because of this that Spain remained excluded from Europe – the great failure of Franco's foreign policy; and even that the country's laws and institutions were not adequate for the new Spanish reality.

Spain finds modernity

These changes help to explain the transition to democracy which took place after the dictator's death, when, contrary to what the hard-line Francoists had hoped, King Juan Carlos (born in 1938) and his advisers encouraged the evolution towards a constitutional and democratic monarchy. This process was accelerated after the appointment of Adolfo Suárez as president of the government in the summer of 1976. Having even won the consent of the Francoist Cortes, and backed by a referendum of the people, Suárez carried out an in-depth political reform on the basis of the Francoist legal framework itself. He legalized the political parties and the trade unions; he called constituent elections which he won by building up a broad centre party; and he achieved a broad consensus with the opposition, reflected in the 1977 Moncloa pacts (an agreement with the trade unions and the parties to combat inflation and unemployment) and, above all, in the 1978 constitution which set up a fully democratic monarchy within which the various nationalities and regions, seventeen in all, had the right to autonomy. Suárez also made special agreements with Catalonia, and failed with the Basque Country only because of the uncompromising violence of ETA, which reached its highest point in 1979 and 1980, and because of the intransigence of traditional Basque nationalism.

In spite of the disappointment of those who would have liked to see a more profound break with Francoism, in spite of the economic crisis which Spain suffered after 1973 and which Suárez was unable to solve, and in spite of the terrorist pressure of ETA and a few ultra-right groups, Spanish democracy turned out to have sufficient strength to survive the fall of Suárez in 1981 and the dissolution of the party which had carried out the reforms, and even the attempted coup d'état of 23 February 1981, led by a lieutenant-colonel of the Civil Guard, Antonio Tejero, and General Milans del Bosch (which failed principally because of its energetic condemnation by King Juan Carlos).

Even more, Spanish democracy adjusted without difficulty to the return of the left to power after fifty years, when the Socialists, led by Felipe González, won the 1982 elections, a success which was to be repeated in 1986 and 1989.

Spanish democracy was not, however, untroubled, faced as it was by problems common to urban and industrial societies: traffic in the cities, lack of security for citizens, social marginalization, youth counter-cultures, drugs, environmental degradation, labour conflicts. To these were added the problems deriving from an irregular, uncontrolled and unplanned development, such as the poor quality of workers' housing and the inadequacy of amenities and social services. The Socialists had to face two great challenges: the decline of traditional industries, particularly severe in regions like Vizcaya and Asturias and in the shipbuilding sector, and unemployment which, in the 1980s, reached 20 per cent of the working population.

Politically, in the 1980s and early 1990s the legacy of more than a century and a half of history was still alive in Spain: the divorce between society and parliamentary politics; the negative image of politics, sharpened by some resounding scandals; the tendency to express protest and pressure via non-parliamentary channels (which culminated in the general strike declared by the trade unions against the Socialist government on 14 December 1989); the weakness of a society accustomed by Franco to depend too much on the protection of the state; and finally, the tendency of governments to seek absolute power. The problem of ETA's violence also remained alive. But there were features in Spain which were historically new. First, Spain had developed a strong economy; this could be seen once the readjustment policy imposed by the Socialists made it possible, around 1985, to overcome the grave crisis which had been dragging on since 1973. Secondly, Spanish society was dominated by the weight of the urban middle classes, linked to the civil service, the management of businesses and the liberal professions, with relatively high levels of well-being and economic affluence – reflected in their high spending on education, housing and consumption – and showing a high degree of homogeneity in their tastes, attitudes and opinions. Thirdly, after joining NATO in 1981 and the EEC in 1986, Spain seemed to have solved the problem of its historical identity and to have found a role on the international scene. From the perspective of the final years of the twentieth century, Spain was a prosperous, democratic and European country, adapted at last, after nearly two centuries of fascinating history, to what can convincingly be called modernity.

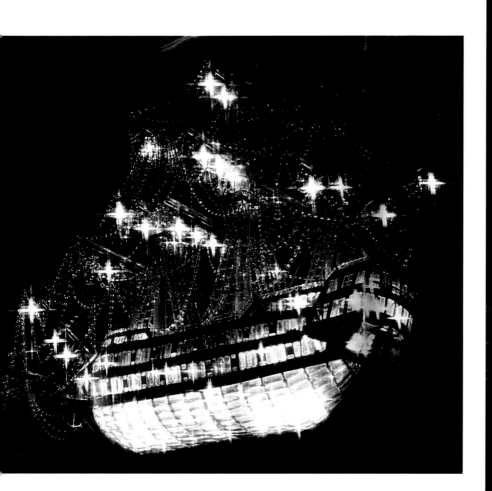

An Accidental Empire

Columbus's landfall was indeed providential in every sense. When he sailed in August 1492, neither he nor his royal sponsors had any thought of founding an empire. Yet within fifty years Spain was governing territories nearly three times the length of Europe from Scandinavia to Sicily.

Columbus himself has assumed something of the status of a myth. When he died in Valladolid in May 1506, his body was taken to Seville, but in 1542 it was exhumed and transported across the Atlantic to Hispaniola to be buried in the cathedral of Santo Domingo. Later it was moved again to the cathedral of Havana, where in 1892 a splendid monument was made by Arturo Melida (*right*). When Cuba was made independent the monument and the remains were moved yet again back to Seville, where they now are. Melida based his design on medieval models with lifesized cloaked mourners, incorporating the arms of the provinces and kingdoms of Spain.

The crystal galleon which forms a chandelier, lit from within by a sort of mystic radiance, in the private apartments of the Oriente Palace in Madrid, is another magical image turning history into symbol.

The triumph of the Cross

Cortés's success with such a small force was so swift and so complete that it still has an aura of the miraculous.

Aztec and Spaniard face each other across a burning temple (*below*): a miniature from a contemporary Mexican manuscript. *Right:* one of a series of paintings by Miguel Gonzalez (1698) showing scenes from the conquest of Mexico. In the background Aztec priests put the severed limbs of sacrificial victims in a pot and Aztec traitors are burned. In the main picture Friar Bartolomé de Olmedo preaches before Montezuma.

The history of the province of Michoacán is represented by Juan O'Gorman in a mural of 1941–42 (*opposite*). In the distance, the Aztecs; in the middle, Cortés and the conquistadors; in the foreground, the subjection of the Indians.

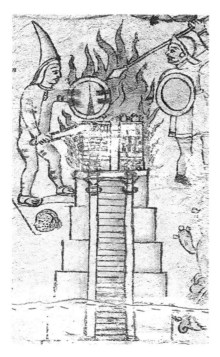

The architectural marriage

Unlike as they were in many other respects, Mexico and Spain sometimes show a strange coincidental affinity in architectural style. Both Aztec, Mayan and Churrigueresque buildings exhibit a fondness for multiplicity of mouldings and ornament piled upon ornament in a sort of decorative frenzy, so that the Baroque churches of Mexico seem uncannily fitting as successors to the Mayan temples of Labná and Uxmal.

Christian churches built and decorated by native Mexican and South American craftsmen have an aesthetic tension that comes from two cultures that have collided instead of coming naturally together. *Left*: the *retablos* of the church of San Luis Potosí, Mexico; the decorative style is imported from Spain and carried to an excess rarely attempted at home, while the two acolytes, the angels and the cherubs who climb over everything reflect Indian inspiration. *Above*: the carved, painted and gilded ceiling of the church of Santa Clara at Tunja, Colombia. The décor includes six-winged cherubim and the emblem of the Sun, which was Inca as well as Christian. *Right*: in the dome of La Compañia at Arequipa, Peru, the details are provincial Spanish rather than pre-Columbian: baskets of fruit, vines, putti and angels dressed as young girls.

Cultural transplant

When the Spaniards came to America, they encountered two high civilizations whose achievements in some ways matched their own, but whose existence – as they saw it – was incompatible with the moral values of Christianity. In grafting these moral values and the symbolic images that went with them on to the older ways of thought, some very bizarre hybrids were produced.

An archangel could, to a Peruvian artist of the late seventeenth century, only be a sort of supernatural Spanish grandee. So he painted him with feathered wings, in flamboyant court dress and wielding a musket.

Local saints crossed the Atlantic and made themselves at home in South America. The Virgin of Potosí (*right*) presided over a mountain city in Bolivia which contained the richest silver mine in the Spanish empire. The miners, who were native Indians, are nowhere in evidence, but she is surrounded by scenes relating miraculous events due to her intercession.

Tota pulchra es, Maria. Et macula originalis non est inte. Tu gloria Ierusalem: Tu laetitia israel: Tu honorificencia populi nostri. Tu aduocata peccatorum. O. Maria i Virgo Prudentissima, Mater Clementis.ᵃ ora pronob.

'Pigmentocracy'

The Spaniards settled in large numbers in Central and Southern America, marrying and interbreeding with the Indians and also importing black Africans as slaves. For a time they tried to maintain rigid social ranks based on ancestry, but as the permutations grew more and more complicated, colour came to be an important criterion.

The racial hierarchy was illustrated by Spanish artists in the eighteenth century. Eight examples out of many more are shown here, reading from top left to bottom right. (1) *Mulatta*, offspring of a Spaniard and a Black. (2) *Castizo*, child of a *mestiza* (Spanish and Indian) and a Spaniard. (3) *Morisco*, child of a *mulatta* and a Spaniard. (4) Spaniard, the child of a *castizo* and a Spaniard (an apparent anomaly). (5) *Barsino*, child of an *albarrasado* (see no. 6) and an Indian. (6) *Albarrasado*, child of a *mulatta* and a *tente en el aire* (who was the offspring of a Spaniard and *tornatrás*, the latter being the offspring of a Spaniard and an *albino*, who was in turn the offspring of a Spaniard and a *morisco* – see no. 3). *Far right*: (7) *Loba*, child of an Indian woman and a *chino* (*mulatto* and Indian); (8) *Barsino*, child of an *albarrasado* (see no. 6) and a *mestiza*. This definition, from a different set of paintings, in fact differs slightly from that given in no. 5.

de Mestiza² y Español
Castizo

De Chino cambuso y India, Loba

de Castizo ³ y Española
Español.

De Albarasado y Mestisa, Barsino.

¹² De Tente en el Aire
y Mulata, Albarrasado

Frutas d la Nu. Esp.ª
Chirimoyas. 1. Uvas. 2. Sandias. 3. Naranjas.
de China. 4. Sapotes Blancos. 5. Sapotes prietos.
6. Mameyes. 7. Melones 8. Camotes. 9. Peras. 10. Agua-
cates. 11. Higos. 12. Piñas. 13. Guayabos. 14. Plane bien-
ca y blanca. 15. Granada. 16. Platanos. 17. Chayote.

Simón Bolívar with New Granada (now Colombia and Panama), represented as a *mestiza* woman: a naive patriotic painting of 1819. Below that, a Mexican scene of 1896; a prosperous family sit on the balcony of their country house overlooking a valley with a church. *Below*: the main square of Lima, Peru, in 1843, thronged with peasants, gentry and priests.

New nations

Like all colonies, those of Spanish America eventually shook
themselves free from the mother country. Bolívar, 'the
Liberator', favoured a united continent, but in the event
each province chose to develop its own individual life-style.

Spanish . . . Hispanic . . . Latino

Recent immigrants from Spanish-speaking countries into the USA have had to face not only poor living conditions and problems of communication. They have also had to sustain their identity in surroundings that are often unsympathetic to their culture and hostile to its expression. Even so, many have achieved success in such diverse areas as property development and show business.

Folk-medicine from rural Mexico still gives comfort to Mexican immigrants in the western USA. Shop-signs (*left*) advertise herbs and religious articles. *Below*: a painting by Carmen Lomas Garza called *Faith healer sweeping away fright*. The little girl is not dead but is being cured of fear through a combination of prayer (the rosaries and the Virgin Immaculate on the wall) and ritual practices. *Right*: three generations of Puerto Ricans in New York.

The public expression of ethnic identity is common and sometimes aggressively nationalistic. *Top*: mural in California representing a farming collective of Mexican workers with a series of familiar motifs: a church, the Virgin, a priest, a pre-Columbian pyramid and a 'Mariachi' band in sombreros. *Left*: 'subway art' in New York includes much work by young Puerto Ricans. One detail (*above*) uses the word 'Latino', a term preferred to 'Hispanic'.

The native American legacy of Mexicans living both in Mexico and the United States is now much more likely to be emphasized than the Spanish. The younger generation calls itself Chicano (from *Mejicano*, Mexican) rather than Hispanic, and motifs from Aztec and Mayan art – this example is in Los Angeles – proclaim the cultural tradition of the conquered rather than the conquerors. Cortés is not a national hero in the land of Montezuma.

2 THE SPANISH CHARACTER AND HERITAGE

The looming silhouette of Nuestra Señora del Pilar (Our Lady of the Pillar) at Saragossa signals one of the great pilgrimage places of Spain. Here, according to tradition, St James in 40 AD saw a vision of the Virgin, who descended onto a pillar and commanded him to build a church in her honour. It has been many times rebuilt. The present one – unique in the number and combination of domes and towers – was begun in 1681 and finished only in 1977.

FROM UNITY TO PLURALISM: RELIGION AND CHURCH W.J. CALLAHAN

Throughout its history Spanish society has existed in close and, since the early nineteenth century, sometimes conflictive relationship with Catholicism. The centuries-old alliance between Throne and Altar lasted until the final collapse of absolute monarchy in 1834. Between the 1830s and the early 1920s, liberal constitutional governments undermined the wealth, privileges and cultural supremacy acquired by the church over centuries, but they maintained Catholicism as the state's established religion. The dictatorial regimes of Miguel Primo de Rivera (1923–30) and Francisco Franco (1936–75) expanded the church's official privileges, while using Catholicism to buttress a right-wing ideology directed against republicanism, liberal democracy, socialism, communism and anarchism.

For a short time, the Second Republic (1931–39) broke the millennial ties between religion and government by separating church and state for the first time in the country's history. But Franco's triumph over the Republic in the savage Civil War of the 1930s allowed Catholicism to recover and enlarge the privileges that it enjoyed prior to 1931. After the general's death, a peaceful revolution saw the establishment of a parliamentary democracy which permitted a definitive, constitutional separation of church and state (1978). This was, however, by no means an unambiguous break between the civil and ecclesiastical worlds. Even the Socialists, in power since 1982, although frequently in conflict with the bishops over issues such as abortion and education, have recognized that Catholicism occupies a distinctive place within national life. The government still subsidizes the diocesan clergy's salaries and finances the Catholic educational system, albeit with certain restrictions.

The existence of an established church does not guarantee religious commitment on the part of a population. An early twentieth-century survey estimated that only five per cent of those living in the southern countryside were practising Catholics; on the eve of the Civil War, an experienced observer noted that in the working-class districts of Barcelona, Madrid, Seville and Bilbao, 'Great contingents of the population living in complete paganism are to be found.' Yet when all is said and done, Spanish Catholicism retains the allegiance of a substantial part of the population. Statistics (1985) on attendance at Sunday Mass show important differences between north and south, younger and older generations, urban and rural areas. Still, on average, one out of four Spanish Catholics practises regularly, a far from modest achievement. A majority of the population observes the traditional rites of passage, from baptism to burial, of the Catholic liturgy. Sociological surveys from the 1970s and 1980s reveal something more striking: there remains a general acceptance of basic Catholic doctrine even among those rarely engaging in religious activities of any kind.

The church's ability to hold its own within the conflicting pressures of the modern world is, in part, a legacy of history. Spanish Catholicism has functioned for centuries without serious religious competition. Well into the twentieth century, clerical apologists maintained that Catholicism was fundamental to the identity of the country and its people. One declared unblushingly: 'All Spaniards are Catholics, either good ones or bad ones.' Neither the limited toleration granted to Protestants under earlier liberal governments nor the full religious liberty established by the constitution of 1978 has led to large-scale conversions to other churches. Religious minorities number less than 100,000 in a population of 40 million.

Imposing religious unity on the Hispanic kingdoms as they emerged from the Middle Ages proved a difficult undertaking. Between 1478, when Ferdinand and Isabella established the Inquisition, and 1609 to 1611, when the forcibly converted Moorish population was sent packing to North Africa, crown and church succeeded in attaining a cherished objective of the early modern state, absolute religious uniformity. The Jews were expelled (1492) and a handful of amorphous Lutheran groups eliminated by the Inquisition during the 1550s. Later, under the influence of the Enlightenment and simple practicality, Catholic absolute monarchs in the rest of Europe granted limited toleration to religious minorities. The Habsburg emperor, Joseph II, did so in 1781; Louis XVI of France restored religious liberty to the Huguenots in 1787. No such concessions were ever made in Spain to the miniscule number of Protestants, largely of recent foreign origin, living in the kingdom during the eighteenth century. Full toleration was established for the first time in the revolutionary constitution of 1869, soon replaced by the conservative charter of 1876 which limited the public practice of religion to the Catholic church alone.

From pluralism to uniformity

The destruction of the religious pluralism characteristic of the medieval Hispanic kingdoms was the first step on the long road to uniformity. Although the coexistence of the Christian population with Jewish and Islamic minorities produced mutual acculturation, the celebrated *convivencia* evoked by historians of medieval Spain, this was in the end no more than a recognition of the facts. By the later fourteenth century, growing hostility against Jews exploded in the Hispanic kingdoms where they already suffered from legal disabilities barring them from office in church and state. In 1391, anti-Jewish riots, often encouraged by fanatical clergy, spread from Seville to other cities of the kingdom of Castile and the Crown of Aragon. It was the beginning of a pattern of violence. Around the middle of the fifteenth century, another wave of rioting began in Andalusia that culminated in a series of bloody massacres.

The turn to violence in 1391 led to a new development in the religious life of medieval Spain. A considerable number of Jews accepted Christianity, the first of successive waves of conversion. As a result, the social condition of those embracing Catholicism changed dramatically. Their civil and ecclesiastical disabilities were removed overnight. *Conversos* found an open road to ascent, moving rapidly into positions in the royal service, municipal governments and in the church itself. This change is illustrated by the career of Selemoh Ha-Levi, a Jewish scholar of renown and principal rabbi of Burgos, who, having accepted Christianity and taken the name of Pablo de Santa María, became bishop of the city in 1415.

This sudden transformation in the condition of subjects previously barred from any public role and despised by much of the population, the Old Christians, produced a strong counter-reaction. Resentment against *conversos*, or New Christians, developed rapidly among the lower classes of town and country, already deeply anti-Jewish, and among ambitious Old Christians who saw choice positions occupied by hitherto scorned individuals. The same intense hostility previously directed against unconverted Jews now focused on the *conversos*. In 1449, there was rioting in Toledo against them, while the municipal government passed the first exclusionary statute, based on the idea of the purity of Christian blood (*limpieza de sangre*), barring New Christians from public office under pain of death. This novel idea did not go unchallenged. In 1465, the Jeronymite friar and theologian, Alonso de Oropesa, argued that the exclusion of *conversos* who accepted their new faith from full participation in Christian society constituted an offence against the unity of the church as the universal, mystical body of Christ, simple charity and the spirit of the gospels. Unfortunately, the time had long since passed when reasoned discourse was capable of stemming the tide of popular hatred.

Ferdinand and Isabella dealt with the religious and social resentments boiling within Christian society in two ways. They moved against unconverted Jews in a ruthlessly straightforward manner through expulsion. Hispanic monarchs had long profited from the services of Jews employed by royal administrations, but whatever the practical advantages derived from these arrangements, they were now sacrificed on the altar of popular antagonism. Moreover, the ideal of religious uniformity as essential to effective royal government had taken firm root by now in the Iberian peninsula, as elsewhere in Europe.

The widespread hostility directed against *conversos* required a more sophisticated response. As baptized Christians with important links to civil and ecclesiastical elites, they could not be summarily expelled through royal fiat. To deal with them, Ferdinand and Isabella created the most notorious institution ever to exist in the long history of Spanish Catholi-cism and the monarchy with which it was so closely identified, the Inquisition. In their representations to Pope Sixtus IV seeking approval for the new tribunal, the sovereigns stated their belief that an inquisitorial body was necessary to eliminate insincere *conversos* whose presence, they argued, posed a danger to the faith.

Whether this ostensibly religious motive was the real reason behind the foundation of the Inquisition has occasioned debate among historians. Few now believe that the *conversos* constituted a threat of any sort to Catholicism. By the late fifteenth century most New Christians were sincerely observing their new faith, although it is likely that Ferdinand and Isabella were influenced by the lurid and unproven tales of mock crucifixions, infant sacrifices and secret Judaic rites widely circulated by the opponents of the *conversos*. It has been suggested that the sovereigns took action either because they wished to secure social stability by appeasing Old Christians, or because they saw the opportunity of creating a powerful, royal institution capable of transcending the historic divisions of the Hispanic kingdoms.

Whatever their precise motives, Ferdinand and Isabella introduced a formidable institutional mechanism for destroying real or imagined dangers to the faith. The Inquisition took decades to develop and refine its apparatus, but the brutal repression of the *conversos* during the first twenty years of its existence set a chilling precedent. More executions were carried out during this period than at any other time in its history. Neither social standing nor high office could save suspect New Christians from inquisitorial clutches. A distinguished prelate of the time, Pedro de Aranda, member of a prominent *converso* family of Burgos, held a series of ecclesiastical and civil posts, serving successfully as cathedral canon, dean of Oviedo and bishop of Calahorra. In 1481, Ferdinand and Isabella granted him the key office of president of the Council of Castile. His career collapsed in ruins when the first Inquisitor General of Castile and the Crown of Aragon, the implacable Tomás de Torquemada, accused him of being a judaizer. The nobility and clergy of Aranda's diocese rallied to his defence, to no avail, although the bishop managed to escape the ultimate punishment by fleeing to Rome.

The fate of Aranda shows how far the Inquisition was prepared to reach, even in its earliest days, to get its way. Although the possibility of torture and execution was real, the number of accused put to death comprised only a small minority of victims. The institution's ability to act in complete secrecy, to confiscate property, to strike at anyone irrespective of office or class and, above all, to destroy the very identity of the condemned within Spanish society formed the basis of its far-reaching power. In a word, it had the authority to assign those surviving its rigours to the status of non-persons, excluded from the life of the community.

For the minority of Islamic origin, the road of persecution was longer, but it led in the end to the same destination as that of the Jews in 1492. Demographically more numerous than the Jews, they were no less despised by Old Christians, but had not endured the same degree of sustained hostility because they lived largely in the countryside, far from the mainstream of Spanish society. In certain regions, notably Valencia, they also enjoyed the protection bestowed by noble landlords on whose estates they worked.

The conquest of Granada and the necessity of absorbing the Islamic masses of Spain's last Moorish kingdom began a new phase in the centuries-old relationship between Christians and Muslims. To ensure the surrender of Granada, Ferdinand and Isabella granted the population the right to practise its religion freely, although from the beginning, they were determined to bring about the conversion of their new subjects. The monarchs secured the appointment of a prominent figure in court and church circles, the Jeronymite friar, Hernando de Talavera, to the new archbishopric of Granada. Talavera knew what was expected of him. In 1492, Ferdinand and Isabella gave him the signal honour of unfurling on the high tower of the Alhambra, palace of the Moorish king, a great banner emblazoned with a silver cross symbolizing the triumphant victory of crown and church after centuries of warfare between Hispanic Christians and Muslims.

Talavera was as firmly convinced of the necessity of converting the Islamic population as his sovereigns. He believed that this goal could be attained without violence through pastoral instruction. When, by 1499, it became evident that peaceful methods were failing, Talavera was pushed aside by the dominant figure in the Spanish church of the period, Francisco Jiménez de Cisneros (1436–1517), archbishop of Toledo. Cisneros arrived on the scene and promptly initiated a policy of bribery and intimidation so extreme that it soon incited popular rioting. Ferdinand and Isabella supported the archbishop's hard line, for in 1502, they revoked the religious liberty granted upon Granada's surrender a decade earlier.

The Moorish population was now forced to accept Christianity. Although some of the Islamic *conversos*, known as Moriscos, did so sincerely, the vast majority remained stubbornly resistant. During the first half of the sixteenth century, royal and ecclesiastical authorities were aware that the conversion of the Moriscos was more nominal than real and that in remote country districts, especially in the kingdom of Valencia, they continued to maintain Islamic places of worship. The response of church and crown was fitful and uncertain at first. The Inquisition ignored the Moriscos until 1526. Thereafter, its policy alter-

nated between repression and indifference. The Moriscos were able to secure limited protection from a campaign of outright persecution through generous financial gifts to crown and church and because of the support provided by noble landlords in some regions.

This fragile *modus vivendi* was undermined after 1550. Intense Muslim pirate activity in the western Mediterranean intensified fears of an imminent attack. Royal authorities increasingly saw the Moriscos as a fifth column of questionable loyalty. Moreover, attitudes among the clergy towards religious dissent, forged by decades of struggle against Protestantism and influenced by the new Catholic militancy instilled by the Council of Trent, began to harden. Archbishop Tomás de Villanueva of Valencia, shocked by the lethargy of his predecessors toward the Moriscos, embarked on an aggressive campaign of evangelization, while Archbishop Pedro de Guerrero of Granada, aided and abetted by the Inquisition, followed a policy of direct coercion which finally provoked the desperate rising of the Alpujarras (1568–71).

Clerical defenders of a pastoral approach to conversion continued to make their case during the 1570s, particularly in Valencia, but the tide of opinion began to shift in the other direction. By the early 1580s, Valencia's inquisitors urged the expulsion of the kingdom's Moriscos, to Newfoundland of all places, for 'the purification of the Christian religion and the security of the kingdoms'. In 1582, the Council of State, concerned with the Turkish threat in the Mediterranean, supported expulsion of Valencia's Moriscos, although not at this stage those of Aragon and Castile. But the die was cast. Expulsion was now a matter of time. The final blow fell between 1609 and 1611 as the Moriscos were sacrificed in the name of religious unity and the security of the monarchy.

The persecution of Jews, Moriscos and *conversos* represented the final working out of the deep antagonisms within Hispanic medieval society. Church and crown never entirely abandoned their obsession with New Christians. As late as the 1720s, several Portuguese *converso* financiers resident in Spain were sent to the stake. By the second decade of the sixteenth century, however, attention shifted toward Lutheranism and its dangers. The Inquisition lost little time in banning the works of Luther. Thereafter, its preoccupation with the Lutheran heresy grew to gigantic proportions. During the 1550s, the inquisitors proceeded against so-called heretical cells in Valladolid and Seville, leaving no doubt of their determination to root out religious dissent root and branch. One of the Seville victims, Constantino Ponce de la Fuente, perished in prison before his trial could be held. Even then, the Inquisition would not relent; it condemned the deceased as a heretic and ordered his bones to be disinterred for public burning.

The obsession with Lutheranism, indeed, with any deviation from the increasingly rigid definition of sixteenth-century Catholicism's corpus of beliefs, arose from different causes than those that led to the persecution of Jews, Moriscos and *conversos*. Lutheranism never threatened Spanish Catholicism's religious monopoly. There is no evidence of the existence of anything even remotely resembling a dissenting church, nor even of adherence to a coherent body of doctrine among those identified as Lutherans by the Inquisition. The influence, moreover, of the diverse groups accused of religious deviationism, whether the *alumbrados* of Alcalá during the 1520s, the Erasmists of the 1530s and 1540s or the so-called Lutherans of the 1550s, was confined to narrow social circles. The urban and rural masses, deeply attached to the practices of medieval Catholicism, remained untouched.

The reason why crown and church perceived Protestantism as a danger from the earliest days of its appearance in Germany was that it threatened the mission of sustaining a European empire united by Catholicism to which Charles V had committed the Spanish monarchy. For Charles, Philip II and their successors, heresy and sedition formed a dangerous combination. Unchecked, they appeared capable of destroying both Catholicism and the monarchies committed to its cause. The military struggle to destroy religious dissent and political revolution took place largely beyond the Iberian peninsula. But neither Throne nor Altar was disposed to allow the smallest seeds of heterodoxy to be planted in the Hispanic kingdoms. Although it is doubtful whether they would have taken root in any case, the Spanish Habsburgs took no chances.

The challenge of reform

By the early seventeenth century, crown and church attained the goal of religious uniformity protected by a vigilant Inquisition. Seeking to realize this objective through force and intimidation was not exclusive to the Spanish monarchy in either Protestant or Catholic Europe. Few states achieved it, however, so successfully and ruthlessly, although at heavy cost. The monarchy lost thousands of productive subjects, while intellectual activity suffered under inquisitorial censure.

But the elimination of dissent, praised by generations of clerics from the late fifteenth to the early twentieth centuries as a spiritual good of incalculable proportions, was perhaps not entirely in the best interests of modern Spanish Catholicism. So long protected from ideological competition, it was ill-prepared to confront a series of later challenges in the form of liberalism, increasing secularization and radical social movements. The intellectual vitality characteristic of a healthy ecclesiastical culture yielded to a stubborn defensive mentality hostile to modern thought and political expression.

Spanish Catholicism looked to the past, to an imagined golden age when it triumphed over its enemies who now appeared in new and sinister guises. 'Rationalism, liberalism, socialism, communism, [and] materialism' were seen as the last links of an unbroken conspiratorial chain forged initially during the Protestant Reformation. The church combatted its new ideological challengers as implacably, though not as successfully, as the Inquisition once proceeded against dissenters. Only under Franco's regime was the church able to impose a narrow, clerical culture completely at variance with the standards of modern intellectual life. Ecclesiastical apologists often evoked Ferdinand and Isabella and Philip II, the glorious monarchs of old, as models for the 'New Spain', the Catholic Spain, that they were determined to create in the favourable circumstances created by Franco's triumph in the Civil War.

This image of a golden age owed more to a powerful sense of nostalgia than to historical reality. Yet like all such images, it contains an element of truth. The strength of Spanish Catholicism during the early modern period had little to do with the imposition of religious uniformity. It developed from several circumstances coming together between the late fifteenth and sixteenth centuries: ecclesiastical reform, the intellectual vigour of a clerical culture closely tied to the secular concerns of the age, the flowering of diverse currents of spirituality and, last, but by no means least, religious vitality at the grass roots.

Like its counterparts elsewhere, the Spanish church suffered from problems created by its socio-economic position within a hierarchical society dominated by a landowning nobility. Its clergy often belonged to that nobility and were administratively and spiritually lax. Bishops were not simple pastors concerned with the eternal salvation of their flocks. With their handsome revenues derived from extensive properties, tithes and other financial resources, they were fully integrated into the complex network of church and crown, moving freely between the civil and ecclesiastical worlds. The attractive prospect of high office and abundant income proved irresistible for nobles seeking comfortable berths for younger sons excluded by law from inheriting family patrimonies.

These circumstances were not calculated to encourage pastoral zeal among the bishops. Diocesan priests, on the other hand, were usually poorly educated and socially isolated from their superiors. Their financial survival depended on a medieval benefice system controlled by lay and clerical patrons often uninterested in their religious mission. So an impoverished and ignorant parochial clergy was left, especially in the countryside, to its own devices, resulting in widespread concubinage, simony and a general neglect of pastoral duties. Other difficulties beset the religious orders, both monastic and mendicant. By the mid-fifteenth century, few were observing the primitive

Detail of a nineteenth-century Holy Week procession in Barcelona with hooded penitents carrying a cross.

.de la Congregación y congregantes con emblemas de la Pasión, hábitos y trofeos de penitenc

rules of austerity and discipline established by their founders.

During the fifteenth and early sixteenth centuries, ecclesiastical reformers throughout Europe were demanding that the church introduce sweeping internal changes to eliminate chronic and sometimes scandalous abuses. These currents swirled and eddied within the Hispanic kingdoms. It was not surprising that Ferdinand and Isabella accorded high priority to ecclesiastical reform.

The Catholic Monarchs focused on improving the quality of bishops and on reinvigorating the religious orders. In an age when more than a few members of the hierarchy had illegitimate children, Isabella insisted upon the appointment of prelates of blameless personal life, and she began what would become established policy by promoting the advancement of university-educated clerics. Reform of the monastic orders, although under way by the 1480s through the efforts of individual religious, was advanced in 1495 by the appointment of Archbishop Jiménez de Cisneros to the primatial see of Toledo. Having promoted a return to discipline within his own order, the Franciscans, Cisneros threw his ample supply of irascible energy into the revitalization of other religious communities. In many respects, the archbishop fulfilled the expectations of his sovereigns. He promoted reform of the orders aggressively, convoked diocesan synods, organized visits of inspection to hundreds of parishes and issued instructions aimed at improving pastoral care.

Historians have debated the effect of these reforms; some maintain that they contributed to Lutheranism's failure to take root in Spain. Protestantism stood little chance, however, of establishing itself whether the church curbed abuses or not. What is important about the early reform is that changes were introduced which would continue, episodically and with different emphases at distinct times, until the end of the eighteenth century. Ecclesiastical reform thus drew new inspiration from the concerns of the Spanish followers of Erasmus during the 1520s and, later, from the determined campaign to stop Protestantism in its tracks through the legislation of the Council of Trent (1545–49, 1551–52, 1562–63).

The Council, firmly supported by Charles V and Philip II, attempted a broad programme directed toward a more precise definition of Catholic doctrine. At a practical level, it sought to improve the quality of bishops and clergy by emphasizing their pastoral mission. The Council's recommendations were received with enthusiasm by Philip II who actively promoted their implementation. The king devoted hours to examining the files of candidates for bishoprics seeking to ensure the appointment of prelates sympathetic to reform. Among those elevated to the hierarchy, none better represented the application of the Tridentine programme to the Spanish church than Juan de

Ribera. University educated, friend of some of the leading intellectual and spiritual figures of his time, Ribera began a campaign of vigorous pastoral action in 1569 upon assuming the post of archbishop of Valencia. His example was widely imitated. In the four decades after Trent, bishops founded twenty seminaries, while more diocesan synods devoted to reform were held than at any time in the history of the Spanish church.

The reforming impulse waned during the seventeenth century, to revive under the eighteenth-century Bourbons, especially Charles III (1759–88). The problems and the solutions of this later reform resembled those of the late fifteenth and sixteenth centuries in many respects. The king, his ministers and reforming clerics looked to the Tridentine model as they sought to improve the education and quality of the parish clergy and instil new vigour in the religious orders.

The extent of ecclesiastical reform over three centuries was uneven and episodic, but much was achieved. The possibility of more penetrating reform was, however, limited. Church and clergy formed an integral part of a traditional hierarchical society in which wealth and status were divided unequally. Members of the hierarchy constituted a privileged minority within the church. The bishops possessed education, wealth and culture which separated them from parish priests. Isabella tried to remedy the situation by promoting middle-class clerics, but this was never realistic. Habsburg and Bourbon monarchs recruited bishops as a matter of course from their own social class. Although the hierarchy never became closed to commoners, as in eighteenth-century France, a majority of bishops came from noble ranks until the disappearance of absolute monarchy.

At the other end of the scale, the prospect of improving the parochial clergy's quality through more attentive episcopal guidance and the creation of diocesan seminaries was limited by lack of resources. Archbishops of Toledo, richest of the Spanish bishops, enjoyed immense revenues. Some donated generously to charity and religious undertakings, but others lived in high style, spending lavishly to uphold their aristocratic station, while parish priests were struggling to make ends meet. In practical terms, there was no radical solution. The parochial clergy stood at the bottom of a top-heavy ecclesiastical superstructure, and overturning it would have required an organizational revolution with profound social and economic implications that neither crown nor church dared contemplate.

The limited reform begun by Ferdinand and Isabella required a corresponding spiritual and intellectual revitalization of Spanish Catholicism. The practices of medieval religion, emphasizing external ceremony, an extraordinary variety of devotions to Christ, the Virgin and the saints, as well as the performance of good works, retained their appeal for the mass of the urban and rural population throughout the early modern period. But during the sixteenth century, for an elite of priests, religious and laypeople, traditional forms of religious expression began to be displaced by innovative spiritual and mystical movements. These emphasized the intense spirituality of the individual in his or her relations to God. They also stressed methodical mental prayer and a rigorous, personal asceticism in contrast to the communal orientation of medieval piety.

Spaniards embracing new forms of religious expression owed a debt to the movement toward spiritual renewal that developed in fifteenth and early sixteenth-century Europe. The influence of Erasmus of Rotterdam (1466?-1536) was especially important, particularly among professors and students of the University of Alcalá, a bastion of humanistic culture and biblical scholarship founded by Jiménez de Cisneros in 1508. Between 1520 and 1530, the Spanish followers of Erasmus profited from the relatively open intellectual atmosphere prevailing during the early years of Charles V's reign to publish virtually all of the great humanist's work. The essential points of Erasmus' message, its emphasis on an accurate reading of the scriptures, its advocacy of a faith based on the moral and spiritual qualities of the individual rather than on merit attained through participation in external ceremonies and good works, its criticism of the excesses of medieval Christianity, were received warmly by a cultivated elite. As the battle against Lutheranism hardened into prolonged war after 1530, however, the influence of Erasmus' thought waned, thanks in no small measure to the activities of an ever more suspicious Inquisition.

The contribution of Erasmus was substantial, but it was by no means the only one. What is striking about the great figures of sixteenth-century religious writing, Juan de Avila (1499–1569), Luis de Granada (1504–88), John of the Cross (1542–91), Teresa de Avila (1515–82) and Ignatius Loyola (1491–1556), is that each, 'sailing the winds of interiority', made a unique contribution to the development of Christian spirituality. Like other mystical writers of the time, they saw the attainment of the pure love of the soul for God as the final stage of a religious search divided into distinct phases: the purification of the soul of all worldly concerns, a period of illumination in which the soul develops an unqualified love of God and, finally, the joyous or ecstatic state of spiritual intimacy between soul and divinity. Moving through these phases was far from easy. It required intense, constant struggle against inner trials and tribulations. Although many individuals may have sought spiritual perfection in this way, few possessed the gift of expressive language, the command of simile and metaphor, essential to the writing of mystical literature capable of reaching a larger audience. Spanish religious writers possessed this gift in abundance.

Considered as a whole, their spirituality wove prevailing mystical threads into distinct patterns. The element of uniqueness arose from the intense and highly personal nature of the mystical experience. Their writings were spiritual autobiographies, however shrouded in metaphoric language. Teresa of Avila, who spent much of her life seeking to direct the Carmelite order to greater spirituality, stressed the centrality of prayer as essential to the attainment of spiritual union within the framework of the conventual life. Her most significant book for the mystical tradition was the *Castillo interior* (1588), usually translated as *The Interior Mansions*. Asked by her religious superiors to write about the life of prayer as she had experienced it, she described the progress of the soul, seen as a 'castle, formed of a single diamond or of a very bright crystal, in which there are many rooms, just as in Heaven, there are many mansions.' The soul had to pass through these rooms, each representing the stages of mystical experience, purification, illumination and, finally, spiritual union, the very centre of the castle 'where the most secret things pass between God and soul ' The intensity of her experience and her ability to offer it as an example to others through the clarity of her rough-hewn writing extended her influence far beyond convent walls.

A close associate of Teresa in the Carmelite reform of the sixteenth century, John of the Cross described the soul's progress through the stages of mystical experience with a sublimity rarely seen before or since among spiritual writers. Unlike Teresa, whose education was limited, he possessed a broad cultural background combining Thomism, Christian humanism and a deep knowledge of the scriptures. Although his works, *Obras espirituales que encaminan a un alma a la perfecta unión con Dios* (1618), were first published years after his death, their literary grace and intellectual subtlety quickly established his reputation as a master of spiritual writing. Like Teresa, he based his method on experience, vastly enriched, in his case, by the cultural milieu of his times. The latter enabled him to make an original contribution to mysticism through a spirituality which redefined the stages of the soul's purification. In common with other writers, he believed that the soul must be purified of all worldly concerns, but he argued that once on this road, it must endure a passive purification, the 'Dark Night of the Soul', a time of difficult trial in which God 'perfects and completes what the soul has begun of its own accord.' As the soul emerges from these tribulations, it enters into the final stages of partaking in 'the Divine Nature'. The appeal of John of the Cross for later generations rests, perhaps, less on his spiritual ideas than on the lyrical, metaphorical beauty of his great religious poems, 'Dark Night of the Soul', 'Spiritual Canticle', and 'Living Flame of Love', the 'songs of the soul' that made him one of the great poets of the Spanish language.

Confraternities of penitents, whose origins go back to the Middle Ages, are still a major – and distinctively Spanish – part of popular religious life. From Spain (*below*) they spread naturally to the New World, where they were often combined with ceremonies deriving from pre-Columbian times. In Guatemala (*right*) patterns of flowers are laid along the path of the procession.

St Teresa of Avila (*left*) and St Ignatius Loyola (*below*) succeeded in communicating the incommunicable – the mystic's experience of the presence of God and the opening out of the soul through prayer. Neither, however, were solitaries who cut themselves off from the world. Teresa's reform and reorganization of the Carmelites and Ignatius's foundation of the Society of Jesus (Jesuits) made those orders powerful forces of the Catholic Reform.

The Spanish founder of the Society of Jesus, Ignatius Loyola, contributed to the richness of sixteenth-century spiritual writing through the *Exercitia Spiritualia* (1548), first published in Latin, although manuscript versions in the original Spanish circulated before this date. Although the *Spiritual Exercises* reflect Ignatius' conversion experience at Manresa in 1522, he was aware of the main currents of European spirituality through his university studies at Alcalá, Salamanca and Paris during the 1520s and early 1530s. In their concern with prayer, a period of spiritual 'desolation' and, finally, the illumination of the soul, the *Exercises* reflected ideas then in general circulation. But in important respects, Ignatian spirituality differed from that of contemporaries. It developed within the institutional framework of the Society of Jesus. Indeed, it was written to provide the order's spiritual directors with a manual to guide the Jesuit to a specific goal, the discovery of 'the design God has for him' in the world. Although mystical elements were present in the *Exercises*, the emphasis was on practical spirituality. The lyrical and metaphorical character of other sixteenth-century writers found scant echo in its pages. The *Exercises* contributed significantly, however, to the forging of a Jesuit identity in the midst of sixteenth-century religious conflict, and in time, the order extended their application to the laity of the Catholic world through the institution of the spiritual retreat.

The new learning

In a parallel renewal of intellectual life, theology and philosophy moved from the narrow confines of academic and clerical discourse to influence official policy. Although the sources of renewal were as diverse as those inspiring the new spirituality, the earliest phase of Spanish Catholicism's cultural reawakening developed around biblical scholarship.

By the late fifteenth century, Italian humanism, with its interest in the pagan authors of antiquity, had penetrated the Hispanic kingdoms. Its influence continued through the first half of the sixteenth century, but soon yielded primacy to a Christian humanism concerned with the recovery and accurate establishment of scriptural texts. Here the ubiquitous figure of Jiménez de Cisneros played a central role. Although feeling no scruples about ordering the burning of thousands of Arabic books and manuscripts during his missionary foray into Granada, he threw much energy and a generous portion of his episcopal income into a great enterprise, the publicaton of accurate biblical texts in simultaneous Greek, Hebrew and Latin versions. Cisneros attracted distinguished linguists, philologists and humanists to his new University of Alcalá where they worked for more than a decade to produce the magnificent *Biblia Sacra Polyglota* (1520), a monument to the printer's art and to the state of biblical scholarship at the time.

In the early years of the sixteenth century, Spanish universities were centres of humanist learning. The Complutensian Polyglot Bible, published by the University of Alcalá, is a monument of biblical scholarship, with parallel texts in Hebrew, Greek and Latin. This is the last page of the Apocalypse, with the Greek and Latin text and a Latin colophon in an ornamental border. *Below*: Renaissance bookcases in the old university library of Salamanca, containing a fine collection of manuscripts and early printed books.

Cisneros also contributed to the revitalization of theology and philosophy by establishing chairs at Alcalá in the principal schools of medieval philosophy, thereby setting in motion a process of intellectual revival and interaction that would endure for decades. It produced a series of important figures, among them the Dominicans, Francisco de Vitoria (1492?–1546), Melchor Cano (1509–60), Pedro de Soto (1496?–1563) and Domingo de Soto (1495–1560), and the Jesuit, Francisco Suárez (1548–1617).

Of key importance was the fruitful combination of two currents, the Thomistic, with its emphasis on those universal or essential qualities characteristic of all humanity, and the Nominalist, according to which individual things and people were real and universals were only names. One viewed men and women in the abstract; the other exalted the person and his or her potential for intellectual, moral and religious development.

This was the philosophical background to the extraordinary debate in sixteenth-century Spain over the treatment of the conquered native populations of the New World. Were they to be exploited and enslaved as chattels of war and used by the colonists solely for economic advantage? In 1511, the Dominican friar, Antonio de Montesinos, appalled by the mistreatment of the native population of Hispaniola, fired the first salvo of a long public debate by asking: 'Are they men? Do they have rational souls?'

Between 1511 and Charles V's issuance of the *New Laws* (1542), which revoked or severely limited the right of Spaniards to exact tribute from native populations, every aspect of Spain's moral, philosophical and legal rights in the New World was subject to intense discussion. The militant 'apostle of the Indians', Bartolomé de las Casas (1474–1566), waged a sustained campaign to secure royal legislation curbing the abuses inflicted on the natives by the colonists. Domingo de Soto rejected outright the argument, based on the Aristotelian concept of natural slavery, that Spaniards could justifiably enslave the native masses in the New World. Together with Melchor Cano, he argued that wars of conquest launched by Spaniards against the Indians were unjust according to natural law. In a series of works, Francisco de Vitoria questioned many of the legal and philosophical claims put forth by advocates of the absolute supremacy of Spaniards in the Indies. Although allowing that there were grounds for Spain's legitimate presence in the Americas, he maintained that the Spaniards were necessarily limited by the fact that the Indians were human beings possessing all the natural rights of men and women everywhere. The passionate and public nature of this debate, in which Charles V took a deep interest, shows how far theological and philosophical issues emerged from academic halls to affect royal policy, even though its practical effects were limited.

The achievements of Spanish humanism were considerable, but further development was limited by the obsession of crown and church with Protestantism. The Inquisition's tolerance of cultural innovation yielded in the 1520s to a hard line when the vindictive Fernando de Valdés became Inquisitor General in 1546. Many of the leading figures of the monarchy's religious and intellectual revival fell under suspicion. 'Silence has been imposed on the learned and a tremendous terror has been inspired in those who would have called themselves scholars . . .', declared one humanist as he viewed the darkening cloud of inquisitorial censure.

The cumulative effects on the cultural and spiritual revival of the sixteenth century proved damaging. The Inquisition's preoccupation with preventing erroneous interpretations of the Bible blighted scriptural scholarship. By the early eighteenth century, the teaching of Greek and Hebrew had virtually disappeared from the universities, although a brief revival occurred after 1750. The innovative aspects of sixteenth-century scholasticism, so closely tied to the burning public issues of the day, gradually yielded to an older pattern of trivial academic argument divorced from reality. And the Inquisition also became increasingly wary of the intense, personal expressions of spirituality, contributing to the decline of the new movement.

The urban and rural masses remained attached to medieval forms of religion, a faith practised through good works and external devotion and bearing little relation to the reforming and spiritual initiatives of a select minority of priests, religious and laypeople. Advocates of the new spirituality, whether the Spanish followers of Erasmus in the sixteenth century, or clerical opponents of 'superstition' in the eighteenth, expressed serious reservations about this older tradition. Popular religious customs were 'so opposed to the simplicity of the Gospel', declared one, that 'they threatened to suffocate the seed of true and healthy doctrine.'

The Council of Trent was no less concerned with the excesses of popular religion, widespread ignorance of Catholic doctrine and low moral standards among the masses. Between the mid-sixteenth and later seventeenth centuries, bishops and priests inspired by the Tridentine programme attempted to communicate knowledge of basic prayers and doctrine to the general population. There is growing evidence, at least for New Castile, that these efforts were partially successful. After Trent, too, the Inquisition devoted more and more attention to enforcing Catholic morality and purifying popular religious practices. A majority of the cases coming before it between 1560 and 1790 were concerned not with formal heresy but with irregular sexual behaviour among clergy and laity, blasphemy, sorcery, magic and mockery of the church's beliefs and institutions.

To do justice to the rich variety of practices and customs existing within the world of popular Hispanic piety is difficult. It represented a grass roots movement seeking to give positive meaning to the fragility of the human condition. Disease, death and natural disaster appeared as imminent dangers, ever ready to strike at city and country dweller. The countless shrines, pious cults, individual and community vows which proliferated throughout late medieval and early modern Spain were not aimed at winning the salvation of which theologians spoke. They sought, rather, to protect men and women from earthly disasters, to bring them good fortune in this life and to secure a sacred intercessor for the passage to eternity. Serving as a kind of protective talisman, they rested on a bargain, an informal contract with God, the Virgin or individual saints, who were represented in an immediate and personal way by a multiplicity of sacred places, statues and intercessory rites.

Holy patrons were chosen, therefore, with the utmost care in view of specific community needs; in particular, they were called upon to intervene in the face of natural disasters. The peasants of New Castile turned to St Sebastian in times of plague, to St Gregory of Nazianus when insects threatened the vines, to St Gregory Ostiense when hordes of locusts appeared. The protector who failed to uphold a contract's terms was soon reminded of his or her responsibilities. The residents of Peralbillo (Ciudad Real) felt no scruples about throwing the statue of St Mark, the village patron, into a nearby river if he failed to heed their prayers for rain in periods of drought. In its own way, popular religion was as deeply felt as that experienced by the followers of the new spirituality. The faith of the masses possessed an earthy realism closely linked to the daily concerns of life itself. Therein lay its strength.

Popular religion owed its vitality to its identification with local needs and aspirations, reflecting the persistence of the strong communal traditions of Hispanic medieval society. Whether in town or country, residents wished to present a united front as they sought to influence holy patrons. Everyone had to participate in these collective religious endeavours. The inhabitants of one small town in sixteenth-century Castile felt so strongly about membership in a village-wide brotherhood, founded years earlier to avert a plague of locusts, that they deprived non-participants of their municipal rights.

Communal piety took the form of processions, pilgrimages (romerías), individual and community vows, devotions and the erection of shrines. These activities were often carried out by an institution widespread in early modern Spain, the brotherhood (hermandad) or confraternity (cofradia). Although such associations appeared late in the Middle Ages, they proliferated during the sixteenth century, the city of Zamora alone possessing 150 in a population of less than 10,000. As late as the

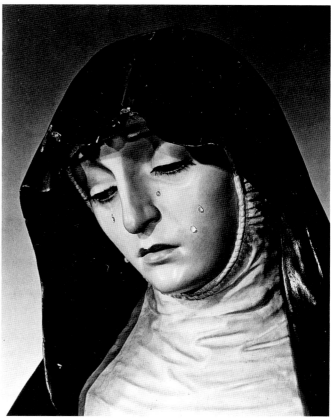

Counter-Reformation preachers urged their listeners to participate fully in the sufferings of the saints by concentrating their thoughts and imagination. Art served the same cause. Sculpture became unnervingly realistic, with naturalistic colours, red blood and crystal tears. *Right*: Dead Christ by Gregorio Fernández, 1614. *Above and above right*: Mary Magdalen by Pedro de Mena, 1664; and the Virgin of Sorrows by José de Mora, 1671.

eighteenth century, approximately 25,000 were still functioning.

In spite of their importance to religious and social life, the organization and objectives of brotherhoods and confraternities did not conform to a single model. Within the Hispanic world, there was nothing comparable to the Santa Casa de Misericordia found throughout the Portuguese empire. In Spain, some associations devoted their attention to purely devotional ends, others to charitable work, still others to penitential exercises, others to all three simultaneously. In Madrid, for example, confraternities and brotherhoods were highly specialized. One took responsibility for burying the poor who died in the city's charity hospitals; another sent its members to visit prisoners in the city's gaols; others donated alms to the impoverished in their homes, while the brotherhood of 'Mortal Sin', as it was popularly known, sought donations in the streets to finance its work of redeeming prostitutes from a life of immorality. In spite of these diverse objectives, the religious dimension was central to all brotherhoods and confraternities. They functioned as 'prayer cooperatives' seeking to merit grace for their members through corporate participation.

The religious practices of many associations were based on an attempt to imitate the lives of Christ and the saints as realistically as possible within the communal framework of local society. Holy Week processions provide a good example. The scenes of the Passion were depicted in graphic detail through elaborately carved statuary groups carried through the streets by members of confraternities and brotherhoods, wearing colourful and distinctive dress. In some regions, notably Castile and León, brothers belonging to penitential associations scourged themselves as the procession made its sombre rounds. These events served a didactic purpose through their realistic portrayal of Christ's last days. But they were more than a device to convey basic knowledge of the faith to the unlettered. They enabled participants to experience the suffering of the Passion in their own persons, to share, in their own time and setting, the agonies endured by Christ to redeem humanity.

This was an elementary faith which was often quite out of touch with the more intellectual, spiritual religion promoted by the ecclesiastical reformers. Even during the sixteenth century, aspects of the Holy Week processions were regarded uneasily by church authorities, particularly after the Council of Trent. By the later eighteenth century, bishops moved by what has been called 'Enlightened Catholicism' attempted to purge excesses. In 1781, they persuaded Charles III to forbid self-flagellation during the traditional rites of Holy Week. Liberalism was less kind. In 1841, the government sold up the property of confrater-

nities and brotherhoods, thereby destroying their economic foundations and undermining their ability to participate in processions, which after this date were conducted only episodically. A revival of sorts took place toward the close of the century thanks to financial support provided by the Catholic middle classes, although, in some cases, as in Seville and Malaga, they drew crowds attracted by both religion and tourism. In some regions, particularly Old Castile, processions retained something of their old communal character. At Malaga, however, the lower classes viewed them with hostility as examples of costly religious display mounted by the bourgeoisie for its own purposes. The invariable presence of the repressive and feared Civil Guard in the line of march did little to assuage popular antagonism.

Within a society full of poor people and beggars, confraternities and brotherhoods provided essential social services in an age when the state assumed little direct responsibility. They formed the backbone of a rudimentary welfare system. The most active charitable association in Madrid, the Holy Brotherhood of Refuge and Piety, thus provided help to nearly a million people during the eighteenth century. The survival of these collective charities shows the strength of older religious ideas. During the sixteenth and eighteenth centuries, ecclesiastical and civil reformers concerned with the damaging economic impact of what they saw as the indiscriminate distribution of alms did their best to discourage it. These efforts foundered invariably on the rock of popular religious attitudes, as the Council of Castile discovered to its dismay during the 1780s. The Council placed almsboxes in Madrid's churches, hoping to clear the poor from the streets and put them in workhouses. The population regarded these institutions as 'houses of abomination'. Clerics adhering to the older tradition of works of mercy argued that confining the poor violated the liberty to which every individual was entitled according to natural law, and that it deprived Christians of the opportunity of giving alms directly to the 'poor of Christ', an essential means of winning grace. Their arguments were identical to those advanced in 1545 by Domingo de Soto during a similar controversy. Not surprisingly, the Council's collectors found the boxes empty as they made their rounds.

In spite of the importance of collective piety expressed through the religious and charitable activities of brotherhoods and confraternities, one should not idealize their contribution. They ameliorated the lot of the poor, but they did not solve the social problems created by the weaknesses of an agrarian economy. Nor were confraternities exempt from the preoccupations of Spanish society as a whole. The Confraternity of the Annunciation of sixteenth-century Zamora thus excluded those who were not of 'pure Christian lineage', a measure directed against the descendants of *conversos*, while the Madrid Brotherhood of Refuge and Piety limited membership to the nobility.

Nor could the confraternities retain their sixteenth-century vigour over time. By the later eighteenth century, signs of decay were evident. The Council of Castile, moved by reports of extravagant spending by pious associations, ordered a general inquiry into their condition. In country villages, the confraternity tended to retain its character as an essential component of religious and community life, but within an increasingly institutionalized framework.

Apostles of the New World

Ecclesiastical reform, intellectual and spiritual renewal and a vital popular religion gave sixteenth-century Spanish Catholicism its resiliency and strength. These developments coincided with one of the extraordinary missionary efforts in the history of Christianity, the conversion of the native populations of Hispanic America and the Philippine Islands. During the twentieth century, few subjects have aroused more scholarly and public controversy. Some maintain that in spite of the linguistic and organizational skills of the missionaries, Christianity was imposed by force, calling attention to examples of torture and abuse, for instance, the 4,500 Mayans subjected to cruel torment in 1562 at the hands of Franciscan missionaries. Conversion, on this thesis, was more nominal than real, not very different, in fact, from that of the Moriscos in Spain itself.

Within this context, there were considerable differences. The harsh treatment of the Mayans eking out a marginal living in the isolated villages of Yucatan, for example, was not characteristic of evangelizing campaigns in the thickly settled, stable farming highlands of central Mexico.

There remains, finally, a simple fact. The missionary campaigns of the sixteenth century implanted Catholicism as a religion and as an integral part of popular culture throughout the Hispanic New World, and political independence, the influence of new ideologies and the competition of Protestant evangelists in the nineteenth and twentieth centuries have failed to dislodge it. This is not to say that modern Catholicism in Hispanic America conforms to a uniform pattern. Far from it. There are substantial differences between countries and, within them, between distinct regions, between areas more or less effectively christianized during the sixteenth and seventeenth centuries and those, like Yucatan, where missionary efforts were less penetrating. There are differences between city and country, between rural faith and urban religion under an institutional church.

The evangelization of native populations commanded constant royal support. Ferdinand and Isabella, Charles V and Philip II took a deep interest in the missionaries and encouraged them in every way possible. Even so, the task of christianizing millions offered formidable difficulties. The failure to convert the Moriscos of Granada was not a favourable precedent.

In 1524, a group of Franciscan friars, symbolically twelve in number, arrived in the central highlands of Mexico, heartland of the recently destroyed Aztec empire. Over the next half century, the Franciscans, later joined by the Dominicans and Augustinians, worked tirelessly to convert the Indians. They mastered the complex languages of those among whom they worked, studied the customs of native societies, published catechisms, built schools and reorganized local populations within a village structure that endures to the present day. Although friars sometimes entertained doubts about the sincerity of their thousands of converts, they developed sophisticated missionary techniques which, they believed, more or less attained the goal of christianizing the Indian masses.

To what extent the friars implanted a doctrinal Catholicism similar to its European counterparts is a matter of debate. Yet in its own terms and with all its limitations, the evangelization of native populations, whether in Mexico, Peru or the Philippines, was a remarkable achievement of organization and determination, especially in view of the relatively small number of religious involved. At the height of missionary activity in sixteenth-century Mexico, the task of converting millions rested with a modest cohort of approximately 800 friars.

Many reasons can be advanced for the relative success of the missionary effort. The pressure of the conqueror over the conquered was important, as was the willingness of the friars to leave native cultures intact, insofar as this was compatible with their religious mission. Evangelization, moreover, was part of the spiritual renewal and ecclesiastical reform taking place within Spain itself. It was not accidental that the crown entrusted the task of converting the Indians to the mendicant orders. Under the influence of Jiménez de Cisneros, the Franciscans returned to the austere discipline of their founder. They attached supreme importance to the observance of the 'evangelical poverty' that they believed characterized early Christianity before the clergy became infected by worldly materialism.

The rediscovery of poverty as a moral good, indeed, as an absolute necessity for salvation, served the friars well in their evangelizing campaigns. Whatever the defects, limitations and abuses involved in the missionary enterprise, the mendicants were never accused of amassing riches either as individuals or communities. Missionary friars lived simply, in sharp contrast to the grasping activities of Spanish colonists, a circumstance which native populations did not fail to notice. But 'evangelical poverty' was more than a way of life for individual religious, more than a model of behaviour for Indian converts. Some

The unbaptized millions of Mexico and Peru presented a challenge to the missionary orders, whose task of converting and saving often found itself at odds with the self-interest of the conquistadors. *Left*: Fray Domingo de Santa María, a famous teacher who spent his life spreading the knowledge of Christ in Mexico. One of the catechisms using the Aztec sign-language is shown below. *Bottom*: an early mission church, San Xavier de Bac, at Tucson, Arizona.

Franciscans saw it as a means of creating in the Americas a moral society, isolated from the corrupting influences of a worldly church and the base materialism of secular society, a 'New Jerusalem' modelled on the simplicity and austerity of primitive Christianity.

So utopian and apocalyptic a programme could not survive harsh reality. The decimation of the Indians through disease during the sixteenth century, the demographic growth of the Spanish and mixed-blood populations and the eventual displacement of the missionary orders by an ecclesiastical organization dominated by diocesan clergy made it an impossible dream. In Mexico, the great age of 'the apostles' was over by 1572, scarcely fifty years after its beginning. The mendicant orders continued to engage in missionary work, primarily in distant, frontier regions, but their central role in the Catholicism of the New World came to an end. Yet they laid the foundations of popular religion in Latin America with its rich variety of devotional practices, often given colourful local variants in their new setting, thereby imprinting Catholicism with an intense, emotional character that survives to this day.

The church in the modern world

Spanish Catholicism's militancy and dynamism, so evident in both positive and negative ways during the sixteenth century, gradually subsided into stability and routine. Its religious and moral supremacy seemed securely anchored through the eighteenth century, however, in the historic relationship between Throne and Altar. The Bourbons asserted greater control over religious affairs than the Habsburgs, although with mixed results. They appointed qualified bishops, supported the foundation of diocesan seminaries and directed the clergy to attend to their pastoral responsibilities. The crown also encouraged a renewal of the cultural life of the church. Less innovative and penetrating than its sixteenth-century counterpart, it produced, nonetheless, figures of importance, especially the Benedictine monk, Benito Feijóo (1676–1764), a trenchant critic of Spanish Catholicism's intellectual stagnation in a time of scientific change. But the aggressive way in which the Bourbons promoted their ecclesiastical policies did not always benefit the church. In 1767, Charles III, a monarch esteemed for piety, expelled the Jesuits from his realms, an action that showed how far the crown was prepared to go to eliminate opposition to its authority in religious matters.

The eighteenth century appeared to later generations of clergy as a silver age, the last period when the church faced no ideological challengers and enjoyed handsome revenues, a time when 'religion, piety, faith and hope' filled every town and village. The reality was somewhat different. A few signs of religious disaffection began to surface in the cities. During the

1780s, the faithful in Madrid wishing to evade the church's Easter communion obligation were able to do so by purchasing certificates of compliance demanded by the ecclesiastical authorities. The certificates, bearing no name or signature, were acquired from inattentive priests by various enterprising individuals, including prostitutes, and retailed to an eager public. The church was also criticized by secular reformers who thought that its wealth should be applied to the benefit of society. The possession of extensive properties by the 'dead hands' of ecclesiastical institutions was seen as damaging to agricultural productivity, while the religious orders were taken to task for contributing little to the kingdom's economic development.

These criticisms were often vociferously expressed, but they were never translated into action. The traditional organization of Spanish Catholicism remained intact until the country entered a period of national crisis provoked by the French Revolution and, later, by the Napoleonic invasion of 1807–08. As the monarchy disintegrated under these pressures, the protective shield of Throne and Altar collapsed along with it. Church and Catholicism stood exposed to challenges for which neither was prepared.

The enforced abdication of the Bourbon dynasty and the installation of a Bonaparte monarchy (1808) led to national revolt and opened the door to Spain's first modern parliamentary assembly, the Cortes of Cadiz (1810–13). Bishops and priests initially supported it. Later, they came into conflict with the liberal majority over the church's role in the new constitutional order. Liberal members were neither anticlerical nor anti-Catholic. On the contrary, they passed a constitution (1812) reaffirming Catholicism as the state's religion and refused to consider even limited toleration for the kingdom's handful of religious dissenters. In spite of these concessions, it became evident that fundamental conflict existed between liberalism, intent on establishing modern political institutions and restricting the clergy to an exclusively pastoral role, and a church committed to maintaining its wealth, power and cultural supremacy. In the face of growing clerical anger, the Cortes abolished the Inquisition (1813) and passed legislation aimed at reducing the size of the religious orders. The conflict between Catholicism and liberalism at Cadiz marked the opening round of a prolonged struggle which, in many different forms, continued over successive generations until the end of the Franco regime.

Nineteenth-century liberalism was scarcely revolutionary. It favoured, however, a redefinition of the relations between church and state. It opened the door to intellectual pluralism within a new society dominated by the middle classes, and economically it pursued a utilitarian policy that cost the church

dearly. Between 1835 and 1860, the vast property holdings of the regular and secular clergy were sold at public auction and the majority of the male religious orders were suppressed.

The intransigent resistance of the church and many Spanish Catholics to liberalism, perceived as 'a rebellion against God and against human society', produced unfortunate religious consequences as well as catastrophic political misjudgments. The church withdrew into a siege mentality, determined to exclude, if not destroy, any group or movement judged hostile to Catholicism. In doing so, it cut itself off from the possibility of reaching Spaniards affected by economic and social changes.

In the later nineteenth and early twentieth centuries, the church proved incapable of halting religious alienation among industrial workers. Its hostility toward radical working-class movements, seen fully as dangerous as liberalism, contributed to the appearance of violent anticlericalism. The church burnings in Barcelona during the summer of 1909, the assassination of clergy during the Asturian rising of October 1934 and the terrible hecatomb of the Civil War in which nearly 7,000 priests and religious perished in Republican Spain, testify to the extent of the failure.

Catholicism retained, however, two bases of support. In regions where popular religion flourished – Old Castile, León, Galicia, Navarre, the rural Basque provinces and some country districts of Aragon and Catalonia – it maintained a connection to the life of agricultural communities. Here, between 1900 and 1920, the church successfully reenforced older loyalties by promoting the establishment of credit unions, cooperatives and agrarian syndicates.

And in the cities, the church had some success in retaining the allegiance of the more conservative middle classes. Here, religious devotion was different in kind from the collective piety of the countryside. It represented an ingenious adaptation of traditional Catholicism to the individualistic society created by liberalism; communal emphasis gave way to something more personal, even during Mass. Reformers emphasizing the Mass as the central act of a community-oriented liturgy viewed individualistic devotional practices with disdain. According to one, many of the faithful attending Mass ignored it altogether in favour of personal acts of worship as they wandered about the church performing devotions to 'Saint Expeditious'. Clerics affected by the movement of liturgical reform endorsed by Pope Pius X disliked what they saw. But the proliferation of new devotions and pious associations, radically different in purpose and structure from traditional piety and its confraternities, provided Catholicism with a convenient means of appealing to middle-class sensibilities within the free-wheeling, individualistic society created by liberalism.

The church's avowed aim was to 'rechristianize' Spain. Whether these middle-class movements would have attained that goal is debatable. In any event, the triumph of Franco offered a more direct means. Bishops and priests saw the general as a providential figure sent to deliver Spain and Catholicism in an apocalyptic battle between 'good and evil, truth and error, Christ and Satan'. With few exceptions, the clergy and Catholic laypeople supported the Nationalist rising. In return, the new regime granted Catholicism exceptional privileges. Protestants were subject to constant harassment; education was delivered into the hands of the church.

As a result of its association with an authoritarian government, the church believed that a 'triumphant Christianity' had acquired, at long last, the tools needed to rechristianize the masses alienated from religion. In fact, the Franco regime presided over a capitalist economic revolution accompanied by profound social changes that made the realization of clerical dreams impossible. Beginning in the late 1950s, economic modernization encouraged secularization and stimulated successive waves of political and social dissent. The simplistic ideological formulas employed by state and church in the years immediately following the Civil War began to crumble.

Some Catholics, aware of the economic transformation of Western Europe during the 1950s, recognized that sooner or later Spain would undergo a similar experience. They believed that the regime needed to adapt to this new reality to ensure its survival. The principal advocates of the authoritarianism-modernization thesis were members of the Opus Dei movement. Founded before the Civil War by a Spanish priest, José María Escrivá de Balaguer, Opus Dei possessed an organization unlike that of a conventional religious order. Its members, recruited from the ranks of lawyers, economists and university professors, were expected to remain in their secular professions and to attract their lay colleagues to religion through good example.

Had the members of Opus Dei fulfilled this apparently simple exercise of faith quietly, the movement would have passed virtually unnoticed into Spanish religious history. From the Franco regime's early years, however, the organization displayed larger ambitions. During the purge of professors carried out during the early 1940s, Opus Dei possessed sufficient influence to place many members in university chairs and to control the country's leading research institutions. In 1957 Opus members gained key economic positions in the government. Opus ministers became the driving force behind successive plans which rescued the regime from bankruptcy and stimulated a boom of unprecedented proportions during the 1960s.

The political ascendancy and key economic role of Opus members in government soon led to controversy. Government

At the same time, devotion to the church retained a deep appeal in regions with strong peasant and communal traditions and among the conservative middle classes of the cities. Religion still occupies a significant place in national life. Protestants are few and non-believers, although more numerous than in earlier times, are still a distinct minority. In the northern countryside, an historic popular faith has managed to hold its own. *Right*: villagers of S. Esteban de Gormaz in northern Castile wend their way to church. *Below*: a charming study of a young girl's first communion, painted by her fifteen-year-old brother – Pablo Picasso.

officials linked to Christian Democracy resented the dominance of a group which threatened their projects to liberalize the regime on the Western European model. Opposition groups saw Opus Dei as a sinister conspiracy, a 'holy mafia' intent on controlling the apparatus of the state for conservative political ends. Opus Dei's administration rejected these charges, arguing that members holding government office were acting in the capacity of private citizens and not as representatives of the movement. From a narrow point of view, this was probably correct, although the obsessive secrecy that has always surrounded Opus activities makes a definitive answer impossible. It was also in good measure a disingenuous explanation. Opus members in government endorsed a political philosophy reflecting the anti-democratic and anti-liberal principles of the organization's founder. Although they favoured limited reforms in civil liberties, largely to satisfy Western European governments, Opus ministers promoted economic development as a means of diverting public opinion away from fundamental political change.

The economic transformation and constrictive reform of civil liberties carried out during the 1960s did not produce the results expected by Opus theoreticians. On the contrary, labour agitation reached unprecedented proportions, while political dissent, far from being stilled, spread among an increasingly vocal opposition. The ambitions of Opus Dei, moreover, were out of tune with important changes taking place within Spanish Catholicism. The liberating effects of the Second Vatican Council (1962–65) were deeply felt among the lower clergy and some bishops who were already questioning the moral validity of identifying Catholicism with an authoritarian government. Basque and Catalan priests broke completely with the established order over its unyielding hostility to regional autonomy, while clerics and laypeople belonging to Catholic social movements indicted the regime for its scandalous neglect of social justice. By the early 1970s, the conditions were present for the momentous changes in the institutional status of Catholicism that would follow Franco's death in 1975.

For the first time in the twentieth century, with the exception of the period of the Republic, church and Catholicism have found themselves faced with many unfamiliar pastoral challenges. Although government financial support is hard to renounce, clergy and committed laity now recognize that Catholicism must look to its own energies and initiatives for the future. How it will fare is impossible to predict, although there are grounds for thinking that it will hold its own. A recent opinion poll (1990) shows that young people place more confidence in the church as an institution playing a positive role within Spanish society than in the Socialist government, a result unimaginable even a decade ago.

Velázquez's *Las Meninas* (The Maids of
Honour) has come to be regarded as the
archetypal Spanish painting. Its subject is
the dignity of the artist: Velázquez is
working in his studio in the palace, and
members of the court have come to
watch. The king and queen, whose presence dignifies the artist's work, are seen,
diminutively reduced, in the mirror
behind him. Centre stage are the little
infanta with her waiting women, two of
the court dwarves and, right in the foreground, a lifelike dog. With its brilliant
technique and its use of devices such as
the mirror, the painting is a subtle
comment on reality, illusion and the
nature of art itself.

ANOTHER IMAGE OF THE
WORLD: SPANISH ART, 1500–1920

JONATHAN BROWN

It is often hard to determine whether the appreciation of Spanish art has been harmed more by its friends or its enemies. To traditional art history, and to the English-speaking public at large, Spanish art is defined by the names of three painters of acknowledged genius – El Greco, Velázquez and Goya. A few more artists are also recognized as admirable – Zurbarán, Murillo and Ribera. All the others, not to mention the architects and sculptors, are considered to be derivative or provincial and have never achieved public recognition. Hundreds of thousands of visitors enter the Museo del Prado every year; no more than a handful know the name of its architect or recognize that he was an important exponent of neo-classicism.

From this ignorance and disdain springs an ill-founded corollary: the artists of Spain, although certainly numerous, contributed little if anything to the evolution of European art. They had no influence (except in Spanish America); therefore they were of little consequence. Behind this attitude lies one of the most solid prejudices of art history. As conceived and taught in the English-speaking world, the course of art history from the Renaissance to the Enlightenment is determined by a cultural mainstream, which derives from Italy, and later from France. Artists who had the misfortune to work outside the mainstream are generally relegated to the category of provincial or derivative.

In dismayed reaction to this 'marginalization' of their country, Spanish writers known as 'the Generation of 1898' went to an opposite extreme and constructed a mythical 'Spanish spirit' which not only explained and excused the isolation of Spain, but glorified it. Spain became a mystery, an enigma, a paradox, a contradiction, and Spanish artists were evoked and interpreted as the visible expression of these qualities of Spanish history. Only those initiated by birth or temperament could truly understand Spanish art. This posture was taken at face value by outsiders, thus greatly reducing the number of potential admirers, and paradoxically reinforcing Spain's isolation from the rest of the world.

The Spanish 'case', however, is in many ways related to those of other countries like Germany and England, which have not been privileged to navigate in the Italo-French mainstream. The process of the development of Spanish art, and especially its relation to the generating centres in Italy, is perhaps best defined by a term borrowed from anthropology, acculturation, which describes how ideas and customs are altered when transplanted from one culture to another. A complex filtering mechanism permits a partial assimilation to occur, which eliminates certain phenomena as unsuited to local conditions, and radically transforms others to serve the needs of the host culture. In practice, the spread of artistic ideas and their alteration when introduced into a new environment is approached through an understanding of patronage.

In Spain, the partnership between artist and patron greatly favoured the patron, whose domination was long assured by insuperable advantages of wealth and social position. Not until the upheavals following the French revolution could a free spirit like Goya take wing. But even in Goya's case, there is a dramatic disjunction between the private man, who created trenchant works of political satire, and the public man, who tirelessly worked to build his position and patrimony and protect his royal pension.

Inspiration from the North

The dynamic of artistic acculturation is at no period more vibrantly at work than during the fifteenth century. Spain was firmly in the orbit of northern art, originating from the Lowlands, Burgundy and the Rhineland. Close commercial ties with the north provided the perfect conduit for the flow of art and artists to Spain, and Spanish collections were rich in Flemish paintings and tapestries.

These works in turn inspired the painters of Castile, who interpreted their Flemish sources with conspicuous originality. The practitioners of what is now called the Hispano-Flemish style seldom travelled to the north; they learned about late Gothic Netherlandish painting by imitating imported works, a practice that might be likened to learning from a student's notes instead of attending the professor's lectures.

Another conditioning factor was the physical context for which the art was intended. Much Spanish painting was created for placement in altarpieces, some of which were gigantic in size, and placed at considerable remove from the viewer. In effect, Hispano-Flemish painters worked at a distance from both their models and their public. Yet the narrative and doctrinal content of the compositions were regarded as of the greatest importance. In response to these circumstances, Spanish painters simplified and schematized the northern styles.

The results are most easily gauged in two versions of the Pietà, one by Rogier van der Weyden, which was owned by Queen Isabella, the other by Fernando Gallego, a leading Hispano-Flemish master active in Castile from 1466 to 1507. Gallego intensifies the emotion of Rogier's image by magnifying the scale of the figures and emphasizing their angularity, thus increasing the visceral, heart-rending power of the tragic event.

The Italian connection

Gallego stands at the threshold of a revealing but little-understood phase of Spanish art, a phase that is characterized by rapid change and dazzling heterogeneity. To those accus

The origins of Spanish painting lie in the Netherlands. *Right: Pietà* by Rogier van der Weyden, owned by Queen Isabella. Fernando Gallego (*below*) follows him closely but increases the scale of the central figures and intensifies the emotion.

The *Aeneid* relates how two serpents emerged from the sea and strangled Laocoön and his sons. To this familiar classical subject Alonso Berruguete (*bottom*) brought an unclassical directness, expressing terror and agony with a power that was to remain a constant element in Spanish art.

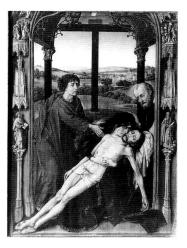

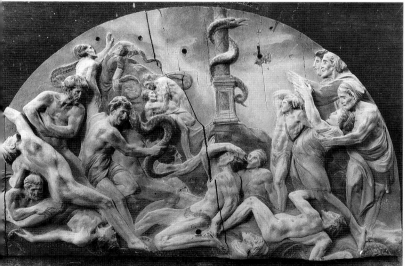

In architecture, Spain experienced her last great flowering of Gothic (only here were huge cathedrals being begun in this style in the mid-sixteenth century) at the same time as the Italian Renaissance was being eagerly adopted for secular buildings. Segovia Cathedral (*opposite above*) is contemporary with the palace of Charles V at Granada (*below left*). The façade of Salamanca University (*below right*) represents a fusion of both.

tomed to the linear progression of Italian art, the period seems all confusion, like a surrealist play in which no one enters on cue and all the actors speak at once. During Gallego's later years and into the first quarter of the sixteenth century, three distinct phases of central Italian painting were telescoped into a short period of time, coexisting with the continuation of the Hispano-Flemish style.

Pedro Berruguete (c. 1450–1503) represents the first phase. Born in Paredes de Nava (Palencia) and trained in the Hispano-Flemish manner, he seems to have spent time in a regional town of north-central Italy, where he acquired a thin veneer of Italianism totally absent from the work of Gallego. Almost before Berruguete died, and while Gallego was still alive, Juan de Borgoña (active 1495–1536), a northern painter well acquainted with central Italian art, entered the scene. Borgoña was sponsored by the archbishop of Toledo, Cardinal Francisco Jiménez de Cisneros. In the new chapter room of Toledo cathedral, executed between 1509 and 1511, Borgoña showed himself to be fully versed in the work of a painter such as Bernardino Pinturicchio, and able to command complex efforts of perspective and a sculpturesque figure style that make the work of Berruguete seem outdated.

The novelty of Borgoña's art was soon eclipsed by the return home of another emigrant artist, Alonso Berruguete (c. 1485–1561), son of Pedro. Alonso was in Florence and Rome from about 1504 to 1517, during the crucial years when the anticlassical style of mannerism was being devised. Mannerism was made to order for an artist trained in the conventions of the Hispano-Flemish style; it offered new possibilities for expressive distortions and Berruguete played them to the hilt. Once re-established in Spain, Berruguete became a sculptor, a great sculptor in fact, who drained all that was normative from the classical style, refilling the empty vessel with powerful, untrammelled emotion.

Thus, between 1490 and 1550, painting and sculpture in Castile quickly passed through three successive stages of Italian art, reworking and recombining these with the persistent northern late Gothic legacy. Those with advanced tastes – the aristocracy – were drawn to the growing prestige of Italian art, but religious patrons tended to be more conservative. Great Gothic cathedrals were therefore initiated at Salamanca (1510–51) and Segovia (1524–99) at the same time that a Roman High-Renaissance palace, intended for the use of Charles V, was begun at a most improbable site, next to the Moorish palace of the Alhambra. And somewhere between these two extremes are buildings in the Plateresque style, such as the famous façade of the University of Salamanca (c. 1525), a Gothic design encrusted with classical ornamentation in a way that would have horrified Bramante (d. 1514), had he lived to see it.

The patronage of Philip II

During the first half of the sixteenth century, the major centres
of patronage were impartially scattered across Spain. Important prelates in cities such as Valencia, Seville, Valladolid,
Burgos, Granada and Toledo had the means and motivation to
sponsor every kind of artistic activity. Leading noble families,
of whom the Mendoza clan is the most important, were also
capable of ambitious projects, secular and religious alike. The
prominence of these bishops and lords was abetted by the
relatively weak presence of the monarchy. To be sure, Isabella
of Castile had been a devoted, canny patron, but after her death
in 1504, a hiatus ensued. Charles V, who reigned from 1516 until
1556, was prepared to dedicate vast sums to the arts in pursuit of
his personal glory, but his itinerant custom of rule diminished
his impact on the arts of Spain.

This situation was dramatically altered upon the succession of
his son Philip II. Even while still prince, Philip had evinced a
profound interest in the arts, and once in power he initiated an
artistic revolution that was destined to have a lasting impact on
his Spanish realms. The first move was to terminate the ambula-
tory court; in 1561, Madrid became its permanent seat. Charles
V had already begun to develop a network of palaces in this
area, with the Alcázar of Madrid at its centre. Once settled in his
new capital, Philip improved the satellite royal houses at
Aranjuez, El Pardo and Toledo, and added to their furnishings.

The establishment of the court, which should have been
favourable to Spanish artists, was accompanied by an unexpected development – the massive importation of foreign art
and artists. This trend had been initiated by Charles V, who
adopted Titian as his court painter. Philip continued to favour
the great Venetian artist and became his most significant client.
Philip also had an architectural project in mind that could be
realized only with outside assistance. This was the Escorial, a
gigantic building complex to be erected at the base of the
Guadarrama mountains, about 27 miles from Madrid.

The Escorial is the greatest architectural project of its time,
and also the least understood, although its origins are clear
enough. Following the victory of his armies over the French at
the battle of St Quentin in 1556, Philip vowed to honour St
Lawrence, on whose feastday the battle took place, by building
a commemorative structure. This purpose, however, was soon
superseded by another. Philip had been charged by his father
to provide a suitable burial place for him, and it was to this that
the Escorial was dedicated.

If the programme was simple, the realization was complex,
although the gigantic building was constructed in the astound-
ingly short time of twenty years (1563–84). In the main, the
building was organized around the royal chapel, under the
altar of which was placed a crypt for Charles V and his

descendants. A monastery for brothers of the Jeronymite order was accommodated in the southern half of the structure, while a seminary and palace quarters occupied the northern part. The Escorial became a sort of prayer factory for the salvation of the royal souls. Thousands of masses were intoned by the monks, whose ranks were replenished from the seminary. All took place under the supervision of the pious king, who when in residence added his own voice to the chorus.

The design of the Escorial was entrusted to artists from or trained in Italy, although the style is unlike any Italian building. The initial architect, Juan Bautista de Toledo, had worked with Michelangelo at St Peter's, but there is nothing of his master's extravagant, complicated manner in the Escorial. Instead, Toledo and his pupil and successor, Juan de Herrera, produced a building in a denuded classical style, which is austere as befits a funerary monument and incomparably grand. At the king's behest, a high-pitched slate roof with prominent corner towers crowned the structure. This wholly original treatment of the classical style converted the Escorial into an emblem of the Habsburg monarchy, and it was not until the end of the dynasty in 1700 that court architects were able to escape from under its shadow.

As for the pictorial decoration, this too was assigned to Italian and Italianate artists, who produced a virtual catalogue of the doctrines of the Counter-Reformation church. Following the example of his father, Philip believed himself to be the leader of the secular forces of Catholicism. The decoration articulates his perfect piety by glorifying Christ as saviour, proclaiming the divinity of the Virgin Mary and reiterating the importance of the saints and the sacraments.

Philip's Italian painters – Luca Cambiaso, Federico Zuccaro and Pellegrino Tibaldi the principal among them – were outstanding figures in their time, although their fame has inexorably diminished over the centuries. Their importance, however, for Spanish painters is inestimable. Zuccaro's *Flagellation of Christ*, executed for the main altar of the Escorial's basilica, does not inspire unbridled admiration, but it made the grand manner of Italian classicism accessible to local artists and influenced the next two generations of painters in and around Madrid.

When Philip began his reign, artists in Spain, and especially Castile, were still experimenting with the new Italian classicism, borrowing motifs and accents but not quite understanding the systems and theories on which it was founded. Philip brought the Renaissance to Spain and then encouraged his artists to rework it in order to express his self-defined status as the Catholic monarch. Through this enormous act of will and intelligence, a new era, the Golden Age of Spanish art, was initiated.

El Greco, the outsider

Philip made only one false step – he dismissed El Greco, the one artist of undeniable genius to cross his path. The king's lack of interest in this great painter has a ready and rational explanation. El Greco was a person whose self-confidence bordered on arrogance, which made him difficult to control. In 1580, the king commissioned him to paint a large altarpiece for the Escorial, the *Martyrdom of St Maurice and the Theban Legion*. El Greco lavished great artifice and artistry on the picture, but committed what the king must have regarded as unpardonable errors. Not only is the scene of martyrdom relegated to the background, but there are portraits of three of Philip's generals in the composition. El Greco's idea was to glorify the king's men as defenders of the faith, but Philip, who was fanatical about doctrinal orthodoxy, would have seen only the anachronism of his contemporaries witnessing an event which had occurred in the fourth century. The *Martyrdom of St Maurice* was thus El Greco's first and last royal commission.

Fortunately, he had a more sympathetic clientele awaiting him in Toledo. The artist had arrived in the city in 1577 after an extraordinary if unsuccessful early career. El Greco was born in Crete in 1541 and was trained as a post-Byzantine painter. Around 1566, he migrated to Venice and began to assimilate the styles of Titian and Tintoretto. Four years later, he moved to Rome and studied the work of Michelangelo. The result of this varied training, which combined elements of Byzantinism and classicism in an unprecedented way, was an art of the utmost originality. For El Greco, however, the classical tradition was like a foreign language which he spoke with a strange accent. The purists in Rome probably found him to be merely eccentric, but in Spain, where classicism was also a second language, he found himself at home.

El Greco might well have flourished in other parts of Europe where the classical style was then being lacquered over a lingering late Gothicism – in Fontainebleau, or Haarlem, or Prague, for example, places all with an ample tolerance for the hybrid in art. But Toledo served his purposes, and there he found an elite group of learned ecclesiastics who accepted his eccentricities without blinking and who, at the same time, encouraged him to paint stirring yet ingenious expositions of Catholic doctrine. Freed from the encumbrances of classical rules, his art began to soar. His masterpiece, the *Burial of the Count of Orgaz* (1586–88), offers a defence of the doctrine of good works, a crucial issue for the Counter-Reformation church. But it is also an encyclopaedia of the entire range of artistic effects, from the uncanny realism of the dead count's armour and the richly embroidered vestments of the priests to the powerful, expressive distortions of the otherworldly judgment scene. El Greco prized imagination as the greatest artistic

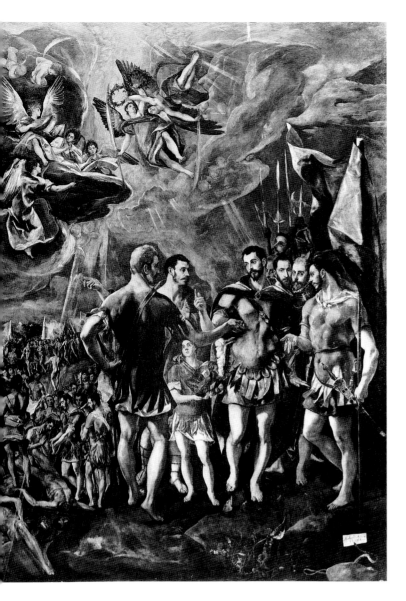

The Martyrdom of St Maurice and the Theban Legion was El Greco's only commission from Philip II. Its subject is the slaughter of a legion of Roman Christian soldiers for refusing to take part in pagan sacrifice. This is seen being enacted on the left. In the foreground are St Maurice and his companions awaiting death – two are portraits of Philip's generals. The unorthodox treatment did not please the king and he gave El Greco no other commissions. *Below*: a detail of the armour of the Count of Orgaz (see p.177), showing the extraordinary realism that El Greco combined with his visionary composition.

faculty, and no painter of the time possessed it in greater measure. For this reason, his art was truly inimitable and he left no followers.

Sacred and secular: a new art for Spain

Although court patronage during the reign of Philip III (1598–1621) was built on the foundations created by Philip II, it was marked by subtle innovations. The king was a passive, rather timid person who surveyed the complexities of governing the Spanish monarchy and decided to devote his attention to hunting and prayer. The reins of power were assumed by the Duke of Lerma, a shrewd and knowing patron of the arts. Rather than importing painters from Italy, Lerma promoted those who had been put into place by Philip II during the final years of his reign, many of whom were the relatives or descendants of the assistants of Zuccaro, Cambiaso and Tibaldi. Yet the religious paintings of these artists are markedly different in tone. The insistent, at times obtrusive, doctrinal orthodoxy required by Philip II is replaced by a more expressive spirituality, which is grounded in natural appearances but then purified of the merely accidental.

Leading proponents of this style were the brothers Carducho, Bartolomé (c. 1560–1608) and his younger brother, Vicente (c. 1576–1638). Bartolomé had come to Spain as an assistant of Zuccaro and remained after his master was sent home. In addition to his activities as a painter, Bartolomé was a picture dealer, specializing in the importation of works by contemporary Florentine painters. These painters, now regarded as among the forerunners of naturalism in Italy, provided models of simple, direct religious art, which were appropriated by the Carduchos and their numerous followers, as is exemplified in Bartolomé's starkly effective *Descent from the Cross* of 1595. Here are found the origins of the spare, soulful interpretations of the Gospel and the lives of saints which are the glory of early Baroque painting in Spain.

Continuity was also the watchword of court portraiture. The distinctive, almost schematic formula of Habsburg portraiture was established by Titian and Antonis Mor in the early years of the reign of Philip II. This formula required the use of stiffly posed figures, wearing elaborate costumes and set against a neutral background. Like flies in amber, the appearance of members of the royal family is preserved in these portraits with pluperfect fidelity. Not even a flicker of emotion is permitted in these visual projections of the hierarchical protocol of the Habsburg court.

The rules of royal portraiture were also applied to an entirely new genre of painting that appeared in the early 1600s. This is the still life, another import from Italy. Italian still-life paintings figure in Spanish collections beginning around 1590, and by

1600 one of the earliest and greatest native practitioners was interpreting the subject in a distinctive way. Juan Sánchez Cotán's (1560–1627) models were the rich, abundant still-life paintings of northern Italy, but he sedulously pruned the harvest to a few well-chosen items. These are placed on a shallow ledge, artfully arranged and illuminated by a powerful light. The sense of stasis and the compelling realism of surfaces and textures are the devices of the portraitist brought to bear on the humble products of nature.

The artists of the court of Philip III became the artists of the early years of the reign of Philip IV (1621–65). Later in life, Philip IV would emerge as the greatest royal collector and connoisseur of the seventeenth century, but until almost 1640, many of the royal painters were the ones put in place by his father and the Duke of Lerma. However, the king's favourite, the Count-Duke of Olivares, was impatient with the status quo in art as in politics, and it was through his initiative that a boy wonder was imported from Seville, Diego de Velázquez (1599–1660).

The permanent presence of the court in Madrid was slowly but inexorably to drain artistic talent from the provinces to the capital. One by one, centres of artistic activity that had been important in the sixteenth century – Toledo, Valencia, Valladolid – fell by the wayside. Only Seville was able to resist, supported by the wealth of the commerce with the American colonies.

Seville was a cosmopolitan centre, with sizable colonies of Genoese and Flemish merchants, and paintings from these areas were obviously known to local artists. The dominant style was in fact an amalgam of these sources, reinterpreted to satisfy the ecclesiastical patrons who dominated the art market. During Velázquez's youth, the preeminent painter was Juan de Roelas (active 1597–1625), who produced several large altarpieces that nicely balance the requirements of legibility and clarity with a sharp sense for the telling naturalistic detail.

The age of Velázquez

The first known works by Velázquez, however, seem to be entirely independent of local tradition and practice. The *Old Woman Cooking Eggs*, for instance, is one of the earliest genre paintings in Seville (its immediate predecessors are by Velázquez as well). It is evident that the artist's point of departure were kitchen scenes of Flemish origin of a kind created by Pieter Aertsen and his followers from about 1550 onwards. But Velázquez has dared to look afresh at nature and to reproduce its appearance as carefully as possible. Too carefully, in fact, because the artist's penetrating gaze imparts an almost frozen quality to the composition.

It was this audacity, novelty and sheer brilliance that soon brought Velázquez to the attention of people at court. In 1623, he

Whereas religious painting could be highly emotional, portraiture maintained a sombre, hierarchic reserve. *Far left: Isabella Clara Eugenia* by Alonso Sánchez Coello. *Left: Descent from the Cross* by Bartolomé Carducho, a darkly powerful painting, but in a style soon to be eclipsed by the bravura of Velázquez. Seville, prosperous and self-confident through its trading links with America, remained as cosmopolitan as Madrid. *The Martyrdom of St Bartholomew* by Juan de Roelas (*below left*) reflects both Flemish and North Italian models.

Velázquez brought a brilliance of technique and an insight into drama and psychology that were new to Spanish art. *The Surrender of Breda (below)* was painted for the palace of El Buen Retiro to celebrate a victory in the Netherlands. Velázquez gives a touching and chivalrous poignancy to the two central figures of victor and vanquished. *The Forge of Vulcan (bottom)* dates from his first period in Rome when he was still forming his style; here heroic myth is depicted with detailed realism.

visited Madrid for the second time in search of royal favour, and his calling card was his greatest genre painting, the *Water-seller* (Wellington Museum, London), which would have made the incumbent royal painters, Vicente Carducho among them, look old-fashioned. Soon after, he painted a portrait of the king and received the much-desired appointment as royal painter. From then on, his career would depend on the patronage of Philip IV.

At first, however, his path to success was beset with obstacles, and his initial years at court were marked by struggle and strife with the older painters, over whom he did eventually prevail. Then in 1628 a friendly rival appeared in Madrid, who showed the young Velázquez that there was more to painting than dreamed of in his philosophy. This was Peter Paul Rubens, then at the zenith of his career as painter, diplomat and courtier. The conversations between Rubens and Velázquez must have been among the most fascinating ever to take place between two artists, but of course there is no record of what was said. Within two months of Rubens' return to the north, Velázquez was on his way to Italy in obvious obeisance to the counsel of the Flemish master.

Velázquez's trip to Italy lasted a little over two years (August 1629–January 1631) and while there, like El Greco before him, he absorbed and then transformed the rules and regulations of classicism. The remaking of Velázquez's art is apparent in the comparison of two mythological compositions; one, *Los Borrachos*, was done just before his departure to Italy, the other, the *Forge of Vulcan*, was executed in Rome in 1630. *Los Borrachos* is a magnificent idea, but an uneven work of art. The juxtaposition of the smooth-skinned Bacchus with the rawboned peasants, flushed with wine and exuding an air of bibulous merriment, is inspired; yet the drinkers are crammed together in the shallow foreground space, compelling the artist to truncate some of the bodies below the chest. In the *Forge of Vulcan*, the prosaic and the classical are successfully conjoined. Velázquez has made an enormous leap in representing the human figure and learned how to construct a credible illusion of space. Nonetheless, he still depicts the small, realistic detail in such a way that the ancient myth is projected forward into the here and now.

Upon his return, Velázquez found the atmosphere at court dramatically changed. In his absence, an heir to the throne, Prince Baltasar Carlos, had been born. In 1632, the prince accepted the oath of fealty from the Cortes of Castile, which occasioned the first of a series of spectacular court festivals during the 1630s. The principal arena of these displays of royal pomp and power was the Palace of the Buen Retiro, constructed along the eastern border of Madrid under the patronage of Olivares. As a work of architecture, the Retiro was cast in the

To bring the supernatural into the sphere of everyday life was the aim of the first generation of Spanish Baroque painters. Francisco de Zurbarán's calm, understated manner makes the miraculous events he depicts all the more effective. *Right: Adoration of the Shepherds. Below right:* the same subject by the sculptor Juan Martinez Montañés.

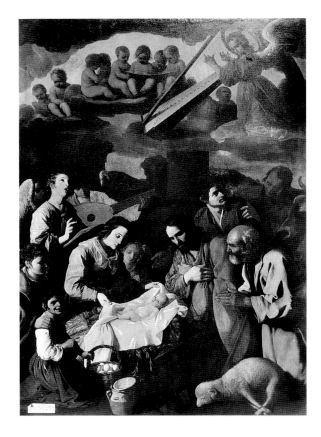

mould of the Escorial, an unlikely model for a pleasure palace. However, such was the power of Philip II's great structure that there was no escaping its influence.

The decoration of the interior fortunately redeemed the rather forbidding façades. As the principal royal painter, Velázquez was much occupied with the pictorial adornment, contributing several works, religious and secular alike, to the ensemble. The greatest of these is *The Surrender of Breda*, one of twelve paintings of victories of the reign which were commissioned from the royal painters and their disciples. The siege of Breda, which was seen as an important victory over the Dutch in the Thirty Years' War, had been won by Spanish troops under the command of the Genoese general Ambrosio Spínola. As represented by Velázquez, the surrender is a brilliant mixture of verisimilitude and imagination. Using topographical prints of the site, Velázquez painted a reasonably accurate landscape of the fortified town of Breda. Also accurate are the portraits of the two generals, Spínola and Justin of Nassau, leader of the Dutch. However, the act of surrender itself is the visual translation of a poetic invention of the event by the playwright Pedro Calderón de la Barca, who emphasized the chivalrous conduct of the Spaniards and their respect for their valorous enemies. Taking this as a point of departure, Velázquez transformed one of the most monotonous artistic subjects, the military scene, into a moving psychological drama of the fortunes of war and a subtle but undeniable glorification of the invincibility of Spanish arms.

Picture collecting and church patronage

The pictorial decoration of the Retiro was an enterprise of enormous magnitude, which required buying pictures in Italy and Flanders as well as Spain. This precipitated one of the most important artistic phenomena of the period – large-scale picture collecting by the crown and the leading nobles. Philip II had imported painters from abroad; Philip IV imported paintings. The impact on painting of these growing collections was manifold, but perhaps the most important consequence was the proscription of certain subjects to Spanish painters. Scenes of everyday life and mythology, as well as landscapes and interior settings, were deemed the province of foreigners and rarely figure in the repertory of Spanish artists, who were restricted to religious subjects, still life and portraiture. In other words, the taste of the time is only partially reflected in the work of Spanish painters, who were compelled to serve the most conservative sector of the clientele, the church.

The predominance of ecclesiastical patronage and its impact on Spanish painters is most vividly illustrated in Seville, where, in the absence of the counterweight of the crown and nobility, the church was unchallenged. The greatest painter in Seville

during the first half of the century was Francisco de Zurbarán (1598–1664), who was born in a small agricultural village in Extremadura and began to find favour with religious patrons in Seville in the later 1620s. His success, which approached near-monopoly in the 1630s, seems to have been predicated on a canny mixture of traditional and novel artistic elements. This is seen to best advantage in his works for the Carthusian monastery in Jerez de la Frontera (1638–40), acknowledged to be among his masterpieces. In the *Adoration of the Shepherds*, Zurbarán employs a composition that had been favoured in the workshops of Seville since the late sixteenth century. This deploys massive, closely grouped figures arranged along the frontal plane of the canvas, which provides optimum clarity and legibility for the viewer. Zurbarán, however, following the precedent of Velázquez, brings the scene to life by casting rustic peasants in the role of shepherds and dwelling with loving care on the textures and surfaces of inanimate objects. The picture is thus solemn but not forbidding, respectful of the content but not remote from the spectator.

This is the tenor of much religious art in Spain during the first half of the seventeenth century, and is found not only in painting, but also in sculpture, as seen in the work of the greatest sculptor of the period, Juan Martínez Montañés of Seville (1568–1649). The *Adoration of the Shepherds* from his most ambitious work, the altar of San Isidoro del Campo, Santiponce (*c.* 1612), is more elegant than the version by Zurbarán, but the artistic presuppositions are virtually identical. Toward the middle of the century, however, and as a further consequence of the importation of the works of an influential foreign master, a radically different approach to religious art came into vogue.

The catalyst was Peter Paul Rubens. Following Rubens' visit to Madrid in 1628–29, Philip IV became his most devoted patron and commissioned numerous works for the royal collection. By the time Rubens died in 1640, Philip had acquired over 200 canvases by the master and his workshop. During the next ten years, these dynamic, colourful paintings slowly fermented in the minds of the younger generation in Madrid, finally breaking to the surface in the 1650s.

An early adherent of Rubens was Francisco Rizi (1614–85), who in 1650 painted one of the first works to break with the static compositions commonly used in the first part of the century. Four years later, a more brilliant painter, Francisco de Herrera the Younger (1627–85), executed an altarpiece for the Carmelite church of San José, Madrid, depicting the triumph of St Hermengild. Herrera's adaptation of Rubens' refulgent style is telling; he captures, and even exaggerates, the surging motion of the master but is indifferent to the sculpturesque figure style which Rubens had derived from the careful study of antiquity

Bartolomé Murillo gave his subjects an irresistible charm that would later lead his followers into sentimentality. In his *Holy Family* the Virgin sits spinning, while St Joseph holds the Christ Child who is teasing a puppy with a tame bird.

and the Italian Renaissance. With its glittering surface and surging compositional energy, this picture demonstrates the pattern of later seventeenth-century painting in Madrid.

Hierarchies of court and church

Untouched by this commotion was Velázquez, who serenely went his way, privately pursuing his personal ambitions. These centred around a desire to elevate his art to the rank of a liberal pursuit and his personal status to that of a gentleman. In the hierarchical society of Spain, this was no easy task. Spanish artists had been trying for the better part of a hundred years to improve their social position and thus to escape the binding authority of their patrons. Painters like El Greco had sued their clients for just compensation, while others like Francisco Pacheco and Vicente Carducho had written lengthy treatises on the subject, bolstering their arguments with evidence gathered from the history of the ancient and modern world. Carducho and his colleagues in Madrid had sought to establish a royal academy of the arts during the 1620s, but this had come to nothing.

Velázquez was not disposed to fight a war on behalf of his colleagues; he merely wanted to win his personal battle by devoting himself to the service of the king, the one person who could solve the problem with a stroke of the pen. This Philip did in 1658 by nominating the artist to membership of the aristocratic military order of Santiago (St James). Although the nobles did everything possible to defeat the nomination, Velázquez, with the king's support, at last achieved his cherished goal.

This struggle for recognition is one component of what many consider to be the greatest picture ever painted, *Las Meninas*. For the purposes of this proclamation of artistic nobility, the royal family is converted into an attribute of the dignity of the painter's profession. The king, the queen and the infanta lend their presence to the painter's workshop, thus proving, in an equation well understood in a monarchical society, that painting is a noble art. But, as every single Spanish painter knew, it was one thing to claim nobility for the art, quite another to achieve it. In *Las Meninas*, Velázquez allows his painting to make his case. Infinitely complex but seemingly effortless, the picture challenges the creative powers of nature herself and emerges victorious.

Velázquez was a reticent person and his is a reticent art, little suited to the new requirements of religious painting for popular consumption. While he provided the models for court portraiture, the field of sacred painting was dominated by the example of Rubens, and not only in Madrid. The leading painters of Seville, Bartolomé Murillo (1617–82) and Juan de Valdés Leal (1622–1691), were equally captivated by the possibilities of the dynamic formulas of Flemish painting. However, during the

1660s, Murillo learned how to tame the exuberance of his foreign models and developed the intimate form of devotional painting for which he has become famous. During the first half of the century, Seville's clients wanted paintings that functioned like billboards of Counter-Reformation Catholicism; that is to say, they commissioned works that were doctrinaire and hortatory. Now the faithful of Seville wished to meet the heavenly beings on familiar terms, and Murillo became their go-between, imbuing the Holy Family with human feelings and projecting their affection and goodness with irresistible warmth and charm.

While Murillo seeks to bestow salvation on the worshipper, for Valdés Leal it is the outcome of an overpowering, all-consuming struggle. However, the exaggerated, at times anguished, emotion of his powerful compositions was not appropriate to the irenic temper of Sevillian religious feelings, and eventually he lost ground to his lifelong rival. For the next one hundred years, the painters of Seville were content to rework the compositions bequeathed them by Murillo.

Dynastic change: re-enter France and Italy

In Madrid, developments were to be far more dramatic. From 1665 to 1700, the Spanish monarchy was nominally ruled by Charles II, the enfeebled son of Philip IV. Although unfit and unable to rule, the king proved to be a devoted supporter of the arts. Indeed, in 1692 he brought the renowned Italian painter Luca Giordano to his court and set him working on a succession of impressive fresco decorations. Giordano commenced where his compatriots of the sixteenth century had left off – at the Escorial – and from there he moved to Madrid, painting half a dozen ceiling frescoes and at least a couple of hundred easel paintings. It may seem odd that this prodigious output made almost no impact on the painters of Madrid, except perhaps to drive the reigning royal painter, Claudio Coello, to an early grave. However, Giordano's relentlessly productive career was cut short by an event of transcendental significance, the death of Charles II and the extinction of the Spanish Habsburg dynasty.

In his last will and testament, the moribund king willed his monarchy to the grandson of Louis XIV, who became Philip V (1700–46) and initiated the Bourbon dynasty which, with certain interruptions, has ruled to the present time. The dynastic change was to make a profound impact on many aspects of Spanish life, but none would be more affected than the visual arts. Philip V and his queen, Marie Louise of Savoy, had been raised at the court of Louis XIV and their idea of a royal palace was Versailles. By comparison, the Alcázar of Madrid, in essence a medieval fortified palace that had been modernized in piecemeal fashion during the sixteenth and seventeenth centuries, was a hopeless anachronism, lacking the fluid Italian classicism which by then was the only permissible style for important secular architecture.

For Philip and his French entourage, the Alcázar was symptomatic of Spanish art as a whole – outdated and provincial. The king therefore decided to improve the situation by importing French architects, painters and sculptors, in effect transplanting the style of French court art to Madrid. In the event, this ambitious programme was forestalled by the War of the Spanish Succession, which did not end until 1713. And when it was over and it was possible to resume the artistic projects, *force majeure* again played a part. Marie Louise died in 1714, and the king almost immediately married Elizabeth Farnese of Parma, who naturally sponsored the careers of Italian artists. This was an important development, as will be seen below, but the imposition of foreign art in Spain needs to be placed in a wider context.

Historians of Spanish art have often been at a loss to deal with much of the eighteenth century, a period when the roster of leading artists contains the names of such foreigners as Filippo Juvarra, Giovanni Battista Sacchetti and Francesco Sabatini among the architects; Carle van Loo, Corrado Giaquinto, Giambattista Tiepolo and Anton Raphael Mengs among the painters; and René Frémin and Giovanni Domenico Olivieri among the sculptors. It is not until the emergence of Francisco de Goya in the 1780s that Spanish art is thought to be redeemed from the foreigners.

This is a narrow view of a period that in many respects mirrors developments in other European courts of the eighteenth century, where an international style, adapted from Italian sources, held sway. Moreover, the sudden predominance of foreign styles is a recurrent phenomenon in Spanish art, and resulted from the perennial imbalance of power between the artists and their patrons. With enough money and will, it was always possible to stop the world and introduce a new race of artist, as was done, for instance, by Philip II in the 1570s and 1580s. In the 1700s, however, this process was extraordinarily eventful and fruitful, and is most readily understood by studying the history of a single, significant monument, the Royal Palace of Madrid.

The plans laid by Philip V to 'frenchify' the Alcázar were dramatically halted by a disastrous conflagration that swept through the building on Christmas Eve, 1734, destroying much of the southern part. The ruins, deemed to be beyond salvation, were demolished. After some deliberation, and through the influence of Elizabeth Farnese, an Italian architect was selected to design the new palace. The choice was a very significant master indeed, the Piedmontese Filippo Juvarra (1678–1736), who had built splendid palaces and churches for the kings of Savoy in Turin. Juvarra arrived in 1735, and produced a plan for an immense, sprawling palace-city, to be constructed on an entirely new site and in an entirely new style, at least for Spain. Juvarra, however, already advanced in years when he arrived at court, died a year later, and his plans were shelved when it was decided to rebuild on the site of the Alcázar and on a more reasonable scale.

The direction of the work, begun in 1738, was given to one of Juvarra's assistants, Giovanni Battista Sacchetti (1690–1764), who produced the handsome if conventional design which adapted the façade elevations from the third of Bernini's conceptions for the Louvre, executed in 1665. The work proceeded apace and by the early 1750s was far enough advanced to begin the pictorial decoration. In the meantime, Philip V had died and been succeeded by his son, Ferdinand VI (1746–59), another in the seemingly endless line of indecisive kings who governed Spain in the Baroque era. However, like many of his faint-hearted predecessors and successors, Ferdinand had exquisite artistic taste, and in 1752 called an important Italian painter to court, Corrado Giaquinto (1703–65). During his nine-year stay in Madrid (1753–62), Giaquinto painted the superb frescoes in the royal chapel and the two entrance staircases, one of which was later enclosed and is now called the Salón de Columnas.

Giaquinto brought to Spain a spirited, refined, sensual late-Baroque style and trained a number of talented Spanish followers, especially Antonio González Velázquez (1723–94) and José del Castillo (1737–93), the first indigenous painters of the eighteenth century to assimilate the ways and means of current Italian painting. Giaquinto also served as director of the Royal Academy of Art (Real Academia de Bellas Artes de San Fernando), which had been founded only in 1752.

Giaquinto's powerful position as an artist and mentor barely survived the death of Ferdinand VI. The king and his queen, Barbara de Braganza, had produced no heirs, and so the crown passed to the first son of Philip V and Elizabeth Farnese, Charles, King of Naples, who would rule Spain as Charles III (1759–88). The new king was another avid patron of the arts, but his tastes favoured a simplified Baroque style, now called classical Baroque. Beginning in 1752, he had sponsored the building of the impressive palace at Caserta, almost 20 miles north of Naples. When he laid eyes on the palace in Madrid, he was horrified. 'What they have done here', he wrote in a letter of 24 January 1760, 'is shameful.'

It was too late to start anew, but Charles determined to make the perpetrators pay with their jobs. Sacchetti and Giaquinto were released and replaced by the cold-blooded architect, Francesco Sabatini, and the more gifted Bohemian painter, Anton Raphael Mengs.

In the eighteenth century, Spanish taste – like that of the rest of Europe – turned from Baroque to neo-classicism. The Bohemian Anton Raphael Mengs' portraits of his patron Charles III (*left*) have a truth to life and a dignity without rhetoric that were to influence Goya; while in his monumental works for the Royal Palace (*second below*), classical Rome reasserts its cultural dominance. *Bottom*: the same development towards neo-classicism in decorative terms: Corrado Giaquinto's *Religion*, a work still in the Baroque tradition, and *Olympus* by Francisco Bayeu, a protégé of Mengs.

Sabatini and Mengs

Sabatini's architectural legacy is difficult to appreciate. His additions to the palaces of Aranjuez and El Pardo were made in order to pump them up to what he and the king considered the requisite size for regal constructions. His independent commissions, such as the Royal Customs House (now the Ministry of Finance) and the General Hospital (now the Centro de Arte Reina Sofia) in Madrid seem to have been intended as a rebuke to Juvarra's fluid manner, on the one hand, and, on the other, to the extravagant Baroque style practised by such native architects as Ventura Rodríguez (1717–85), Sacchetti's assistant. Sabatini's designs are therefore stern lessons in correct court architecture, and were eventually displaced by an imaginative version of French neo-classicism.

Mengs (1728–79), by contrast, made a profound impact on Spanish art. He was lured to Madrid in 1761, where he spent eight productive if unhappy years. He returned to Rome in 1769 to recuperate, and then came back to Madrid a second time (1774–76). At the outset of his initial stay, Mengs encountered considerable opposition from Spanish artists, especially at the Academy, where he sought to carry out a thorough and unwanted reform of the pedagogical programme. He also faced a challenge from a formidable Italian rival, the great Venetian decorative painter Giambattista Tiepolo (1696–1770), who arrived in Madrid with his sons Domenico and Lorenzo in 1762. Tiepolo's fresco for the Throne Room, executed in 1764, is undoubtedly the most renowned work of all the Italians who worked at the Bourbon court, but the king's taste was already turning away from the delicate, decorative style of the Rococo toward the sterner stuff of Mengs.

Mengs' work for Charles III falls readily into two categories – portraits and history painting. During the first part of the century, Philip V and Ferdinand VI had employed a succession of French and Italian painters who specialized in portraiture. The best of these was Louis-Michel van Loo (1707–71), who served Philip V and Ferdinand VI from 1737 to 1752. Mengs' renditions of members of the court follow the French manner of court portraiture, which is characterized by dazzling effects of costume and scintillating colours. However, Mengs' astonishing virtuosity of technique elevated the court portrait to new heights of splendour.

As a history painter, Mengs was equally gifted. His role in the formation of neo-classicism is common knowledge, and in his works for Charles III he intensified his understanding of the twin pillars of the movement – Greco-Roman antiquity and the classical strain of Italian painting, exemplified by Raphael, Annibale Carracci and Domenichino. Mengs was undoubtedly a greater painter than was Sabatini an architect, but their common dedication to a more rigorous exploration of classicism carried the day. The frescoes executed in the Royal Palace by Mengs, culminating in the *Apotheosis of Trajan*, mark the triumph of classicism in Spanish painting.

Among his many virtues, Mengs was a gifted, generous teacher, and took under his wing two young Spaniards who would rise to positions of prominence at court, Francisco Bayeu and Mariano Salvador Maella. Bayeu, the older of the two (1734–95), was a prolific painter who was called to Madrid from Saragossa by Mengs in 1763 and promptly established his reputation with a series of excellent frescoes in the palace. Maella (1739–1819), now remembered only by specialists, began to work at court in 1765, following his return from Rome, where he was a pensioner of the Royal Academy. During the 1770s and 1780s, the two artists often worked at the same sites and even on the same commissions. As the memory of Mengs receded in their minds, they borrowed ideas from Giaquinto and merged his warm sense of colour and lively touch with the compositional balance and measure of their mentor.

A new golden age

With Mengs' final departure from Madrid in 1776, the waves of foreign artists who swept over the court during the eighteenth century at last receded, and a new golden age of Spanish art was starting to dawn, which reached its zenith in the career of Francisco de Goya. This pattern of development may seem familiar, and indeed it is. In the sixteenth century, Philip II sponsored a comparable importation of Italian artists to decorate the Escorial, and their pupils took what they learned and transformed it to suit the institutions and ideologies of Counter-Reformation Spain. During the eighteenth century, a succession of Bourbon monarchs invited more foreigners and once again precipitated an artistic revolution. However, in this instance, the assimilative phase was interrupted by an outside force that temporarily altered everyone's plans. This of course was the upheaval of Spanish society that transpired in the confusing aftermath of the French Revolution and the Napoleonic invasion, an upheaval that was witnessed and memorably interpreted by Goya.

Such is the greatness of Goya that it is tempting to skim over all the other art and artists of his time. This temptation must, however, be resisted, or at least postponed, to avoid losing sight of a major patron, Charles IV (1788–1808). Charles is usually graded half a step behind Charles II as the most inept ruler of post-medieval Spain, although this is debatable. He essentially abdicated his rule to his wife, Maria Luisa of Parma, and her corrupt, opportunistic favourite, Manuel Godoy. No one in the government was equipped to deal with the machinations of Napoleon, who usurped the Spanish crown in 1808, precipitating almost two decades of chaos, violence and bruta-

lity in Spanish society. It is no surprise, then, that historians have been slow to recognize Charles as the enlightened sponsor of the neo-classical style in Spain or to acknowledge the special virtues of some of the artists he employed.

Charles' career as a patron began in 1771, while he was still prince of Asturias (the title of the heir to the throne), with the construction in the grounds of the Escorial of a casino, which was completed in 1774. (The building was later enlarged by a perpendicular addition constructed between 1781 and 1783.) The Casita de Abajo, as it is known, set the pattern for the future king's style of patronage. Almost as if fleeing from the grandiose building projects of his father, the prince preferred to work on a small scale and to pay loving attention to the exquisite decoration of the interior, carefully coordinating every aspect of the objects and furnishings.

As his architect, Charles selected Juan de Villanueva (1739–1811), Spain's major neo-classical architect. Unlike Sabatini, who practised a simplified Baroque style, Villanueva, having spent his formative years in Rome (1759–65), was thoroughly grounded in Greco-Roman art. Thus, his command of the vocabulary and syntax of ancient architecture is complete, although he handles it with great freedom and originality and so avoids the merely archaeological repetition of types.

Villanueva designed a second casino for the prince in 1784, the Casita del Principe of the Pardo Palace, which was once again decorated with exquisite taste. The plan of the building, which consists of a square central pavilion flanked by two smaller units and connected by narrow galleries, looks forward to the architect's greatest achievement, the Gabinete de Ciencias Naturales, now known as the Museo del Prado. The gestation of the design and the progress of this famous but little-appreciated building, which was never completed during the architect's life, are too complex to be discussed here. Suffice it to say that Villanueva's ambition was to create a temple of science consisting of laboratories at the extremities, connected by galleries to a large central lecture hall in the form of an ancient temple. The principal exterior elevation, which is constructed of the traditional Castilian building materials, brick and granite, is enlivened by the refined, decorative treatment of the classical vocabulary. The Prado, like the Escorial, is a totally original response to the major tradition of Western European architecture.

As a patron of painting, Charles also charted an independent course, favouring almost exclusively Spanish artists, and thereby terminating the eighty-year hegemony of the French and the Italians. The king's tastes in painting are little studied, except of course for his relations with Goya. Indeed, Goya's enormously fertile and complex career is not to be understood without considering his relationship with the crown.

Goya's genius is many sided but always true to his own personal vision.

Upper row: The Family of Charles IV, painted when he was at the height of his career – the king, queen and their children represented without flattery (the painter himself on the extreme left, facing the easel). And (*far right*) one of the late enigmatic paintings that he made for his own home, *La Leocadia*, a veiled woman, dressed in mourning and leaning against an unidentifiable mound surmounted by an iron railing.

Lower row: three examples of Goya's social comment, always bitter, often ironic, sometimes horrifying: 'For Being Born Somewhere Else' (an innocent victim of the Inquisition); 'Divine Liberty' (celebrating the fall of Ferdinand VII in 1820); and 'Love and Death' (a satirical comment on the victim of a duel for love).

Goya: the first modern painter

Goya was born in 1746 in a town in Aragon; his father was an artisan from Saragossa. The young Goya was educated with the Piarist Fathers, but he was no man of letters. His powerful intelligence was channelled into the art of painting which, like his hero Velázquez, he saw as a passport to wealth and status. Velázquez, however, had the right connections and from an early age enjoyed the protection of the king. Goya, by contrast, had to fight his way slowly to the top, and once having achieved success he was prepared to hold onto it for dear life.

Until 1773, Goya's career advanced gradually and with difficulty. But in that year he married the sister of the royal painter Francisco Bayeu, María Josefa, an event that made it possible to find employment at court. In 1775, he began to design cartoons for the royal tapestry factory, creating original, often witty compositions that were used to decorate the royal residences. These attracted the favourable notice of the Prince and Princess of Asturias and enhanced his standing at court. Patiently the artist waited his turn, avidly seeking the favour of the aristocrats who commissioned him to paint their portraits, missing no opportunity to demonstrate his superiority over his rivals. In 1786, his efforts were rewarded by the appointment as royal painter, and three years later the new king Charles IV named him as painter of the privy chamber. Finally, in 1799 he reached the pinnacle; he and Mariano Maella were appointed jointly as first painters to the king.

The rationale behind this dual appointment can be inferred from the works of the two painters. Goya was regarded as the specialist in portraiture, Maella in religious and allegorical compositions. Portraiture was, in fact, the staple item in Goya's repertory and the means by which he earned a comfortable living. His renditions of Charles IV and Maria Luisa, painted in 1789, show Goya as the heir to the formulas of virtuoso portraiture devised by Mengs.

Yet, had Goya painted only splendid portraits, he might be remembered as a latter-day Van Dyck and not as the first, and possibly the greatest, interpreter of the maddening uncertainties and mindless brutalities of modern times. Goya the courtier lived in the same skin as Goya the social critic, who had seen the light of reason and was dedicated to banishing the shadows of Spain's backward social system. During the eighties, Goya made contact with a coterie of *ilustrados* (men of the Enlightenment) in Madrid, who profoundly influenced his thought and led him to reexamine the premises and values of the system he had so eagerly wished to master. Thus, the artist found himself locked in an irreconcilable conflict, serving the ideas of the old and new regimes simultaneously. In the very same year that he became first painter to the king, he published *Los Caprichos*, a series of eighty etchings with aquatint that mercilessly satirize

Divina Libertad

the human foibles and institutional failures that were inexorably leading to the collapse of the monarchy.

Goya's solution to his quandary now seems like cowardice; he kept his thoughts to himself in the form of sketchbooks and prints that were never published and in paintings that were never displayed in public, while he put his brushes at the service of those who would pay. The later portraits, although more allusive in technique and probing in their analysis of personality, fit comfortably within the conventions of Romantic portraiture. In the sketchbooks and prints, however, Goya abandoned the prevailing fashions and turned to the rough-and-ready style of the French and English political and satirical print – an underground art for an underground artist. The appropriation of low art for high purposes constitutes an astonishing feat of intelligence and audacity and permitted Goya to engage the world around him with unprecedented and undiminished immediacy.

During the troubled period that followed the defeat of Napoleon and the restoration of the reactionary Ferdinand VII, Goya's delicate balancing act nearly collapsed. The new king had little use for this deaf old man (Goya lost his hearing in 1792), and Goya was appalled by the cruel repression of Spanish liberalism. The prints and drawings of these years are furious in their criticism of the ignorance, superstition and cruelty of the old order that Ferdinand was reimposing on Spanish society. But the most moving testimony to those desperate times are the Black Paintings, the series of fourteen fantastic, gruesome images created by Goya to decorate two of the rooms of his country house, known as the *Quinta del Sordo* (the 'Deaf Man's Cottage'), which he acquired in 1819. At last, Goya's demons escape from the confines of his sketchbooks and invade the real world.

Salvation from Ferdinandine repression miraculously arrived the very next year, when a coup d'état toppled the king from the throne and reinstated the liberal constitution of 1812. Goya expressed his joy in a pungent ode to liberty, contained in Album C of his collected drawings, but his happiness was short-lived. Only three years later, the French sent an army to restore the king, and the darkness of tyranny again descended over the land.

For three months – from late January to mid-April 1824 – Goya went into hiding, apparently fearing the retribution of the king, but either he had nothing to hide or Ferdinand was not disposed to punish the ancient painter. He personally granted Goya permission to leave for France to take the waters at Plombières. In the event, he settled in Bordeaux, where many of his liberal friends of earlier days had gone into exile. There he lived the remaining few years of his life (he died in 1828), frail in body but still vital in spirit, producing drawings, prints and paintings that are miracles of wit and passion. However, despite ill health he returned to Madrid in 1826 to petition the king for his pension, which was granted in the amount of 50,000 reales. Until the end, Goya never allowed his politics to interfere with his perquisites.

To this degree, then, Goya remained a man of the old regime. Spanish artists had traditionally centred their aspirations on the figure of the monarch, and Goya was far too old to trust his future to dispossessed liberals and fiery revolutionaries. Goya's vision of a new Spain remained safely hidden in his sketchbooks and unpublished etchings for future generations to discover, to ponder and to analyse. These remarkable works seem to open a new chapter in Spanish art. There is undoubtedly a measure of truth to this notion, but Goya's highly original works are readily comprehensible to anyone who knows the history of Goya's artistic ancestors. Like his predecessors, Goya enjoyed the incomparable advantage of working on the margins of the classical tradition, which afforded the opportunity to create another and powerfully affecting image of the world.

The discovery of Spain

Up to Goya's time, the depth and originality of Spanish painting was little known beyond the Pyrenees. The Grand Tour, by which cultivated English gentlemen bridged the distance between northern Europe and Italian civilization, only served to emphasize the geographical and cultural isolation of Spain. However, where tourism failed, politics succeeded. The French invasion of Spain in 1808 unintentionally opened the floodgates of a massive exportation of Spanish pictures to France and then to England. Unscrupulous French generals, notably Nicolas Soult, sequestered sizable collections of paintings, which they took home after the defeat of the Napoleonic armies in 1812. Soult lived off his booty for the rest of his life, selling pictures as the need or opportunity presented itself. After his death, his heirs disposed of the remainder of the collection in a sale held in Paris in 1852.

The plunder of artistic treasures begun by the French army was finished by the Spanish government. Just before he died in 1833, Ferdinand VII decreed the suppression of the monastic orders, a decree that was fully implemented in 1835 by the chief minister, José Alvarez Mendizábal, whose name has become synonymous in Spain with the dispersion of works of art. The monasteries and nunneries of Spain were shuttered (called the *exclaustración*) and their movable goods were sequestered by the state (known as the *desamortización*). In practice, the government was not very efficient in expropriating the possessions of the religious orders, and into the breach stepped a number of opportunistic, well-financed operators, who made

Only in the nineteenth century did Spanish art make its impact on the rest of Europe. In 1865 Edouard Manet went to Spain and 'discovered' Velázquez. He adapted the latter's *Pablo de Valladolid* (*right*) for his own portrait of another famous actor, *Philibert Rouvière as Hamlet* (*below*).

huge collections of Spanish Golden-Age painting almost overnight and took them away.

The most famous and influential of these collections belonged to Louis Philippe, king of France (1830–48), and was assembled between 1835 and 1837 by his emissary, Baron Isidore Taylor. In 1838, the king placed his collection of some 446 canvases on view at the Louvre, under the rubric of the Musée Espagnol. In 1841, it was enriched by 220 additional pictures through the bequest of an eccentric Englishman, Frank Hall Standish. When Louis Philippe fell from power, he was allowed to keep his Spanish pictures, which after his death were sold in London in 1853.

The effect of the arrival of these hundreds of Spanish paintings in Paris, and later in London, was little short of revolutionary. Artists known mostly by name – Velázquez, Murillo, Ribera – came into full view; other masters of the stature of El Greco and Zurbarán were introduced to the French public for the first time. The enthusiasm aroused by Spanish art is communicated by an anonymous critic writing in the *Journal des Artistes* just before the Musée Espagnol went on public view:

It is truly something marvellous and unexpected, this sudden appearance of so many masterpieces that reveal an entirely new language that explains, no less well than the plays of Calderón and Lope de Vega, a neighbouring country we still hardly know.

The term 'entirely new language' encapsulates the profound importance of Spanish art for the French art world of the mid-nineteenth century. This was the moment when a small vanguard of painters and critics was starting to search for alternatives to the stagnating system of academic art, and the paintings of Spain offered them a different system of artistic values already sanctioned by history and genius. Thus, they became a beacon to the artists we now consider the first modernists.

The epitome of these painters is Edouard Manet, whose trip to Spain in 1865 brought him face to face with Velázquez's work, an experience that confirmed the rightness of his chosen path. As he wrote to a friend in Paris, 'The most astonishing piece of his splendid oeuvre, and perhaps the most astounding bit of painting ever done, is the picture listed in the catalogue as: *Portrait of a Famous Actor of the Reign of Philip IV* (*Pablo de Valladolid*). The background disappears: it is only air that surrounds the good man, all dressed in black, and alive.' Manet, who was already acquainted with Spanish painting then so abundant in Paris, translated Velázquez's jester portrait into his own idiom in the *Portrait of Philibert Rouvière as Hamlet*. However, no single work can adequately demonstrate Manet's debt to Spanish art, for he was canny enough to see the possibilities offered by its independent stance toward the

Renaissance conventions of picture-making that were finally proving inadequate to express the dynamic complexities of the industrial world. French art was about to break away from its centuries-long connection to Italy and form a new partnership with Spain. Out of this Franco-Spanish alliance would come the makers and masters of modern art.

A continuing tradition: Picasso and Miró

The pivotal role played by Pablo Ruiz Picasso (1881–1973) and Joan Miró (1893–1983) in the history of twentieth-century art is taken for granted. However, the Spanish elements in their artistic personalities are not so easily identified, although it must be admitted that the question has scarcely been examined. Indeed, the endeavour is fraught with every kind of peril, especially since both artists were profoundly affected by their experiences of French art (and of course Picasso never returned to Spain after the start of the Civil War). Yet, to someone versed in the history of Spanish painting from El Greco to Goya, the earlier works of these two modern masters follow a familiar pattern.

The similarities are not found in specific motifs appropriated from the old masters, although these do exist, but in the stance taken by these Spanish modernists toward the dominant artistic mode of the day, in this instance French painting. Like their great predecessors – El Greco, Velázquez and Goya – Picasso and Miró are simultaneously insiders and outsiders to the prevailing style.

Picasso, more than Miró, was thoroughly immersed in the traditional painting of Spain; he spent time in Madrid at various periods during his youth (1895, 1897, and again in 1901), when he became acquainted with the collections of the Prado (of which he served briefly as director during the Spanish Republic). In El Greco and Velázquez, Picasso could have seen perspectival space exposed for the artificial convention that it is, and the classical canons of figure drawing as merely one option for depicting the human body. Picasso, on whom no visual experience was ever wasted, ingested these non-normative elements of Spanish painting and used them to remake the art of painting. Recent studies of the *Demoiselles d'Avignon*, that thunderclap of a picture painted in 1907, have demonstrated specific links to a masterpiece of El Greco seen by Picasso in Paris, the *Apocalyptic Vision* (now in the Metropolitan Museum of Art, New York). Other influences were obviously at work on Picasso's imagination, but the *Demoiselles d'Avignon*, like *Las Meninas* and the *Burial of the Count of Orgaz*, is one of those great declarations of artistic imagination and independence which define the creative summits of Spanish art.

For Miró, the insider-outsider duality forms the core of *The Farm*, the key picture of his early period, executed partly in France, partly in Catalonia, in 1921–22. During his formative years in Barcelona, Miró had been profoundly affected by the idea of a Catalan nationalism espoused by certain cultural critics who defined the native spirit within a somewhat amorphous tradition of Mediterranean classicism. In *The Farm*, Miró places the pictorial strategies of Cubism at the service of this nostalgic Catalan idea. The farm is a *masia*, the characteristic complex of simple buildings that dot the rural landscape, which evokes the ordered life of the Catalan peasant, here filtered through the modernist optic of avant-garde French painting.

The Spanishness of Picasso and Miró will long be debated, but, one hopes, never denied. And it was they who at last delivered their native land from its honourable position on the margin of European art. For, to a greater or lesser extent, every painter of the twentieth century has been one of their disciples.

'All Spaniards are Catholics . . .'

Religious conformity, not a divisive issue in most other European countries until the Reformation, had long been a major Spanish concern because of the Jews and Muslims. Even today, when full liberty of belief is guaranteed, fewer than one in four hundred Spaniards belong to non-Catholic churches. If official Catholicism was strong, popular Catholicism was stronger. Devotion to local saints, membership of local confraternities, participation in local ceremonies, all were the main channels through which faith was made manifest and important elements in uniting society.

Notre Dame du Sublon was a miraculous image venerated in Brussels when it was part of the Spanish Netherlands (*left*). Here, richly dressed, crowned and hung with jewels, she is carried through the streets by barefoot friars. *Above*: a modern procession in South America, the Corpus Christi festival at Cuzco, Peru. Here too the image has been crowned and dressed in a special robe depicting the chalice and the consecrated host.

The suppression of dissent

Although there were periods, often prolonged, when Jews, Christians and Muslims lived peacefully together, and the practice of all religions was tolerated (the Muslims had a better record in this respect than the Christians), the clear tendency, as the Reconquest drew to its fulfilment, was towards forced conformity.

To convert the Jews, preferably by persuasion but when that failed by force, was a persistent expectation of the medieval rulers of Spain. Alfonso X's *Cantigas de Santa María* contains stories in which the miraculous intervention of the Virgin convinces even the Jews of the truth of Christianity and they end dutifully worshipping her image (*above left*).

When the Moors were finally conquered in 1492, they were promised that they should be allowed to go on practising their religion. Ferdinand and Isabella were confident that through vigorous preaching and proselytizing, they too could be converted. That did not happen, and after ten years the promise was broken. Muslims were given the choice of baptism or expulsion. A coloured relief (*left*) on the altar of the Chapel Royal at Granada shows the mass baptism of Moorish women.

Cardinal Jiménez de Cisneros was appointed Archbishop of Toledo in 1495. Highly devout and a patron of learning, he threw himself into the task of spiritual and ecclesiastical reform in Spain, and was a champion of religious conformity and of continuing war against Islam. This relief portrait (*right*) catches the austerity of his character; the Baroque frame features the cardinal's hat on the top, flanked by Franciscan cords.

Act of Faith

The rigid Catholicism of the Counter-Reformation was maintained at home, promulgated in the empire overseas and imposed forcibly upon the incipiently Protestant Netherlands. In Spain itself the instrument of conformity was the Inquisition, formed to crush first the lingering faiths of Judaism and Islam and then the more insidious heresies of dissident Christianity. Repentant heretics were made public examples; stubborn ones were handed over to the secular arm for execution.

The Plaza Mayor in Madrid, 1680. A great ceremony of penitence and punishment (*auto-da-fé*) is taking place. On a dais at the back sits the king, Charles II, the queen and the queen-mother. In the screened-off area in the centre we see episodes from the trial, with the figures of Dominican friars prominent and the accused dressed in red cloak and tall red hat. Massed spectators occupy the galleries of the square and specially built ramps of seats. In the central area the accused men are seen accompanied by priests, often being exhorted to repent by being shown the crucifix. The Inquisition itself went back to the thirteenth century, when it had been founded to crush the Albigensian heresy of Catharism. Pedro Berruguete's altarpiece (*detail below*) ostensibly illustrates an execution of that time, but it reflects the conditions of a later period. Berruguete, born about 1450, was strongly influenced by Netherlandish painting.

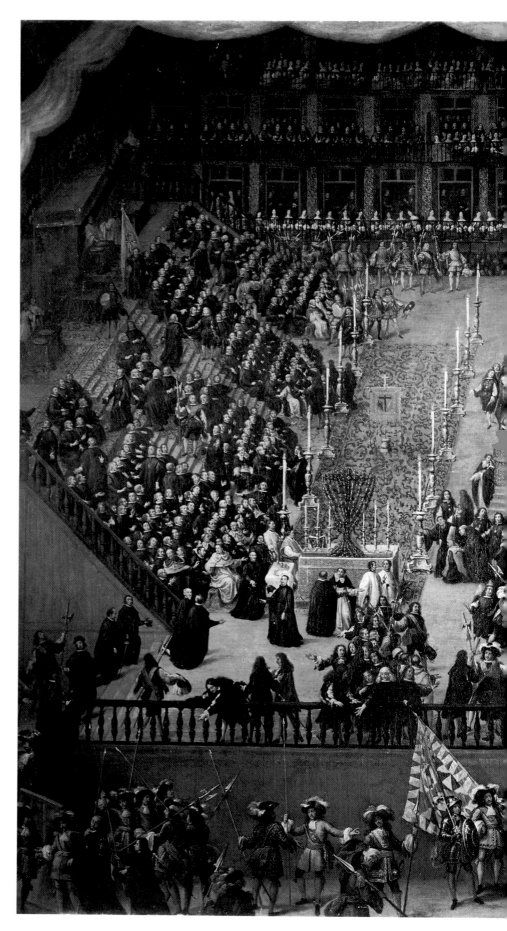

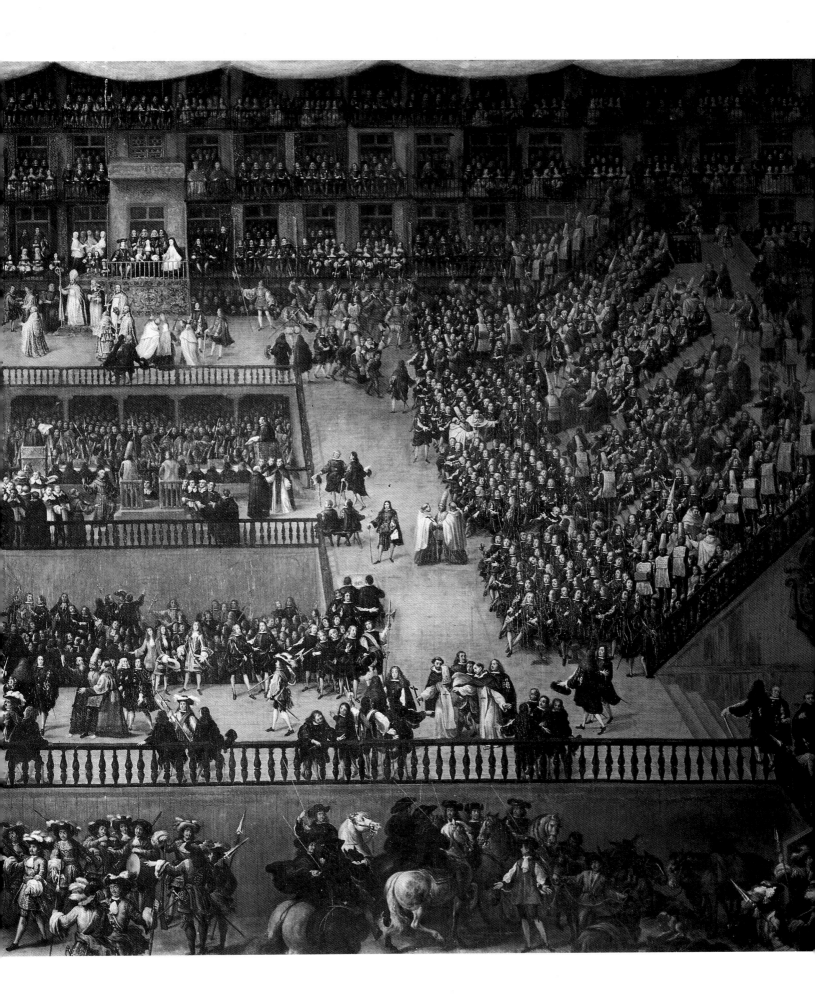

The genius of El Greco does not fit easily into the main-stream of Spanish, or indeed of European, painting, uniting Byzantine abstraction, Venetian colour and Spanish intensity. His *Burial of the Count of Orgaz* (*right*) is as complex theologically as artistically, a miraculous confirmation of the efficacy of good works. At the funeral of Gonzalo Ruiz de Toledo, Count of Orgaz (he had died two centuries earlier, in 1323), those present saw 'visibly and clearly, the glorious saints Stephen and Augustine descend from the heavens, their features and dress easily recognizable by everyone; going to where the body lay, they took it up and placed it in the tomb, saying: ''Such is the reward of him who has served God and His saints''.'

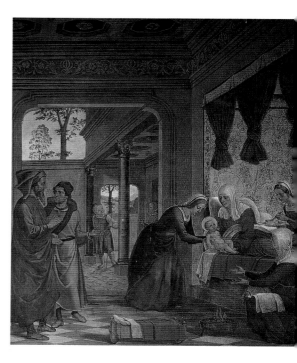

Art for the church

In medieval Spain the church had been virtually the only patron of the arts, and even in the sixteenth century painting and sculpture were predominantly religious. The Flemish style represented by Berruguete was soon supplemented by that of the Italian Renaissance.

For Toledo Cathedral Cardinal Cisneros initiated (1509–11) a new chapter room (*above*) reflecting the prestige of his diocese. The wooden ceiling was probably made by Moorish craftsmen. Along the base of the wall run two rows of portraits of bishops. Above them is a cycle of paintings of the story of the Passion which marks the first major eruption of Italian influence into Spanish art. The artist was Juan de Borgoña and he was clearly aware of the work of such painters as Pinturicchio in Italy. *Right*: two of the panels, the birth of John the Baptist and the Deposition.

The holiness of the everyday

Spanish artists of the Golden Age adopted two further types of painting from the Netherlands and Italy, but made them peculiarly their own: genre and still life. To both they brought a sense of reverence that has been called religious but is rather the result of the intense powers of concentration and abstraction with which the artist represents his subjects.

The still figure of the *Old Woman Cooking Eggs* by Velázquez has a dignity that would not be inappropriate in one of his aristocratic portraits or even in a Madonna. Something of the same contemplative air hangs over the still lifes of Luis Meléndez (*left*), where the subject has been reduced to a few mundane objects painted with the concentration of portraiture.

In his study of peasants carousing, *Los Borrachos*, Velázquez goes as far as possible down the social scale but avoids the mockery with which Dutch painters habitually treated their (or their patrons') inferiors. These are true devotees of Bacchus, worthy companions of the god of wine.

Juan Sánchez Cotán was the inventor of the classic Spanish still life (*right*). His models were the abundant, overflowing still lifes of Flanders and northern Italy. He reduced the clutter of these compositions to a few simple objects, arranged in imaginative groupings, and illuminated them with a strong, powerful light that makes them seem more real than life.

The Age of Goya

It is difficult not to see Spain's revolutionary years (1790–1825) through Goya's eyes. His art embraces all aspects of life and society. Beginning as a fashionable portrait painter, he came to see virtually all classes, the exploited as well as the privileged, as decadent and corrupt. His middle period is one of disillusioned realism, and at the end of his life his pessimism turned to unsparing visions of human conduct gone mad.

The Unequal Wedding (*below*), painted in 1791–92, is a light-hearted satire on a marriage of convenience.

Saturn, the horrifying image of the father of Jupiter eating his own children (*right*), comes from the end of Goya's career (1820–23), when he was over seventy. It was painted on the wall of his own house outside Madrid, known as the Quinta del Sordo, 'the house of the deaf man'.

In his royal portraits of King Charles IV and his Queen Maria Luisa (*below right*) Goya represents the royal couple with a brilliance that almost overwhelms them, human yet strangely vulnerable in their dignity.

The hidden genealogy of art

When Picasso's *Demoiselles d'Avignon* was first exhibited in 1907 it aroused shock and outrage by its novelty and apparent disregard for tradition. It is now clear that it had many roots, not the least vital of them being those in the soil of Spain.

El Greco in his *Apocalyptic Vision* (detail, *left*) was portraying the end of the world, when 'the souls of them that were slain for the word of God' should be raised and 'white robes given to every one of them'.

Picasso had no such mystical intention, but his enigmatic nudes have a fierce, concentrated energy that has a direct impact on the spectator. Picasso had seen El Greco's painting in Paris, and was impressed by its brilliant disregard for the major conventions of Renaissance painting – perspective, proportion and reverence for classical antiquity.

To Joan Miró, living in France in 1921–22, the typical peasant farm came to symbolize the enduring qualities of his native Catalonia. However, he views the simple farm buildings, animals and household objects through the avant-garde prism of Parisian cubism.

THE FAMILY AND SOCIETY

JAMES CASEY

Ties of family are sometimes seen as substitutes for alternative forms of political and economic organization, destined to wither as the state takes over the function of protecting the citizen and the market economy renders dowry and inheritance less significant as ways of acquiring wealth. The Hispanic world may suggest some variations on this model. Here was a society which showed a surprising ability from an early date to number, identify and control its citizens and their territory, from the great *Relaciones Topográficas* of Castile and the Indies (1575–85) to the uniquely detailed survey of the Marquis of Ensenada (1750). Such investigations were paralleled by those of the church into the life events of the people, their baptisms, marriages and deaths (especially, perhaps, in the seventeenth century, when the state was rather weaker). The diocesan archives of Spain particularly, with their thousands upon thousands of case histories of young men and women who left their parish of origin, are a testimony to a pioneering attempt at policing the citizen, which would later be taken over by the state in its own interest. If the voluntary use of notary and judge to regulate property and inheritance and, indeed, status, is added to this imposed surveillance, one has the impression of a much-governed society, attuned to the use of contract and professional adjudication in the regulation of its relations.

The problem for the historian of the family, then, is to discover what role was left for house and kin. Clearly, the abundance of official documentation presents a difficulty in its own right, given what the social anthropologist tells us about the evasion of law in the small-scale communities of modern Spain. It seems legitimate to infer that informal networks – kinship, godparenthood, ritual friendship – must have had a great role to play in the early modern period in linking these communities with a wider trading and political empire. Patronage is less an institution than a culture. It reflects ultimately, perhaps, certain patterns of education, of child-rearing, of 'piety' towards household and lineage. Foreign travellers commented upon the unusual features of the family as they observed it south of the Pyrenees – the seclusion of women, early marriage, the stress on honour (yet accompanied by an ease of relationships between the social classes). It is too easy to conclude, as Alexandre Dumas said, that 'Africa begins at the Pyrenees.' Cervantes and his contemporary Fray Diego Haedo, who had experience of life in Algiers, tell us that the role of women was quite different from one shore of the Mediterranean to the other. Rather than a borrowing from the Arabs, may not the family system of Spain ultimately have been conditioned by the long struggle against them – by the opportunities of a frontier society, prolonged into the Indies in the early modern period, which created a certain pattern of migration of men and inheritance by women? The very flexibility of the Spanish (or, at least, the Castilian and Valencian) system is, indeed, its most striking feature. For, by stressing lineage rather than the house, it permitted a great deal of geographic and social mobility, while, at the same time, maintaining those threads of dependence which held a great world empire together.

A mobile population

The impression of travellers in the early modern period that Spain was an underpopulated country tended to be shared by her statesmen. After all, the Reconquista had only really come to an end in 1609 to 1614 when large tracts of land in Valencia and Aragon were emptied of their Morisco inhabitants in a last great wave of persecution. The internal colonization of Andalusia, meanwhile, was proceeding apace in these years with the sale of common lands and the foundation of hamlets – a movement interrupted round the middle of the seventeenth century, then resumed with Charles III's colonies in the Sierra Morena (1767). Clearly the Spanish situation was not at all comparable to that in Eastern Europe at the time: there was relatively little good land available for settlement and even in Spanish America, despite the dramatic decline in the Indian population, there was remarkably little free land in the core areas of Mexico and Peru. Nevertheless, the filling up of empty spaces was a distinguishing feature of the Hispanic world not shared by other West European countries during the early modern period.

Spain's population reached a maximum of about $8\frac{1}{2}$ million towards 1600 (about half that of France, about twice that of the British Isles). After a slump of a quarter or so during the next century, it recovered to its old level by the middle of the eighteenth century or before, and then went on expanding to $15\frac{1}{2}$ million by the middle of the nineteenth century – a figure which the Spanish historian Jordi Nadal regards as its 'natural' level under an agrarian regime. The Spanish American population is somewhat harder to estimate – probably $2\frac{1}{2}$ million inhabitants around 1600, rising to somewhere between 12 and 20 million on the eve of independence in 1825. By the latter date some 60 per cent may have been Indian, 20 per cent of Spanish origin, and the rest mostly of mixed blood, together with a substantial black element. Already equivalent numerically to the mother country in terms of population, America was increasingly differentiated from it by the new social weighting of urbanized half-breeds.

Both in Spain and the Indies one has the impression of considerable opportunity for growth, combined with a certain sluggishness in meeting the challenge. Birth and death rates were both high. Women tended to marry young – Spanish women perhaps at 20 in the seventeenth century, rising to 22 to 23 in the later eighteenth century, Moriscos and Indians (though

The lineage pattern at two social levels. *Top*: middle-class Mexican father and son. *Below*: the Duke of Alburquerque with his son in front of a tapestry bearing the family's coat of arms.

there are very few studies of either) at about 18. Much depends, of course, on social class; aristocratic women regularly married in their teens, while peasant women in the Basque Country or Galicia – possibly because so many eligible men emigrated – waited until 24. But, in general, it seems fair to conclude that Spanish women tended to marry rather younger than their West European counterparts. One can invoke the greater opportunities of a frontier society (and some comparisons might be made here with seventeenth-century New England, where the age of brides was also quite low); but cultural tradition and the desire of the Catholic church to foster monogamy among its new converts probably counted as well.

One of the chief factors may simply have been a response to high mortality among the older generation. According to the census of 1787, only one Spaniard in seven was aged fifty or above, while an observer of 1871 in Navarre commented: 'Those who earn a living by the spade are already old at forty.' One in five children would not survive the first year of life, and only a little over half could expect to reach adulthood – even in 1901, when Spain had one of the worst rates in Europe. In Mexico, as in Spain, the death rate seems to have begun to come down tardily from about 1900 to 1920. To judge from the number of treatises devoted to it, diphtheria (*garrotillo*) was the great killer of infants; and Spain may have been specially prone to epidemic diseases like bubonic plague in the seventeenth century. But surely the most important single cause of death was the wasting battle with hunger.

It was the search for subsistence which threw large numbers of Spaniards onto the roads – some 25,000 or more leaving Galicia (with a population of about one million) every year in the eighteenth century to look for seasonal employment in the harvests of southern Spain, and sometimes never returning home. Diego de Torres Villarroel, mathematician and author of a classic autobiography (1743), tells us of the wanderings of his artisan forebears. His great-grandfather Francisco wandered penniless from Soria to Salamanca, where he was hired by a pharmacist, 'to take water from the well, wash pots, pound roots and sing lullabies now and again to a child of the family.' Francisco studied pharmacy, and set up shop for himself after his master's death, marrying the latter's widow, 'as was the done thing'. Francisco's son Jacinto left as a soldier for Flanders, where he learned tapestry, before returning home to Salamanca to set up shop at the age of thirty-four. Jacinto died young while his son Pedro was still at school; Pedro drifted into service in various parts of Spain, before settling down in Salamanca again as a bookseller. Finally, the author of our autobiography, Pedro's son, had to leave home (where there were eighteen children) in order to make his way in the world, acquiring an education in his employer's household. It is a

familiar pattern, which one can find nearer our own day in the autobiography of the great biologist Santiago Ramón y Cajal (1852–1934). Although the guilds of Spain and of the New World became increasingly restrictive during the seventeenth century, excluding those of mixed blood or non-Christian ancestry, there seems to have been none of the rigour of the German or Elizabethan settlement laws.

Leaving the land

If demography suggests that the Hispanic world was slowly 'filling up' in the early modern period, the lawyer will want to ask: 'But who controlled the resources?' The classic studies of Joaquín Costa (1846–1911) show the importance of communal landholding in Castile, which corresponded in part to the strength of transhumant pastoralism. An interesting feature of the early modern period is the continuing break-up of these commons, as characteristic of Andalusia as it is of the ranching frontier of north-west Mexico in the seventeenth century. The traditional communal landholding of the Indian villagers began to give way rather later (surviving longest in Peru) as Indians moved out to work for the ranchers, and half-breeds moved in. Certainly the rise of private property over this period must have subtly influenced family structure. As did the relative weakness of the manorial system in Spain. Where the lord controlled the land (as in much of Eastern Europe), it was often in his interest to keep the peasant farm intact as a unit of rent and labour. What is interesting in Spain is how quickly new allotments to colonists – even in areas of strong seigneurial jurisdiction like Valencia after 1609 – were split up among their children and bartered or sold.

The Castilian peasantry were required to subdivide their estates equally among all their children, both male and female. They could, however, dispose freely of one-fifth (usually for masses for their souls), and leave an advantage or *mejora* of one-third to a favoured child. Rather than a strict institution, the *mejora* was a flexible arrangement whereby a child looking after the parents would take more than his siblings. The practice of the society was essentially egalitarian – as it was in Valencia, where the law technically allowed a father to leave virtually everything to one child and disinherit the others with token legacies of five *sous* apiece. This enactment was modelled on the inheritance laws of the Crown of Aragon, of which Valencia was a part. Interestingly the Bourbons in the eighteenth century imposed the civil law of Castile on Valencia as part of their centralization programme, but not on Catalonia, where the inheritance customs were just too different.

Partible inheritance possibly survived longest in frontier areas where land was available. The limited testamentary freedom of the Castilian father to favour one child through the

mejora seems often to have been imposed by royal legislation from the thirteenth century as the Reconquista was completed, being finally codified in the Laws of Toro (1505), which became the basis of the modern law of property in Castile and Spanish America. In fact, subdivision among several heirs was not quite the threat to established fortunes that it seemed to Costa and others. As Lockhart and Schwartz have pointed out for the Indies, 'often the most powerful heir bought the others out, or all the heirs let the most capable or the oldest operate the unit as before in the interest of all'. In Andalusia it was quite common for richer peasants to establish pious trusts (*capellanías*), whose funds would be used to dower girls or educate boys of the lineage, thus ensuring that the family perpetuate its elite status within the community from one generation to the next.

Another resource was open to the successful: the adoption of the *mayorazgo* or perpetual entail. The Laws of Toro codified a growing practice here, allowing a testator, without special permission, to place the *mejora* (one-third plus one-fifth of his estate) in trust for just one of his descendants at each generation. The *mayorazgo* became a popular institution, at least down to the middle of the seventeenth century, spreading even among the ranchers of Mexico's northern frontier. It was bitterly criticized at the time for denying younger sons a fair share of the estate, and for encouraging a drift to rentier status among the elite. It had, indeed, some uniquely harsh features: it was perpetual unlike, for example, French or English entails which were limited to grandchildren or great-grandchildren, and it made no legal provision for younger children unlike, for example, the perpetual Italian entail. For such an important instrument, it has attracted comparatively little social (as distinct from legal) analysis.

Arranging marriage

The general rule of subdivision of inheritance made it necessary for children to marry well if they were to maintain status, for daughters shared equally with sons. Even where the estate was tied down by entail, parents made enormous sacrifices in order to give marriage portions to their female offspring. Laws of 1534, 1573 and 1623 attempted vainly to stop the upward spiral in dowries; and that of 1623 refurbished old enactments that a groom should not endow his bride with more than one-tenth of his property.

The problem of how to find marriage portions for daughters was a major headache. Don Luis de Requesens, on the eve of his departure for Flanders in 1573, made his will and noted that, if he had any more daughters, he would not be able to leave them 'anything of substance'. His executors were to 'try to persuade them to become nuns'; otherwise their future was bleak – a small annuity and refuge with some cousin, 'for out of the many

we have, I trust in the mercy of God that there will be some who will do us this favour.' But how many parents could afford even to place their daughters in convents? The Cortes of 1586–88 and those of 1615 protested that convent dowries were also too high. No doubt the solution was to place some girls as lay sisters. In the enormous nunnery of La Concepción in Lima, with over one thousand inmates at its peak around 1700, there was only a small minority of fully endowed sisters 'of the black veil'. These lived comfortably in huge cells of their own, with patios and gardens attached, educating 162 young boarders or *educandas*, who were sometimes their relations. They supervised the second-class nuns 'of the white veil', who acted as housekeepers, and the unendowed lay sisters, often *mestizas*, together with a regiment of maids and slaves. Since nuns tended to live in the towns where they were born, their interaction with their families continued to be intense. Unfortunately we still know surprisingly little about how their lives were actually organized within their convents.

Not all girls could afford, or would wish to become nuns – there was a big drop in numbers in the eighteenth century, though part of this may have been due to a reduction in the size of aristocratic families at the time. Their options in the marriage market were limited. The Portuguese essayist Francisco Manuel de Mello, in his *Carta de Guia de Casados* of 1651, suggested that they might have to marry a little below their own class if they were not given an adequate endowment. His essay is interesting because it is one of the few in the Iberian world penned by a layman in a field dominated by ecclesiastics. It therefore pays more attention than usual to crassly material problems like dowry. Mello's solution, that the girl marry slightly beneath her, seems to echo another practice among middle-class townsmen: the daughter became, in effect, her father's heir, while her brothers travelled abroad and she married an immigrant of good family but little fortune. One finds the type among the silk merchants of Valencia described in Blasco Ibáñez's great novel, *Arroz y Tartana*, in the autobiography of Diego de Torres Villarroel (1743) and in the diary of the Cadiz merchant Raimundo de Lantery at the end of the seventeenth century. But the system has been best analysed for the merchants of Buenos Aires at the end of the eighteenth century. The merchants there tended to place their sons in the army, the law or the church. One of the daughters would marry an immigrant from Spain, with a smallish dowry, and he would be brought into her father's firm as an associate, taking over the business in due course.

One major problem was that of ensuring that the migrant was a man of character and background. Marriage negotiations could be extremely lengthy and complicated, and intermediaries had an enormous burden of trust placed upon their shoulders in checking the wealth or origin of prospective partners. In many cases this caution would lead to marriage with cousins. It was rare enough to seek out a partner who belonged to the same lineage, even among the aristocracy; though when an ancient patrimony or title passed to an heiress, she appears to have looked to marriage with a cousin in the male line. What tended to happen more often was intermarriage within a group of families over several generations, exploiting and consolidating the trust between them (the links between Olivares and the Zúñiga and Velasco families seem an example of this). The label 'cousin marriages' can mask a multiplicity of strategies of qualitatively different kinds. In *Los Pazos de Ulloa* (1886), Emilia Pardo Bazán has left an unforgettable portrait of the proud hidalgo of Santiago de Compostela, Don Manuel de la Lage, who had no money to dower his four daughters but could not contemplate the alternative of marrying them down to some local bureaucrat. He seized the chance of a visit from his nephew and fostered an attachment between him and one of the girls – no difficult task since his daughters' sheltered lives made them peculiarly susceptible to the young man's charm.

Technically such marriages were forbidden by the Catholic church, whose 'Prohibited Degrees' of incest extended before 1917 to the descendants of great-great-grandparents. Spanish ecclesiastical writers of the period repeated the ancient canonical principle that marriage was a way of extending fraternity within a commonwealth and should not be used to consolidate the exclusivist tie of consanguinity. But the diocesan archives are full of concessions – an enormous documentary record which still awaits its historian. Though the Papacy had to authorize each dispensation in peninsular Spain (delegating such authority to the bishops in the Indies), the bulk of the investigation was everywhere conducted at diocesan level. At a time when the government became concerned to limit the fees payable to Rome, it conducted nation-wide investigations into the working of the system. In 1762 it was calculated that ten or eleven thousand dispensations were negotiated every year for Spain. One may estimate, given a population of about 10 million at the time, that this represented one marriage in every ten.

The classes chiefly affected seem to have been aristocrats at one end and peasants at the other. Aristocrats were generally granted dispensation on the grounds which would have been used by Don Manuel de la Lage, that their daughters were too poor to find a partner of their own social status, except for a kinsman who, through piety, would take them unendowed. For the peasants a reason sometimes adduced was that the groom had 'dishonoured' the girl by too frequent visits to her house – grounds for a dispensation, certainly, though attracting a penance of a pilgrimage in person to Rome or several months

sweeping out the church. In fact, these ritual pretexts seem to have concealed other motives. Spanish bishops were extremely informative about what they saw as the real reasons in reports to the government between 1778 and 1813: the tendency of each village to be a little world of its own, given the poor state of communications, traditional intercommunal rivalries, and the occupational specialisms of each community which made it difficult for outsiders to fit in. Some of the strategic arrangements about property might not actually necessitate a dispensation – for example, where a brother and sister married a sister and brother of another household, thus cancelling the transfer of dowries. Much remains to be studied in this domain. No doubt the importance of dowry and female inheritance, combined with male mobility, kept alive interest in family background. Property on one side had to be balanced by 'respectability' on the other.

Pride in ancestry

The popularity of genealogies was a significant feature of early modern Spain. Don Joseph Pérez de Orozco, silk merchant of Granada, kept two velvet-lined books, trimmed with gold braid, recounting his maternal and paternal descent, with reproductions of coats of arms, copies of marriage and baptism certificates, and other documents. All were prefaced by a few general comments in his own hand on the exemplary record of honest dealing therein contained which should spur his own children to live well. He possessed another book, published a century before, relating the genealogy of the Orozco counts of Miranda to whom he claimed to be remotely connected. All three books were submitted in 1770 as proof of his nobility and his right to sit as town-councillor of Granada.

The presentation of the self is one of the most fascinating features of any civilization. In Italy and France there began to appear at this time journals recounting the life of the household, the birth and death of its members, which were often inserted in the account books of merchants in whose milieu the genre first developed. This was complemented in seventeenth-century England by the growth of the Puritan diary, a kind of inner accounting with the self. Both kinds of record are somewhat rare in the Hispanic world, or rather – as with the religious autobiography – take non-secular forms. The autobiographies of laymen tend often to be a 'narration of deeds' – *Libre de Feyts*, to quote the title of one of the earliest and most famous, that of the thirteenth-century King James I of Aragon. They were meant to illustrate the providence of God and to serve as a moral exemplar for descendants rather than to explore the mind of the author. Sometimes they aimed merely to tell a good story, and the 'lives' of the soldiers and adventurers of the Golden Age are hard to distinguish from the picaresque novels

of the time. Rather than the self or the household, it was the lineage which seems to have captured the imagination of Spaniards.

Although building and entailing a fine home was one of the features of the creation of a *mayorazgo*, the rules of succession led to much amalgamation, absenteeism and neglect. *Mayorazgo* houses tended to accumulate and, rather than being bartered or sold in the interests of consolidation, they would be temporarily allocated to different members of the lineage. The dukes of Alcalá kept about four big houses in various parts of Seville, where they placed cousins and dowager duchesses. Much more work needs to be done on vernacular architecture in Spain, but some foreign travellers, like Barthélemy Joly (1603), were inclined to criticize the construction of houses for being cramped. Physical subdivision of the building – even among some patricians – seems to have been not uncommon; adobe walls would be run up on the inside, and torn down again if necessary, in order to cater to the needs of the wider family. The 'plasticity' of the Castilian house was, indeed, a noteworthy feature of its design.

The mobility of the physical setting was accompanied by a certain lack of the kind of moral tradition that characterized the Catalan-Aragonese household. At the death of parents the building might be split up or sold off, and its possessions auctioned in order to ensure a fair division of the assets among the heirs. Gonzalo de Amezúa speculated that the absence of family portraits, noticeable even among the elite, may be due to this kind of pressure. We know that Castilians liked to commemorate family events – Pantoja de la Cruz recorded in his will of 1599 the picture of the daughter of Don Cristóbal de Moura, 'dressed in white, which I painted when her marriage was arranged.' But few portraits of husband and wife, or parents and children (of the kind becoming fashionable in northern Europe at the time) have survived. Whether they ever existed is doubtful; inventories of Granadan patricians list landscapes and devotional pictures, but few portraits even of individual family members.

Family correspondence certainly did exist, but was equally a victim of the mobility of the Castilian household. Don Luis de Requesens, in his will of 1573, resolved to group his scattered records in one residence, but asked for only certain kinds of letter to be kept – those from the king and his ministers, and those from his wife and mother. The valuable caches of letters which have been found are mainly in court archives, where they were deposited as a form of identification.

If the household was transient, it was the tomb and the burial chapel which took over the role of providing a physical identity for the family. As the charter granting a chapel to the Quesadas in the cathedral of Jaén noted in 1412: 'The things of this world

The enduring vestiges of ancient nobility in Spain are family mausolea. In the late Gothic period these tombs reached a climax of artistry and extravagance, with richly displayed heraldic decoration. *Above left and above*: the Chapel of the Marquis of Los Vélez, Murcia Cathedral, and the Chapel of the Constable at Burgos. *Left*: tombs of Alvaro de Luna and his wife, Juana de Pimentel, in the Chapel of St James in Toledo Cathedral and (*far left*) the tomb in Sigüenza Cathedral of Martín Vázquez de Arce, a young knight who died in 1486 fighting the Moors in Granada.

are passing, but these tombs remain for ever as a memento of the founders.' Not all were as splendid as the famous chapel of the marquis of Los Vélez in the cathedral of Murcia. Many disappeared in the reorganization of church interiors in the later eighteenth century, while more perished with the suppression of the convents by the liberals after 1837. The *Viage de España* of Antonio Ponz (1771–91) is probably the best guide to what they must have looked like. They seem to have been founded mainly in the fifteenth and sixteenth centuries, and were adorned with funerary sculptures which seem often to have depicted the founder and his wife, and, more rarely, their children. The best examples of such sculpture occur in Old Castile, then the centre of Spanish wealth and power. In Andalusia they seem less frequent, being replaced by the family coat of arms. But firm conclusions are hazardous in a domain which has barely begun to be explored. Certainly Ponz noted a decline in funerary architecture from the later seventeenth century. This may have owed something to the dislike of the Counter-Reformation church for lay pomp within the sacred precincts.

Nevertheless, remembering the dead of the lineage continued to be important, not only because of the possibility of claiming a perpetual entail which had become vacant, but also for obtaining access to those numerous benevolent trusts, the *capellanías*. In Cadiz between 1772 and 1779 some seventeen girls, many married to 'poor wage-labourers', claimed that they were related to a certain Captain Fernando de la Barrera who had set up a dowry fund for girls of his lineage in 1656.

A genealogy was also essential for the coveted post of familiar (lay associate) of the Holy Office in order to establish the Old Christian ancestry required by the statutes of 'Purity of Blood'. In their defence, Bartolome Ximénez Patón, chronicler of Jaén, stressed that, though hard on individual Jews who might be good Christians, they served an important social function: they 'buttressed' religious orthodoxy with the strong support of honour, family pride and tradition (1638).

A similar debate engaged those concerned with the definition of 'nobility'. There was basic agreement that a man was first and foremost the child of his own works, but these might be fostered and set off by good family background. For the Granadan silk-merchant Pérez de Orozco the study of his ancestors was a means of encouraging a 'sense of honour', in the fullest sense, among his own children. Although Spain was a frontier society, with great possibilities of geographic and social mobility, it remained fascinated by genealogy as a guide to character – a way of 'situating' an immigrant. As one old priest in early seventeenth-century Granada put it, recalling his childhood: 'In those days . . . there was talk about everyone's background, for the disturbances and upheavals in this king-

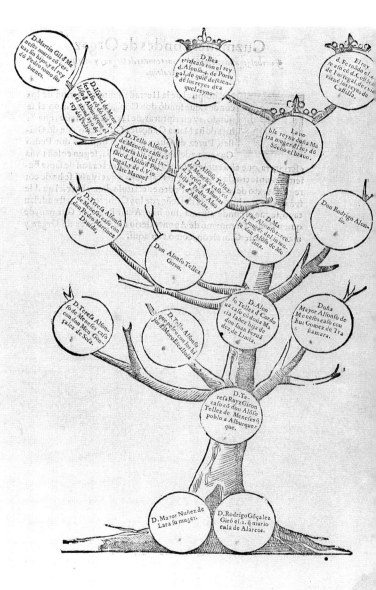

Large families have been traditional in Spain, partly as a means of compensating for high infant mortality, and the inheritance laws, which varied from province to province, often led to the division of estates and complicated disputes over property. Juan Bautista del Mazo (*above*) painted his own family in the mid-seventeenth century, when he and his wife had six children. This is meagre compared to the fairly typical family (*right*) photographed at Puerto Llano in 1910, where the grandmother can count seventeen children and grandchildren. *Left*: part of the family tree of the Girón family, who married into the royal line, from a book printed in 1577.

dom were still recent, and there were so many Moors.' Even in the early nineteenth century, the radical politician Antonio Alcalá Galiano (born in 1789) devoted the first part of his memoirs to tracing his noble ancestry, so that (as he tells us) people should not think he was an adventurer created by the troubled times.

The concept of 'caste' underwent an interesting mutation in the Indies, where it became bound up with notions of race rather than religion or nobility. In spite of the proliferation of terms in the seventeenth century to describe people of mixed race, the basic criterion of social status in the Indies seems to have been 'utilitarian'. Pure Indians enjoyed the same civil rights, in principle, as Spaniards, according to the decree of 1697 – probably because their strong family and community structures were a guarantee of their 'honour'. But those of mixed blood, particularly urban drifters, were discriminated against as untrustworthy – unless they were able to acquire 'letters of grace', deeming them 'white' (that is 'reliable').

A basic problem in both Spain and the Indies was the unreliability of genealogies. Family trees were never, as it were, pruned. Instead, the memorialists meandered through a maze of overlapping branches. The sheer complexity of these documents (which makes them such a fascinating 'who's who' guide to a local community) must be due, in part, to the perpetual nature of petty entails, which made it desirable to retain a record of distant connections on all sides of the family. As Bernabé Moreno de Vargas commented in his treatise on the seventeenth-century nobility: 'I have seen more quarterings in a family coat of arms than kingdoms in a map of the world.' Some 10 per cent of the population had latent claims to petty nobility – like Martín de Ayala, archbishop of Valencia, who died in 1566, the son of a sawyer from Jaén, who tells us in his memoirs that his family had lost the papers proving its nobility. What had been lost – or never owned – was sometimes invented. When asking for the documents establishing his noble ancestry to be burnt, one childless Sevillian commented in his will (1774): 'They would not be the first certificates to be bought and sold by individuals who go off to America, from where their descendants turn up again in Europe alleging connections and rights to which they have no claim.' It was before the chancery courts that such claims were contested and authenticated – leaving an enormous fund of documentation on social mobility and family structure in the early modern period, which is only now beginning to be explored.

The web of kinship

Awareness of family connections may have been a factor in knitting together the scattered parts of a far-flung empire. Where members of the clan had distinguished themselves, they were more likely, of course, to be kept in mind. The Cuevas were one of those rambling Spanish clans which, from an original base in Ubeda, had fanned out over the kingdoms of Granada, Jaén and Extremadura. Although the wealthiest branch of the clan was that of the dukes of Albuquerque, and although they descended only in the female line, they were regularly enrolled as part of the clan by the 'senior kinsmen' (*parientes mayores*) of Ubeda; while in 1662 the Granadan branch organized a poetry tournament to commemorate the return of Albuquerque that year from his Mexican viceroyalty. These remote connections could serve the purposes of patronage. Also in 1662, a minor gentleman of Granada, Don Fernando de Teruel, got his 'uncle', the Marquis of Santa Cruz, to testify to his noble ancestry. The marquis was, in fact, only a second cousin of the boy's maternal grandfather, related through a series of marriages 'downwards' by female cousins of the Santa Cruz into the petty gentry and professional class of Granada.

The fact that lineage could sometimes be used as a source of patronage does not mean that it compelled its members to reciprocate. Quarrels over entails and over headship of the clan drove a wedge between the branches of Guzmán and between the branches of Fernández de Córdoba for much of the sixteenth and seventeenth centuries. In these two cases the name conferred a dignity of which its members were proud, but it was a poor guide to political alliances. Much remains to be studied about the building up of factions in this period, and their connections with family networks. Nor is the way in which these networks influenced the decisions of a bureaucracy trained to operate with professional impartiality sufficiently explored. The correspondence of Lope de Vega's patron, the Duke of Sessa, with ministers and judges suggests some of the tension between 'professionalism' and 'friendship'.

In the business world of the early modern period, family played a crucial role in building networks of credit and confidence. One of the best-studied of the Spanish mercantile houses, that of the Espinosa, regularly employed nephews and cousins in the sixteenth century, in a chain of contacts linking Medina de Ríoseco and Madrid with Seville and the Indies. Large numbers of children, marriage into petty seigneurial and lawyers' families, and service with the aristocracy or crown created a formidable network of information and influence. One of the clan, García Ortiz de Espinosa, was appointed by the municipality of Lima as its envoy to the chief minister Cardinal Espinosa 'because of his merits and because he is a kinsman of Your Lordship and of his house' – though the cardinal is not known to have been related to these Espinosas at all.

The tendency of the family to annex useful outsiders no doubt underlies the institution of *compadrazgo*, the ritual tie between

a child's godfather and parents, which came to assume great importance in Latin America particularly. In spite of the horrendous infant mortality, the baptism of a child was an occasion for great celebration, and the choice of godparents a solemn decision for most parents. Raimundo de Lantery, merchant of Cadiz, recorded 'the many pangs in my heart and that of his mother' when they decided to delay the baptism of their second son in 1675 because the chosen godfather was away in the Indies. It would be interesting to know more about the kinds of men and women selected for this honour. In Spain itself, especially among the aristocracy, they seem to have been chosen from among members of the family, thus consolidating existing ties. In the Indies they were more often outsiders – testimony, perhaps, to the greater mobility of the New World.

The *compadrazgo* was not the only way of acquiring allies. As the *Siete Partidas*, the great thirteenth-century lawbook, puts it, 'To rear him from childhood is among the greatest benefits one man can bestow on another.' Such a person was thenceforth bound by ties of devotion, 'whether he is a son or a stranger'. The foster-child (*criado*) has become, by an interesting transferral of meaning, the Spanish term for servant. This is, perhaps, hardly surprising, given that many 'servants' in the big houses of the Golden Age were children – sometimes orphans, sometimes the illegitimate offspring of the master of the house, sometimes the sons or daughters of his poorer neighbours for whom he would find a position. When the third Duke of Alcalá embarked for his Roman embassy in 1625 he took with him a household of 150 people, including 32 pages from among the lesser noble families of his native Seville. Such households also seem fairly typical of government officials in the Indies at this time.

But the household itself was less significant than the multiple ties which linked it to the surrounding community, as *criados* grew up, married and set up their own families. One of the interesting features of Spanish towns or villages is the presence of members of a wider family at several different social levels, creating useful openings for patronage. In later eighteenth-century Granada, for example, one of the notaries – José Fernández de Córdoba y Zayas – was the great-great-grandson of the first Marquis of Valenzuela in the illegitimate line and thus related to one of the two or three big aristocratic landlords of the area. Such networks honeycombed a town like Granada and made difficult the formation of a self-conscious middle-class identity among the professional or even mercantile groups. The career of the Pizarro brothers, conquerors of Peru, illustrates the possibility of collaboration among step-siblings who were raised in different households – some by their father, a petty aristocrat of Trujillo, and some by their mothers, his lower-class ex-mistresses.

Affairs of honour

Lineage was very important for status, but the conduct of womenfolk was scarcely less so – in spite of the impression to the contrary produced by the Pizarros. For moralists of Renaissance Spain, learning how to dominate the sexual urge was a step necessary for becoming fully human. As the court preacher Martín de Cordoba told the seventeen-year-old Princess Isabella in 1468: 'We despise those who follow the promptings of the flesh, for it is a sign that . . . they do not use reason as men should, but give way to passion like the beasts.' Women had to be particularly vigilant, he thought, since they had fewer distractions than men; but their sense of modesty or shame was more highly developed than that of men.

The literature on the family in early modern Spain was dominated by ecclesiastics. Their contributions took so many different forms that it is hard to reduce them to a few categories. At one extreme there were the texts of the canon lawyers, concerned with laying out guidelines for marriage litigation, and sometimes giving the feeling of a certain 'remoteness' from real life. Then there were the books of moral advice, more accessible to the lay reader. Though written by a celibate clergy, these could be knowledgeable about married life, since they often grew out of confessors' manuals. The family seemed to interest confessors more as a special topic in the seventeenth and eighteenth centuries than it had done before. A few of these texts became classics – for example, *The Ten Books of Marriage Controversies* by the Cordoban Jesuit Tomás Sánchez (1592). Although Sánchez's book achieved swift recognition in the Catholic world, its cautious legalism and the fact that it was written in Latin made it more suited to confessors than to laymen. His concern with sexual relationships, shocking to some, seems to have been aimed more at establishing guidelines for penance than offering moral counsel and was perhaps not typical of Spanish books of guidance on the family. These examined the family as a set of social roles, and emphasized that marriage was primarily a spiritual rather than a sexual partnership; because it is a sacrament, conferring grace on the participants, it must be entered into freely.

In all this – their emphasis on free consent and their relative lack of concern with property or kinship – the theologians must have seemed remote from the real preoccupations of laymen. There was, indeed, major controversy in sixteenth-century Europe over control of marriage, with the Protestant Reformers rejecting the interference of church courts between parents and children. The Council of Trent would accept an amendment to tradition only to the extent that parents should be informed of what their children intended through the publication of banns on three successive holidays, and that a priest and two others should witness the ceremony. But on the point that a boy of

fourteen and a girl of twelve could make their own life-long commitment to each other, free of parental interference, it would not budge. As a result, situations reminiscent of *Romeo and Juliet* became rather characteristic of early modern Spain. The Cortes of 1579–82, followed by those of 1586–88 and those of 1588–90, drew attention to the fact that parents need not even know what their children were planning, since the latter could contract clandestine betrothals which were almost as binding as a marriage. Although Philip II promised to 'write with great insistence' to the pope, nothing was achieved. Denouncing the system, Joaquín Amorós in 1777 alleged that a youth who wanted to marry a girl against her parents' wishes had only to appeal to the bishop's court: 'Generally the parents would not dare place the slightest obstacle to the almost forcible removal of their daughter.' Equally any girl could allege that her suitor had made a clandestine betrothal with her; with only 'a summary hearing of witnesses (mostly of doubtful character)', a boy of good family could be gaoled until he agreed to marry her. The institution, in spite of its abolition by laws of 1776–1803, was partially continued in the practice of elopement in nineteenth-century Cuba.

A variety of reasons for the church's stance can be identified. In defending its right to come between parents and their children, the eighteenth-century Jesuit Matías Sánchez suggested that the former sometimes adopted the wrong course of action 'through passion'. Underlying much theological discussion was the danger that a child would be forced into an arranged marriage when the salvation of its soul might be better served by entry into the religious life. But the Spanish theologians were generally moderate men, and emphasized the obligation of 'piety' – setting the wider family interest above the satisfaction of individual desire. As well as piety, however, there was 'charity', by which the theologians meant basically 'fraternity', or good fellowship within the community. Charity required the avoidance of bitterness and feuds, which could be caused by a dishonourable marriage – but also by the unreasonable rejection of a suitor, or by the compromising of a girl's reputation. The diocesan courts of Spain seem to have been guided more by social need than by the letter of canon law in their handling of marriage litigation, though their voluminous records are only now beginning to be explored. The role of the civil courts needs to be investigated too; but it would appear that it was extremely rare in practice – and virtually impossible under Castilian law – for a Spanish father to disinherit a daughter who insisted on using the church courts to defy his plans for her future.

The seventeenth century French traveller, Madame d'Aulnoy, remarked that the risk of elopement made the seclusion of girls all the more necessary in Spain. Camos noted in 1592 the custom of women in Castile and Valencia (but not, apparently, in Catalonia) of going about the street 'with their face covered, showing only one eye'; while the novelist Alarcón has left a grimly humorous description of the 'sequestration' at home of the respectable women of small-town Granada in the early nineteenth century. The houses of Seville or Cadiz in the seventeenth century, like those of Lima, seem often to have lacked windows onto the street – though there seems to have been a considerable remodelling, with more use of balconies, from then on. Within the house the *estrado* (dais), with its cushions, seemed to mark off an exclusively female space, until the spread of the chair broke down the barrier in the eighteenth century.

In all this literature of popular customs, the historian has to pick his way cautiously. He should distinguish, in the first place, between the roles of women in different areas of the peninsula. From at least the early eighteenth century we have descriptions of the *veladas* or 'conversations' in rural Aragon, 'in the long nights of winter', which brought together peasants of both sexes to spin and talk, pay court and make merry. The setting was the big kitchen which characterized these mountain homes. In the south of Spain, where the kitchen was a less prominent feature of the house and where women worked less in the fields, sociability took different forms. Pilgrimages (*romerías*) to shrines of the local patron saint, a day's walk or ride from the village, were an imaginative way of breaking the rigid code which governed sexual relationships in the village or town itself (as dismayed moralists began to point out in the early modern period). And there were the nightly meetings between boy and girl, at the half-opened door just before curfew or at a balcony or window, which came to typify the romantic notion of Andalusia. But perhaps the Romantics did not have to invent – one seventeenth-century betrothal suit from Granada refers to a serenade with guitar.

Much information on marriage customs comes from these suits. What strikes the reader initially is the language of love used in the seventeenth century – the refusal to give up the suitor ('first the sun will have to fail'), the defiance of parents ('they will have to break me into a thousand pieces first'). One wonders where the popular classes – for most of the litigation concerns them (but artisans rather than peasants) – got their ideas from. Were they influenced by the theatre, increasingly popular from the middle of the sixteenth century? In middle-class circles, however, open discussion of affairs of the heart did not become fashionable until the birth of the periodical press in the 1760s. The language of love is a convention, of course, which need not have much connection with reality – as in *The House of Bernarda Alba* (published in 1940), where the old matriarch is prepared to countenance the nightly trysts of

Children of the nobility, and especially royal children, were treated as adults from an early age, moving, in the words of the sixteenth-century novelist Mateo Alemán, 'straight from the cradle to the horse'. This was almost literally true in the case of the young Don Baltasar Carlos, painted here by Velázquez as a military leader in miniature.

the suitor with the daughter whom she has arranged for him to marry. The tragedy arises when his affections slip to another daughter who did not figure in the mother's plans.

What seems clear from the marriage customs of Castile and the Indies is that there could be much confusion over what constituted an undesirable match. Race, wealth, family background all had to be taken into account. Given that men tended to migrate and women to inherit property, the 'purity of blood' of the one would have to match the wealth of the other – a delicate adjustment which might generate controversy. The courts of the church might serve to cut the Gordian knot. Antonio Alcalá Galiano tells us in his memoirs how his aristocratic mother, short of money, had to allow her daughter to marry into trade, but, in order to save face, insisted that the church court should order the marriage (around 1800). Equally it seems rare for these courts to enforce a real mésalliance. The aristocracy had its mistresses, but, at most, these would have recourse to the civil courts in order to obtain a dowry with which to marry someone of their own station. The third Duke of Alcalá's career illustrates the problem. Born in 1583, he was married off at the age of fifteen to Don Cristóbal de Moura's daughter (this must have been the occasion of the Pantoja de la Cruz portrait mentioned above). He had several liaisons in his young married life, one with one of his ladies-in-waiting, Leonor Manrique de Lara, by whom he had seven children. After he abandoned her, she took him to court, demanding a large dowry to cover her shame. Alcalá defended his conduct. He had been ready to place her in a convent nor had he caused her shame, even though she was of gentle birth: 'Rather, while I was having a relationship with her, her mother and brothers and her other kinsmen paid court to her as though she were their lady and the head of their lineage.' One of the children of this liaison, Pelayo de Ribera, went on to become archbishop, and then viceroy of Mexico (1673). The numbers and high standing of illegitimate children, at least of the aristocracy, is an interesting feature of Spanish society down to the later seventeenth century.

Demographic historians are beginning to make us aware of the significance of bastardy in this period. In the urban areas – Granada, Seville, Madrid – between 5 and 10 per cent of births may have been illegitimate. The exact figure is hard to establish because of the number of foundlings, not all of whom were necessarily born either in the town where they were found or to unmarried parents. In the countryside bastardy seems to have been more tolerated in the north of the peninsula (Galicia, Asturias) than in the south, where the rates may have been one per cent of births or less. In the Indies the Spaniards of the first generation produced many illegitimate children by the native women with whom they cohabited; but their half-breed descendants seem to have contracted church marriages, as did the Spaniards themselves in the seventeenth century, given the greater availability of women of their own race.

One of the problems in this field is that of understanding what the people of the time recognized as a true marriage. The Jesuit missionary to the barely Christianized peasantry of Andalusia in the 1580s, Pedro de León, recalled finding couples 'betrothed for two, three or more years, waiting for one harvest, then another, in order to get married, burdened, meanwhile, with children and living in mortal sin.' This practice of cohabitation after the betrothal was something that Counter-Reformation synods did their best to stamp out. But the betrothal was deemed a binding contract by the church courts. And in form it differed only slightly from the marriage itself, which was a simple exchange of words, sometimes in the bride's own house (but after 1563 with a priest in attendance). The formal ceremony in church with the nuptial blessing – the *velación*, or 'placing of the veil' over the head of the bride and shoulder of the groom (modifying slightly the custom of ancient Rome) – was not technically necessary. No blessing was given to widows or widowers remarrying, and no veiling could be conducted in the penitential seasons of Lent or Advent, when the public festivities which accompanied the church ceremony were deemed inappropriate. The *velación* was, in fact, an announcement to the community that the couple were ready to set up their own house; it usually accompanied the effective transfer of the dowry, and it might be delayed for months or years after the actual marriage. The confusion which this caused about who was or was not legitimately married seems to have been one of the reasons for the campaign of seventeenth-century synods to have the church ceremony follow the marriage as quickly as possible.

During this period the church mounted an energetic campaign to control the matrimonial customs of its flock. From the 1580s the diocesan archives of Spain began to keep full records on those marrying outside their parish of origin; and parish records of marriages, births and the taking of annual communion permitted the building-up, by the later seventeenth century, of a fairly precocious system of identification and control of the citizen. Repression of 'public sins' was certainly called for by the Council of Trent, and the synods and councils which tried to enforce the recommendations in Spain expected the parish priest to act as a policeman, checking on vagrants, visiting inns, denouncing concubines. That he actually did so seems doubtful. The canons of the cathedral of Granada pointed out in 1565 that accusations of adultery would cause more scandal than moral reformation. The dreaded Inquisition, though quick to pounce on bigamy and talk of fornication, did not concern itself with concubinage as such.

Generally it was the *alcalde*, the local secular judge, who would punish prostitutes and concubines, but probably only if there was a disturbance, or if he needed to conscript young men for the army. The diocesan courts – so concerned with moral reformation in early Stuart England – seem to have acted in Spain only if called upon by the parties: to enforce a betrothal contract, or to take a daughter from her father's control so that she could marry the suitor of her choice.

The quest for discipline

In 1777 the essayist Joaquín Amorós drew attention to a defect of the moral control exercised by the church courts: the way in which it undermined the authority of parents, when human beings, more than other creatures, needed long years of education in order to achieve maturity. Although Spanish writers were aware of the 'ages of man' in the classical sense, they were perhaps slower to see the importance of psychological development. In the eyes of canon and criminal law, full responsibility for one's actions came around puberty, or perhaps a little later. For the rest, concepts of 'childhood', 'youth' or 'maturity' corresponded more to a gradual emancipation from the authority of mother, father or master. Many aristocrats, like the duke of Alcalá, moved from the classroom to the headship of a household while still in their teens.

The household itself lacked the autonomy which it came to have in more modern times. Patrons were a powerful rival to parental authority – as Lope de Vega found out when he reluctantly agreed to forgive his errant son at the suit of the Duke of Sessa. The proliferation of step-children and foster-children must have further complicated the pattern of control. Although nuclear families predominated in the censuses of the old regime, one has to remember that because of remarriage – and the presence of illegitimate children or slaves among the servant-body – lines of authority were not as clear-cut as at the present day. Affection between spouses and between parents and their children is not in question; we have too many moving tributes in diaries, autobiographies and testaments for that. But, with the man's domain being essentially the street and the public square, his role as 'companion' of his wife and children was perhaps diminished.

Children tended to learn the social norms from their peers, outside the home – indeed, until quite recently, as the autobiographies of the biologist Santiago Ramón y Cajal and of his fellow Aragonese Ramón Sender suggest. The experience of youth was that of rebellion against fathers and teachers seen as too remote and uncomprehending. Antonio Alcalá Galiano recalled in his autobiography that it was the servants who gave him one of the first books he read with pleasure, a romance of chivalry forbidden by his father: in England too, imaginative literature, other than the classics, was often regarded as frivolous and denied to children at home until this century. Games were also slow in becoming integrated into a system of education for the young. Ramón y Cajal describes the contests of strength among the nineteenth-century Aragonese peasants (tossing iron bars, lifting sacks of wheat); but the 'games' of the children of Aragon were largely anarchic warfare among themselves, waged with much spontaneous craftiness. When the novelist Mateo Alemán (1547–1609) described the youthfulness of participants in the tournaments of Andalusia, he commented: 'Children are brought straight from the cradle to the horse, as they say here.' This precocious initiation into adult tournaments typified a readiness to confer responsibility on the young – and to ignore what Amorós called that long apprenticeship before maturity.

During the early modern period, however, the seeds of a complete change of attitude were sown. From the Renaissance, a succession of major treatises indicated the growing preoccupation of Spaniards with the proper education of the young. What is notable about Diego de Gurrea (1627) or Pedro López de Montoya (1595) is a new awareness of 'discipline' as an element in the formation of character. López de Montoya signalled the new mood with his warning about illegitimate children, who were not so much a badge of guilt for their parents as objects of social concern 'since generally they cannot be reared in a befitting manner.' Concern with public order was particularly marked in Bourbon Spain, with a series of edicts aimed at more efficient policing and at the restriction of occasions of disorder – bullfights, charivaris, carnivals and popular pilgrimages. As part of this, the law of 1745 extended the definition of vagrant widely to include disobedient children, concubines and those who did not have regular employment. There also seems to have been an attempt by the government to reinforce the authority of the head of the household. An edict of 1788, recalling the obligation on the justices to punish 'public sins', warned them not to interfere too much 'within the household' – such as coming between man and wife, master and servant or parents and children.

It is the great series of marriage laws between 1776 and 1803, for Spain and the Indies, which really marks the triumph of patriarchalism. Henceforward a girl could no longer sue for marriage unless there was a written contract, while no boy under twenty-five or girl under twenty-three could marry without parental consent. The edict of 1776 spoke of a recent spate of 'unequal matches', and there may be some grounds for thinking that the old ecclesiastical system was too easily exploited by fortune-hunters and the upwardly mobile. The problem may have been greater in the Indies, with its quite thriving economy in the eighteenth century and the advance of

the *mestizos*. In peninsular Spain one is perhaps more reluctant to see such dramatic social change. There the chief argument may simply have been that it was desirable, in the general interests of public order, to reinforce parental authority within the home. Certainly the whole drift of social thought was in that direction, and the church itself seems to have offered little resistance to the new laws. Much still requires to be investigated about the growing encouragement given by the church (in imitation of the Protestant Reformers) to the father as moral head of his family and teacher of the young.

It remains to note that the marriage laws of 1776–1803 were complemented by the Civil Code of 1888 which broke with the old egalitarian inheritance practices of Castile and allowed a father to leave up to two-thirds of his estate to a favoured child. The preceding debates suggest that this legislation was intended to increase the moral authority of the head of the family. As indicated earlier, these debates really laid the foundation for the study of the family as a moral system. For nineteenth-century reformers like Joaquín Costa, disorder in the family lay at the root of political instability and economic backwardness in Castile. His agenda is an immensely challenging one for the historian; but it may help to throw light on some of the fundamental paradoxes of Spanish history, such as the contrast between political centralism and the vitality of local community life.

Towards a modern world

The slowness of modernization in Spain was inevitably reflected in a certain conservatism of family structures. Birth and death rates did, indeed, begin to fall after 1900 in harmony with trends in the rest of Europe, and decisively so after the Civil War of 1936 to 1939, which seems in retrospect to have definitively interred an older Spain. But down to recent times Spain remained an overwhelmingly agrarian country, a land of small-scale rural communities, where family structures changed only gradually. Inevitably the great expansion of population, from $10\frac{1}{2}$ to just under 28 million between 1800 and 1950, created pressure of a new kind – more poverty within the rural sector, more emigration abroad in search of work. As in the rest of Europe, foundling rates seem particularly high in the first half of the nineteenth century among the dispossessed, accounting, for example, for between 15 and 18 per cent of births in Seville in this period. Yet, in spite of the massive fall in church attendance from the later nineteenth century, most Spaniards seem to have solemnized their marriages officially – testimony, no doubt, to the continuing strength of community ties. These survived the upheavals of migration, in many cases, as wives and mothers remained in the village to look after the farm and transmit traditional ideals to the young. It is only in our own day that the structures of rural Spain have been massively shaken.

The political changes brought about by the liberal revolutions of the nineteenth century, of course, also affected the family – the abolition of entails, for example, or the opening of careers to individual talent and the abolition of requirements of nobility for commissions in the army. But despite the good intentions of the legislators, an older hierarchy based on dynastic pride continued to survive. Good birth and advantageous marriage long remained the key to social success. Luis María Ramírez y Las Casas-Deza (1802–74), doctor of medicine and eminent historian of Cordoba, made the point eloquently in his memoirs for his children: look to your lineage, marry well, and do not expect to be able to live respectably on your professional earnings alone. Concern with ancestry seems to have been a continuing feature of liberal Spain, to judge by the numbers of genealogies published at the time. However, the broadening of economic opportunity and the lack of protection provided formerly by entails did lead to a certain decline of regional dynasties by the later nineteenth century. When the historian José Martínez Aloy came to survey the palaces of the old families of Valencia around 1920 he found that many had changed hands, victims of 'the insidious invasion of small-time capital'.

These new families were orientated more towards careers than lineage. Education, training and discipline were the hallmarks of the bourgeois family in Spain as in the rest of Europe. The home, as a place of training for the young, acquired a new sanctity. But the new closeness of relationship between husband and wife, parents and children, which the bourgeoisie sought, and which was reflected in Spain (as elsewhere) by the spread of terms of endearment (*papá* and *mamá* becoming fashionable after 1800), veiled a subtle authoritarianism. The church and state courts ceased to provide, as they had done in the old regime, an alternative to paternal control. Indeed, the purged and more evangelical church of liberal Spain tended to strengthen the sanctity of the home by its teaching. It was, no doubt, unfair of the novelist Ramón Pérez de Ayala to blame the sexual repressiveness of the middle-class home on the church (1923); the problem was a much wider one. The new puritanism of Spanish life drew on old roots, but it was essentially nurtured by the Enlightened governments of Charles III (1759–88), and their liberal successors.

Conclusion: questions and evidence

The 'family' is a subtle thread which can guide us through some of the labyrinthine changes of Spanish life, but only if we take the trouble to identify it properly. The risk is that we ask, perhaps, the wrong questions of the evidence. For example, because femininism was a significant issue in northern Europe and because of the prestige of family studies there, there may be a temptation to fit the divergent Spanish material into a framework which does not particularly suit it. The family is less an institution which can be compared directly from one culture to another than a prism through which some of the profoundest strains of a civilization can be brought into view.

Another problem lies in the evidence itself. Although it has become a commonplace to pay tribute to the influence of the family in the Hispanic world, there is in fact a relative lack of detailed studies. Much work has been done, indeed, on historical demography (though this seems considerably more advanced in Spain than in Spanish America). However, these studies have usually been set in the context of economics, and rather less attention has been paid to their broader social significance. It is interesting, for example, how little demographic comparison has been made between the different cultures within the Hispanic world – notably Moriscos, Indians and Christian Spaniards. Though the parish records are not at all easy to exploit for this purpose, they do constitute an almost unique source of information about non-European populations.

Cultural traits have been more the concern of social anthropologists, or occasionally of students of literature, interested in the seventeenth-century background to the 'drama of honour'. Yet, where the social anthropologist has concentrated on closed, rural communities, the historian is more likely to be aware of movement – expulsions of Jews and Moriscos by the hundreds of thousands, the southward march of the Reconquista, the colonization of the Indies . . . While the social anthropologist portrays communities richly textured through a multiplicity of internal ties, the historian is conscious of Spain as a great world empire, with threads of political and economic contact running from periphery to centre and back. Both perspectives are inherently valid in their own right. It is, indeed, the dialogue between them which is likely to advance our understanding of the Spanish family as an important bridge between the local community and the outside world.

Antonio Pereda's painting *The Knight's Dream* has no precise literary connotation (although it has been linked with Calderón's play *Life is a Dream*), but it brings together so many of the preoccupations of Spanish writers from the Middle Ages to today that it can stand as an allegory of what makes Spanish literature so distinctive and so unlike the literature of other languages and cultures: its unembarrassed combination of ordinary life and the supernatural; its obsession with heroic aspiration and death; its playing with the shadowy barrier between illusion and reality; and its questioning of the values that this barrier implies. The angel bears a scroll with the inscription 'It pierces perpetually – flies quickly through the air and kills' (a sentence capable of many meanings) and gestures towards the table piled high with objects that symbolize wealth, military glory, worldly power, beauty, knowledge, time and the vanity of all things. Such concerns are, surely, as fundamental to the author of a modern Latin-American novel like *One Hundred Years of Solitude* as they were to the authors of *Amadis de Gaula* and *Don Quijote*.

THE LITERARY HERITAGE

B.W. IFE AND J.W. BUTT

Like all great novelists, the Colombian writer Gabriel García Márquez is often asked about his favourite reading. His replies usually include a mention of Garci Rodríguez de Montalvo's romance of chivalry, *Amadís de Gaula*. This book, published in 1508, was the first of the great cycles of chivalresque romances which dominated literary taste in Spain for most of the sixteenth century, and García Márquez's fondness for it is instructive and intriguing. In one sense it reminds us that the enormous success of the contemporary Latin-American novel has its roots in the classic writers of the Spanish Golden Age, and points to a broad continuity underlying the literary heritage of two continents across five centuries. Yet at the same time, García Márquez shows how frequently life imitates art in the culture and politics of Spain and Spanish America: there is no evidence to show that he has ever read *Amadís de Gaula* and plenty to suggest that he has not.

The fact that a fashionable novelist should tease gullible interviewers about the sources of his work is not as trivial as it may appear, for García Márquez's piece of harmless fun poses the first of two central questions which underlie this essay: is the primary responsibility of the writer to the real world or to the world of the imagination, and how are these responsibilities to be reconciled? The issue is a key one for Cervantes and his generation, and it continues to dominate the practice of fiction in the Spanish-speaking world to this day. By holding up the authentic Amadís in place of his more obvious comic counterpart, Don Quixote, García Márquez seems to challenge the received wisdom that the natural mode of Spanish literature is one which debunks fantasy in favour of a disillusioned vision of the real. Spanish-speaking writers have risen at least as often to the challenge of creating a literary reality out of a fantasy world.

The second question is implicit in the very use of the word 'heritage'. If there is such a thing as a Spanish literary heritage, what does it consist of and what makes it specifically Spanish? With the union of the crowns of Castile and Aragon in 1479 came the need to create a homogeneous cultural identity which would help to underpin the fragile political unity of the new nation state. This was not easy in a country which had for so long been at the crossroads of Jewish, Muslim and Christian traditions, particularly at a time when Italian Renaissance culture was so influential throughout Europe. The balance between an inherited but necessarily selective cultural tradition and one imported from abroad posed difficult problems which have never been fully resolved. The result has been a suspicion of unorthodoxy from within and hostility to outside influence which has haunted Spain for much of its cultural history, and has a direct parallel in the long-standing problematic relationship between the national cultures of Latin America and the influence on them of a Spanish and European cultural elite.

The knight, the shepherd and the rogue

The origins of a purely Spanish literary heritage might perhaps be traced to the great series of experiments in prose fiction which took place in Spain throughout the sixteenth century, culminating in the work of Cervantes. These developments, the test bed of the modern novel, were dominated by the popularity of a single genre: the romances of chivalry. Built out of late remnants of the great Arthurian cycles of twelfth and thirteenth-century France, these books made an unprecedented impact on the new reading public which grew up in the wake of the printing press. Nearly 50 titles were published and republished in 251 editions between 1508 and 1605, the year of publication of *Don Quijote*.

It is difficult to be certain why the genre was so successful. In some ways, it testified to the continuity of a crusading spirit in a society newly inspired by the completion of the Reconquest in 1492, by the discoveries overseas and the imposition of a dominant Christian ideology by the Catholic Monarchs. Ferdinand and Isabella could not have wished for a more appropriate corporate image for the new Spain than the knight, the white Christian in a multi-racial society. He embodied a tradition of militant Christianity which looked back to the Cid and which was reassuring to an aristocracy under threat from the new meritocrats who were beginning to run the country. At the same time, the Christian virtues which the knight exemplified, and his constant struggle for good against the forces of darkness, were useful adjuncts to the religious reform which the Catholic Monarchs were pursuing with such energy.

In purely literary terms, however, the popularity of the chivalresque raised important questions of propriety. Harsh words were directed at the lack of verisimilitude in the romances, and critics complained that they peddled falsehoods and corrupted young and impressionable readers. These criticisms were not entirely without substance. *Amadís de Gaula* was one of the first books to show the general reader how literally anything was possible in fiction. Subsequent contributions to the genre developed their own logic. If the plot required a decapitated man to make a rapid recovery, considerations of plausibility were not allowed to stand in the way. And if the violence was implausible, the sex was often casual and alarmingly explicit. The opening chapter of *Amadís* contains one of the most powerful evocations of instantaneous lust in the literature of early-modern Europe.

The success of chivalresque romance undoubtedly has something to do with the way in which it managed to appear to be upholding Christian values while simultaneously offending against truthfulness and decency. But the chivalresque was not the only form of romance to find favour in sixteenth-century Spain. The sedate, platonic and frequently lachrymose introspection of Renaissance pastoral also had its appeal, with the shepherd emerging as a more fashionable counterpart to the knight, sharing his fine feelings, but making up in cosmopolitan sophistication for what he lacked in muscularity. Sannazaro's *Arcadia* appeared in Spanish in 1549 and the genre was taken up with some enthusiasm by Jorge de Montemayor (*Diana*, 1559), Gaspar Gil Polo (*La Diana enamorada*, 1564), Cervantes (*La Galatea*, 1585) and Lope de Vega (*Arcadia*, 1598).

Pastoral romance was widely seen as the natural successor to the chivalresque, and Don Quixote's proposal that he and Sancho should follow their career in chivalry with one in shepherding caused understandable alarm among the members of his household. But the pastoral genre in Spain largely escaped the backlash suffered by chivalresque romance and was widely used as a flexible medium for the discussion of issues ranging from the nature of love and emotional distress to the structure of a stable society. And in purely technical terms, pastoral fiction made substantial contributions to the development of new ways of constructing long narratives and of integrating prose and verse.

The knight had another influential counterpart in the person of the picaro, the roguish hero of the picaresque novel. Though deriving in part from the social world of Fernando de Rojas's novel in dialogue *La Celestina* (1499), where the ideals of courtly love are brought low in a sleazy setting, the picaro has more in common with the knight than might appear obvious at first glance. The prototype of the genre was established with the publication of *Lazarillo de Tormes* in 1554. This short, sketchy pseudo-autobiography tells the story of a young man who serves a succession of masters and learns to survive, and even to achieve limited prosperity, in moral, social and economic adversity. Like the chivalresque hero, with whom Lazarillo is explicitly compared in the opening lines, the picaro is an outsider engaged in a struggle for survival and his efforts are no less heroic for his being an anti-hero. He may lack the idealized motivation of the knight, but his adversaries are just as vicious and cynical, and they too fight to the death. The social satire of the *Lazarillo* is trenchant and frequently anti-clerical, and its lessons are deeply disturbing.

The low-life setting of the picaresque has often been interpreted as a conscious move to establish a form of realism in early-modern Spanish fiction, as a corrective to the escapist exoticism of the chivalresque. There may be something in this; it must make a difference to a reader whether he is spirited off to far-away places like Brittany or England, or is asked to consider events which were taking place in his own neighbourhood on a daily basis. The urban poor who dominate the world of the picaresque were a fact of life in sixteenth-century Spain. To that extent the picaresque may well have satisfied those who called

for more responsible forms of literature and more engagement with the real world. Yet the 'realism' of *Lazarillo de Tormes*, and particularly that of its successors such as Mateo Alemán's *Guzmán de Alfarache* (1599, 1604) and Francisco de Quevedo's *El Buscón* (c. 1605, published 1626), is frequently spurious. It is mostly literary in origin, and as the genre develops, the 'realism' becomes increasingly formulaic. For all the local colour, the taverns, the clutter of the real world and the squalor, the picaresque is fundamentally concerned with the great intangibles: power, wealth, corruption, hypocrisy and human folly.

'Reality' and wonder: the New World to Cervantes

The great period of experiment in narrative fiction which took place in sixteenth-century Spain was not restricted to the three genres already mentioned, and, indeed, was not restricted to fiction at all. One of the most important non-fictional vehicles for narrative experiment was the series of reports which came back from the discoverers and conquerors in the New World. The writers of these reports were not always educated men and certainly not usually practised in narrative skills. But the nature of their task made it necessary for them to develop ways of making their readers relive the incredible events in which they had taken part and conceptualize what was for European readers well nigh inconceivable. The effectiveness and popularity of this body of writing, and the role it played in developing literary taste in Spain, is not always given its full due. Of all the writers of early-modern Spain, it was perhaps the men serving abroad as part of the imperial mission who had to face up to and resolve the tension between the accurate reporting of matters of fact and the need to impress.

Using different language, the chroniclers of the New World were addressing from the 1490s onwards the very issues which Miguel de Cervantes Saavedra (1547–1616) would put at the centre of his own work a century later: the reconciliation of verisimilitude with the writer's obligation to surprise and delight his readers, to provoke wonder. With hindsight, it seems clear that Cervantes set himself the task of producing a synthesis of the Spanish literary heritage as he saw it around 1600. He certainly turned his hand to virtually every literary form available to him at the time, including drama and poetry, and the only genre to which he did not contribute in the standard format of that genre was the picaresque. This omission may or may not be significant, given his frequent use of picaresque conventions in other ways; what is surely significant is the way in which he consistently moved back and forth between high romance and his own literary version of contemporary Spain.

This emphasis on Cervantes's interest in the full spectrum of genres available to him is important in view of the popular

Cervantes's *Don Quijote* both mocked the romance of chivalry and immortalized it, the saintly knight and his worldly squire Sancho Panza representing the two poles of the Spanish nature – indeed of human nature. *Left, top*: Cervantes in 1600, when he was writing his masterpiece. *Centre*: the first image of Don Quixote, in the Portuguese edition of 1605. *Bottom*: the nineteenth-century's Don Quixote, an English photographic reconstruction of 1854.

The symbol of Don Quixote, appealing at once to so many associations and layers of meaning, has fascinated artists through the centuries, evoking characteristic responses in different countries. *Above left*: Daumier's warrior, a gaunt, anonymous figure on a skeletal Rosinante. *Left*: Salvador Dali's abstract contrast between linear knight and volumetric squire. *Below*: ink drawing by Picasso: the Don, Sancho, Spain itself reduced to the minimum of expressive marks.

conception of him as a debunker of romance. The origin of this view is undoubtedly tied up with the success of his own sprawling, two-part romance of chivalry, *Don Quijote de la Mancha* (1605, 1615). This work may have started life as a short story restricted to the first sally covered in the opening chapters. In a fairly conventional piece of satire, Quixote's hare-brained determination to re-enact the fantasies of chivalresque literature is shown to fail in the face of the 'real' world. References to the standard works abound (Cervantes had certainly read *Amadís de Gaula* and expected his readers to have done so), and Quixote's attempt to impose chivalresque ideals on an unreceptive and hostile public are made to look ridiculous. The standard lesson is drawn in a wide-ranging critique of Quixote's library. Most of what he read was rubbish and should be burned, and that which had literary merit needed to be handled with caution.

Fortunately, the lesson is lost on Quixote and he returns to the fray, accompanied this time by his trusty squire Sancho Panza. Two things are surprising about the way in which the book subsequently develops. One is the extent to which literary issues dominate Quixote's thinking, and the other is the way in which Quixote is able so often to make the world, not himself, look out of step. Towards the end of Part I, Quixote engages another character, the Canon of Toledo, in a long debate about the merits of novels of chivalry. The Canon puts up the standard points about their implausibility, their poor construction and the adverse effects they can have on impressionable readers, like Quixote himself. Quixote's replies range from the daft to the beguiling. He asserts, for example, the historicity of fictional characters and the reliability of the printed word. But in his reply he also, through the story of the Knight of the Boiling Lake, evokes brilliantly the ecstasy of reading and being transported to another world with a reality of its own.

Don Quixote's ability with words makes him a curiously effective exponent not just of the chivalresque ideals but also of the power of fiction. What begins as a fairly routine swipe at a tired old genre becomes, in practice, rejuvenated and compelling. By undermining a particular case of chivalry, Cervantes makes us rediscover the power and value of fiction in general. It has been the overlapping of these concerns which has undoubtedly led to the Romantic view of Quixote as a noble idealist engaged in a tragic struggle with a world which did not understand him. The comedy of Quixote, on the contrary, is real and intended: it is foolish to presume that values, however worthy, can be imposed in the way that Quixote tries to implement them. The power of the fiction, though, lies in the way in which readers can be led to regret this.

Cervantes's finest example of the way in which, in skilful hands, fantasies can be made real comes in his collection of twelve short stories, the *Novelas ejemplares* (*Exemplary Novels*, 1613). Cervantes makes several interesting observations in the Prologue to this collection. He stakes his claim to be the first Spanish writer of original short stories, and asserts that they are intended to be both entertaining and harmless, an interesting gloss on both the Italian origins of many of the plots and the numerous rapes and murders they contain. Furthermore, they are called 'exemplary' because each one contains a moral, as does the collection as a whole. The exemplarity of the stories is, however, a good deal more problematic than this. As far as explicit moral lessons are concerned, they appear to contain none, at least nothing more than an occasional, very banal gesture towards the conventional morality of fables. What does make them exemplary is the way they constitute an anthology of the writer's art, and the way in which the stories individually and collectively offer a convincing sample of the richness and complexity of human emotions and experience.

Underlying all the short stories is an implied challenge, to Cervantes himself as well as to the reader. The task is to extend the boundaries of what is possible in fiction without losing the reader's goodwill in the process, something the writers of romance rarely achieved, if indeed they ever aspired to it. To do this successfully means stretching the reader's credulity while retaining credibility, and having led the reader often further than he might otherwise have been prepared to go, not leaving him exposed and stranded but bringing him back to safety. It is often only when we look back that we see how far we have been led by the power of the fiction.

This process is most clearly illustrated in the final two stories of the collection, *El casamiento engañoso* and *El coloquio de los perros* (*The Deceitful Marriage* and *The Dogs' Colloquy*). They are linked thematically and formally by the device of presenting the second story as having been written by the protagonist of the first. He prepares the ground with a conventional tale of confidence trickery and then forces his interlocutor to read an account of a conversation between two dogs he claims to have overheard while recovering in hospital from a dose of the pox. His reader's understandable reluctance is gradually overcome as he is engulfed in a deepening spiral of implausibility. At the end of the story, which marks the end of the volume, the reader concludes that even though it was incredible it was very well done. Any reader might conclude the same of the collection as a whole. The most unlikely plots and coincidences are carefully prepared and lovingly presented in the most convincing settings, usually real places in contemporary Spain. Outrageous outcomes develop with inexorable logic. And all this is done with the imperceptible craftsmanship of the pickpocket.

Readers who are used to the sedentary introspection of much modern fiction are sometimes surprised by the broad scale and constant movement of Spanish Golden-Age narrative. No one ever seems to sit still for five minutes unless it is to listen to (or read about) another character recounting his own travels and travails. There is a restlessness in Golden-Age prose which is both epic in its origins (all narrative is essentially an answer to the questions 'Where have you been?', 'What have you been doing?') and symptomatic of an energetic, imperialist mentality. The characters, like the nation, are searching each for their own goal, the knight his grail, the shepherd a cure for his sorrows, the picaro respectability and survival. There is a fourth type whom Cervantes and others came to see as part of this picture, the seeker after truth, the pilgrim.

In *Los trabajos de Persiles y Sigismunda* (*The Travails of Persiles and Sigismunda*, published posthumously in 1617), Cervantes attempted his most daring feat, a seventeenth-century challenge to Heliodorus, whose *Ethiopic History* was frequently held up by sixteenth-century humanists as a model for the epic in prose. The work tells of the long quasi-allegorical journey of two lovers, marooned in the Arctic as a result of misfortune, through Scandinavia and the Baltic, France, Portugal, Spain and Italy, to Rome, the centre of the Christian world. The scope of this work and the profusion of characters and incident is breathtaking. The northern setting outdoes both the exoticism of medieval romance and that of the New World, while the later chapters bring the reader into a warmer climate familiar from the *Novelas ejemplares*, a recognizably contemporary Mediterranean world suffused with the atmosphere of popular fiction, star-crossed lovers, recognitions of long-lost relatives, tearful reconciliations, murder, rape, piracy and transvestite disguise. *Persiles y Sigismunda* is Cervantes's least read novel and his noblest failure, but it is the clearest sign of the height and breadth of his literary aspirations.

Poetic contraries: Góngora and Quevedo

The years leading up to 1617 had also seen the production of another work in which a pilgrim is the central figure, the *Soledades* (*Solitudes*), a long, unfinished poem by Luis de Góngora y Argote (1561–1627). Góngora's role in Spanish literary history is as problematic as Cervantes's was statesman-like and conciliatory. Where Cervantes tried to bring together the many strands of experiment and weave them into a finished product, Góngora took up an outstanding poetic tradition and developed it almost to the point of self-destruction. After his apprenticeship in the conventions of Italianate verse and the artistic reworking of popular ballads, Góngora stunned the literary world of Madrid with two long poems written in an elaborate decorative style based on extreme syntactic flexibility, extended metaphor and mythological allusion. Although the origins of this style are clearly visible in his own early work

and in that of some of his sixteenth-century predecessors, the concentrated effect of the new poetic language in his *Polifemo* and *Soledades* was unprecedented.

Whereas the *Polifemo* is a reworking of the story of Acis and Galatea in fairly tightly structured eight-line stanzas, the *Soledades*, of which only the first and most of the second were completed of the intended four, is an original narrative written in an extremely free combination of seven- and eleven-syllable lines. This form allowed Góngora maximum scope to aspire to his goal of making Spanish poetry the equal of Latin. The lack of grammatical inflexion in Spanish and the extreme complexity of Góngora's metaphorical language make this poem very difficult to read. The effect is clearly intended to be like cutting one's way through the forest, or *silva*, after which the verse form is named, and the reading experience is, again consciously, akin to that of the protagonist or pilgrim washed ashore in a strange and beautiful land. The pilgrim's past life at court, his disillusion with the power games of love and politics, interact almost surrealistically with a world of great natural beauty constantly intercut with images of decay.

Góngora's impact on the literary establishment in Madrid was quickly rebuffed. He was, after all, a marginal figure, from Cordoba in southern Spain, not from Castile, a new Christian with *converso* blood in his veins and a face that did not fit. His work was ridiculed in particular for its adoption of a Latinate vocabulary in which the etymology of common Spanish words was frequently overridden by a morphology which was closer to classical roots. Other poets wrote macaronic verses in 'gongorine' vocabulary, treating it as gibberish, and coined the form *culterano* (one who follows an affected, high-flown style) by analogy with *luterano* (a follower of the heretic Luther). In its more extreme manifestations, opposition to Góngora's work took the form of accusations of an international conspiracy to destroy all that was best in the poetic legacy of sixteenth-century Spain. This opposition could be disregarded were it not for the fact that it was spearheaded by a man who could reasonably claim to be Spain's greatest living writer, Francisco de Quevedo y Villegas (1580–1645).

Quevedo's career is one of immense achievement and shocking waste. He wrote some of the most trenchant satire in Spanish, the most brilliant of the picaresque novels, the *Buscón*, a huge body of poetry, some glorious, much scurrilous, and a large number of historical, philosophical and devotional works. Yet the picture which comes across is of a deeply unhappy, unfulfilled and dissatisfied man. His youth was wasted in frivolity at court, in his early thirties he tried to turn over a new leaf and took up a political and administrative post in Italy, he narrowly survived the downfall of his patron amidst political scandal, and spent the last twenty or more years of his life

Luis de Góngora (*top right*) was an outsider, from Andalusia rather than Castile, and for his greatest work, the unfinished *Soledades*, he virtually invented a new language which his readers found as difficult as his personality.

Francisco de Quevedo (*centre right*) was Góngora's literary opponent and personal enemy. Aristocratic, conservative, inhibited, he resented change and looked back with longing to the Catholic Monarchs and Charles V.

desperately trying to ingratiate himself with a political regime which he despised. Much of his work is viciously misanthropic, and even his love poetry is marked by a deep hatred of women.

Quevedo did and said many unforgivable things in his life, but his hounding of Góngora must be one of the worst cases of personal malice in literary history. However, their differences were not just personal. It is true that Góngora represented everything that Quevedo – an impoverished, anti-Semitic aristocrat from Old Castile – most hated. But Quevedo brought a political dimension to literary life which is more frequently associated with the modern period. Quevedo was a 'young fogey', a brilliant, youthful, old-fashioned right-winger whose approach to politics and art was, like that of so many of his generation, based on nostalgia. The great days of Spain, he felt, had gone, the moral and religious discipline had disappeared with the Catholic Monarchs and Charles V, and the political authority of Spain in Europe had not survived Philip II. The reigns of Philip III and Philip IV were marked by withdrawal, appeasement, spinelessness, indulgence in luxury, domination by corrupt favourites and a decline into social chaos.

As if these disasters were not enough, he had also to contend with artistic novelty and the threat of cultural domination from Italy and France. Quevedo conspicuously championed the poets of fifteenth and sixteenth-century Spain – the poets of the *Cancionero general* (1511), Garcilaso de la Vega (1501–36), Fernando de Herrera (1534–97), Fray Luis de León (1527–91) whose works Quevedo edited and published for the first time, and St John of the Cross (1542–91) – on the grounds that they represented the true tradition of Spanish poetry – clear, simple and direct. He conveniently turned a blind eye to the Provençal and Italian origins of much of their work.

In reality the dichotomy between Góngora and Quevedo in terms of technique and achievement is almost entirely false. Where Góngora tended to favour experiment in syntax and lexis, Quevedo was more fascinated by the intellectual complexity of the conceit. But neither writer had a monopoly. Góngora's lexical innovation is usually based on an intellectual as well as a physical association between two objects or concepts in a comparison. Quevedo is equally fascinated by the expressive and investigative power of poetic language and its ability to bring forth semblances between things apparently unlike. At bottom, both writers shared the common poetic legacy of the time, a rich compound of Petrarchism, Renaissance Neoplatonism and religious and satirical verse.

The drama of honour

Quevedo's frequent backward look at the writers and values of an earlier age was characteristic also of the dramatists of Golden-Age Spain. Though the kind of drama developed by

Lope de Vega (1562–1635) for the popular theatre of seventeenth-century Spain was in many ways revolutionary in form, the themes and the ethos seem strikingly conservative. Lope de Vega established and wrote extensively for an outdoor theatre set up in a courtyard or *corral*, and for a largely popular audience. His output was phenomenal – some 500 plays are extant – but there is a sameness about his productivity which is hard to reconcile with the image of a public with a voracious appetite for novelty. Lope's success, however, clearly shows that he was closely in touch with his audience. His dramatic manifesto, the *Arte nuevo de hacer comedias* (*New Art of Writing Plays*, 1609), is marked above all by the need to give the public what it wanted. And what they clearly wanted was his own home-grown format of the *comedia*, a three-act play usually performed with *entr'actes*, observing none of the unities of classical drama, and written in flexible and largely octosyllabic verse.

Lope drew his subjects from a variety of sources – mythology, the Bible and ancient history – but he had a particular liking for plots derived from Spanish history and with peasant themes. Taken as a whole, his work seems to underwrite the dignity of the individual and the value of stable and responsible social relationships. His most famous peasant dramas, *Peribáñez* (*c*. 1610) and *Fuenteovejuna* (*c*. 1613), show the common man acquiring the dignity of his social superiors through an attack on their monopoly of entitlement to honour. As Lope himself said, cases of honour are the best subjects for drama because everybody finds them interesting. Honour, which can entail a host of qualities from arrogance and sexual possessiveness to personal integrity and mutual respect, is the most common cause of conflict in Golden-Age drama, and its fascination for a public willing to go over and over again to watch what were essentially the same half-dozen plays seems to have been endless. To say this is not to criticize, but to recognize the sustained commitment of Spanish Golden-Age society to an artistic form which clearly satisfied a deep-seated need.

What a Golden-Age audience saw when it went to the theatre was in fact a quite subtle expression of anti-establishment values. All literary forms were subject to local authority control and censorship by the church. The implementation of the system was often surprisingly liberal, but the theatre, in Spain as in many other countries, was viewed with the greatest suspicion, especially during the moral re-armament period of the 1620s. In these circumstances, the value-systems of the *comedia* were carefully tuned. The cult of the happy ending, for example, and its implication that order is always restored by judicial or regal intervention, was often subjected to heavy irony. Tidy, multiple marriages are made to look hollow in the wake of murder and rape. Female desire, which is portrayed

Lope de Vega (*bottom right*) – with Calderón – made the seventeenth century as important for Spanish drama as it was for English. Most of his plays turn on honour, especially cases where the demands of honour conflict with the principles of morality. Their intellectual vigour and intense emotion keep them alive, even when the codes of conduct they assume are unsympathetic.

with surprising frequency and directness, is made to undermine established views about the relationship of the sexes. Lust at first sight offers a direct challenge to marriage and the family, and the gentry's cloak and dagger sexual hypocrisy is mimicked and mocked by their servants.

A second generation of playwrights, including Tirso de Molina (1580–1648) and Pedro Calderón de la Barca (1600–81), emerged as Lope's successors and built on his achievements in establishing the theatre as a legitimate form of cultural expression. Calderón both identified with and distanced himself from Lope by rewriting many of his plays. In doing this he recognized their popularity and their success, but also their limitations. Calderón tried to inject more order and dignity into the construction and the language of the drama, and became fascinated by the way in which the conventions of the *comedia* could be used to produce a new form of tragedy. Tragedy in the classical sense has often been seen as incompatible with a Christian society for whom fate must always be divinely providential. Calderón developed his own form of tragedy by using social and artistic orthodoxy in place of fate. His wife-murder plays, for example, illustrate the tragedy of public duty in conflict with personal desire. These jealous husbands are driven to murder their wives against their wishes and their better judgment because of some imagined slur on their honour, and simply because that is what dishonoured men in Golden-Age plays are supposed to do.

The best illustration of Calderón's reworking of the conventions of the *comedia* comes in his own powerful peasant drama *El alcalde de Zalamea* (*The Mayor of Zalamea*, c. 1642). The play examines a number of interpretations of honour, mocking some, apparently approving others. The protagonist, and tragic hero, Pedro Crespo, a rich peasant with pure blood, desperately tries to head off an inevitable disaster when troops are billeted at his house. He refuses to buy his way into the minor nobility, which would bring him exemption from the billet, on the grounds that a bald man in a wig is still bald. Instead, he locks up his daughter. The visiting Captain and blackguard sniffs out the daughter, abducts and rapes her. That much is conventional. But Crespo is appointed mayor of Zalamea and overrules the military authorities by having the Captain arrested. There follows one of the most complex and tragic encounters in all drama. Crespo tries to force the Captain on pain of death to marry his daughter and restore her honour. The Captain refuses on the grounds that he is noble and she is not. Crespo begs on bended knee, but the Captain continues to refuse, even as he is garrotted. What Crespo cannot see is that no amount of justice can put this injustice to rights. He may kill the Captain, but he cannot make him marry the girl; he cannot make them social equals; he cannot defy the system.

Calderón wrote extensively for the popular theatre, and later increasingly for the more elaborate court theatre with its taste for more classical themes and mythological subjects, and for early forms of the opera. He wrote over 100 *comedias*, and also dominated the production of open-air allegorical drama presented regularly on the feast of Corpus Christi. He wrote two *autos sacramentales* every year for thirty years, all illustrating the theme of the Eucharist, and these dramas, presented on mobile carts, show how successfully he reconciled complexity of thought, construction and language with the demands of a popular audience watching under makeshift conditions. In some ways, the *autos* represent a final flowering of the synthesis of aristocratic and popular culture which is one of the finest achievements of the Spanish Golden Age.

Enlightenment and Romanticism

After the death of Calderón, literature in Castilian went into a decline which lasted, with few exceptions, until the 1880s. Thereafter it revived spectacularly. There was a Hispanic Enlightenment, especially in Spain, but its authors contributed little to eighteenth-century European thought: its concerns were too local and its rationalism too prudent for it to produce Humes or Voltaires. Poetry and fiction in eighteenth-century Spain were also handicapped by the country's isolation from the literary life of northern Europe, and no numerous readership receptive to neo-classical tastes existed anywhere in the Hispanic world.

But the literary models of France and other developed countries spread far and deep enough among the elites to ensure that literature suffered from the Enlightenment's aesthetic prejudices. Rhetoricians and critics in eighteenth-century Spain organized a sustained attack on much of the literature of the Golden Age and succeeded in discrediting most of its distinctive qualities: its extravagance, wit and ingenuity, anarchic lexical wealth and grotesque lack of 'verisimilitude' – in other words, its preference for aristocratic, military or peasant themes and its neglect of middle-class life. Neo-classicists disliked the sprawling excesses of Baroque literature. They found its popular element vulgar, its religion fanatical, its language 'unnatural', its poetry remote from everyday life, its morals dubious and its social and political attitudes indecorous or destabilizing: they were disturbed by the lack of social distances in Golden-Age drama. They proposed to replace it by a largely utilitarian literature pledged to the Enlightenment project of rational social reform and expressed in sober language likely to communicate ideas clearly and effectively.

This anti-Baroque campaign inaugurated a period of some two centuries in which Hispanic literary criticism was to be heavily influenced, at times quite dominated by, essentially realist ideals of the writer's social and political responsibility. These principles, more than anything else, checked the growth of literature in Castilian by limiting the imaginative freedom of authors, and its negative influence persisted into the last years of the following century. Neo-classical influences lingered late in Spain, and even in the 1880s we find the verse and prose of some highly esteemed writers peppered with the peculiar dead vocabulary of the neo-classics, which called the sky 'the celestial vault', water 'lymph' and breezes 'zephyrs'.

The Romantic movement in Spain should have revolutionized literary language as it did in northern countries. But prejudices about the immediate social function of literature did much to ensure that Spanish Romanticism in the 1830s was a pale reflection of its northern counterparts. The movement produced a number of authors who, in a more adventurous aesthetic climate, could have achieved European stature: Mariano José de Larra (1809–37) and José de Espronceda (1808–42) come to mind. But both were intensely political writers and much of their short literary careers was taken up with journalism or propaganda for the liberal cause, which is hardly surprising since Spanish Romanticism had to compete for attention against a violent civil war between the liberal regime in Madrid and Carlist counter-revolutionaries in the north and east of Spain.

Spanish Romantics also had little to react against. The absence of a powerful Hispanic rationalist tradition meant that there was little call for a Romantic revolt against it. Spanish Romanticism therefore lacked the essential ingredient that made the movement so revolutionary elsewhere: a renewed interest in the creative powers of the unconscious mind, in dream, intuition, vision and imagination. Such an interest would in turn have generated pressures for a renewal of literary language, but these things do not really appear in Castilian until some forty years later with the posthumous publication in 1871 of the *Rimas* of Gustavo Adolfo Bécquer (1836–70). Spanish Romanticism was essentially a worldly literary movement, concerned less with exploring inner states and the possibilities of language than with defining the nature and limits of social and political freedom, or with reasserting national identity or reinstating medieval culture and literature.

The victory of realism

The great revival of literature in Castilian came first in Spain and in the genre of the novel. Spanish literature in the 1880s and 1890s is dominated by the realist novel and by the figure of the first Hispanic writer of truly international status to appear for more than two hundred years, Benito Pérez Galdós (1843–1920), the author of 80 novels and 24 plays that virtually

The chronicler of late nineteenth-century Spain, a novelist and social observer who ranks with Balzac in France or Dickens in England, was Benito Pérez Galdós. Beginning, like Dickens, as a journalist, he too turned to fiction and in a prolific output of over eighty books explored Spanish society and history at all levels. In this photograph of 1897 he is reading to a circle of literary friends.

Miguel de Unamuno – poet, novelist, philosopher, teacher – represents the end of the great nineteenth-century humanist tradition. His liberal principles, which he fearlessly proclaimed, brought him into conflict with several governments; he died under house arrest in 1936.

constitute a literature in themselves. Although he wrote a series of 46 historical novels, the *Episodios nacionales*, dedicated to elucidating the mysteries of nineteenth-century Spanish history, the great works of his naturalist phase, for example *La desheredada, El amigo Manso, Lo prohibido, Angel Guerra* and, above all, *Fortunata y Jacinta*, all written between 1881 and 1887, are closely focused on middle-class life in Madrid. The city he depicts is very much a provincial town with an immensely strong sense of community and a passion for gossip and social contact. This atmosphere of bustle and gaiety, and a certain instinctive optimism on the author's part – he rounds on one depressed character at a tragic moment in *La desheredada* for forgetting that every cloud has a silver lining – give many of his greatest novels an attractive emotional balance which will refresh readers accustomed to the tragic gloom of Tolstoy, Flaubert or Zola. Such readers will recognize the mood of the other great Spanish realist of the period, Leopoldo Alas (1852–1901). *La Regenta* (1884), a magnificent but acid study of adultery in a provincial town, portrays a world quite unlike Galdós's: superficial, hypocritical, vicious and irredeemably cruel.

The great successes of these and other realist novelists in the 1880s and early 1890s reinforced a critical prejudice that had its roots in the eighteenth century: that the natural mode of Spanish literature is realism, and preferably that sort which, like *Don Quijote* and the picaresque in these critics' view, shows ideals and illusions failing the test of real life. The realists of the '80s and '90s were all encouraged by the feeling that they were the heirs of Cervantes, and the vogue of positivism and science encouraged their belief that Spanish backwardness was due to the impractical idealism of Spaniards.

The balance had now tipped too far towards realism. Even in the late 1880s, Madrid literary circles seemed unaware of developments in European post-Romantic poetry, an indifference that contrasts markedly with changing attitudes elsewhere in the Iberian peninsula, notably Portugal and Catalonia. Poetry was in a sorry state: 'There is not a single name, not one, that gives grounds for hope [for Castilian poetry]', Leopoldo Alas wrote in 1896, and a year earlier the talented novelist Emilia Pardo Bazán (1852–1921) had lamented that 'among us one sees no signs of the birth of decadents or symbolists; among us a Baudelaire would arouse horror and disgust; among us, in the land of St John of the Cross, the mysticism of a Verlaine would seem suspect.' Her remarks indicate the extent to which anti-clerical fears about 'neo-Catholicism' and 'mysticism' were as much to blame as conservative dislike of foreign innovations for the long-delayed exposure of Spanish literary language to the invigorating example of French aestheticism and *symbolisme*.

Modernismo and modernism

The good news about developments in French poetry in fact came from Latin America, in the shape of a movement led by the Nicaraguan poet and diplomat, Rubén Darío (1867–1916), and dubbed by supporters and enemies *modernismo*. Rubén Darío's first visit to Madrid in 1892 was premature: he complained that the only modernists in the country were the Catalans. But by the time he returned in 1898, the time had come for a literary revolt, and his imitations of French Parnassian and symbolist verse caused a furore among the budding poets and novelists who had established a modest literary Bohemia in Madrid.

This was the first instance of the renewal of Spanish literature by the example of Latin-American writing, and *modernismo* signalled the end of Spain's literary hegemony in the Spanish-speaking world. It was not to be the last time that the realist excesses of Castilian literature in Spain would be checked by trans-Atlantic experimentalism. Despair at Spanish backwardness had been one motive of the Latin-American revolutions of independence in the first two decades of the century, and the scattered and tiny intellectual and literary elites of the new republics inevitably looked directly to northern Europe, especially to France, for ideas and inspiration. On several occasions since the 1890s, Latin-American literature has played Góngora to the peninsular Quevedo and has hauled Spanish literature out of its realist rut.

Rubén Darío's example sparked off a striking and sustained literary renewal which soon left behind his own occasionally grotesque imitations from the French. Spain's real achievements in literature since 1895 have been essentially modernist in character, 'modernist' here used in its normal European sense of post-realist, experimental and avant-garde and not in its usual, more limited Spanish meaning of *fin-de-siècle* or *symboliste*. It is a severe problem of modern Spanish studies that one cannot talk intelligibly about literary modernism in Spanish since the word *modernismo* is used in that language for what was merely the earliest and embryonic stage of modernism, that is imitations of French *Parnassiens* and *symbolistes* inspired by Rubén Darío.

But modernism, in its European sense, was the making of modern Spanish literature. Despite the splendid achievement of the realists of the 1880s and '90s, nearly all the most famous Spanish writers of this century, Ramón del Valle-Inclán (1866–1936), Juan Ramón Jiménez (1881–1958, Nobel Prize 1956), Gabriel Miró (1879–1930), Miguel de Unamuno (1864–1936), Ramón Pérez de Ayala (1881–1962), Federico García Lorca (1898–1936), Rafael Alberti (born 1902), Jorge Guillén (1893–1984), Miguel Hernández (1910–42), Luis Martín Santos (1924–64), Juan Goytisolo (born 1931), were or became, to varying degrees and with different levels of self-awareness, experi-

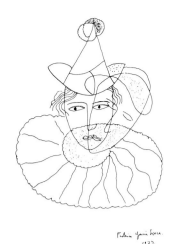

Federico García Lorca, murdered by supporters of Franco at the beginning of the Civil War, is best known abroad for his plays exposing the tragic plight of women in the prejudice-ridden south. But he was a brilliant and highly sophisticated poet and also an artist with affinities to Cocteau and Dali. Here, *Clown Mask* of 1927, and *Signature*, a weeping moon above the name 'Lorca'.

mental writers who broke with realism and with traditional literary forms and language.

Even the two poets who most dramatically reacted against the innovations and obscurities of 'modern' literature, Antonio Machado (1875–1939) and Luis Cernuda (1902–63), were heavily marked at the beginning of their careers by the then avant-garde influences of *symbolisme* and surrealism respectively. Only two well-known writers of the period from 1900 to 1936, the novelists Pío Baroja (1872–1956) and Vicente Blasco Ibáñez (1867–1928), were more or less unaffected by modernist literary experiments, and the artistic reputation of both is rather uncertain. Spain may have been isolated from the rest of Europe in the first seventy years of the twentieth century, but her literature has at certain periods during this time been daringly innovative, sometimes extravagantly so. This boldness has precedents: Góngora was the most avant-garde poet of seventeenth-century Europe. Although his work was not consciously resuscitated and revalued until his tercentenary in 1927, the spirit of his refusal to allow literary language to be impeded by subservience to colloquial speech is alive in the most characteristic works of Hispanic *modernismo* of the turn of the century and in the experiments that followed it.

The most brilliant of the Spanish modernists (the term used again in its European, not its Hispanic meaning), and the greatest international literary success of modern Spain, was the poet and playwright Federico García Lorca. The trajectory of his career traces the development of Spanish literature in the first thirty years of this century and brings out that literature's strong points. His early poetry was heavily influenced by Darío, Jiménez and other imitators of the French *symbolistes*, despite the fact that the rarefied vocabulary of such poetry, with its eternal jasmines, lilies, swans and sunsets, was bankrupt stock by the First World War. The melancholy vagueness and somewhat wishy-washy transcendentalism of the symbolist Ivory Tower were also ill-suited to a poet who was anything but a dreamy recluse and had an extraordinarily sharp sense of visual detail and a deep familiarity with the popular culture of his native Andalusia. It was Andalusia that inspired the striking imagery of *Romancero gitano* (*Gypsy Ballads*, 1928) and *Poemas del cante jondo* (1931), the former work especially exemplifying that fusion of traditional elements and the avant-garde that typifies much – though not all – of Lorca's best work.

For Lorca was in no sense a 'poet of the people' exclusively interested in rural Southern culture, although foreigners exposed only to his internationally famous rural tragedies, *Bodas de sangre* (*Blood Wedding*), *Yerma* and *La casa de Bernarda Alba* (*The House of Bernarda Alba*), might be tempted to think so. Lorca was by taste and temperament more at home in select and very sophisticated avant-garde artistic circles. His

surrealist works, for example the poems of *Poeta en Nueva York* (*Poet in New York*) and the play *El público* (*The Public*), both of them full of a strange intensity, enigmatic and unforgettable, are extremely cosmopolitan works as far removed as possible from the flamenco music and gypsy feuds with which he is often associated. If Lorca could write brilliant plays and poems about Spain, it was because he had a connoisseur's eye for the artistic potential of certain popular forms, not because he was an untutored or plebeian poet.

The fact is that, viewed overall, there is a sense in which Spanish literature of the period 1900 to 1930 was struggling not to establish its links with Spanish culture, but to break out of provincialism by building new bridges with the rest of Europe. Hence the importance of the various '-isms' of the period, *modernismo*, *creacionismo*, *ultraísmo*, surrealism, which all offered writers an escape from the ossified literary language of Spain and from the overpowering strength of popular Spanish culture. So much of the literature of 1900 to 1930, with its difficult, sometimes far-fetched imagery, tortuous structures and occasionally obscure arguments, is not so much an expression as a rejection of everyday Spanish life.

The critic and philosopher José Ortega y Gasset argued, in his *La deshumanización del arte* (*The Dehumanization of Art*, 1925), that the basic aim of avant-garde arts is to humiliate and exclude the man in the street so as to reestablish a proper distance between minority and majority culture – the latter, according to him, being always 'realist' and representational. His essay is no doubt a homage paid by ignorance to modern aesthetics, but it contains a grain of truth: modern Spanish literature had to fight for the right to be elitist in order to distance itself from majority and traditional tastes, whether they were the Academy's or the common people's. This was the only path that would lead it to discover the potential of the Spanish language as a vehicle for a literature of innovation.

This battle was eventually lost for a period that lasted almost thirty long years. The position of Spanish modernism in the 1920s and 1930s was vulnerable enough without Ortega y Gasset imputing to it the motive of snobbery: it badly lacked theoretical defences. The best avant-garde works of the period, for example the poetry of Lorca, Alberti, Guillén, Miguel Hernández and the early poems of Luis Cernuda, the plays and novels of Valle-Inclán and Pérez de Ayala, seem to exist in a kind of critical vacuum in the sense that they are not accompanied by a body of powerful and learned intellectual justifications written by the authors themselves or by prestigious supportive critics. In this respect Spanish literature of the period differs from that of France, Germany or the English-speaking world. One need only contrast the disarming theoretical innocence of Lorca's literary lectures with the essays of

T.S. Eliot, Yeats or Paul Valéry, to see the point of this argument.

Spanish modernism thus entered the 1930s unprepared for the fray. The left viewed the experimental arts as the swansong of a decadent bourgeoisie on the eve of revolution. The right hated its lack of Catholic, national and traditional roots, its 'intellectualism' and dubious liberalism. The authors themselves were, of course, generally indifferent to the arguments of the right, but left-wing complaints about 'escapism' and elitism troubled liberal consciences. One sees in the later works of Lorca (especially in the, for him, colourless play *La casa de Bernarda Alba*), and of Alberti, Cernuda and Guillén, concessions to 'ordinary language' or social relevance that are alien to the spirit of their best work and to the whole modern experiment in Spanish literature.

The Franco years

Some of the great modernist writers, for instance Juan Ramón Jiménez and Jorge Guillén, continued the experimentalist tradition in exile after Franco's victory in 1939: Juan Ramón Jiménez, the last great mystical symbolist of Europe, doggedly refined the vision of *fin-de-siècle* aestheticism until his death in Puerto Rico in 1958. Others, like Alberti and Cernuda, also continued to write in exile, although alienated from modernist experimentalism. Some – Lorca, Miguel Hernández – were victims of the Civil War. Pérez de Ayala gave up novel writing in 1926. Ramón del Valle-Inclán and Gabriel Miró both died before the Civil War began. Unamuno, the grand old man of modern Spanish letters, author of volumes of poetry, plays, novels and religious and secular essays, and, perhaps unwittingly, intensely modern in the experimentalism of many of his works and in his philosophy, died in despair in 1936, confined to his house at Franco's orders. The modernist generation was dead or dispersed.

But the brutality and mediocrity of Franco's long dictatorship were only indirectly to blame for the fact that the next generation of Spanish writers neither profited from their example nor showed much interest in their works. The excuse often heard even today for the post-Civil War generation's indifference to the achievements of most authors of the period 1900 to 1936 is that their works were suppressed by Franco's censorship. But it is not easy to reconcile this argument with the fact that everywhere in the 1950s and '60s young intellectuals were reading texts by Marx, the anarchists, Lukács, Antonio Machado and other authors who were likely to disturb the dictator's supporters. The fact is that in the 1950s and '60s the *samizdat* and clandestine distribution services in Spain were simply not interested in modernism, either in its early form as *modernismo* or in the works of Lorca, Alberti, Guillén, Unamuno and others; and the reason was that they were judged

in some sense to be the products of a liberal vision of life and were therefore condemned as 'bourgeois'.

The most vigorous novels and poetry published in Spain by the generation that came of age after about 1955 were, given the circumstances, inevitably left-wing, although their political message had to be disguised behind more or less transparent codes: veiled socialist realism was, for example, called *literatura social*. Surprising numbers of 'social' novels were published in Spain: Franco's censors were inefficient and semi-literate when it came to poetry and novels, though they were impossibly severe with the mass media, including the theatre.

The anti-modernist bias of this 'social' literature reflected a prejudice against anything smacking of 'elitism'. The young literary critics of the day were much influenced by the Hungarian Marxist-Leninist Lukács and by the Marxist ideal that great literature should represent 'typical' social characters in 'typical' social situations, and their essays constantly hold up *modernismo* and the avant-garde as deplorable examples of artistic individualism indifferent to the class struggle. The examples of pre- or anti-modernist writers, Antonio Machado (who was a cult figure in these years), Pío Baroja, Leopoldo Alas, even the Golden-Age picaresque novelists, were adduced to show how great literature could be written in the realist mode and in ordinary language intelligible to the victims of oppression.

The result, as it seems to a foreign reader spared the experience of life under Franco, is flat and insipid, not because the accounts of deprivation are inevitably dreary, but because the language these writers used is so artistically inhibited. The post-Civil War reaction against modernist elitism cut Spanish literature off from all those energies of baroque excess and adventurous experimentalism that have been one source of its strength since the seventeenth century. In the 1950s and 1960s Spanish literature to a large extent returned to those formulas – social responsibility, easy, everyday language, decorum and moderation (now adjusted to proletarian norms) – that governed its decline in the period 1750–1880. 'Social literature' – that is anti-Franco, socialist realism – eventually became a strait-jacket. But by the time Spanish writers finally fought their way out of it in the late 1960s, the growth point of Hispanic literature had definitively shifted to Spanish America.

The triumph of Spanish-American literature

One fundamental reason for the successes of Spanish-American literature since the Second World War is that, unlike peninsular Spanish literature between the 1940s and the mid-60s, it was never shut off from the influence of experimental writing in Europe and North America. (The term 'Spanish American' is used purely as a convenient shorthand method of indicating the limited areas of Latin America under discussion.) The 'boom' of

the 1960s and after in the Spanish-American novel would have been unthinkable without the influence of surrealism (a source of the novelist Alejo Carpentier's ideas about 'magic realism', first formulated in the mid-1940s) and, above all, of Joyce and Faulkner, whose work inspired many of the formal innovations that characterize Spanish-American writing in the period.

This openness to modernist experimentation has funded a dizzying success: the international prestige of Spanish-American literature has risen to extraordinary heights since the 1950s. One need only list the names of Alejo Carpentier (Cuba, 1904–70), Jorge Luis Borges (Argentina, 1899–1986), Julio Cortázar (Argentina, 1914–84), Manuel Puig (Argentina, 1934–90), Juan Rulfo (Mexico, 1918–86), Pablo Neruda (Chile, 1904–73), Octavio Paz (Mexico, born 1914), Mario Vargas Llosa (Peru, born 1936), Gabriel García Márquez (Colombia, born 1928), Carlos Fuentes (Mexico, born 1928), Augusto Roa Bastos (Paraguay, born 1917) to be reminded that the continent has recently produced some of the greatest, possibly the greatest novels, short stories and poems in the world.

Openness to European and North-American literary influences guaranteed this success, but this is not to imply that recent Latin-American literature is merely a local version of European avant-garde. Latin America is an original and uniquely privileged environment for imaginative writing. It is very much part of the Third World in the sense that all its republics are ex-European colonies, none of them independent for more than 160 years; to this extent Latin-American experience is markedly un-European. But these republics all differ from other Third-World countries in that their populations are heavily, in some cases overwhelmingly, European in origin. Only in Paraguay has an indigenous non-European language been adopted by nearly everyone for daily use; even in strongly *mestizo* countries like Peru, Ecuador and Mexico, Amerindian cultures are marginalized and beleaguered.

Latin-American intellectuals and artists have thus been much more intensely cosmopolitan, much more distanced from traditional culture, than their Third-World counterparts elsewhere, and this has given them a unique vantage point from which to survey both their own continent and the First World on which it so heavily depends. They have lived surrounded by, or in some cases have been the products of, Amerindian, African or *mestizo* societies, but they have also usually moved in heavily Europeanized circles and have had life-long familiarity with European and North-American values and ideas.

Culture shock is central to Latin-American experience, which inherits a bitter and conflict-ridden legacy. On the one hand Latin Americans are part of a world that owes nothing to Europe: the deserts, mountains and huge rain forests of Latin America were the site of singular and splendid civilizations such as the Aztecs, Mayas and Incas, and millions of Latin Americans still carry the blood of these defeated peoples. On the other hand, Latin Americans are also usually the descendants of the European adventurers who ruthlessly enslaved their forefathers and all but eradicated native America.

Racial, religious and class conflict are inevitably acute in such an environment and they are inscribed in the very identity of Latin Americans. In fact the whole concept of cultural and historical identity is problematic when one inherits both the pain and shame of one's defeated forebears and the dubious legacy of their conquerors. But such a world is an endlessly suggestive environment for writers of fiction and poetry, and the real secret of the unparalleled success of Spanish-American writing since the Second World War is that its authors have learned to profit from these complexities and contradictions, so as to produce works that are totally 'First World' in their sophistication, erudition and complexity, but dramatically unfamiliar in their techniques and themes.

The literatures of some regions inevitably seem less exotic than others to European readers. Whereas many Latin-American republics are pretty obviously ethnically *mestizo* to the extent that a pure European face is something of a rarity, modern Argentina and Chile are societies produced by recent mass European immigration.

Their nineteenth-century literatures are, like those of all Latin America, generally unimpressive: Argentine gaucho or cowboy literature, for example the dialect poem about the gaucho Martín Fierro, reads nowadays like the product of a vanished world. But in the twentieth century the region has produced a remarkable number of fine writers whose work, with the possible exception of the poet Pablo Neruda, differs from other Spanish-American writing in that both its techniques and its themes have been distinctly cosmopolitan. The work of the Argentines Borges, Cortázar, Manuel Puig, Bioy Casares, Ernesto Sábato and of the Chilean José Donoso has a number of characteristics not typical of other parts of the Spanish-speaking world, including Spain: it is preoccupied, even obsessed, with private mental states or philosophical questions, but it is not markedly 'Latin American' in its concerns. In fact Argentine literature has a strong and distinctive streak of fantasy and solipsistic introspection; this may reflect a society that has cultivated self-contemplation – psychoanalysis is a national pastime – in the absence of strong collective ties and roots.

The further north one goes, the more historically self-aware the literature seems to become. Mexico is in many ways the opposite case from Argentina: most Mexicans have strong if ambiguous roots in a non-European past. Whereas the Amerindians of Argentina had been effectively exterminated by the late nineteenth century, some 60 Amerindian languages are still spoken in Mexico and surrounding areas, which were also the site of two splendid Amerindian cultures, the Mayan and the Aztec. Mexico is, moreover, distinctive in that it is the only Latin-American country in a supposedly revolutionary continent to have had a revolution of lasting social consequences.

It is no surprise, therefore, that all creative activity in Mexico from literature to cooking has a strong and unique national identity: exhibitions of Latin-American art tend to be overwhelmed by Mexican images. Nor is it surprising that Mexican literature is much preoccupied by the Amerindian and *mestizo* components of Mexican identity and by the nature and fate of the revolution of 1911 that signified the partial and uncompleted irruption of *mestizo* Mexico into the nation's historical life and raised vast and still unsatisfied hopes for social justice. One of the most famous works of the poet, essayist and recent Nobel Prize winner Octavio Paz, *El laberinto de la soledad* (*The Labyrinth of Solitude*, 1950), brilliantly expresses the peculiarities of the Mexicans' relationship with their own past, and the causes and consequences of the failure and eventual institutionalization of the revolution are central themes in the work of Carlos Fuentes, particularly *La muerte de Artemio Cruz* (*The Death of Artemio Cruz*, 1962); of Juan Rulfo – *El llano en llamas* (*The Burning Plain*, 1953) and *Pedro Páramo* (1955); of Mariano Azuela – *Los de abajo* (*The Underdogs*, 1915); and, indirectly, of Elena Poniatowska (especially in *Until we meet again*, 1969).

It is perhaps less appropriate to speak of the 'national literatures' of the other seventeen Spanish-American countries, despite the fact that most of them have produced writers of international importance. Since these are too numerous to name individually, we conclude this brief survey with a few general remarks about the Spanish-American novel, the novel being the richest genre of the region.

English-speaking readers new to Spanish-American novels are often struck by the violence and bizarreness of the world they portray: novels like Alejo Carpentier's *El reino de este mundo* (*The Kingdom of this World*, 1949), García Márquez's *Cien años de soledad* (*100 Years of Solitude*, 1967), Carlos Fuentes's *Terra Nostra* (1975), José Donoso's *Casa de campo* (*A House in the Country*, 1978), Mario Vargas Llosa's *La guerra del fin del mundo* (*The War of the End of the World*, 1981), must be catalogues of prodigies and horrors to anyone used to the typically minor scale of many British and even American novels. In fact, the ordinary foreign reader might conclude that Latin America is a madhouse that defies rational analysis, beyond hope of reform. It is not impossible that such pessimism is a secret belief of many Spanish-American writers. But there are also reasons of method and technique that explain the 'weirdness' of much Spanish-American writing.

One of these reasons is the novelists' belief that the categories of everyday Latin-American life are radically different from those of Western Europe and North America, and that they are politically and morally obliged to acknowledge this fundamental strangeness. This is the key to the technique of 'magic realism' that many non-Hispanic readers wrongly assume is characteristic of all Latin-American writing. Alejo Carpentier argued, in the early 1950s, that the Latin-American novelist's situation was analogous to that of those first Spanish chroniclers who found themselves almost incapable of describing intelligibly the mind-boggling new world that they had discovered. Alejo Carpentier, who was half French and very much an outsider to the ordinary life of Latin America, initially wrote novels, for example *El reino de este mundo* (*The Kingdom of this World*, 1949), *Los pasos perdidos* (*The Lost Steps*, 1953), that reflect the surprise of a cultivated Parisian in an exotic place: he focuses on the superstitions, barbarism and peculiarities of the Caribbean region and portrays this world as deeply alien to ordinary European experience.

Many other Spanish-American novelists have done the same thing in different ways. In innumerable novels the superficial rationalism of European culture and ideas is brutally confronted with the 'otherness' of Amerindian or African civilization, or with the vicious 'irrationality' of native Latin-American political and social life with its incomprehensible violence and vindictiveness. The results of this approach often read like fantasy, but the writers would claim that a certain 'fantastic' or 'magical' quality is typical of ordinary life in Latin America, and that no muted and decorous realism like Tolstoy's, Dickens's or Flaubert's could ever do this intrinsic bizarreness justice.

It is debatable whether this is in the long run an accurate or helpful way of presenting Latin America to the foreign reader, but it certainly makes for absorbing and strange novels. The international success of recent Latin-American fiction, with its nightmare holocausts and irruptions of superstition and fantasy into everyday life, has been very much due to the fact that it offers an exciting alternative for an international readership tired of the restrained and comparatively limited individual tragedies of Western literature.

Spanish-American literature makes much recent European and North-American writing seem very grey and flat. The Spanish-speaking authors may often overreach themselves or confuse formal complications with profundity of vision, but no one can accuse them of setting their artistic or conceptual sights too low. There is no sign, at the time of writing, that Spanish-American literature has exhausted its potential to shock and surprise. This potential will last as long as the world it comes from remains neither wholly European nor wholly removed from or indifferent to European history and culture.

A patent conferring nobility (*hidalguia*) upon Diego Aranguiz, sixteenth century. To be made a *hidalgo* was to join a hereditary aristocracy with many practical advantages: its members had the right to a coat of arms, were addressed as Don and were exempt from taxes. But they did not always become rich.

The bizarre pantheon of the Condes de Buenavista (*below right*), a sixteenth-century burial chapel in the church of El Cristo de la Victoria, Malaga, reflects a certain tendency in Spanish art to play with the furniture of death.

Marriage was a contract, often involving the transfer of property. This miniature from the thirteenth-century Catalan *Liber Feudorum Maior* shows such an occasion, with the couple on either side of the bridegroom's father, who symbolizes their union by his crossed arms.

The eldest son inherited the rank and honours of his father but not necessarily all his property. Here (*right*) the first Marquis of Santillana kneels in prayer in a monastery church, with behind him his son and heir who became the first Duke of Infantado.

Family identity

Spanish history, compared to that of England or France, is curiously lacking in family portraits. For Spaniards, partly because the laws of inheritance tended to sub-divide fortunes, family identity was something less tangible, embodied in documentary records (like the velvet-lined books trimmed with gold of Don Joseph Pérez de Orozco) or in family tombs and mausolea, rich with coats of arms and heraldic emblems.

The bonds of kinship

Beneath the complex web of legal obligations and property transactions, the reality of family life is harder to document. But from descriptions by foreigners, from popular stories and from vernacular art, it is clear that emotional ties binding relatives together were at least as strong in Spain as elsewhere.

A family meal draws together the generations in a vivid tile-picture from Valencia (*left*). *Above*: another Valencian tile of a servant preparing food and beneath that a picnic scene in a Peruvian watercolour, one of a series made for Don Baltasar Compañon, later bishop of Trujillo, between 1782 and 1788.

The two peasant women in Velázquez's *Christ in the House of Mary and Martha*, painted around 1620, are taken straight from vernacular Spanish life.

Little St Margaret by Zurbarán is clearly a local girl from his native Seville, with her red woollen skirt, white blouse, blue over-dress and sheepskin waistcoat.

María Teresa de Borbón y Vallabriga gazes out of Goya's picture with that mixture of pride and vulnerability so characteristic of Spanish royal children.

The bride of Christ. A girl whose dowry was insufficient for marriage might become a nun. In Mexico (*below*, *c*. 1777) she would be richly dressed to take her final vows.

Women: freedom and duty

Contrary to the beliefs of romantic foreigners, Spanish women were not the slaves of their menfolk. In many areas and at many times, their rights were greater than in most other European countries. Daughters shared inheritances equally with sons, nor could they be coerced into marrying against their choice. This selection of female portraits illustrates a range of historical periods, geographical regions and social classes.

A criollo beauty painted in 1794 (*left*) is an early example of the new demand for portraits by the wealthy Mexican middle-class; hence the many allusions to Doña Juana María Romero's money.

Goya's duchess of Alba (*below left*) presents so powerful an image of femininity that she has become almost the icon of 'Spanish womanhood. The rings on her fingers with the names 'Goya' and 'Alba' and the inscription in the sand to which she points, 'Solo Goya', strongly suggest a love story which, however, remains unproven.

Women's plight in twentieth-century Spain did not improve as rapidly as elsewhere, so that they came to seem relatively underprivileged. Lorca's plays and poems present a bleak picture of blighted lives and submission to social conventions. *Above*: his sketch for the gypsy Soledad Montaya in *Romancero gitano*:

> 'Soledad, whom do you seek,
> Alone and at this hour?'

Signing the register: a charmingly realistic painting by Mariano Fortuny (died 1874). Nineteenth-century marriages in Spain – especially a fashionable one like this – were still both affairs of the heart (since the women were entirely free to choose their husbands) and matters of property, the careful regulation of family status. Here the bridegroom bends down to sign under the eye of the priest while the bride and her friends look on. Behind them is a typical Spanish *reja*, the ornate screen that surrounds the *coro* of a church.

3 CREATIVE DIVERSITY

A decorative sixteenth-century map of the Iberian peninsula, showing the regions of Spain, the Balearic Islands, Portugal and the tip of Africa.

CREATIVE DIVERSITY
GALICIA

C. LISON-TOLOSANA

For the last thousand years Spain has remained the most heterogeneous socio-cultural mosaic in Western Europe. A land of changing frontiers, of differing self-images and of numerous partners in dialogue, it has proved, with its cultural tidal waves surging from the centre to the periphery and back again, that the power of myth, of regional beliefs and separate languages, together with local visions, symbols and values, are factors as powerful as any others in determining both the development of the internal history of a people and its necessary dealings with near neighbours and with distant foreigners. Galicia, with its nearly 3 million inhabitants and more than 11,000 square miles divided into 4 provinces, is one of those multiform regions which actively contribute to making up the whole.

At once rural, urban and seafaring in its character, archaic in its folklore yet innovative in its moments of glory, Galicia has throughout its history exhibited unusual features. Since the sixth century BC its territory has received successive waves of invaders such as Celts, Germans, Romans and Suevi who have left their mark, sometimes more in fantasy than in reality. Its political-administrative division into 50 *vilas*, 315 municipalities, 2,777 rural parishes and more than 32,000 villages gives it today distinctive and traditional characteristics, as do such features as the structure of the family and the system of inheritance with their Suevo-German and seigneurial origins. The theory and practice of a house founded on lineage and expressed in the lineal family is important in explaining some periods of Galician history.

The nuclear family with cognate succession and bilateral inheritance coexists not only with a system of families organized on the fraternal principle, in which the bride and groom each continue to live in the house of their parents, but also with two other modes: the patrilineal and the matrilineal. In the patrilineal system there is only one heir, the wife goes to live with the husband's family and virtually the whole inheritance goes to the first-born son. The matrilineal family is another variation on the same theme, but only in Galicia is it instituted as a positive principle, not just in the case of failure of the male line, as in Catalonia. In this system the filiation is also lineal but the succession, the inheritance, the adherence to the house and to the lineage, the rights and the duties are transmitted by the mother to just one daughter, ignoring all the other sons and daughters; a young couple lives with the wife's family. It is the heiress, not her husband, who represents the lineage, who wields authority and makes the decisions both inside and outside the house; the money is in her pocket, she – not her husband – directs the work in the fields and it is her voice that counts in local public affairs.

Lineality creates a link between the living and the dead – always influential in Galician beliefs; it bestows a feeling of permanence, a vision of human life which transcends the individual. The lineal family system is related to the rural belief in the nocturnal procession of the dead – *a compaña* – which leaves the parish cemetery at night to make a premonitory visitation to someone who is about to die. The corpus of Galician beliefs is partly revealed in the rich vocabulary connected with the subject. The multitude of witches, visions, apparitions, possession by the devil, and so on, are elements in a system of representing symbols and values which flourishes in an oral tradition, in rural isolation, in certain professions, emblems, rites, pathways, hermitages, monasteries and in numerous pilgrimages typical of the region. All these provide foci and structures for the establishment and retention of beliefs.

Lineality, in conjunction with other important factors, has also led inevitably to emigration. This has been massive in numerical terms and has taken place over a long period, first to Castile, then to South America and now to Europe. There are more Galicians in the New World than in Galicia; some of the Galician Centres which have been founded there have had more than 100,000 members. Emigration has contributed to the use of the word 'Galician' to mean 'Spanish' and to Spaniards being called 'Galicians'. Significantly, this is nothing new, as the Arabs gave the name Galicians to all the Christians in the north of the peninsula.

Their own beliefs and Islam have an even greater significance in the history of Galicia; its geography, its mythic and imaginative creative powers and the stimuli of the socio-political situations it has experienced have brought about processes of cultural growth in Galicia that are truly unique and extraordinary. Its position in the extreme north-west of the peninsula favoured from the beginning its isolation. This isolation in turn contributed to the internal development of a politico-cultural system dominated by great noble houses, by bishops and by monasteries; that their control was not always benign is shown by a fifteenth-century revolt. But the course of the history of this remote corner of the peninsula was changed in the Middle Ages, when Galicia was transformed into the lodestar for all the Christian kingdoms of Spain.

Towards the middle of the eighth century, when the Arabs conquered Spain – it is, perhaps, significant that the two events happened at the same time – there arose, or at least there reemerged with great strength, the belief that the Apostle St James had preached in the west of the peninsula. By the ninth century there is documentary evidence of the tradition according to which some angels revealed the spot in which his body was buried, where the cathedral of Santiago now stands. King

Galicia is synonymous with the pilgrimage centre of Santiago. *Left*: a sixteenth-century representation of a pilgrim wearing traditional garb – a voluminous cloak against bad weather, a stout walking staff, satchel and water bottle. Prominently displayed on his cloak are scallop-shells, the symbol of St James and pilgrimage. *Below left*: a section of the original pilgrim road, the stones smoothed by the feet of countless travellers.

Alfonso III (866–910) later ordered the construction of a new cathedral in keeping with so precious a relic. And just as the Moorish conquest had expanded from the south northwards, so the opposite process, beginning in Galicia, expanded southwards. The cathedral chapter, its bishops and the monarchs transformed the city of Santiago into the third most important centre of Christianity, not only for Spain but for the whole of Europe. The monarchs called the bishop of Compostela 'Pontiff of the whole world', and he adopted the title 'Bishop of the Apostolic See' (tenth century). What is more, during the eleventh century Santiago became a rival of Rome itself. The apostle, for his part, assisted the process by emerging from his tomb in order to support the Christian monarchs. He appeared during difficult battles to bring the Christian forces final victory and became, in popular parlance, Santiago Matamoros ('St James the Moorkiller').

The efforts of chapter and bishops caused the tomb of the apostle to attract ever greater numbers of Spanish and European pilgrims as the eleventh century progressed; Santiago talked to Rome and Jerusalem on equal terms. The cosmopolitan capital of Christendom received 'Gascons, Bretons, Germans, English, Burgundians, Normans, people from Toulouse, Provençals, Lombards and many others', wrote an anonymous chronicler proudly. Since then saints, kings, nobles, rogues and beggars have made the pilgrimage to Santiago. Thanks to the powerful creative imagination of its elite, the city succeeded in transforming the periphery into the centre; Galicia was no longer the end of the world (*Finisterrae*) but its starting point (*Principiumterrae*). The same is true of the city's economy: through a daring stroke of imagination in the formulation of the Vow of Santiago, both Castiles, Extremadura, Murcia and Andalusia paid tribute to the cathedral of Compostela. The brilliant idea of the pilgrimage, which began at a time of changes affecting social life, warfare, economics, politics and religion, also went on to give rise to the production of miniatures, goldsmithry, sculpture, reliquaries, paintings, tympana, capitals – a whole iconography of St James in Europe and beyond. It also led to the building of roads, hermitages, churches and hospitals, the formulation of laws and the writing of books essential for any account of the history of Europe.

But there is yet more: with the pilgrims came French literature, the Roman rite, new architecture, monastic orders and troubadours who reactivated the traditional Galician lyric forms. The people, their folklore, their legends and local stories, their songs and dances were, then as now, the source of inspiration for the medieval Galician lyric. The songs of love and friendship, pilgrim songs, songs to insult and songs to curse, demonstrate not only poetic creativity but also the popular infrastructure of the poetry: the sea, fiestas, pilgrimages, indigenous songs and dances. Galicia with its incomparable troubadours, such as Macías, Meogo, Ruy López, Ayras Nuñes, Rodríguez de la Cámara, came to be the most important centre of medieval poetry, to such an extent that Galician became the common literary language in which Hispanic literature was written because it was considered more appropriate and more subtle than Castilian. The musical and poetic language has helped to make present-day Galicia one of the great homelands of poetry, authentically local in character and popular in tone: proof of this is the impromptu sung poetry, governed by its own rules, used for toasts and at local fiestas.

The wonderful Romanesque Pórtico de la Gloria, the Baroque towers of the Obradoiro, which have been called 'the highest achievement of Hispanic Baroque', the monasteries (Sobrado, Osera, Samos), the manors, soul-shrines, wayside crosses and granaries bear witness to the artistic creativity of the people at all social levels. The popular dances and tambourine music can bear comparison with the sculpture of Gregorio Hernández, the nostalgic paintings of Pérez Villaamil (1807–54) or the piercing social criticism of the drawings of Castelao. But it is in literature that the Galicians have gone beyond their frontiers. By describing their own local reality they have attained a privileged position at the national level. Coinciding with the Romantic movement and with the awakening in certain circles of the feeling of regional identity – for instance, Benito Vicetto (1824–78), novelist, historian and journalist, and Manuel Antonio Martínez Murguía (1833–1923), historian and art-critic – Galician literature was reborn with the melancholy poetry of Rosalía de Castro (1837–85), the regional novels of Emilia Pardo Bazán (1851–1921), and the local background of a good part of the works of the exceptionally innovative novelist and playwright, Ramón María del Valle-Inclán (1869–1935). In this guise, the reality of the Galician world appears as literature: gatherings, meals, pilgrimages, envy, irony, lawsuits, mistrust and beliefs, the nostalgia of emigrants, poverty and *caciquismo* (the dominance of local political bosses). This resurgence culminated in the generation of *Nos* with Vicente Martínez Risco (1884–1963), who consolidated Galician regionalism politically and also created a new myth – that of 'Celtic' Galicia – by proclaiming a Celtic origin for the main body of Galician culture. This elitist invention, which both differentiates and exalts Galicia in contrast to Castile, has become part of Galician historiography.

On the other hand, the age-old constant emigration, mainly to Madrid, has served as the basis for creating a stereotype of the Galician as a simpleton, or a person of no consequence. 'The Galicians never count, because they are nobodies', wrote the unknown author of *La Tía Fingida* ('The False Aunt'). *Gallegada* ('the Galician mob') was already in the seventeenth century a contemptuous term to refer to the unwelcome groups of Galicians passing through on their way to or from the harvest in Castile. The Galician bourgeoisie responded to this negative image by inventing the stereotype of the labourer or peasant, endowed with irony and astuteness – the classical clever fool, adept at dissimulation, argument and politics. The people, for their part, created symbolic bourgeois types such as the scrivener, the lawyer and the political boss which reflect the subtlety of their judgments and values. There was a singular capacity at all levels for creating myths – distorting mirrors which pass themselves off as reality. And which operate as if they were real.

I have selected representative moments of the creative history of a people, constructive moments which consolidate and empower different Galicias, which show in action the imaginative genius of a people who, without ceasing to be rooted in the land and culture, manipulate, remember and redefine their situation and their past. History is also made by sentiment and imagination.

ASTURIAS

GONZALO ANES

The Principality of Asturias (it is called a principality because John II bestowed the title 'Prince of Asturias' upon the heir to the throne of Castile) lies between the Cantabrian mountains and the sea, separated from Galicia by the rivers Eo and upper Navia and their flood-plains. The river Deva flows between it and present-day Cantabria.

The mountainous outcrops of the cordillera are cut by valleys which at their highest points become passes, the natural exits and entrances of Asturias, which have always been points of transit between the lands of the northern and southern slopes. The trails made in the Paleolithic Age by animals migrating between their winter and summer pastures were turned into primitive roads by the hunters who preyed on them. When the seasonal migration of flocks became organized, their routes followed the same ancient tracks. Roman and medieval roads, and the highways of the eighteenth and ninteenth centuries and of today, use the same routes. Even the Madrid-Gijón railway follows the line of a primitive cattle trail.

The difficulty of reaching Asturias from the Meseta and the laborious climb up to the passes from the coast and from the valleys explain why Asturias remained so isolated in ancient times. Only in the Roman period did it attract some interest by the discovery of gold and possible deposits of copper and tin. It was this, and the warlike attitude of the tribes who inhabited the craggy lands beyond the passes, that caught the attention of the geographer Strabo, who described the tribal organization of the peoples of the north of the Iberian peninsula, and how they made their living by gathering food and rudimentary cattle raising. This primitive way of life tended to persist, hardly influenced at all by the Romans and Visigoths.

So when the Moors reached the valleys of the northern slopes of the cordillera, they encountered stiff Asturian resistance and were driven back in several skirmishes. One of these formed the basis of the legendary battle of Covadonga, the starting point of the Kingdom of Asturias. Pelayo, the victor of Covadonga and leader of the peoples of the lands of Cangas de Onís, used the prestige he had gained from his triumphs over the Moors to lay the foundations of this small kingdom.

The original grouping, organized as an elective monarchy, managed to enlarge its territory and the number of people living in it. Pelayo died in 739 and was succeeded by his son Favila, who was killed two years later while out hunting. Pelayo's son-in-law, Alfonso I, was then proclaimed king. It seems that he was the son of Pedro, the Visigothic Duke of Cantabria, who had perhaps been able to survive in the mountains of his duchy without submitting to the Moors. Alfonso, the true founder of the Asturian monarchy, took advantage of the internal rebellions and struggles of al-Andalus to extend his kingdom. He attacked the Moors who remained in the territories of Galicia and Astorga. He and his brother Fruela organized forays into the north-east of the peninsula, northern Portugal and towards the east and the south-east: in Alava, la Bureba, la Rioja and the Tierra de Campos, reaching as far as the Tagus valley. Because Alfonso lacked the resources to establish garrisons in the territories he raided, he was unable to make his conquests secure. Nevertheless, he ensured that the area which coincides with the present-day principality and with Cantabria was flanked by two frontier zones: part of Galicia to the west, and to the east a somewhat imprecise zone inhabited by the Basques. Here Christians fleeing from Moorish domination took refuge.

Fruela (754–69) transferred the court to Oviedo, and a city began to grow up around what had been a religious community and perhaps a Roman camp before that. Here the road from the Pyrenees to Galicia crossed that leading from the sea up to the mountain pass of Pajares. Under Alfonso II (791–842), its population began to increase as the town acquired palaces and churches, baths, a defensive wall and, in the surrounding countryside, country houses and places of recreation. Its urban development coincided with the late Carolingian Empire, and Gothic and Carolingian influences are evident in its cultural flowering with examples of what has been called 'Asturian art'. Alfonso II ordered the building of the basilica of San Salvador and the Cámara Santa, and the churches of Santa María, San Tirso and San Julián de los Prados. The interior walls of the latter are covered with paintings similar in style to late Roman examples.

In Oviedo, the sovereign aimed to restore the Visigothic traditions and the rituals of the Court of Toledo. Thus the Kingdom of Asturias saw itself as the continuation of the Visigothic kingdom which the Asturian monarchs were called to restore, a notion that might have been fostered by refugee Mozarabic clergy. The late-eighth century *Chronicle of Albelda* indicates that Alfonso II decreed the establishment in Oviedo of 'the entire order, as it had been in Toledo, both in the Church and in the Palace'. Chroniclers called the Asturian monarchs 'the Visigothic kings of Oviedo'. Nevertheless, there still existed those indigenous elements which had made possible the birth of the Kingdom of Asturias and which were to be gradually eliminated as the new institutions came into being. Until then, there had been no difference between the Cantabrians and their neighbours in the organization of their societies. In spite of the evolution of all the social orders since the time of the Romans, including their own tardy, and only partial, conversion to Christianity, the peoples who lived to the north of the Cantabrian cordillera had neither been politically absorbed by the Visigoths nor become dependent on the court of Toledo.

The widest territorial expansion of the Kingdom of Asturias took place under Alfonso III (866–910), who was elected king by a council of magnates on the death of his father Ordoño I (850–66). After this, the elective system seems to have given way to the principle of hereditary kingship. Alfonso was deposed by Froila, the Count of Galicia, who was later killed by those loyal to the young deposed monarch. The *Chronicle of Albelda* relates the military successes and conquests of Alfonso III who, like his father, had to fight against the Basques. He repelled the Moors and gained control of the Duero valley through successive campaigns, and also of Galicia and northern Portugal. Simancas, Dueñas and Toro were repopulated, while settlers from the north occupied lands in the valley, and more Mozarabs came to live in the Kingdom of Asturias. At the same time the power of the monarchy was being consolidated.

The reign of Ramiro I (842–50) saw the construction of palaces and churches with vaulted domes, combined with interior wall arcading and external shallow buttresses or pilaster strips. The

The magnificent late Gothic south tower of Oviedo Cathedral, Asturias, capped by a lacy pyramidal spire of outstanding delicacy (*below right*). Among the treasures of the cathedral is a twelfth-century 'Book of Testaments', which records the most important gifts made to the church in Oviedo. The codex contains seven magnificent illustrations of the most notable donors. *Right*: King Alfonso presenting his gift to the bishop.

decoration shows Byzantine and Lombard influences. The palace of which the great hall is now Santa María del Naranco and the church of San Miguel de Lillo, on the slopes of the Monte Naranco, both date from this period, as does the hermitage of Santa Cristina de Lena. Under Alfonso III, Andalusian influences began to appear, alongside inherited traditions: the horseshoe arch appears along with other decorative elements originating in Moorish Spain. In the Kingdom of Asturias artistic and cultural development came together just as they were declining in almost the whole of Europe. This conjunction was important not only as an example of the resurgence of Christian art but also for the rise of the Romanesque style. A number of examples of Asturian gold work survive: the *Cruz de los Angeles* ('Cross of the Angels') from the reign of Alfonso II and the *Cruz de la Victoria* ('Cross of Victory'), both in Oviedo Cathedral, the casket of Astorga Cathedral and the 'agate chest', all from the reign of Alfonso III.

The Kingdom of Asturias was a place of pilgrimage in the ninth century because of the sanctuary of San Salvador in Oviedo and its relics. It also became a stage on the road to Compostela after the spread of the news that the remains of St James had been discovered there. Alfonso III erected a new church with marble pillars over St James's sepulchre, transforming the one built by Alfonso II (the Chaste), and made other major donations.

The expansion of the Kingdom of Asturias had several effects. On the death of Alfonso III in 910, the court was transferred to the city of León, because Asturias was too far from the lands of the Duero valley which had by then been incorporated into the kingdom. It became necessary to rebuild or erect castles. It was also essential to encourage people to settle and cultivate the newly conquered lands. The plains traversed by the river Duero, between the Cantabrian cordillera and the Gredos and Guadarrama mountain ranges, had become almost depopulated because of the destructive campaigns of Christians and Moors. There was a growing number of cities in ruins, agricultural undertakings abandoned, hamlets and villages destroyed and deserted, barren and ownerless fields full of weeds and scrub. In the valley, military action was followed by repopulation, as it was in Galicia, in the Bierzo and in the areas to the north of the upper Ebro. What made these resettlements different from that of the Duero plains was the fact that in the valley, nearly all the cultivable land lay abandoned. In the Duero valley settlement began in the middle of the ninth century. It took place in a variety of ways, but all of them were based on the free initiative of individuals to occupy barren lands, bringing with them their families, cattle and farm equipment. Sometimes, the settlers came to the area which was to be repopulated either with the king, or much more frequently with one of his representatives. 'Sounding the horn and waving the royal standard' they took possession of the barren fields by a process known as *pressura*. On other occasions, a count would on his own initiative give people land to cultivate in some barren area of his district. In a 'settlement charter' he would set out the rules which the settlers were to abide by. Settlers also established themselves in the neighbourhood of some sanctuary or religious community, constructing their dwellings next to it and occupying the nearby fields under the system of *pressura*, in what amounted to an ecclesiastical or monastic repopulation, since it took place around churches or religious communities. Sometimes the monarchs granted general or special authorization for people to occupy certain lands by *pressura*, but what seems to have happened most commonly was that the settlers dispensed with any such authorizations: they could later apply for royal confirmation of their *pressura*.

Because the settlers had freely occupied the barren lands, their society was made up of free men and women, not subject to any lord through ties of personal dependency, nor through the land they cultivated, since the extent of the unoccupied territory far exceeded the ability of the settlers to colonize it. Therefore, in Asturias proper, serfdom was not found to the same extent, or in the same forms, as in the rest of Western Europe during the late Middle Ages. Indeed, evidence exists that there were no tied serfs in the Duero valley even during the second half of the twelfth century. The historian Sánchez-Albornoz has attributed the absence of 'tied serfdom in the Kingdom of León and Castile from an early date' to emigration for the purpose of resettlement. This absence of a true feudal system also led to the liberties attained by the country people of the plains of Castile-León and the great strength acquired by the councils of the two kingdoms. The movement of colonists into the Castilian plains was, for Sánchez-Albornoz, the first historical enterprise of the Kingdom of Asturias, resulting in 'an appetite for ever increasing assimilation, across an ever open frontier'.

After the removal of the court to León, Asturias was governed from the new capital, becoming a province of the Kingdom of Asturias-León, and subsequently of León-Castile. In Asturias, as elsewhere in Christian Spain and the rest of Western Europe, the area of cultivated land increased from the end of the tenth century and methods of cultivation improved. Agricultural production also increased and urban growth developed, encouraged by the pilgrims on their way to Compostela along the coast. Pilgrims also travelled from León to Oviedo to venerate the relics in the Cámara Santa.

During the twelfth and thirteenth centuries several Romanesque churches were built in Asturias, and it was then that Asturian art reached its purest form in such works as the statues of the apostles in the Cámara Santa. Bishop Gutierre de Toledo ordered several buildings to be demolished on the site of Alfonso II's church, and construction of the cathedral began at the end of the fourteenth century. The work continued for four hundred years, although it was in the fifteenth century that the basic structure which establishes the character of the whole edifice was completed, in the Flamboyant Gothic style. Oviedo Cathedral is a model of elegance and sobriety in which balance and harmony reign. The late Gothic new tower, in the words of Jesús E. Casariego, is 'one of those . . . architectural triumphs whose majesty and beauty . . . conquer each generation.'

As the construction of the cathedral was nearing completion, that of the University of Oviedo was just beginning. It was founded by Archbishop Fernando Valdés who died in 1568, and built by his heirs following his intentions. The university finally opened its doors in 1608. Because of the excellence of its reputation for classical studies, it attracted men like Campomanes and Jovellanos, who later distinguished themselves as writers and politicians during the period of the Enlightenment in Spain. Their thinking helped to form the basis of the legislation which overturned the institutions of the ancien régime and encouraged the establishment of a new juridical order.

During the seventeenth century, agricultural practices in Asturias underwent considerable changes. The cultivation of maize was introduced in its coastal regions and valleys, and the area devoted to maize increased.

As more food became available, the population rose. This tendency continued through the eighteenth century, until it reached a level where emigration became essential, and it was to remain a constant factor in the history of Asturias. At the end of the eighteenth century, Jovellanos was already drawing attention to the number of Asturians who were leaving for Madrid, Seville, Cadiz or America. At the end of the nineteenth century, emigration to America began to reach a peak which it maintained until the 1920s.

The influence of the Asturian emigrants on the countries of America to which they travelled has not yet received the attention it deserves. The cultural and leisure activities of the Asturian centres founded there by emigrants are well documented, as is their charitable and welfare work, but there have been no studies of their economic, political and cultural influence. Some managed to make a fortune in their new country, others were not so lucky. All of them merit recognition of their adventurous spirit in leaving home and risking the uncertainties of life in their adopted countries. When their economic activities are investigated, it will be seen how important was their labour and how much they contributed to the economy, the politics, the culture and the science of the countries which received them.

THE BASQUE COUNTRY: ALAVA, GUIPUZCOA AND VIZCAYA JUAN PABLO FUSI AIZPURUA

The first book written in the Basque language was published in 1545. The earliest work on the systematization of the language was begun in the eighteenth century by the Jesuit Manuel de Larramendi (1690–1776). The first general histories of Alava, Guipúzcoa and Vizcaya were also written in the eighteenth century and modern scholars discovered the Basque world in the same period. On 28 November 1799, after a visit to the Basque Country, Wilhelm von Humboldt (1767–1835) wrote to Goethe: 'I have never encountered a people who have preserved such a strong national character and a physiognomy which appears so distinctive at first sight.' The sense of a separate Basque identity had emerged early. This was already evident in the ideas expressed by some sixteenth and seventeenth-century historians such as Garibay and Poza about Basque nobility of blood, egalitarianism and original liberty, claims supported by the very antiquity of the language, which many have identified with that of the first inhabitants of the Iberian peninsula. For Basque apologists, it was the Basque lineage which had produced the nobility of Castile.

Such arguments did not challenge the integration of the Basque territories into the kingdom of Castile and the Spanish state, which was indisputable from the twelfth century onwards, if not before. On the contrary, they served to justify the administrative privileges enjoyed by the Basque provinces, enshrined in their Codes of Law (*fueros*), and to reinforce the position of power of the Basque elites who were particularly prominent in the administrations of Charles V and Philip II. Spanish – which developed in the north of Castile alongside the Basque language – became a vehicle for the expression of Basque identity as much as the Basque tongue itself. The Basque *fueros*, ancient laws by which each of the Basque provinces was separately governed and which remained in force until 1876, were written in Castilian.

In spite of the fact that for a long time the population of Alava, Guipúzcoa and Vizcaya was low – it was reckoned to be about 300,000 at the end of the eighteenth century – the Basques played an important role in Spain's American empire and in the imperial administration. They were explorers and colonizers, sailors, churchmen and evangelizers, soldiers, secretaries of state (like the powerful Idiáquez family in the sixteenth century). In 1522 Juan Sebastián Elcano completed the first voyage around the world, begun by Magellan. Paraguay was colonized by Irala, the immense territories of western Mexico by Francisco de Ibarra, the Philippines by Legazpi and Urdaneta. It was a Basque, Lope de Aguirre, who symbolized the mad lust for power which possessed the conquistadors in their search for the fabled El Dorado. Juan de Zumárraga, the first bishop of Mexico and 'the protector of the Indians', brought printing to America in the mid-sixteenth century. The Basques were at that time excellent calligraphers: Juan de Icíar created the splendid Spanish imperial typescript of the Golden Age. The first Spanish ambassador to the United States, Diego María de Gardoqui (1735–98), was a Basque and so was Pedro A. Olañeta (1770–1825), the last general to die fighting against the independence of Spain's colonies in America.

Another Basque, Ignatius Loyola (1491–1556), tenacious, ascetic, reserved and authoritarian in nature, in whom Unamuno saw the finest expression of the Basque character, founded in 1534 the Society of Jesus, the principal instrument of the Catholic Counter-Reformation of the sixteenth and seventeenth centuries. The order has always been particularly linked with the Basque Country, the birthplace of many Jesuits and, since 1886, the site of an influential Jesuit university. By contrast, distinguished members of the small Basque aristocracy, such as the Count of Peñaflorida, who in 1765 founded the Royal Society of Friends of the Basque Country, adopted the spirit and ideas of the eighteenth-century Enlightenment. Several Basques, among them Mariano Luis de Urquijo (1768–1817), the translator of the works of Voltaire, were members of the pro-French government set up by Napoleon when he invaded Spain in 1808. Bilbao and San Sebastián, the provincial capitals, with an important role in Castilian foreign trade, were at that time small, but relatively active and modern cities. They soon became the centre of liberalism in the Basque Country. The strongly Catholic rural areas became pillars of support for Carlism, the Catholic, popular and anti-liberal counter-revolution which gave rise to the civil wars of 1833 to 1840 and 1872 to 1876 (and which would survive to be one of the principal forces supporting General Franco's military uprising in 1936).

The Basque Country was transformed after 1876 by a formidable process of industrialization based on the export of iron ore to England and driven by the dynamism of a small number of highly ambitious and talented entrepreneurs such as Victor Chávarri, José María Martínez Rivas, Horacio Echevarrieta, Eduardo Aznar, Ramón de la Sota, Federico Echevarría, Juan Tomás Gandarias and the Ibarra family. The area around Bilbao became the centre of the iron and steel industries and naval shipbuilding. Basque capital, supported by strong industrial banks, was the driving force of the national economy. Guipúzcoa diversified its production into the manufacture of paper, armaments, railway equipment, tools, textiles and bicycles. Only Alava, the most Castilianized of the provinces, stagnated until the 1960s. The population, due to the immigration of workers from other provinces, grew spectacularly from 450,000 in 1877 to 600,000 in 1900 and 890,000 in 1930.

The uniqueness of their language and the peculiarities of their history conditioned the Basques' perception of themselves. Miguel de Unamuno (1864–1936), the Bilbao-born writer

Basque liberty through the ages. *Left*: King Ferdinand of Aragon pledging to respect the *fueros* (or codes of law) of Vizcaya at a ceremony in Bilbao, the region's capital. *Below left*: during the forty years of Franco's dictatorship, Basque culture was fiercely suppressed. But in 1979, after his death, the Basque people were granted a wide measure of autonomy and celebrated their new freedom at a huge, emotional gathering at which the previously forbidden *ikurriña* (Basque flag) was proudly flourished.

who was the intellectual leader of the Spanish 'Generation of 1898', saw in the universal presence of the Basques in America the principal element in their historical personality. He thought that the Basques were an inseparable part of the Castilian spirit and regarded Bilbao as a liberal, Spanish city. Ramiro de Maeztu (1874–1936), another Basque member of the same 'Generation', saw the economic dynamism of Bilbao in the early twentieth century as the essential fact in Basque history. By contrast, the novelist Pío Baroja (1872–1956), a writer captivated by the rural Basque world and the region's maritime tradition, depicted a Basque Country peopled by Carlist guerrillas, seafaring adventurers and smugglers. Other Basque intellectuals, such as Sánchez Mazas or Mourlane Michelena, preferred the enlightened tradition of the eighteenth century as the ideal representation of their people.

These theories were literary and speculative, not directly political. By comparison, the theories of Sabino Arana (1865–1903) implied a real political revolution. By defining Basque identity as a distinctive nationality in its own right, based on race, language and religion, Arana created Basque nationalism, which aspired to independence, or self-government, for the Spanish Basque provinces plus Navarre and the Basque territories in France. The Basque Nationalist Party was a minority party until the First World War, based mainly in Vizcaya and Guipúzcoa. Moderate, popular and Christian in orientation, even though the separatist and racial ideas of Arana were never abandoned, the party became the major force in Basque politics in the 1930s. The Second Republic (1931–36) gave autonomy to the region in 1936, a privilege withdrawn by Franco even before he had achieved victory in the Civil War of 1936 to 1939. The bombing of Guernica by Franco's German allies remained a symbol of the crushing of the ephemeral experience of Basque self-government. Later, in the last years of the Franco dictatorship (1939–75), the terrorist organization ETA, founded clandestinely in 1959, revived nationalist aspirations and continued its violent struggle for Basque independence even after the return to democracy in 1975 and after political autonomy was once again granted to the Basque provinces in 1979.

Nationalism, which was to a great extent a cultural reaction to the disappearance of the traditional Basque order, idealized the rural and ethnic elements in the Basque world. However, because of the economic and social changes of the nineteenth and twentieth centuries, the Basque Country ceased to be an organic community and became a predominantly industrial, urban and mass society. Since the beginning of the twentieth century, a strong pluralism defined both the cultural and political life of the region. Nationalism revitalized rural Basque culture as reflected in the language, dances, music and popular songs, ancient rural and maritime sports, customs, festivals and

Detail from Picasso's *Guernica*, painted as a protest against the bombing of the ancient Basque capital by Franco's German allies.

traditions of many localities. As a result, there was a revival of literature written in Basque which had its first golden age in the 1930s with the work of the poets Lizardi, Lauaxeta and Orixe and reached new peaks in the 1960s with the poet Gabriel Aresti and in the 1970s and 1980s with the emergence of a generation of new writers. At the same time, Basque-Spanish culture flowered in the work of a notable number of personalities highly influential in the culture of Spain: Unamuno, Baroja, Maeztu, Salaverría, Sánchez Mazas, Basterra, Tomás Meabe, the painter Zuloaga, the architects Zuazo and Aizpúrua, the philosopher Xabier Zubiri, the poets Juan Larrea, Blas de Otero and Gabriel Celaya, the writer Ignacio Aldecoa. Bilbao was transformed into an industrial city of great energy, with modernistic buildings of undeniable interest. San Sebastián became an elegant summer resort. Modernization generated a new demand for culture in society. In the first third of the twentieth century a school of modern Basque painting emerged – Iturrino, Regoyos, Zubiaurre, Arteta, Ucelay, Echevarría and others – regional in themes and outlook, but whose work shared in the principal artistic tendencies of their time. They paved the way for a later generation of artists some of whose members, like the sculptors Oteiza and Chillida, became prominent in the vanguard of modern art in the 1960s and 1970s. Finally, industrial society produced a mass culture. From the 1920s onwards, modern sports – football, cycling, athletics, boxing and others – for all of which the Basques were to show a great talent, became the most important form of collective entertainment in Basque society.

Modernization also brought about an increasing socialization of politics. The appearance of mass parties, such as the Socialist Party, strong in Vizcaya since the end of the nineteenth century, and the Nationalist Party itself, changed Basque politics. Until 1936, the marked pluralism of the region meant that no single party achieved political hegemony and that the three provinces of Alava, Guipúzcoa and Vizcaya even had different party systems. Carlist traditionalism was the dominant force in Alava;

the Catholic right and Basque nationalism dominated in Guipúzcoa; the Republican and Socialist left, nationalism and the Spanish right controlled politics in Vizcaya. All this changed after the forty years of the Franco dictatorship (1939–75) which for the Basque Country meant on the one hand a fresh impetus for economic, industrial and demographic growth – between 1950 and 1970 the population increased by 900,000 to reach about 2.1 million in 1980 – and on the other hand, a long period of assimilation and centralism involving discrimination against Basque culture. The emergence of ETA in 1959 marked the crystallization of a new violent and revolutionary nationalism which in a few years deeply radicalized politics in the Basque Country.

Since 1975 the hegemony of nationalism – both traditional and radical – became apparent, although the Socialist party, deeply opposed to ETA, retained part of its old influence in Bilbao and even extended it to San Sebastián and Alava, whose capital Vitoria experienced since 1960 a rapid process of industrialization and growth. Ironically, the political hegemony of nationalism was achieved when the rural and ethnic Basque world had become merely residual. In 1985 only 7 per cent of the working population were in agriculture or fishing; only 20 to 25 per cent spoke Basque. The Basque Country of the last third of the twentieth century bore little resemblance to that seen by Humboldt two centuries before: the views of life and society, the organization of work, the forms of leisure and entertainment, human relations, were all simply variations of late twentieth-century European social life. Its political, cultural, linguistic and territorial problems resulted from the different conceptions of Basque nationality; its social and economic problems derived from the industrialized and urban nature of its economic structure. Above all, the Basque Country had its own political order: in 1979 it received a broad autonomy which provided it with a government, a parliament, a university, schools, television and police of its own, none of which existed when the Basque Country was governed by its ancient *fueros*.

Spain's landscape changes dramatically from region to region. The snow-capped Pyrenees seem to belong to a different world from the sub-tropical coasts of Andalusia.

In the province of Vizcaya, not far from the north-east coast of the peninsula, a loop of the River Plencia flows round fertile farmland (*top left*). The northern province of Navarre is similarly green and fertile. In the Baztán valley (*centre left*), cows graze in fields divided by dry-stone walls.

Spain's chief physical feature is the vast elevated central plateau, or *meseta* – dry steppes that make up two-fifths of the country. La Mancha, famous for its windmills (it is the setting of *Don Quijote*), occupies part of its southern reaches (*left*). In the far south of Spain lies Andalusia. At Motril (*above*), the land slopes down from the Sierra Nevada to the sea. Olive and almond trees flourish on the hillsides.

A copse of palm trees shades a house at Elche, near Alicante in Valencia (*top right*), close to the eastern Mediterranean coast. By contrast, deciduous trees and a stony stream in a valley overshadowed by the snowy peak of the Encantats represent the alpine climate of the mountainous north.

NAVARRE

MARIA CRUZ MINA

It has become commonplace to present Navarre as a region of contrasts, but that is indeed what the evidence forces upon us. First nature played its part. From the Pyrenees and their interspersed valleys to the fertile valley of the Ebro and Bardenas deserts, the most varied climates and landscapes are found. Such disparate forms of geography inevitably produce different life-styles and in many ways condition the temper of its peoples. Then time worked its effect on nature. Navarre has been a crossroads of peoples, cultures, languages and, in medieval times, also of religions. But in spite of everything, a long and unique history has endowed it with a strong sense of community.

The first to come were the Vascones, the ancient tribe from which the name Basque derives; from them the land was called Vasconia. Rome arrived in the first century BC, bringing its own language, culture and urban life and eventually the Christian religion. The present capital Pamplona was then Pompeiopolis, the city of Pompey, whom it supported in his struggles against Sertorius. By that time the Romans had already come to appreciate the military qualities of the Vascones.

After the Romans, the Visigoths, and after them the Muslim invasion. Vasconia was divided. The southern part made a pact with the new arrivals. The north had not yet entered into history: neither Romans nor Visigoths had penetrated its valleys. Its peoples are still enveloped in legends, among them the one that inspired the *Chanson de Roland*. Christian resistance was organized in a small area in the middle western area, Old Navarre, and its first kings were installed at its head. Little Navarre became identified with its geography and the ancient Vascones took the name of *Navarros*, the people of Navarre.

If Navarre as a kingdom was born to resist, the crisis of Islam allowed it to go on to reconquer. In the first decades of the eleventh century it was to exercise an unquestionable hegemony over the remaining centres of Christian Spain. Sancho the Great (1004–35), appointed by the Pope as *rex Hispaniae*, was the first to take the title of king 'by the grace of God'. The same King Sancho invited to Spain and protected monks from Cluny. His successors were to establish monasteries and later to encourage the mendicant orders.

The road to Santiago exercised a similar influence. This path – at one and the same time of piety, adventure, trade and culture – crosses Navarre. Protected by kings who granted them chartered rights and privileges, cities arose along its route which received new immigrants from France, bringing their language and customs, and their commercial expertise and craftsmanship. Pamplona by then was speaking Latin, Occitan,

Spanish and its native Basque. Romanesque and early Gothic architecture was also brought in along the road, leaving valuable traces in Roncesvalles, Leire, Sangüesa, Eunate, Puente la Reina and Estella.

But medieval Navarre comprised a great deal more than this. A city in the south, Tudela, where Christians, Jews and Moors lived peacefully together, was in the twelfth century one of the most important meeting points between Muslim science, the heir of both Greek and Oriental knowledge, and European scholars eager to take advantage of it. Benjamin of Tudela was the leading figure of the Hebraic synagogue. These central centuries of the Middle Ages were the pinnacle of Navarre's importance, not only within Spain, but in Europe as a whole.

In the thirteenth century, the kingdom was reduced to an area roughly the same as it has now, its outlet to the sea had been lost, and it was hemmed in by the powerful kingdoms of Aragon and Castile which prevented its expansion on the Spanish side. Its kings therefore turned their eyes to France. But not before another King Sancho, the Strong, still taking part in the task of the reconquest alongside the Castilians, endowed Navarre with the Andalusian chains, captured during the victory of Las Navas de Tolosa (1212), that it displays to this day on its coat of arms. When France and Navarre were not ruled by the same person, as was the case with Philip the Handsome, the dynasties of Navarre's kings (Champagne, Evreux, Foix, Albret) were French. The people of Navarre joined the French in the Third and Sixth Crusades, the latter headed by St Louis; and, like the French, they gave their allegiance to the Avignon papacy. French influence was seen in court customs, art, poetry and the music that the kings enjoyed listening to in their palace at Olite, one of the most beautiful royal mansions on the peninsula, and also of French inspiration.

Mistrusting a foreign power, the Navarrese grandees, lesser noblemen and clergy forced the kings to recognize their rights and privileges. This is the origin of the *Fuero General de Navarra* (c. 1238), the chartered rights and privileges of the kingdom. The king was obliged to consult with them on major decisions and in the fourteenth century to convene the Cortes, which was also attended by ordinary citizens. The 'first estate' was not the nobility, as in Aragon and Castile, but the clergy, a reflection of their acknowledged power.

The end of the medieval period was, as in much of Europe, a time of crisis and the breakdown of order, of plagues leading to depopulation, of urban decline and violent clashes between factions among the nobles. The sixteenth century saw the rise of the modern system of national states, and Navarre had to

Navarre past and present. *Right:* the wax seal of King Theobald I (1234–53). The king, a vigorous crusading knight, bears on his shield and horse's trappings the chains captured from the Moors at Las Navas de Tolosa in 1212, symbol of Navarre. *Bottom right:* looking across the town of Olite from its early fifteenth-century castle, once the home of the kings of Navarre. *Centre right:* the statute of autonomy of 1978 restored to Navarre its own parliament. Here its president and other democratically elected representatives stand outside its entrance.

choose between the French and Spanish monarchies, themselves in the grip of a frontier war. The different options exacerbated the division which the Navarrese were already experiencing in a long civil war. One party, the Agramontese, supported France, while the Beamontese backed Ferdinand the Catholic. The Spanish option triumphed and the old kingdom of Navarre became the last to be incorporated into the new monarchy (1512–15). It contributed barely 2.1 per cent of the total territory (4,630 square miles) and 1.6 per cent of its population (185,000 inhabitants), but its strategic location turned it into a loyal sentinel of the frontier. Later, in 1530, the Navarre beyond the Pyrenees was lost by Spain. Incorporated at a later date into the neighbouring monarchy, its kings ascended the throne of France as 'Kings of France and Navarre', its chains uniting with the fleur-de-lys on its coat of arms.

The new Spanish monarchy combined political centralism with administrative decentralization. Navarre under the Habsburgs not only retained but consolidated and enriched its institutions. Navarrese took part in the great tasks of Imperial and Counter-Reformation Spain. There were Navarrese legions in Flanders and Catalonia, and the Colombian cities of Pamplona and Tudela, as well as the New Kingdom of Navarre (*Nuevo Reino de Navarra*) in present-day Costa Rica, bear witness to the Navarrese origin of their founders. Many Navarrese were viceroys in America, who also formed part of the royal administration.

The Bourbon attempts at modernization in the eighteenth century clashed with entrenched local traditions, particularly in the area of customs regulations and privileged taxation. Again the Navarrese were divided. The enlightened, such as the Marquis of San Adrián, immortalized by Goya, supported the change. Modern Navarre was born amidst discord and war, first the opposition to the French Agreement (1794), and then the struggle against Napoleon (1808). The moving spirit was not so much a patriotic desire to expel the foreigner as a reawakened crusading fervour, directed this time against 'godless' liberalism.

Spanish society faced modernization and secularization and the forces of resistance to change found their strongest bastion in Navarre and the Basque region. In this Spanish Vendée, the Holy Alliance had, at the Congress of Verona, already seen 'the spiritual reserve of Europe'. The Carlist Wars against liberalism (1833–39 and 1873–76) found ready sympathy there, and Franco's military uprising of 1936, unlike in other regions, encountered genuine popular support among some Navarrese, ready to take up arms enthusiastically in a new crusade. The main, if not the only explanation is to be found in religion. Navarrese Christianity is more inward-looking, perhaps more

sincerely lived than elsewhere in Spain. It is also more intransigent and belligerent: Caro Baroja has called it 'the strongest force operating in society, one which has been crucial at decisive moments in the past.' Navarre was the preferred refuge of religious orders expelled from France, and has always been rich in religious vocations. St Francis Xavier, the great missionary saint, is in many ways a typical Navarrese.

But Navarre, land of contrasts, has also produced notable liberal figures such as Mina el Mozo, Espoz y Mina and Moriones, and ministers occupying national positions, such as Madoz, and Ansó and Irujo, the Republican Ministers of Justice at the height of the Civil War. By the law of 1841 Navarre claimed considerable administrative and fiscal autonomy and this continued to be recognized under Franco. Indeed, Navarre's typical independent spirit has found ways of surviving absolute monarchy, liberal state and Franco dictatorship, to find new scope in the decentralization of the 1978 constitution.

But tradition, a rejection of innovations and a clinging to old values closed the door to real progress. 'More bell towers and fewer chimneys' was a typical slogan. And the results were ruralization, economic and demographic stagnation and massive emigrations to escape hunger and poverty. Then in the 1960s everything changed. Navarrese embarked on a spectacular programme of industrialization which fearlessly faced up to European integration. In 1900 72 per cent of Navarrese worked the land; now barely 11 per cent do.

However, Navarrese are also divided today, though unequally, between two distinct political cultures. The majority look towards Madrid and, remembering the Reconquista and the Spanish, crusading origin of their ancient kingdom, think of the Navarrese as exemplary Spaniards. The minority, barely 20 per cent, look towards the Basque Provinces. This uneasy and sometimes violent division, which is explained more by psychology than economics, seems to be forgotten only on 7 July each year, when the proverbial Navarrese hospitality opens the doors of its capital to people of the whole world to celebrate the feast-day of their first bishop, St Firminus. This is the festival that Hemingway immortalized in *The Sun also Rises*. It provides Navarrese with an opportunity to prove their valour, not in any sort of crusade but in the midst of the bulls that are allowed to run freely in the streets.

Although it is true that the Navarrese have made history more with the sword than with the pen, and have been moved more by blind faith than by reason and interest, the democratic experience of present-day Spain, here as well as in other communities, has produced a growing taste for freedom and tolerance – a happy parallel with the spirit of medieval Navarre where Christians, Jews and Moors lived together in peace.

ARAGON

ELOY FERNANDEZ CLEMENTE

Aragon has an area of about 19,300 square miles, but a small population (barely 1.2 million) and considerable physical limitations: an arid land; extensive mountainous areas unsuitable for its main crops of cereals, grapes and olives; a lack of rain; and rivers with little water, except for the Ebro and some tributaries descending from the Pyrenees. On the other hand, its location at an important crossroads always made control of the region politically and militarily desirable to various peoples.

Its valuable archaeological remains suggest little more than a tribal society until the Roman conquest of the Ebro valley. The Romans founded Caesaraugusta (now Saragossa), together with many other small towns, constructed roads, fortifications and bridges, and provided the territory with its first political and military organization. The period of the Visigoths is obscure, remembered in the Christian Church for St Braulio and for the tradition that the Virgin Mary appeared standing on a pillar in a vision to the Apostle James, a belief commemorated by the Basilica del Pilar in Saragossa.

In the eighth century the Muslim invasion occupied almost the whole country. With the collapse of the caliphate of Cordoba, an independent kingdom (*taifa*) was set up in this area, the splendour of which is revealed in the Aljafería palace and in the work of the philosopher Avempace. It was a period of tolerance between the Muslims and the Christian and Jewish communities (a particularly distinguished member of which was the poet Ibn Gabirol at the end of the eleventh century). Irrigation was developed in the narrow valleys, handicrafts and trade were promoted. Because of the weakness and lack of unity of Spanish Islam and the protection offered by the Carolingian system in France, more or less autonomous earldoms reappeared in the high valleys of the Pyrenees.

The Christian reconquest of Aragon, which required barely a century of warfare, from the end of the eleventh to the end of the twelfth century, created a kingdom with a system of feudal relations in which a dominant role was played by the monasteries (the most prominent of which was San Juan de la Peña) and the military orders, an extensive network of castles and fortifi-

Saragossa, the capital of Aragon, endured two terrible sieges by the French during the Peninsular War (1808-09). *Right*: the Condesa de Bureta, a heroine of the fighting. When the French broke into the town on 4 August 1808, she organized troops and drove them back. *Below right*: an aerial view of Saragossa in more peaceful times. In the centre, the domes and towers of Nuestra Señora del Pilar. The seven arches of the fifteenth-century Puente de Piedra span the River Ebro.

cations, and a series of special rights (*fueros*) and privileges designed to encourage the risky repopulation of land to the south. The monarchs, forced to come to an agreement with the powerful nobility, were subjected to tests and oaths before their Cortes in exchange for economic benefits, until in the mid-fourteenth century they managed to impose an authoritarian government.

Over these lands, crossed by El Cid and the scene of frequent battles with neighbouring kingdoms, a diverse and tolerant culture flourished, as exemplified by the Tarazona school of translators and by the Aragonese schools of law: the great Huesca codification of 1247 was carried out by Bishop Vidal de Canellas in the Aragonese language. Beautiful Romanesque and Gothic churches were built, as well as those built in Mozarabic and, later, Mudejar styles.

The kingdom of Aragon attained great power and considerable geographic expansion through a dynastic union with Catalonia: Valencia was reconquered from the Moors and lands were secured north of the Pyrenees and in Sardinia. Naples, Sicily and even a part of Greece were for a time ruled by the Aragonese. But the old homeland which gave its name to this 'Crown of Aragon', while retaining its uniqueness and institutional independence, remained an agrarian and cattle-herding hinterland, dependent upon a flourishing commercial and cottage industry economy in the coastal areas of Catalonia, Valencia and Mallorca.

An unusual conflict caused by the death of a king without a clear succession led to the famous Compromise of Caspe (1412), whereby debate and agreement took place between representatives of all the various interests. The result of this peaceful solution was to place Aragon in the hands of the reigning dynasty in Castile, so paving the way for the future union of the kingdoms. At the same time the support given in the Great Schism to the Aragonese candidate Pedro de Luna, as Pope Benedict XIII (1394–1423), raised the problem of relations between the secular and ecclesiastical powers.

The marriage of Ferdinand II of Aragon and Isabella I of Castile produced an external unity of action, but in fact the kingdoms retained their own Cortes, laws and customs, including currency and customs regulations. Although Aragon contributed considerable sums towards the conquest and colonization of America, it was to remain on the fringe of the process, the Aragonese being regarded as 'foreigners' in Castile. Nevertheless, many Aragonese were to distinguish themselves in the New World: soldiers, such as M. Díaz de Aux alongside Hernán Cortés in Mexico; experts in navigation, such as Martín Cortés, author of the *Compendio de la Esfera y Arte de Navegar*; sailors like Porter, who explored California, or missionaries like Fray Francisco Garcés.

In the Renaissance period, though a certain prosperity was reflected in the beauty of its *lonjas* (exchanges) and civil official buildings, Aragon was more notable for the inventive genius of its people than for its political or economic power. It produced Miguel Servet, who studied the circulation of the blood and, a notable theologian, was burned at the stake in Geneva by the supporters of Calvin; Jerónimo Zurita, the great chronicler of his time, who compiled a well-documented history of the Crown of Aragon; the anonymous author of the apocryphal *Quijote* of Avellaneda; the Argensola brothers, poets whose work is regarded as a model of the Spanish language; the Jesuit Baltasar Gracián, essayist and political commentator and one of the most critical and profound minds of his time; the heresiarch Miguel de Molinos, whose *Spiritual Guide* was a forerunner of modern nihilisms; and José de Calasanz, founder of the Pious Schools. The spirit of the Baroque and the Counter-Reformation dominated the period.

Meanwhile in the struggle with centralized power in the reign of Philip II, Aragon defended its ancient privileges such as *Manifestacion*, which permitted a man imprisoned under Castilian law to appeal to the *Justicia*. This right was exercised in 1591–92 to protect the persecuted former royal secretary Antonio Perez. This conflict reached its peak when the Justiciar Juan de Lanuza defied the king and was beheaded. The Spanish crown had administered a serious blow against the integrity of the kingdom.

Its economy was weakened in 1609 by the expulsion of the Moriscos (Muslims who had converted to Christianity), a measure which the Aragonese nobility unsuccessfully opposed, and then damaged further by the adverse result of the War of the Spanish Succession (1701–13). After this the independent political institutions of Aragon were abolished, and with them its existence as a state, and it was absorbed into the absolute and centralized kingdom of the Bourbons.

But the spirit of Aragon survived. Paradoxically, the second half of the eighteenth century, the period of the Enlightenment, represented a genuine golden age for the old kingdom. This was undoubtedly the result of the prestige and power wielded at court by a handful of nobles, artists and intellectuals: the Count of Aranda, who presided over the Council of Castile (a position equivalent to Prime Minister); Roda, Secretary for Mercy and Justice; the diplomat José Nicolás de Azara (most renowned in Rome or Paris, a famous patron of the arts); his brother the botanist Félix de Azara, an expert on South America; General Ricardos, hero of the war against the French Convention; F.M. Nipho, the creator of the first Spanish newspaper; and above all, one of the greatest Spanish artists, Francisco de Goya.

Many of them, forming a kind of 'Aragonese party' were concerned about their native country and helped its residents to develop its economy, education and culture. Thus, Ramón Pignatelli, a member of the Royal Aragonese Economic Society of Friends of the Country, one of the chief among such societies in Spain, supported the building of the Imperial Canal, which had a decisive effect on trade and was also a source of irrigation for extensive areas. Men of great learning, such as the bibliographer Latassa, the historian Traggia and the economist Ignacio J. de Asso, represented a society in favour of progress.

This progressive trend was cut short first by fear of a revolution like that in France and then by the war against Napoleon. During this war, Saragossa endured two catastrophic sieges (1808–09) which brought it glory, but reduced it to ruins.

Shortly after the death in 1833 of the absolutist monarch Ferdinand VII the first of the Carlist Wars broke out. Aragon was one of the main theatres for these conflicts.

But in Saragossa the liberal bourgeoisie grew. There were insurrections and risings, and attempts to transfer ecclesiastical and state assets into the private sector. Industrialization increased, stimulated particularly in the 1860s when Saragossa became a junction for the new railways. A certain development of republicanism and the workers' movement (socialism and anarchism) counterbalanced the city's conservative society, while the modern sciences were being accepted onto the curriculum of the university, where in the 1870s the future Cuban hero José Martí studied and in the 1880s S. Ramón y Cajal, who went on to win a Nobel Prize.

Aragon was also the launching point for the Spanish Regenerationist movement, headed by Joaquín Costa, lawyer and politician, who fought the oligarchical and cacique system of the Restoration, promoted a policy for hydraulic power (to be carried out in the 1920s by the dictatorship of Primo de Rivera), and promoted the groupings of peasants with small and medium-sized holdings spread across the whole of the Spanish interior. A great Hispano-French World Fair held on the hundredth anniversary of the war demonstrated the wish to improve economic and cultural relations with its neighbouring country, the opportunities for which were increased twenty years later by the Canfranc railway.

On the cultural level, the 1920s and 1930s were a silver age, with significant figures such as the novelists B. Jarnés and R.J. Sender, the artists P. Gargallo and F. García Mercadal, and the film director Luis Buñuel. In Saragossa, the industrial and financial centre of Aragon, there was no lack of ambition to modernize and develop. One example was the iron and coal mining industry of the Teruel mountains.

Between 1936 and 1939 the Civil War resulted in a very serious social and economic collapse. The terrible battles of

Belchite, Teruel and the Ebro, and the enforced exile of many public-spirited citizens, combined with economic deprivations under a harsh political, social and cultural dictatorship, represent a long silence in the history of Aragon, broken only by the voices of a few writers and poets such as Miguel Labordeta. Nevertheless, outside their own land major intellectual and artistic work was produced by Pedro Laín and Manuel Alvar, Pablo Serrano and Carlos Saura, and F. Grande Covián. Aragon, however, never renounced the struggle for freedom, democracy and social change; active groups of university students and workers resisted the most severe repressions.

Saragossa, designated a development zone, reached half a million inhabitants in the 1960s. Its industrial importance was enhanced after the return to democracy by the addition of a large General Motors factory. After 1975 the new regime allowed a renewed Aragonese national consciousness to develop, which found expression in 1978 when more than 100,000 people called for a Statute of Autonomy. This facilitated the development of forms of regional government (the *Diputación General*, or General Council), its own parliament (evoking memories of the medieval Cortes) and a *Justicia* or ombudsman. In little more than ten years, the town halls and democratic provincial corporations had provided considerable evidence of town-planning and cultural transformation.

Today, Aragon is aware of the importance of the formation of a united Europe, which it very much desires and values. But many of its old problems (communication, irrigation, territorial segmentation) remain and new ones arise, such as ecology and protection of its energy resources. Within its limited human and economic dimension, it can claim to have a significant contribution to make to world progress.

Moreover, although a number of nationalist or regionalist parties (such as PSA, PAR, CHA) have arisen with various degrees of success, the large majority of Aragonese feel that they are fully integrated in Spain (while nevertheless clearly affirming their distinctive identity). Proud of their own liberal history tending to compromise and unity, they view with hope and sympathy the processes of democratization and the difficult economic recovery of Latin America, which they see as an authentic extension of their past.

CATALONIA

JOSEP FONTANA

At what point does a community which one might describe as Catalonia make its appearance? It is always difficult to define the origins of national identity. In the case of Catalonia, some have placed its political foundation at the end of the ninth century and at the present time the thousandth anniversary of its independence is being celebrated.

This claim turns out to be too simplistic. But a thousand years ago, the Catalan counties already felt themselves to be no longer either part of the French empire or part of Spain, and, as Pierre Bonnassie has written, they were beginning to show signs of an economic growth which would give birth to a society very different from that developing in Castile: 'There [Castile] the cities, designed essentially for military purposes, will grow slowly; here they will expand under the pressure of the development of craft activities, of internal trade and, very shortly, of great international trade.'

Between birth and full maturity there is always a formative stage. The names 'Catalonia' and 'Catalan' are not found until the beginning of the twelfth century. But the Catalan language was already being spoken in the eighth century; the first written texts which have been preserved date from the twelfth century, as does the first important flowering of literature (the poetry of the Catalan troubadours, written in Provencal, a language closely related to their own). The first great writer to employ Catalan – a figure of European stature in the field of thought – was Ramon Llull, born in about 1235 on the island of Mallorca, shortly after its conquest by James I.

One cannot understand the historical evolution of Catalonia if one forgets that its development was shaped by these converging streams of influence. Initially the most important was the one linking it to what is now the south of France, with which it was united linguistically; it was during its economic and political expansion in the Mediterranean region that Catalonia achieved its great period of splendour; its relationship with the peninsular territory began to be dominant only from the fifteenth century, when Catalonia started to decline.

In 1137 the Count of Barcelona, Ramon Berenguer IV, who exercised undisputed hegemony over the combined Catalan counties, married the heiress to the throne of Aragon. His successor, Alfonso – who bore the titles of King of Aragon and Count of Barcelona – made a pact with the King of Castile regulating how the two of them would share out the lands of al-Andalus as they were reconquered from the Muslims. For the Catalans and the Aragonese this process ended with the conquest of the kingdoms of Mallorca and of Valencia by James I (1213–76), but in Castile it lasted for another 250 years.

In the course of those 250 years, the Crown of Aragon (the name given jointly to the Catalan counties and the kingdoms of Aragon, Mallorca and Valencia) turned towards the east those energies which were no longer absorbed by its 'reconquest' and which could not be directed towards expansion north of the Pyrenees, because of the penetration there of French domination following the crusade against the Cathars. In the east, however, the Crown of Aragon managed to form a Mediterranean empire made up of the Western Islands (the Balearics, Corsica, Sardinia and Sicily), Naples and part of Greece. At the height of its power, Pedro the Ceremonious (1336–87) was concerned that a guard should be placed on the Acropolis in Athens to guard the Parthenon, at that time a church dedicated to the Virgin, in order to preserve what he considered to be one of the most admirable monuments in the world.

A man who typifies the whole epoch, and the kingdom's Mediterranean dimension, is the chronicler Ramon de Muntaner (1265–1336). Born in the north of Catalonia, he lived in Mallorca, Sicily and Valencia, took part in the battles in Greece, was governor of the island of Djerba, near Tunis, and died in Ibiza. His work expresses to perfection the 'national' pride of empire builders.

The succession to the throne of a new Castilian dynasty in the fifteenth century, the Trastamara, coincided with the beginning of the decline of Catalonia, a decline hastened by the confrontation with John II in the civil war of 1462–72, which was waged in the midst of serious social conflicts. It was to be his son and successor Ferdinand's marriage to Isabella I of Castile which would lead to the unification of the two monarchies in the persons of their descendants, the Spanish Habsburgs.

Dynastic union did not imply fusion of the 'states', which, as we have seen elsewhere, preserved their own legislation, parliaments, currency, and so on. However, the association between a Crown of Aragon in decline and a Castile which, having in 1492 completed its 'reconquest' and begun its expansion in America, was becoming the major world power of the period, could not help being an unequal one. It is not surprising that Catalonia should have remained overshadowed by Castile during this century and a half and that it should have played little part in the world enterprises of the Habsburgs.

The first serious conflict arose in the middle of the seventeenth century. Castile had carried the major burden of the costly European adventures of its kings and when its own treasury had been squeezed dry, the Count-Duke of Olivares demanded from the kingdoms of the Crown of Aragon a contribution which he considered just, not only because of their obligations to the monarch, but so that they should share the costs of defence from which they all benefited. As he put it, from the time of the union the military efforts of Castile 'have given protection to those kingdoms and diverted to other areas the enemies who would have made war on them'. He also hoped that this 'union in arms' would be the beginning of a closer relationship between the subjects of the various kingdoms, overcoming 'that dryness and separation of hearts that has existed up till now'.

The result was a long-term crisis which began with the revolt, or War of Separation, of 1640 but which was not resolved until the end of the War of the Spanish Succession in 1713. The half-century between the two conflicts was marked by indications of mistrust and prejudice on both sides. It was rather like a prolonged armistice in which none of the fundamental problems was sorted out. The Castilianization of the Catalans' patrician culture might indicate an 'assimilation' of their ruling classes. On the other hand, the Catalan economic expansion which was taking place, although on a modest scale, along the lines of the capitalist development model then triumphing in Western Europe, contrasted with the backwardness of the Castilian economy, whose industry had been ruined and which was content simply to act as an intermediary in the exchange of industrial products for precious metals which was taking place between Europe and the American colonies of Castile.

Thus the latent conflict began to change its nature. If the War of Separation had been fought in the name of two opposing conceptions of the internal structure of the state – in defence of the 'privileges' of the Catalans against the interference of the 'Castilian' government – the War of Succession brought into conflict two different visions of society. On that occasion the struggle was for more than the preservation of privileges which initially did not appear threatened. The Catalan supporters of the Habsburgs would maintain to the end that they were fighting for Spain and for the liberty of all Spaniards, while the partisans of the Bourbons would terrify the Castilians with the fear of an enforced 'Catalanization'.

The defeat of the Crown of Aragon meant the end of the political and institutional separateness of its kingdoms – parliaments, autonomous government, viceroy, codes of law – and an attempt was made to assimilate them as provinces of Castile. A monarchy which claimed to be absolute could modify laws, proscribe the language and impose a regime of military occupation. (For nearly 300 years, whatever the political system in power, the ruling authority in Catalonia has been that of its military chiefs, the Captains General.) There were some things, however, which it did not even understand and consequently could not change.

The policy of the so-called 'enlightened despotism' of the eighteenth century – which was much more despotic than enlightened – was to concentrate all its efforts on Castile; but even so it failed in its attempt to promote Castile's growth.

Catalonia has always been proud of its institutions and cultural traditions. *Right*: James I presiding over the Catalan Cortes at Lérida. *Centre right*: a political celebration in Barcelona. On the float is depicted the origin of the region's flag, symbol of local pride. Count Wilfred, wounded while fighting the Moors, draws his bloody fingers across his golden banner, to produce the four red stripes preserved ever since. *Below right*: the Palace of Catalan Music, Barcelona, built in 1908 by Domenich i Montaner. The hall is decorated in the variant of the Art Nouveau style typical of Catalonia.

Meanwhile, the Catalan economy continued to develop by the same methods which it had used since its origins: by specializing its agriculture in the production of brandy for export and by promoting industrial activities which met the internal demand and were already beginning to penetrate the Castilian market. It is the continuity of this process, based more on contacts with European markets than on the fleeting and unreliable predominance of colonial trade at the end of the eighteenth century, that explains such a difference in economic progress. Not only did it owe nothing to the 'enlightened' policy of the government, it was carried on either without its knowledge – Jovellanos was unaware of it until he found himself obliged to cross Catalonia on his way to exile in Mallorca – or in the face of its open hostility (men like Campomanes or Cabarrús refused to accept this 'English-style' model of urban industrialization).

In the first years of the nineteenth century, with the bankruptcy of the Exchequer and the shameful surrender of the monarchy to the Napoleonic invasion, absolutism rapidly lost prestige and a new hope was born. During the so-called War of Independence (1808–14), the struggle was not only to expel Napoleon's troops from the peninsula but also to endow Spanish society with new political and social bases (a constitution, parliamentary government, economic liberalism) more in accord with the needs of the times. Although the Spanish liberals were no less centralist than their predecessors – they were as obsessed with combatting 'the hydra of federalism' as with driving out the French – the Catalan bourgeoisie participated enthusiastically in this collective project and in the long struggle to impose it in the face of absolutist resistance throughout the reign of Ferdinand VII (1808–33).

The Catalan ruling classes were prepared to be integrated, to abandon definitively their language and their culture, in order to take part in the creation of a society in which they could realize their collective aspiration towards progress. The most clear-sighted of the Castilian politicians seemed to think in the same way. Antonio Alcalá Galiano said in the Cortes in 1835: 'One of the principal objectives which we must set ourselves is to make of the Spanish nation one nation, which it is not today and has never yet been.'

The nineteenth century, however, was to see the frustration of these hopes of building a modern 'Spanish nation'. A government dominated by the interests of the great landowners of Castile and Andalusia systematically rejected any move towards modernization. The disagreements between the central government and the Catalan bourgeoisie were presented to public opinion as a dispute between 'protectionism' and 'free trade'. In reality what lay behind it was the refusal of the government to adopt the programme of political liberalization which was needed in order to obtain the social consensus on

which European nation states were based. Instead of founding a modern nation, the rulers of Spain contented themselves with establishing a centralized government.

The results of this choice were to show themselves in the failure of the process of industrialization, in the political backwardness of the state – Spain was the only European power which in the second half of the nineteenth century continued to lose colonies rather than to acquire them – as well as in the assimilation of the diverse components of the country. The so-called *Renaixença* of Catalan language and literature in the nineteenth century is not so much the renaissance that its name suggests, as the disillusioned patricians reclaiming their cultural heritage. The language had been kept alive in the popular sectors, thanks to its neglect in public education.

At the beginning of the twentieth century the Catalan bourgeoisie, who had now lost all hope of actively participating in Spanish politics, once again made common cause with the rest of society and initiated a complicated and prolonged game of threats, negotiations and pacts with the central power, in the name of Catalonia and the defence of its interests. There were phases of concessions: for instance 1914–25, when the four Catalan provincial councils (*diputaciones*) were allowed to combine in one *mancomunidad* (or 'union'), to which the state granted a fair measure of devolution; and 1932 and 1979, when further measures of autonomy were passed. But these alternated with phases of repression, especially during the dictatorships of 1923–30 and 1939–75, when autonomy was reduced in the name of safeguarding 'Spain's national unity'.

The fact that movements similar to that in Catalonia were developing at the same time in the Basque Country, were starting in Galicia and were embryonic in other regions (Andalusia, Valencia and the Canaries) reveals the failure of Spanish nation-building plans in the nineteenth century.

As far as Catalonia is concerned, neither the forty years of Francoist repression, which carried out a policy of cultural genocide against it, nor the massive immigration of Castilian-speaking workers, were enough to weaken the desire for self-government which, after the death of General Franco in 1975, manifested itself in the largest mass demonstration ever seen in the country (one million people demanding an autonomy statute in September 1977).

In the years since the implementation of the 1979 autonomy statute, the principal characteristics of Catalan political life have been, without doubt, peaceful coexistence with the immigrant population and the consolidation in the government of a conservative force favouring a nationalism based on pacts. This has made difficult the growth of more radical sectors favouring independence. At the same time, the prospect of European integration has produced a powerful attraction towards the focal points of the Rhone valley and the Mediterranean coasts. Catalonia once again stands at the crossroads of influences which spread beyond the boundaries of the peninsula.

CASTILE

ANGEL GARCIA SANZ

The history and language of Castile are without any doubt the key factor in the whole of Spanish history and culture; so much so that 'Castilian' has often been used to mean the same as 'Spanish'. But over the centuries the name 'Castile' has signified such widely differing geographical areas and historical entities that we must begin by making clear exactly how it will be used in this essay.

It is first documented at the end of the eighth century, when Arab sources begin to use *al-Qila* ('the castles', Latin *castella*) to refer to a small mountainous area around the upper basin of the River Ebro between what is now the province of Burgos and Cantabria. At that time it formed the most easterly enclave of the kingdom of Asturias, and it was the Asturian king Alfonso II (791–842) who, in order to impede the advance of the Moors along the Ebro, had built the castles that gave it its name. During the ninth century the territory of Castile expanded as lands were reconquered further south and repopulated by, among others, Basques, Asturians, Galicians and Mozarabs from al-Andalus. At first Castile was merely a feudal dependency of the crown of Asturias-León. It was governed by counts, who gradually accumulated more power until Count Fernán González (*c.* 930–70) is credited with achieving complete independence.

In 1035, through a series of dynastic mergers, King Ferdinand I (1035–65) succeeded to all the territories that had been the county of Castile, the kingdom of León and the lands of Galicia and Asturias. This new kingdom of Castile and León covered most of north-east Spain, including the present provinces of Cantabria, Burgos, Soria, Segovia and Avila.

By 1230 the new kingdom had become permanently established and formed the strategic and ideological base for the reconquest of the whole of the territory occupied by the Moors. The kingdom of León had always seen itself as the legitimate heir of the ancient Visigothic kingdom, and consequently responsible for its restoration. The Castilian kings thus became the leaders of the reconquest of the western half of the peninsula.

The newly conquered territories were given new names. The western part, the most southerly outpost of the old kingdom of León, came to be called Extremadura. The eastern part became first the kingdom of Toledo (Toledo itself had been recaptured in 1085) and then 'New Castile', to distinguish it from 'Old Castile'. Finally, between the thirteenth and the beginning of the sixteenth centuries, the monarchs of Castile-León conquered all the southern and south-eastern parts of the peninsula (Andalusia and Murcia respectively), together with the Canary Islands and the vast territories of Spanish America.

The meaning of Castile has thus fluctuated widely. In this essay it will be used to mean only the lands ruled by the kings of Castile in the Middle Ages, including León but excluding Galicia and Asturias. This huge territory – over 90,000 square miles, almost half the area of Spain – comprises six present-day Autonomous Communities: Castile and León, Cantabria, La Rioja, Castilla, La Mancha, Madrid and Extremadura.

The most important contribution of medieval Castile to the Hispanic world was its institutions – political, administrative and social. These institutions, which were unique in their time, were adopted throughout the whole of the peninsula and later transported to America.

First, the monarchy. The Castilian monarchy was always strongly centralized. The nobility and gentry did exercise some power but it was indirect and precarious. Some historians have even maintained that there was not even such a thing as feudalism in Castile (as there certainly was in Aragon). Consequently, Castile was socially much more open and flexible. Because of the need to repopulate the territories conquered from the Moors, conditions were made attractive, while regional and local charters and codes of law promised a wide measure of independence.

These two factors – weak seigneurial power and strong legal safeguards – determined the form of Castilian society. Its level of personal freedom was one of the highest in medieval Europe. The Edict of Medina del Campo (1480), for instance, re-affirmed the obligation of nobles to respect the Castilian peasants' rights of movement. Catalonia and Galicia saw uprisings in the fifteenth century against oppressive seigneurial power, but this never happened in late medieval Castile. That is not to say that there were no feudal lords in Castile, nor that they may not have sometimes imposed very hard conditions upon the peasants. But there was a climate of greater freedom and there was always the supreme power of the king before which seigneurial excesses could be denounced.

Up to this time, Castle was predominantly rural. The towns and cities were under the control of a patrician nobility whose interests were centred on military activity and the profits of their landed estates. As elsewhere in Europe, the eleventh century saw the beginnings of an urban bourgeoisie founded upon crafts and trade. This bourgeois class was particularly in evidence in the towns along the pilgrimage route to Santiago de Compostela which crossed the northern part of the Duero basin. In cities that had been recovered from the Moors, like Toledo, there was already a vigorous tradition of economic activity and this continued after they passed into Christian hands.

Another pre-eminently Castilian institution, which appeared as an organized body in the twelfth century, was the Mesta, the association of the owners of flocks of sheep and goats to protect the annual migration route of 500 miles between the winter pastures of the south, in La Mancha and Extremadura, and the summer pastures in the north, on the southern slopes of the Cantabrian Cordillera. Migration of flocks and the intensive exploitation of natural pastures was a rational use of the great extent of newly reconquered land which was difficult to repopulate because of lack of manpower, and it was the only economic activity whose territorial range coincides exactly with that of the region described in these pages. The export of Castilian wool through the Cantabrian and Basque ports from the end of the Middle Ages was a decisive factor in the rise of the maritime and commercial cities of the Cantabrian coast.

In the fifteenth and sixteenth centuries, as we have seen, Castile became the political centre of the Spanish empire, a position which brought it both advantages and disadvantages. The royal court and the administration of the imperial state were always situated in genuinely Castilian territory: first in Valladolid and from 1561 in Madrid. It was in these cities that the Cortes used to meet, attended by deputies from the cities of the Crown of Castile, to discuss fundamental questions which affected the whole empire, such as the financing of wars. The domain of Vizcaya and the territories of the Crown of Aragon remained at a greater distance, and therefore more sheltered, from the affairs of empire. It is clear that a good part of its bureaucracy, as well as the greater part of its financing, was provided by the territories of Castile.

From the beginning, these demands were seen as impositions upon the Castilians, and from time to time resentment blazed into insurrection. Under Charles V, in 1520–21, the Comuneros of Castile rose in revolt. His son Philip II faced opposition to higher taxes from the cities of Castile united in the Cortes. Philip III had the same problem; and Philip IV managed to extract money from the Castilians only by surrendering certain areas of royal jurisdiction.

The relationship between Castile and the Indies in the modern period is one of great interest. Old Castile, New Castile

An allegorical representation of Castile, from a seventeenth-century copy of the *Triumph of Maximilian* by Dürer. The nobleman holds aloft a banner bearing the region's heraldic sign of castles. *Below*: until Madrid was chosen as Spain's capital by Philip II in 1561 it was a relatively insignificant town. During the reign of Philip III, churches, hospitals and monasteries were built, and considerable expansion took place under his successors. It was in Philip III's reign that the Plaza Mayor was built (1617–19), and here he rides in procession through the new square.

and Extremadura were the regions which, after Andalusia, sent the greatest number of immigrants to America between 1493 and 1600. The language and the institutions of Castile were likewise transplanted to America. From the Indies, Castile obtained immediate benefits, the greatest of which was 'the American treasure' – gold and, above all, silver – although this finally caused violent inflation.

Castile's most brilliant period, economically and socially, is the sixteenth century. It was the most densely populated and the richest of all the Spanish provinces. It boasted a vigorous bourgeoisie living in a network of numerous cities and important centres whose various functions were perfectly distributed. There were predominantly industrial cities like Segovia, Toledo and Cuenca; commercial and financial cities like Burgos, Medina del Campo and Medina de Rioseco; the political and administrative centres were Valladolid and Madrid, while Salamanca and Alcalá de Henares were the intellectual capitals.

The seventeenth century was a period when the different regions of Spain got out of step chronologically, with unequal degrees of development. The coastal areas, after a brief decline, recovered and enjoyed more prosperity at the end of it than at the beginning. The interior, on the other hand, suffered severely. Only Madrid escaped because it was the capital and seat of the court.

By the eighteenth century Castile no longer held the dominant position in the peninsula that it had enjoyed up till then. This came about, paradoxically, by the very extension of Castilian institutions to the rest of Spain. Previously, each province had had its own juridical, constitutional and economic structure; there were even customs barriers between them. The only unifying factor was the person of the king, whose dynastic rights varied from province to province. But under Philip V, by the Decrees of Nueva Planta, all this was given up and the whole of Spain was 'Castilianized'.

From now on, and especially after the introduction of the liberal state in the early nineteenth century, the history of Castile becomes indistinguishable from that of the rest of Spain. The territories of the interior did not benefit from the development of capitalism. They remained agrarian, and in more recent times have suffered from disastrous emigration of people and resources to the more industrialized coastal areas. Although Madrid is in Castilian territory, its prosperity is not Castilian, but national. In sharp contrast with the situation in the sixteenth century, the territories of Old Castile and León, New Castile (excluding Madrid) and Extremadura are now three times less densely populated than the Spanish average.

Today, the living heritage of Castile is not economic but cultural. The language that we know as Spanish is in fact Castilian, though Catalan, Galician and Basque are also Spanish languages. Originally there were many more, most of them descended from the vulgar Latin spoken at the time of the later Roman Empire. Castilian, the first written evidence of which dates from the tenth century, was a flexible mixture of the Navarre-Aragonese dialect, Basque and Mozarabic. The earliest texts are glosses in the margins of Latin manuscripts. The first literary product is the famous *Cantar de Mío Cid*, an epic about the Castilian hero Rodrigo Díaz de Vivar, written at the end of the twelfth or beginning of the thirteenth century. This was the time when Castilian was establishing itself as the literary language of Spain. Gonzalo de Berceo, a monk of the monastery of San Millán de la Cogolla, was writing his poems to the Virgin and King Alfonso X, the creator of Castilian literary prose, his stories inspired by Arabic tales. We also find the first legal documents (*Las Siete Partidas*) and scientific treatises (*Libros del saber de astronomía*).

Linguists have found in early Castilian certain features which made it the most innovative of the Spanish Romance languages, and this is doubtless one of the reasons for its extraordinarily wide diffusion later on. But the most important factor was political: it was the language of the region with most influence in the peninsula and, subsequently, in America. Castilian pushed down towards the south of the peninsula, dislodging Mozarabic, and also spread laterally, isolating Galician and Catalan on the western and eastern fringes of the country, respectively. It thus overflowed the historical limits of the territories of the Crown of Castile and implanted itself in the kingdom of Aragon.

In 1492, a year laden with significance for Castile and for Spain for so many reasons, the great humanist Elio Antonio de Nebrija, Andalusian by birth but a professor at the Castilian universities of Salamanca and Alcalá de Henares, published the first Castilian grammar, *The Art of the Castilian Language*. He dedicated it to Queen Isabella, referring to the language as 'the companion of empire'.

The process of 'Castilianization' reached its peak at the beginning of the eighteenth century after the Decrees of Nueva Planta, which affected language as well as institutions. Castilian was now accepted as the official language of Spain, and by 1812, when the Constitution of Cadiz established the liberal state, it was not even necessary to raise the point at all.

The first Spanish universities were in Castile. Palencia, the oldest, was created in 1212 by Alfonso VIII of Castile. Salamanca was founded in 1218–19 by Alfonso IX of León; Valladolid dates from the middle of the thirteenth century. The University of Salamanca, which modelled itself on that of Bologna, was the most prestigious and its system of organization was copied by the universities created in America (those of Lima and Mexico were founded as early as 1551). In the sixteenth century the University of Salamanca was particularly sensitive to the problems generated by the discovery and colonization of America. The Dominican Francisco de Vitoria of Burgos, who held a chair at Salamanca, made a fundamental contribution to the future development of international law in discussing the legitimacy of the Spanish occupation of the Indies. Salamanca was also the home of the 'School of Salamanca', a group of theologian-economists, including Domingo de Soto and Martín de Azpilcueta, as well as Francisco de Vitoria, whose deep moral concern about the inflationary effect of the precious metals from the New World led them to make early contributions to the theory of value, of money and of exchange.

In the final years of the fifteenth century Cardinal Cisneros founded the university of Alcalá de Henares, also known as the Complutensian University. This was intended to accommodate all the intellectual currents of the era. It was an eminently humanist and critical university which produced the Polyglot Bible, one of the most splendid examples of Spanish humanism. One must not forget, moreover, that the great attention paid by these Castilian universities to the teaching of juridical sciences helped to train the bureaucracy of the Spanish empire.

Up to the sixteenth century, Castile was the meeting place of intellectual currents from all over the world, but the Counter-Reformation brought a relative cultural isolation, especially after 1559, which was to last until the eighteenth century. It was also, as we have seen, a period of prolonged economic recession (except for Madrid). Paradoxically, however, these very centuries saw an extraordinary flowering of arts and letters, the Golden Age of Spain. With *Don Quijote* Miguel de Cervantes set the seal on Castilian as the literary language of Spain, a position consolidated by many more outstanding works that have been discussed in a previous chapter. *Don Quijote* is indeed deeply Castilian in other ways. Cervantes was born at Alcalá de Henares and his characters constitute a panorama of contemporary Castilian society.

A second period of extraordinary cultural richness occurred between 1875 and 1936, the so-called Silver Age. The principal members of the 'Generation of 1898' who flourished then were not from Castile, but most of them (especially the Basque Unamuno, rector of the University of Salamanca, 'Azorin' from Alicante, and Antonio Machado, an Andalusian) found their chief inspiration in Castile, its history, its people and its landscape. The history of Castile, once rich and powerful but now sunk in poverty and neglect, caused them to reflect upon the meaning of 'Spanish' in contrast to 'European'. A century ago, Spanish intellectuals and artists, in the main not themselves Castilians, saw Castile as a symbol of what is essentially Spanish. But now, after so many centuries when 'Castilian' and 'Spanish' were thought of as identical, twentieth-century Castile is seeking its own identity in a very different and diverse Spain.

Galicia has its ancient dances accompanied by drums and bagpipes. Note the Galician granaries in the background.

In Navarre the difficult 'Danza de los Zancos', or 'Stilt Dance', is performed in the town of Anguiano in July.

A dance of Asturias, the 'Llanes', danced by men and women dressed in the regional costume of the Pericote area.

Murcia, the southernmost province of New Castile, preserves its 'Parranda' dance with castanets.

The dances of the provinces are as distinctive as their architecture or their language, and as redolent of the past.

The Basque village of Marquina specializes in the 'Espatadanza', a dance with swords, at the end of which a warrior is lifted into the air.

Catalan dance in the eighteenth century is shown on this charming painted tile, formally dressed ladies and gentlemen revolving hand in hand.

The Flamenco, the dance of Andalusia, retains its gypsy and Moorish origins and has come to sum up Spanish dance for the rest of the world.

The Aragonese dance called 'La Jota' is characterized by extremely fast rhythms and wild leaps.

VALENCIA

ALFONS CUCO

The year 1238, the date of the entry of the troops of King James I into the Muslim city of Valencia, has traditionally been regarded as that of the founding of the kingdom of Valencia, although the final fixing of its borders did not come until 1308. The Christian conquest created a new state within the Catalan-Aragonese Confederation that rapidly became a community with its own political structure. Its legal instruments, *Els Furs*, were very much influenced by Roman law and endorsed the authority of the monarchs. Even so, fluctuations in relations between the dynasty and the feudal nobility were complex and were not settled until well into the fifteenth century. Moreover, the kingdom of Valencia from the very beginning had a dual character: the interior was fundamentally Aragonese but the coast, including the main urban centres, was basically Catalan. Beyond the borders of the free cities a feudal regime predominated, with overlords who were mainly Christians and vassals who were mainly Moriscos (Muslims who had converted to Christianity). Later expulsions and repopulations gradually balanced the demographic equation.

Valencia integrated smoothly and promptly into the framework of the Confederation. Characterized by a strong agrarian base, intensive on the coast, and by an increasingly buoyant manufacturing industry, the Valencian economy contributed, particularly from the 1300s, to the strengthening of the important trade routes of the Crown of Aragon.

Although their political institutions were separate, the principality of Catalonia and the kingdoms of Valencia and Mallorca shared homogeneous 'national' features, such as language, architectural style and commercial organization, including the *Consolata de Catalans*, which lasted until well into the seventeenth century. All of this contributed to their identification by foreigners as members of the same nation.

The city of Valencia played a crucial role in the kingdom's fortunes. Already during the thirteenth century it was a great manufacturing and commercial centre, though its peak came only in the fifteenth century. Dominated by a powerful bourgeoisie, to which must be added a rich Jewish minority, Valencia in the 1400s had more inhabitants than Barcelona. It became the financial capital of Spain under the Catholic Monarchs and the centre of the spectacular cultural achievements of Catalan literature. However, Valencian prosperity was not firmly founded; it involved an increased public debt and the tying up of commercial capital. All of this, together with a strengthening of the aristocratic regime, led to social tensions that reached breaking point in the popular uprising of the *Germanías* in 1520.

The union of the crowns of Castile and Aragon was a personal and dynastic one, which did not involve the institutional integration of the two kingdoms except on specific, though not thereby less important, matters. These included the introduction of the Castilian model of the Inquisition, the siting in Castile of the *Cancillería* (the supreme legal tribunal), commercial consulates and the concept of viceroyalty. In all other aspects their autonomy was complete. The American conquest and colonization, for instance, were exclusive to Castile until the eighteenth century.

Within the new historical framework created from the 1500s, however, Castile strengthened its *de facto* domination and the states of the Confederation (including, of course, the kingdom of Valencia) were slowly brought into a domestic role, limited to the defence of their traditional institutional structure. Even so, during a good part of the sixteenth century Valencia continued to be economically the most dynamic territory of the Crown of Aragon. The founding of the university in 1501 encouraged the spread of the liberal Christianity associated with Erasmus, but this was soon neutralized by the official ideology of the Counter-Reformation and, finally, by the Inquisition. As a consequence, a significant number of intellectuals of this period, including the humanist Joan Lluís Vives, who was of Jewish origin, had to take the path of exile.

The establishment of Castile as a leading Western power and the consolidation of the autocratic policy of the Habsburgs inevitably affected the political and social structure of Valencia. The privileged classes increasingly came to identify themselves with the ruling dynasty. The nobility and senior clergy became 'Spanish' in language and manners. This process was voluntary at first, but from the eighteenth century on was imposed by force. As royal authority increased, Valencian institutions declined. The disunited Cortes, defender of private and elitist interests, could not reverse this process. Political weakness, combined from the last third of the sixteenth century with economic weakness, the formation of the Barcelona-Genoa trade axis, a worsening of the Morisco question, all help to explain Valencian docility vis-à-vis the new order. In fact, and in spite of a normal appearance of continuity, the Valencian institutional structure was dying. By the middle of the seventeenth century it was already a legal fiction. The old kingdom had become a 'province'.

The War of the Spanish Succession (1702–13) may be analysed both as a dynastic struggle and also as an international conflagration. In the Valencian region it was an agrarian war in which, generally, the lower social strata (particularly the pea-

After its reconquest from the Moors in 1238, the kingdom of Valencia formed part of the Crown of Aragon, and it is the Aragonese coat of arms that is held aloft by angels on the façade of the Lonja de la Seda (silk exchange) in the city of Valencia. Nevertheless, Valencia retained its own institutions: members of the Cortes sit in the Valencian Palacio de la Generalidad (parliamentary building).

sants of the large estates) sided with the Habsburgs, and the nobility and senior clergy with the Bourbons. One consequence of this was the end of the unofficial agreement that traditionally existed between the monarch and the kingdom of Valencia. The 'New Plan' (*Nueva Planta*) of 1707, the codification of the government's reform policy, abolished the ancient autonomous Valencian institutions and imposed, by 'the just right of conquest', complete assimilation to the Castilian legal and political code.

In spite of these changes and the consequences of the war, the eighteenth century was a period of considerable prosperity marked by high demographic growth, indeed, one of the highest in the Europe of its time. Population was concentrated in coastal areas, where towns grew rapidly. The cause of these increases was economic. Agriculture was being commercially developed, and more land was being brought into cultivation. Industries like paper and silk helped to strengthen a commercial bourgeoisie which was consolidating its markets on the Atlantic coast of Europe and establishing initial contacts with America. Economic prosperity was accompanied by notable cultural achievements. The Valencian region became one of the centres of the Spanish Enlightenment, both from the humanistic and the scientific point of view, although the centralizing of the political structure involved the withdrawal of some of its most distinguished men to Madrid and the progressive provincialization of Valencian intellectual life.

The crisis of the ancien régime, already obvious since the end of the eighteenth century, marked the beginning of a prolonged stage of social and political instability which did not in fact end until the mid-nineteenth century. It was a turbulent period, during which the old feudal society finally collapsed to give way to a new system based on a market economy and, in political terms, Spain became a modern nation state. The new system involved not only the legal disappearance of the old Valencian kingdom, but also the incorporation of some Castilian districts into the new provinces of Valencia and Alicante.

Capitalism now penetrated into rural areas as a result of expropriations; many rich peasants and holders of long leases were able to secure ownership of land. Town dwellers, particularly merchants, invested in the country, seeking high profits from a strong export-directed agricultural trade based on rice, wine and later citrus fruits, which were to become the most characteristic product at the end of the nineteenth century. Many day-labourers and tenants were excluded from this process, and we find them playing a leading role in various social disturbances until the first third of the twentieth century. Industrial development was not always smooth: silk declined between 1850 and 1860, but other manufactured products, particularly ceramics, wood and later footwear, were successfully developed. During the second half of the nineteenth century, the Valencian region became the third leading Spanish industrial area after Catalonia and the Basque region, though only the area of Alcoy, the centre of the workers' movement, adopted a 'Manchester-type' system.

These economic transformations involved the formation of a powerful agrarian and commercial bourgeoisie which profited from the railways, banks and speculative urban businesses. High profits encouraged them to make large agricultural investments. In fact, 'agrarianism' became an essential part of Valencian ideology and survives to this day. The bourgeoisie maintained its hegemony through cacique methods, while the working classes passed from liberalism to a determined republicanism, very active in the big urban centres and characterized by a considerable rebellious streak. Reorganized by the novelist Blasco Ibáñez at the end of the century, the Republicans dominated the municipal life of Valencia until the early days of the Civil War. Within the movement the influence of workers' organizations, both anarcho-syndicalist and socialist, increased particularly under the Second Republic, leading to demands, supported by the whole Left, for a Statute of Autonomy.

After the defeat of the Republic (Valencia was its capital city from the end of 1936 to 1938) and the long period of political repression that followed, the Valencian region experienced, from the 1960s onwards, a strong economic recovery based on the expansion of the traditional export-directed agriculture, a revival of industry and the beginning of tourism. Its social consequences are not unrelated to the opposition that had been growing under late-Francoism. The slogan 'Liberty, Amnesty, Statute of Autonomy' became a reality during the democratic transition that ended in 1982.

ANDALUSIA

ANTONIO DOMINGUEZ ORTIZ

The southernmost region of the Iberian peninsula has always had a strongly individual character, which has enriched the whole of Spain. At the same time, it has also been a link with the outside world, sometimes receiving influences from abroad, sometimes becoming a source of influences radiating out on a global scale.

This dual role is largely the result of Andalusia's geographical position – open on its landward side to the rest of Spain and to Europe but with a coastline on both the Mediterranean and the Atlantic. At the Straits of Gibraltar, where the two seas meet, Andalusia and Africa are only nine miles apart. Its historical connection with the East is not only by sea across the Mediterranean, but also overland along the North African coast. And then, later, after the Atlantic had been opened up by the fifteenth-century explorers, Andalusia found itself the gateway to the New World. This position as crossroads and meeting-place encouraged the mingling of races and cultures. And when armies invaded the peninsula or immigrants arrived, they were often tempted to stay here and settle down among Andalusia's natural riches: a fertile land, a plentiful sea and mineral resources, now nearly exhausted.

If, however, the complexity of Andalusian history is to be understood, it is important to remember how extensive the region is. At 33,200 square miles, it is larger than a number of European states, with a local diversity that for the sake of simplicity can be expressed as three great natural regions: the broad and fertile alluvial plain through which flows the River Guadalquivir; to the north, in contact with Castile, the low highlands of the Sierra Morena, an extensive area of ancient rock, poor and underpopulated, but endowed with mineral resources; and finally, an area of high mountains to the east, constituting the nucleus of the kingdom of Granada.

If Andalusia has a striking geographical diversity, history has also introduced further profound differences of its own. The territory that now constitutes the province offered little resistance to Roman might and became integrated into the Mediterranean economy, benefiting from a climate of both internal and external peace. While Italica provided Rome with two of its most notable emperors, Trajan and Hadrian, Cordoba, elevated to the rank of capital of the province of Baetica, was the birthplace of such important Roman writers as the two Senecas (the rhetorician and the philosopher), and Lucan, author of the epic poem, *Pharsalia*. Both Lucius Annaeus Seneca and Lucan fell victim to the tyranny of Nero.

Just as Baetica was the most Romanized of the Iberian provinces, it was also the earliest to be converted to Christianity, a logical development in view of its contacts with the outside world. The first Spanish council was held in Iliberis (Granada) at the beginning of the fourth century. Its proceedings provide a valuable record of the internal workings of the early Christian communities.

Baetica became integrated into the Visigothic state, though without receiving a significant infusion of Germanic blood, since most of the invaders settled in central Spain. The differ-

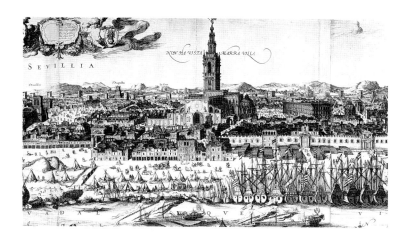

After the conquest of Granada and the voyage of Columbus (both 1492), Andalusian ports, in particular Seville, rose to prosperity through the rich trade with America. In an engraving of 1617, its quayside is crowded with tall ships.

ence in religions also strengthened a certain mutual repugnance, since the Hispano-Romans remained orthodox Christians, whilst the Visigoths adhered to the Arian heresy. This was the basis for the secession attempted by Hermenegild, son of King Leovigild. The projected creation of a Catholic state in the south of Spain came to nothing, but the troops sent by the Byzantine Emperor Justinian were well received. For a while there existed a Byzantine Baetica on the coast, while the Visigoths dominated the interior regions.

The desperate efforts of the cultured minority, largely ecclesiastics, to preserve the remains of an increasingly impoverished Romano-Christian culture were exemplified in the figure of St Isidore (c. 560–636), a brilliant beacon in the obscurity of the Dark Ages. He was archbishop of Seville and architect of the conversion of the Visigoths to Catholicism. He founded a school, which included a library and a *scriptorium* where the copyists reproduced classical works. St Isidore's own books, particularly his encyclopaedic *Etymologies*, were read throughout the Western world over several centuries, as can be seen by the large number of surviving manuscripts.

Religious unity could not save the Visigothic kingdom from a marked decline, culminating in their rapid defeat and conquest by the Arabs and Berbers who crossed the Straits at the beginning of the eighth century. Nevertheless, for a long time thereafter there remained a large community of Mozarabs.

The territory dominated by Islam was called al-Andalus, a word of Arab appearance, albeit dubious etymology. At first this referred to the whole of Spain, but later on, as the Christian reconquest progressed, it came to mean only the southern portion. The period of greatest splendour for Islam was the tenth century, and specifically the caliphates of Abd al-Rahman III and al-Hakam II. Freed from obedience to the caliphs of Baghdad, the caliphs of Cordoba made their city into the most brilliant in the Western world.

When Paris had 20,000 inhabitants and London even fewer, Cordoba had more than 100,000. This required continuous extensions to the great mosque, until it attained the splendid dimensions so admired today. Here can be seen the mixture of cultures whose synthesis created the splendour of al-Andalus. The columns are Roman and Visigothic, the horseshoe arch also had precedents, and the mosaics of the mihrab were executed by artists brought from Byzantium, while the domes and the delicate finishing in gesso and wood are in some cases oriental in origin and in others are the product of the creative genius of Spanish Muslims.

Although relations with Christian Europe were open and there was an exchange of people, products and ideas, the most dynamic influence came from eastern lands, where the Arabs had encountered a still living Hellenistic cultural tradition, had translated the works of the philosophers and scientists of antiquity and enriched this tradition with their own contributions. While economic activity was revitalized by the cultivation of oranges and sugar-cane and by the silk and paper industries, themselves of Arab origin, intellectual life was at an apogee, with a proliferation of mathematicians, astronomers, theologians and philosophers, not all of them working within the strict norms of Islamic orthodoxy.

The decline of the caliphate and its division into small kingdoms did not mean that cultural traditions were abandoned. In the courts of Toledo, Saragossa, Granada, Seville and elsewhere, art, poetry and music continued to occupy a privileged place, but the invasions of the African tribes of the Almoravids and Almohads in the eleventh century had disastrous consequences. Not only were Jews and Mozarabs persecuted, but within the Islamic community itself a climate of intolerance took root, epitomized by the exile of the two great philosophers and internationalists, Averroes – commentator on Aristotle – and Maimonides, the Jew.

Andalusia was reclaimed for Christianity in two phases. During the first (thirteenth century), the whole of the Guadalquivir valley was conquered and colonized, largely by Castilians, but also by Jews and people from Navarre, Galicia and France. The kingdom of Granada was the last redoubt of Islamic civilization, of which the most celebrated product is the castle-cum-fortress of the Alhambra. The history of modern Andalusia begins with the conquest of Granada in 1492, which is also the most crucial year in the history of Spain as a whole. The birth of a united Andalusia coincided with that of the Spanish state itself, thanks to the concerted efforts of the Catholic Monarchs, Ferdinand and Isabella.

All the important events of that vital reign took place in Andalusia. The violence of the religious and racial strife is epitomized first in the creation of the Inquisition, and then in the decree exiling the Jews, signed shortly after the conquest of Granada. This in turn was followed by the departure of Columbus and his three historic caravels from the Andalusian port of Palos. From Seville, Cadiz, Sanlúcar and other Andalusian seaports other expeditions sailed, including that which, under the command of Magellan and later Sebastian Elcano, would be the first to circumnavigate the globe.

After 1560, when Madrid became the capital of the whole of Spain, Andalusia inevitably suffered a loss of autonomy, but remained rich and influential. Madrid was the centre of power and decision-making, but Seville was the seat of the *Casa de Contratación*, from which the dispatch of the armadas and merchant fleets to the Americas was directed. Seville, with 150,000 inhabitants, was for a long time larger than Madrid and in its *Casa de la Moneda* were minted gold and silver coins,

The rich diversity of peoples who make up the Spanish nation is impossible to ignore anywhere in Spain. Indeed, the constant problem faced by Spain's rulers throughout history has been that of regionalism versus centralization. Monarchs and ministers up to the early nineteenth century laboured to minimize regional differences and make Spain into a single nation state. In the following decades, however, Spaniards began to look back nostalgically to their provincial roots and think of themselves as Galicians, Andalusians, Catalans . . . Regional art, regional literature, regional history, took on new values. Franco's dictatorship was hostile to these feelings and tried to suppress them, but since his death the pendulum has swung back the other way and local loyalties are now as strong as they have ever been. Here, in a demonstration by Andalusian workers in Barcelona, the Andalusian and Catalan flags are prominent – the red stripes of Catalonia and the green of Andalusia.

whose excellent quality assured their overwhelming acceptability in the world's financial market.

This material prosperity attracted to Seville – and to a lesser extent to the other Andalusian cities – a large number of foreigners, from rogues and criminals to wealthy merchants and artists of repute. In this manner the international vocation of Andalusia was affirmed, thanks to the tolerance of its inhabitants and their ability to assimilate. There are today in Andalusia many families of French, English, Italian and Flemish origin. The shortage of labour brought about by emigration to America, epidemics and the expulsion of Jews and Moriscos resulted in its becoming a land of immigration and a melting pot of diverse races. This racial mix, continually in contact with the outside world, together with the favourable conditions for acquiring wealth and overcoming social barriers, and an atmosphere of relative freedom and tolerance, all helped to create an Andalusian model that was very distinct from the Castilian. Moreover, the abundant vestiges of earlier cultures, particularly that of Islam, reinforced this impression of distinctiveness, conveyed to every traveller. Gradually the florid south replaced the austere centre as the characteristic image of Spain, and although this change was not complete until the Romantic period, it was clearly discernible much earlier on.

The fluctuating fortunes of the Habsburg monarchy had a profound effect on Andalusia, and the general crisis of the seventeenth century was strongly felt in the region. The drain on manpower and money and the consequences of incessant warfare led to a long period of economic decline, aggravated by the tendency of merchants to limit themselves to the entrepot trade, which left most of the benefits in the hands of other countries. It was also common practice to retire from commerce and invest the profits in land. Even families of foreign origin were affected by these ambitions and by the desire to acquire titles and honours which were regarded as incompatible with industrial and commercial activities. Thanks to tithes and donations, the church was largely able to avoid this impoverishment. This explains why most of the artistic works from the seventeenth century are ecclesiastical buildings and sculptures, and paintings with religious themes, like those of Martínez Montañés, Murillo and Alonso Cano. Velázquez was the exception, having abandoned Seville at an early age in order to work at court.

The establishment of the Bourbon dynasty in the eighteenth century led to a partial recovery. External conflict decreased and the problem of piracy was gradually brought under control, breathing new life into the coastal regions. Cadiz succeeded Seville as the centre of the Atlantic trade and Malaga also became very active, which accounts for its numerous foreign colony. Andalusia remained a meeting point of new and old ideas. Its antiquated universities needed modernization, but this proved to be an onerous task, and the authorities, conscious of Spain's scientific backwardness, pushed for the establishment of extramural centres of investigation like the Academy of Medicine in Seville and the Astronomical Observatory of San Fernando. The economic societies and private circles, analogous to the French *salons*, also contributed to the intellectual revival. In spite of the best efforts of the Inquisition, many foreign books were read. During this period writers like Cadalso, Lista, Marchena and Blanco White (the last-named of Irish origin) were active.

When Andalusia was invaded by Napoleon's troops, many inhabitants found refuge behind the impregnable walls of Cadiz, and it was there that the constitution of 1812, a document that was to have a profound influence throughout Europe, was prepared.

During the nineteenth century Andalusia's activity did not decline, rather the reverse. Writers, artists and travellers of the Romantic Age identified its image as that of Spain as a whole, a Spain of tambourines, bulls, flamenco, bandits and beautiful women. True, the Andalusia of *Carmen* and *The Barber of Seville* had a genuine basis in the gaiety and colour of those southern lands. But it was not the whole truth, since there were also serious problems in Andalusia: economic problems brought about by the independence of the American colonies and the failure of the attempts at industrialization; social problems due to the large landholdings and the misery of the landless day-labourers; cultural problems arising from the high level of illiteracy and the crisis in the ancient faith; and political problems created by all these factors. Real power was in the hands of the aristocracy and a section of the middle class known as the caciques, while the labouring masses lacked leadership or abandoned themselves to a sterile anarchy. Many of the Spanish political leaders were Andalusians – Mendizábal, Narváez, Castelar, Cánovas, Lerroux, Primo de Rivera – but none of them produced effective solutions to the problems of their own land.

Contemporary Andalusia is making determined efforts to resolve these underlying problems. It continues to be a land of great artists and literary figures. Excluding those still living, one only need mention Picasso, Manuel de Falla, Federico García Lorca, Juan Ramón Jiménez and the Machado brothers. An ambitious programme of popular education is also being pursued. It remains the same welcoming land it has always been, though at the present time many of its inhabitants have had to emigrate for economic reasons. Since 1980 it has benefited from an autonomous status, which, without in any way loosening its bonds to a unified Spain, has proved a more effective device than earlier ones for solving its internal problems.

257

The language of loyalty

Heraldry was a way of proclaiming one's allegiance at all levels – to the family, the province and the nation. In Spain the language of heraldry was universal and much of Spanish history is displayed in heraldic terms, in sculpture, manuscripts, stained glass and painting.

Navarre, Aragon and Castile as they appear in one of the most splendid of heraldic manuals, the *Armorial Equestre*. Navarre is the most complicated, containing five major quarterings, one of which is the chains captured from the Moors at the battle of Las Navas de Tolosa (1212). Aragon has plain red and yellow stripes. Castile unites the castles of Old Castile with the lion of León.

Architectural dialects

Until recently the regional styles of vernacular Spanish buildings were so individual that one could tell roughly where one was merely by looking at the architecture. Some of these building types are unique to a single province. Pictures are described from top left to bottom right.

Galicia is notable for its extraordinary stone granaries raised on stilts as protection against rats. They are large, gabled and often decorated with crosses, so that they look almost like small chapels. Here, one at San Paio de Narla.

Andalusia has inherited traditions from the Moors and from the European Baroque. This row of whitewashed houses with iron balconies is at Priego, near Cordoba.

Asturian villages have long arcaded streets, the houses rising above them, frequently jettied out over the road. This is the main street of Avilés.

Old Castile evolved a farm-type consisting of two very thick walls linked by an open balcony at first floor level and with a large arched entrance for carts. This example, dated 1670, is at Carmona.

Valencia is the home of a distinctive house-type called *barraca* whose origin goes back to palaeolithic times: walls made of earth mixed with rice-husks and roofs of heather.

Navarre makes a speciality of large houses under wide spreading gables, the walls mostly whitewashed but the doors and windows outlined in stone. This nineteenth-century street is at Baraibar.

A modern heraldy

In the twentieth century the regions of Spain have sought to assert their identity in more overt ways, both through politics and through art. Two of the most patriotic provinces, where local pride has culminated in movements for separation, are Catalonia and the Basque Country.

Catalonia has produced more outstanding modern artists than any other region of Spain and many of them would characterize their work as specifically 'Catalan' rather than 'Spanish'. In Barcelona a distinctive brand of Art Nouveau became widespread around the opening years of this century, of which Antoni Gaudí is the best-known practitioner. His Guell Park (*right*) uses a variety of exotic forms and materials to produce a highly original effect. Later, Joan Miró, an equally staunch Catalan, designed a mosaic for the Ramblas in Barcelona (*opposite below*) that marks it as different from other cities.

The Basque Country finds its artistic voice in the sculptor Eduardo Chillida. His *Combs of the Wind (opposite top)* are giant constructions of iron fixed to the cliff near San Sebastián. For him, they express the Basques' relation to the sea, their 'best friend and master'.

A new spirit of integration into Europe after centuries of proud isolation is symbolized by Ricardo Bofill's huge monument at La Junquera on the French-Spanish border. Built between 1974 and 1976, it stands next to the new Catalan highway linking the two countries and consists of a giant pyramid 100 metres square and 80 metres high; its volume is equivalent to the volume of earth removed to make the road. At the summit is a structure designed to express both the spirit of Catalonia and the brotherhood of nations. It is said that in the ninth century Count Guifré el Pelós (Wilfred the Hairy) was wounded in battle against the Moors. The king of France, his hand wet with the Count's blood, drew his fingers across a golden banner and said: 'This shall be your flag.' The four irregular red stripes have been the emblem of Catalonia ever since.

SELECT BIBLIOGRAPHY

A Pluralist Society: Medieval Spain

Baer, Yitzhak *A History of the Jews in Christian Spain* (2 vols, Philadelphia, 1978)
Beinart, Haim *Conversos on Trial: The Inquisition in Ciudad Real* (Jerusalem, 1981)
Bisson, T.N. *The Medieval Crown of Aragon: A Short History* (Oxford, 1986)
García de Cortázar, J.A. *La Epoca Medieval* (Madrid, 1973)
Hillgarth, J.N. *The Spanish Kingdoms, 1250–1516* (2 vols, Oxford, 1976, 1978)
Iradiel, P., Moreta, S., and Sarasa, E. *Historia Medieval de la España Cristiana* (Madrid, 1989)
Lomax, Derek W. *The Reconquest of Spain* (London and New York, 1978)
MacKay, Angus *Spain in the Middle Ages: From Frontier to Empire, 1000–1500* (London and New York, 1977)
O'Callaghan, Joseph F. *A History of Medieval Spain* (Ithaca and London, 1975)
Tate, Brian and Marcus *The Pilgrim Route to Santiago*, photographs by Pablo Keller (Oxford, 1987)
Valdeón, J., Salrach, J.M., and Zabalo, J. *Feudalismo y Consolidación de los Pueblos Hispánicos (Siglos XI–XV)* (Barcelona, 1980)
Watt, W. Montgomery *A History of Islamic Spain* (Edinburgh, 1965)

Unity and Empire, 1500–1800: Spain and Europe

Domínguez Ortiz, Antonio *The Golden Age of Spain, 1516–1659* (1971)
Elliott, J.H. *Imperial Spain, 1469–1716* (1963, 1970)
—*Spain and its World, 1500–1700* (1989)
Fernández Alvarez, Manuel *Charles V* (1975)
Herr, Richard *The Eighteenth-Century Revolution in Spain* (1958)
Kamen, Henry *Inquisition and Society in Spain in the Sixteenth and Seventeenth Centuries* (1985)
—*Spain, 1469–1714. A Society of Conflict* (1983)
Lynch, John *Bourbon Spain, 1700–1808* (1989)
—*Spain under the Habsburgs* (2nd edn 1981, 2 vols)
Parker, Geoffrey *Philip II* (1979)
Stradling, R.A. *Europe and the Decline of Spain* (1981)

Spanish America: Empire and its Outcome

Bethell, Leslie (ed.) *The Cambridge History of Latin America*, vols 1–8 (1984–91)
Blakemore, Harold, and Smith, Clifford T. (eds) *Latin America: Geographical Perspectives* (2nd edn 1983)
Bushnell, David, and Macaulay, Neill *The Emergence of Latin America in the Nineteenth Century* (1988)
Clendinnen, Inga *Ambivalent Conquests: Maya and Spaniard in Yucatan, 1517–1570* (1987)
Dealy, Glen *The Public Man. An Interpretation of Latin American and other Catholic Countries* (1977)
Hemming, John *The Conquest of the Incas* (1970)
Kubler, George, and Soria, Martín *Art and Architecture in Spain and Portugal and their Dominions, 1500–1800* (1969)

Liss, Peggy K. *Mexico under Spain, 1521–1556. Society and the Origins of Nationality* (1975)
Lockhart, James M., and Schwartz, Stuart B. *Early Latin America. A History of Colonial Spanish America and Brazil* (1983)
Lynch, John *The Spanish American Revolutions, 1808–1826* (2nd edn 1986)
Morner, Magnus *Race Mixture in the History of Latin America* (1967)
Morse, Richard M. 'The heritage of Latin America' in *The Founding of New Societies*, Louis Hartz (1964)
Parry, John H., and Keith, Robert G. (eds) *New Iberian World. A Documentary History of the Discovery and Settlement of Latin America to the Early 17th Century* (5 vols, 1984)
Véliz, Claudio *The Centralist Tradition of Latin America* (1980)

The Hispanic World in the United States

Acosta-Belén, Edna, and Sjostrom, Barbara R. (eds) *The Hispanic Experience in the United States: Contemporary Issues and Perspectives* (New York, 1988)
Acuña, Rodolfo *Occupied America: A History of Chicanos* (New York, 1981)
Bean, Frank, and Tienda, Marta *Hispanic Population in the U.S.* (New York, 1988)
Boswell, Thomas D., and Curtis, James R. *The Cuban-American Experience: Culture, Images, and Perspectives* (Totowa, New Jersey, 1983)
Deutsch, Sarah *No Separate Refuge: Culture, Class, and Gender on an Anglo-Hispanic Frontier in the American Southwest, 1880–1940* (Oxford, 1987)
García, Mario T. *Mexican Americans: Leadership, Ideology, and Identity, 1930–1960* (New Haven, 1989)
Gómez Quiñones, Juan *Chicano Politics: Reality and Promise, 1940–1990* (Albuquerque, 1990)
Hendricks, Glenn *The Dominican Diaspora: From the Dominican Republic to New York City – Villagers in Transition* (New York, 1974)
López, Adalberto (ed.) *The Puerto Ricans: Their History, Culture, and Society* (Cambridge, Mass., 1980)
Moore, Joan, and Pachon, Harry *Hispanics in the United States* (Englewood Cliffs, New Jersey, 1985)
Padilla, Flix M. *Latino Ethnic Consciousness: The Case of Mexican Americans and Puerto Ricans in Chicago* (Notre Dame, 1985)
Rodríguez, Clara E. *Puerto Ricans: Born in the U.S.A.* (Boston, 1989)
West, John O. *Mexican American Folklore* (Little Rock, Ark., 1988)

Adjustment to Modernity: 1800–1992

Ben Ami, Schlomo *Fascism from Above* (Oxford, 1983)
Carr, Raymond *Spain 1808–1975* (2nd edn Oxford, 1982)
Juliá, Santos *Manuel Azaña. Una biografía política* (Madrid, 1990)
Lannon, Frances *Privilege, Persecution and Prophecy: The Catholic Church in Spain, 1875–1975* (Oxford, 1987)

Malefakis, E.E. *Agrarian Reform and Peasant Revolution in Spain* (New Haven, 1970)
Payne, Stanley *The Franco Regime 1936–1975* (Madison, 1987)
Prados de la Escosura, L. *De imperio a nación. Crecimiento y atraso económico en España (1780–1930)* (Madrid, 1988)
Preston, Paul *The Coming of the Spanish Civil War* (London, 1978)
Romero Maura, J. *La Rosa de Fuego: el obrerismo barcelonés de 1899 a 1909* (Barcelona, 1974)
Sánchez Albornoz, N. (ed.) *La modernización económica de España* (Madrid, 1985)
Thomas, Hugh *The Spanish Civil War* (revised edn London, 1965)
Varela Ortega, J. *Los amigos politicos. Partidos, elecciones y caciquismo en la Restauración (1875–1900)* (Madrid, 1977)

From Unity to Pluralism: Religion and Church

Bilinkoff, Jodi *The Avila of Saint Teresa* (1989)
Callahan, William J. *Church, Politics and Society in Spain, 1750–1874* (1984)
Christian, William A. *Local Religion in Sixteenth-Century Spain* (1981)
Clendinnen, Inga *Ambivalent Conquests: Maya and Spaniard in Yucatan, 1517–1570* (1987)
Flynn, Maureen *Sacred Charity: Confraternities and Social Welfare in Spain, 1400–1700* (1989)
Kamen, Henry *The Spanish Inquisition* (1976)
Lannon, Frances *Privilege, Persecution and Prophecy: the Catholic Church in Spain, 1875–1975* (1987)
Payne, Stanley *Spanish Catholicism: An Historical Overview* (1984)
Phelan, John Leddy *The Millennial Kingdom of the Franciscans in the New World* (2nd edn 1970)
Ricard, Robert *The Spiritual Conquest of Mexico*, trans. L.B. Simpson (1966)
Sánchez, José M. *The Spanish Civil War as a Religious Tragedy* (1987)

Another Image of the World: Spanish Art, 1500–1920

Baticle, Jeannine, and others *Zurbarán*, exhibition catalogue, Metropolitan Museum of Art (New York, 1987; expanded Spanish edition, 1988)
Baticle, Jeannine, and Marinas, Cristina *La Galerie Espagnole de Louis-Philippe au Louvre 1838–1848* (Paris, 1981)
Bottineau, Yves *El arte cortesano en la España de Felipe V (1700–1746)* (Madrid, 1986)
—*L'Art de cour dans l'Espagne des Lumières, 1746–1808* (Paris, 1986)
Brown, Jonathan *The Golden Age of Painting in Spain* (New Haven and London, 1991)
—*Velázquez, Painter and Courtier* (New Haven and London, 1986)
Brown, Jonathan, and Elliott, J.H. *A Palace for a King: The Buen Retiro and the Court of Philip IV* (New Haven and London, 1980)
Gassier, Pierre, and Wilson, Juliet *The Life and Complete Work of Francisco de Goya* (New York, 1971)
Kubler, George *Building the Escorial* (Princeton, 1982)

Mann, Richard E. *El Greco and his Patrons* (Cambridge, 1986)
Marías, Fernando *El largo siglo XVI* (Madrid, 1989)
Martín González, Juan J. *Escultura barroca en España* (Madrid, 1983)
Moleón Gavilanes, Pedro *La arquitectura de Juan de Villanueva. El proceso del proyecto* (Madrid, 1988)
Morán, Miguel, and Checa, Fernando *El coleccionismo en España. De la cámara de maravillas a la galería de pinturas* (Madrid, 1985)
Pérez Sánchez, Alfonso E. *Pintura española de bodegones y floreros de 1600 a Goya*, exhibition catalogue, Museo del Prado (Madrid, 1983–4)
Sambricio, Carlos *La arquitectura española de la Ilustración* (Madrid, 1986)

Joan Miró: A Retrospective, exhibition catalogue, Solomon R. Guggenheim Museum (New Haven, 1987)
Bartolomé Esteban Murillo (1617–1682), exhibition catalogue, Royal Academy of Arts (London, 1983)

The Family and Society

Altman, Ida *Emigrants and Society: Extremadura and America in the Sixteenth Century* (1989)
Chacón, Francisco (ed.) *La Familia en la España Mediterránea (siglos XV–XIX)* (1987)
Costa, Joaquín (ed.) *Derecho Consutudinario y economía popular de España* (1879)
Dillard, Heath *Daughters of the Reconquest: Women in Castilian Town Society 1100–1300* (1984)
Lockhart, James *Spanish Peru 1532–60: a Colonial Society* (1968)
Lohmann Villena, G. *Les Espinosa: une famille d'hommes d'affaires en Espagne et aux Indes à l'époque de la colonisation* (1968)
Martín, Luis *Daughters of the Conquistadores: Women of the Viceroyalty of Peru* (1983)
Martínez-Alier, Verena *Marriage, Class and Colour in Nineteenth-Century Cuba: a Study of Racial Attitudes and Sexual Values in a Slave Society* (1974)
Nadal, Jordi *La Población Española (siglos XVI a XX)* (revised edn 1984)
Redondo, Augustin (ed.) *Les Parentés Fictives en Espagne (XV–XVIIe siècle)* (1988)
Seed, Patricia *To Love, Honour and Obey in Colonial Mexico: Conflicts over Marriage Choice 1574–1821* (1988)
Socolow, S.M. *The Merchants of Buenos Aires 1778–1810: Family and Commerce* (1978)
Torras i Ribe, Josep Ma *Evolució Social i Econòmica d'una Família Catalana de l'Antic Règim: els Padró d'Igualada (1642–1862)* (1976)

The Literary Heritage

Butt, J. *Writers and Politics in Modern Spain* (London, 1978)
Franco, J. *An Introduction to Spanish-American Literature* (Cambridge, 1971)
Gallagher, D. *Modern Latin-American Literature* (Oxford, 1973)
Green, O.H. *Spain and the Western Tradition* (Madison, 1963–66)

Ife, B.W. *Reading and Fiction in Golden-Age Spain* (Cambridge, 1985)
Jones, R.O. (ed.) *A Literary History of Spain* (London, 1972)
Labanyi, J.M. *Myth and History in the Contemporary Spanish Novel* (Cambridge, 1989)
Martin, Gerald *Journeys through the Labyrinth: Latin-American Fiction in the Twentieth Century* (London, 1989)
McKendrick, M. *Cervantes* (Boston, 1980)
Parker, A.A. *The Mind and Art of Calderón* (Cambridge, 1988)
Rico, F. *The Spanish Picaresque Novel and the Point of View*, trans. Charles Davis (Cambridge, 1984)
Russell, P.E. (ed.) *Spain. A Companion to Spanish Studies* (London, 1973)

Creative Diversity

GALICIA

Aponte, Vasco de *Casas y Linajes del Reino de Galicia* (15th century)
Beramendi, J.G. *Vicente Risco no Nacionalismo Galego* (2 vols, Santiago, 1981)
Lisón-Tolosana, C. *Antropología Cultural de Galicia* (2 vols, Madrid, 1979)
López Ferreiro, A. *Galicia en el último tercio del siglo XV* (Santiago, 1883)
Menéndez Pidal, R. *Poesía juglaresca y juglares* (Madrid, 1942)
Vázquez de Parga, L., Lacarra, J.M., and Uría, J. *Las peregrinaciones a Santiago de Compostela* (3 vols, Madrid, 1948)

Historia Compostelana (12th century)

ASTURIAS

Anes, G. *Economía y sociedad en la Asturias del Antiguo Régimen* (Barcelona, 1988)
Anes, R., San Miguel Cela, J.L., Ojeda Gutierrez, G., and Nadal Oller, J. *Edad Contemporánea II. Economía y sociedad (siglos XIX–XX)* (Historia de Asturias 9, Vitoria, 1981)
Barbero, A., and Vigil, M. *La formación del feudalismo en la Península Ibérica* (Barcelona, 1978)
Barrau-Dihigo, L. *Historia política del reino asturiano (718–910)* (Gijón, 1989)
Benito Ruano, E., and Fernández Conde, F.J. *Alta Edad Media* (Historia de Asturias 4, Vitoria, 1979)
Cuartas Rivero, M. *Oviedo y el Principado de Asturias a fines de la Edad Media* (Oviedo, 1983)
Diego Santos, F. *Asturias romana y visigoda* (Historia de Asturias 3, Vitoria, 1978)
Fernández Alvarez, M., Tuero Bertrand, F., and González Novalin, J.L. *Edad Moderna II* (Historia de Asturias 6, Vitoria, 1979)
Fugier, A. *La Junta Superior de Asturias y la invasión francesa (1810–1811)* (Gijón, 1989)
Gonzales y Fernández-Valles, J.M. *Asturias Protohistórica* (Historia de Asturias 2, Vitoria, 1979)
Jorda Cerda, F. *Prehistoria* (Historia de Asturias 1, Vitoria, 1978)

Madrid Alvarez, J.C. de la *El viaje de los emigrantes asturianos a América* (Gijón, 1989)
Martínez Cachero, L.A. *La emigración asturiana a América* (Gijón, 1976)
Mateo del Peral, D., García San Miguel, L., González Muñiz, M.A., Diaz Nosty, B., and Baragaño Alvarez, R. *Edad Contemporánea I. De la caída del Antiguo Régimen a la Guerra Civil* (Historia de Asturias 8, Vitoria, 1981)
Ocampo Suarez-Valdes, J. *Campesinos y artesanos en la Asturias preindustrial (1750–1850)* (Gijón, 1990)
Ruiz de la Peña Solar, J.I. *Baja Edad Media* (Historia de Asturias 5, Vitoria, 1979)
Sánchez Albornoz, C. *Despoblación y repoblación del valle del Duero* (Buenos Aires, 1966)
—*Origenes de la nación española. Estudios críticos sobre la historia del reino de Asturias* (3 vols, Oviedo, 1972–75)
Sangrador y Vitores, M. *Historia de la administración de justicia y del antiguo gobierno del Principado* (Gijón, 1989)
Vigil, C. *Asturias monumental, epigráfica y diplomática* (2 vols, Oviedo, 1887)

THE BASQUE COUNTRY: ALAVA, GUIPUZCOA AND VIZCAYA

Aranzadi, Juan *Milenarismo vasco* (Madrid, 1981)
Barañano, Kosme Ma de, and others *Arte en el País Vasco* (Madrid, 1987)
Caro Baroja, J. *Introducción a la historia social y económica del Pueblo Vasco* (San Sebastián, 1986)
Collins, Roger *The Basques* (Oxford, 1986)
Corcuera, Javier *Origenes, ideología y organización del nacionalismo vasco, 1876–1904* (Madrid, 1979)
Extramiana, José *Historia de las guerras carlistas* (San Sebastián, 1980)
Fernández Albaladejo, P. *La crisis del Antiguo Régimen en Guipúzcoa 1766–1833* (Madrid, 1975)
García de Cortázar, Fernando, and Montero, Manuel *Diccionario de Historia del País Vasco* (2 vols, San Sebastián, 1983)
García de Cortázar, J.A., and others *Introducción a la historia medieval de Alava, Vizcaya y Guipúzcoa en sus textos* (San Sebastián, 1979)
González Portilla, M. *La formación de la sociedad capitalista en el País Vasco* (San Sebastián, 1981)
Granja, José Luis de la *Nacionalismo y II República en el País Vasco* (Madrid, 1986)
Juaristi, Jon *El linaje de Aitor* (Madrid, 1987)
Michelena, Luis *Historia de la literatura vasca* (Madrid, 1960)
Mitxelena, K. *La lengua vasca* (Durango, 1977)
Otazu, Alfonso de *El 'Igualitarismo' vasco: mito y realidad* (San Sebastián, 1973)
Unzueta, P. *Los nietos de la ira* (Madrid, 1988)

NAVARRE

Boissonade, P. *Histoire de la réunion de la Navarre à la Castille. Essai sur les relations des princes de Foix-Albret avec la France et l'Espagne (1479–1521)* (Paris, 1893)
Campion, A. *Navarra en su vida histórica. Euskeriana (Novena serie)* (Pamplona, 1929)

Caro Baroja, J. *Etnografía histórica de Navarra* (3 vols, Pamplona, 1971–72)
—*La hora Navarra del XVIII* (Pamplona, 1969)
Lacarra, J.M. *Historia del Reino de Navarra en la Edad Media* (Pamplona, 1976)
—*Historia política del reino de Navarra desde sus origenes a su incorporación a Castilla* (3 vols, Pamplona, 1972–73)
Leroy, B. *La Navarre au Moyen Age* (Paris, 1983)
Marichalar, A., and Manrique, C. *Fueros de Navarra, Vizcaya, Guipúzcoa y Alava* (San Sebastián, 1971)
Mina, M.C. *Fueros y revolución liberal en Navarra* (Madrid, 1981)
Moret, J. *Anales del Reino de Navarra* (4 vols, Tolosa, 1890)
Sánchez Albornoz, C. *Origenes del Reino de Pamplona. Su vinculación con el Valle del Ebro* (2nd edn Pamplona, 1985)

Navarra (Barcelona, 1988)

ARAGON

Armillas, J.A. (ed.) *Los aragoneses en el Nuevo Mundo* (1986)
Beltrán, A. (ed.) *Historia de Aragón* (1985–90)
Biescas, J.A. *La estructura económica de la región aragonesa* (1977)
Colás, G., and Salas, J.A. *Aragón bajo los Austrias* (1977)
Fatás, G. (ed.) *Aragón en el mundo* (1988)
Fernández Clemente, E. *Aragón contemporáneo* (1975)
—*La Ilustración Aragonesa* (1972)
Lacarra, J.M. *Aragón en el pasado* (1972)
Peiró, A., and Pinilla, V. *Nacionalismo y regionalismo en Aragón* (1981)
Ubieto, A. *Historia de Aragón* (1981–89)

Enciclopedia Temática de Aragón (1988–90)
Gran Enciclopedia Aragonesa (1978–80)
Jornadas sobre el Estado actual de los Estudios sobre Aragón (1979–85)

CATALONIA

Bisson, T.N. *The Medieval Crown of Aragon. A Short History* (Oxford, 1986)
Bonnassie, Pierre *La Catalogne, du milieu du Xe à la fin du XIe siècle. Croissance et mutations d'une société* (2 vols, Toulouse, 1975–76)
Dufourcq, C.E. *L'Espagne catalane et le Maghrib aux XIIIe et XIve siècles* (Paris, 1966)
Elliott, J.H. *The Revolt of the Catalans. A Study in the Decline of Spain* (Cambridge, 1963)
Nadal, J., and Wolff, P. (eds) *Histoire de la Catalogne* (Toulouse, 1982)
Vicens Vives, J. *Noticia de Cataluña* (Barcelona, 1954)
Vilar, Pierre *La Catalogne dans l'Espagne moderne* (3 vols, Paris, 1962)

CASTILE

Bataillon, Marcel *Erasmo y España* (Mexico-Buenos Aires, 1950)

Bennassar, Bartolomé *Valladolid en el Siglo de Oro. Una ciudad de Castilla y su entorno agrario en el siglo XVI* (Valladolid, 1989)
Carande, Ramón *Carlos V y sus banqueros* (Barcelona, 1988)
Castro, Américo *La realidad histórica de España* (Mexico, 1954)
García Sanz, Angel *Desarrollo y crisis del Antiguo Régimen en Castilla la Vieja* (Madrid, 1986)
García de Valdeavellano, Luis *Historia de las instituciones españolas* (Madrid, 1968)
Jiménez Lozano, José *Guía espiritual de Castilla* (Valladolid, 1986)
Klein, Julius *La Mesta* (Madrid, 1981)
Pérez, Joseph *La revolución de las Comunidades de Castilla (1520–1521)* (Madrid, 1977)
Ruiz Martín, Felipe *Pequeño capitalismo, gran capitalismo. Simón Ruiz y sus negocios en Florencia* (Barcelona, 1990)
Sánchez Albornoz, Claudio *España, un enigma histórico* (Buenos Aires, 1956)

Historia de Castilla y León (Valladolid, 1985–86)

VALENCIA

Burns, Robert I. *Jaume I i els valencians del segle XIII* (Valencia, 1981)
Casey, James *The Kingdom of Valencia in the Seventeenth Century* (Cambridge, 1979)
Cucó, Alfons *País i Estat: la qüestió valenciana* (Valencia, 1989)
Fuster, Joan *Nosaltres els valencians* (Barcelona, 1962)
Martínez Serrano, J.A., Reig, E., and Soler, V. *Evolución de la economía valenciana (1878–1978)* (Valencia, 1978)
Peset, Vicent *Gregori Mayans i la cultura de la Il.lustració* (Valencia-Barcelona, 1976)
Reglà, Joan *Aproximació a la història del País Valencià* (Valencia, 1968)
Sanchis Guarner, M. *La ciutat de València* (Valencia, 1972)

Història del País Valencià (3 vols, Barcelona, 1975, 1975, 1989)

ANDALUSIA

Chaunu, Pierre *Sevilla y América, Siglos XVI y XVII* (Seville, 1983)
Cuenca Toribio, José Manuel *Andalucia, Historia de un pueblo* (Madrid, 1984)
Moreno Alonso, Manuel *Historia General de Andalucia* (Seville, 1981)

Actas del I Congreso de Historia de Andalucia (9 vols, Cordoba, from 1978)
Andalucia (2 vols from *Tierras de España*, Barcelona, 1981)
Gran Enciclopedia de Andalucia (7 vols, Seville, n.d.)
Historia de Andalucia (9 vols, Barcelona, 1986)
Historia de Córdoba (4 vols, Cordoba, from 1985)
Historia de Granada (4 vols, Granada, 1983–86)
Historia de Sevilla (7 vols, Seville, revised edn from 1984)

PHOTOGRAPHIC CREDITS

References are to page numbers, followed by position on the page.

Museums and Libraries

Barcelona, Archivo de la Corona de Aragon 218 top & bottom
—Museo de Arte Moderno 99
—Museo de Historia de la Cividad 98–9, 245 top
—Picasso Museum 147
Bilbao, Fine Arts Museum 211, 235
Boston, Museum of Fine Arts 178 bottom, 209 top
Bruges, Museum Gruuthuse 44
Copenhagen, The Royal Library 47 bottom, 68 (all)
Cuzco, Regional Museum 72, 77
Edinburgh, National Gallery of Art 178 top
Escorial 22, 35 bottom, 46, 172 top, 155
Gerona, Cathedral Treasury 18 left
Granada, Cathedral Treasury 13 top left
Grenoble, Musée de Peinture 158
La Paz, Bolivia, Museo Nacional de Arte 120
León, Cathedral Treasury 35
Lima, Biblioteca Nacional 221 bottom, 196 bottom
London, British Library, 18 top, 23 left, 24 left, 26, 34, 49 bottom, 144 middle, 190, 226, 241
—National Gallery 59, 60 top, 222 top left and right
—Victoria and Albert Museum 102, 205 bottom
—The Wallace Collection 198
Los Angeles, Southwest Museum 87 bottom
Madrid, Biblioteca Nacional 102, 211, 248
—Instituto de Valencia de Don Juan 205, 209
—Museo de América 116, 122–123, 124
—Museo de Arte Moderno 99, 224
—Museo Lazaro Galdiano 209 bottom
—Museo Municipal 248
—Museo Nacional de Artes Decorativas 220–21
—Museo Romantico 98
—Prado 12 top left, 49, 51, 55, 96, 148, 150, 157, 159, 160, 162, 164, 167, 174, 174–5, 177, 179, 180–81, 218 right
—Real Accademia de S. Fernando 202
—University 173
Mexico City, Museum of Fine Arts 124 bottom
—Museo Nacional de Historia 222 bottom right, 223 top left
—Universidad de Mexico 73 bottom
Munich, Neue Pinakothek 205 below left
New York, Hunter College, Centro

de Estudios Puertorriquenos 94 bottom
—Metropolitan Museum of Art, The Wrightman Collection, 1980, 64
—Museum of Modern Art 83 bottom, 183
—Pierpont Morgan Library 19 top
Oviedo, Cathedral Library 231 top
Pamplona, Museo de Navarra 239
Paris, Bibliothèque de l'Arsenal 258–9
Pontevedra, Museum of Pontevedra 228 top
Potosi, Bolivia, Casa Real de la Moneda 73 top, 121
Princeton University Library 144 centre
Puebla, Mexico, Accademia de Bellas Artes 144 top
San Antonio, Texas, The Daughters of the Republic of Texas Library 86
San Diego, Museum of Fine Arts 179 bottom
San Marino, California, The Huntington Library 86 top
Santa Fé, Museum of New Mexico 87
Saragossa, Museo de Bellas Artes 163
Seville, Museo de Bellas Artes 113, 157 bottom left
Simancas, State Archives 47
Stuttgart, Staatsgalerie 13 bottom
Turin, Galleria Sabauda 170–1
Valencia, Museo Nacional de Ceramica 221 top
—Palacio de la Generalidad 29 bottom, 253
Valladolid, National Museum of Sculpture 141
Vich, Diocesan Museum 54
Vienna, Kunsthistorisches Museum 45, 193
Washington, National Museum of Art 167 bottom, 184
Zumaya, Zuloaga Museum 182

By courtesy of the following private individuals

Baring Brothers, London 124–5
Sir Alfred Beit, Ireland 12 bottom
Professor J.H. Elliott, Oxford 60 bottom
Palacio de Liria, Madrid 37, 50
Lidia Serrata, Victoria, Texas 126

Photographers

Ansel Adams: Trustees of The Ansel Adams Publishing Rights Trust 144 bottom
A.G.E. Fotostock, Barcelona 42, 57, 245
Anaya, 193, 245 centre, 257

Mike Andrews/Camera Press 80 bottom
Artephot/Oronoz, Paris 116, 122–23, 124, jacket subject
Bantam Books 91
Camera Press 71 below
J. Allan Cash, London 151 top
F. Catala-Roca, Barcelona 263 top
Henry Chalfant 127 centre right
Rafael Maximo Colon, New York 89 bottom, 94 top
Martha Cooper 127 centre left
Efe Grafica 106 top
Ermo/Camera Press 215 (Octavio Paz)
Editorial Everest, León 35, 138 top
Giraudon, Paris 60–61, 183
Globe Photos, New York 95
Julie Goodson-Lawes, New York 127 top left and right
Benoit Gysembergh/Camera Press 112
N. Herzog Verrey/Camera Press 235
Jacques Huillot/Camera Press 112
Martin Hürlimann 139 bottom, 151, 256
Illustrated London News 146 top and bottom
F.L. Kennett 13 top left, 141
Emily Lane, London 262
Charles Lenars, Paris 135 right
Melba Levick 128
H. Nils Loose 40, 138 bottom
Salvador Lutheroth and Y.S. Uribe, Mexico City, 124 bottom
Archivio Mas, Barcelona 12 top left and bottom, 23 bottom, 24 centre, 29, 33, 36, 36–37 bottom, 43, 45 top, 46, 49, 51, 55, 113, 148, 150, 155, 159, 160, 162, 164, 167, 173–77, 179 bottom, 180–81, 218 top, 219, 223, 224, 253
Ramón Masats *Spain from the Heights*, Lunwerg Editores 38–39, 111
Miami Information Centre 89 bottom
P. Lopez Mondejar (Ed. Viso) 193
Nicholas A.J. Philpot 260–61
Rizzoli Press/Camera Press 186
Roger-Viollet, Paris 106, 108, 109
RTVE Archivo Madrid 105
Scala, Florence 58
Beryl Sokoloff/Camera Press 215 (Carlos Fuentes)
The Spanish Tourist Information Centre 26, 103, 236–7, 250–1
Susan Griggs Agency, London 171
Sven Simon/Camera Press 215 (Vargas Llosa) 112
Wim Swaan, New York 73 top, 118–19, 120–21, 190–91, 217
Serena Vergano, Barcelona 264
M. Wolgensinger 12 top right
Photographie Yan, Toulouse titlepage, 16, 24 bottom, 25, 30 (all), 47, 150 bottom, 152, 169, 228
Earl Young/Camera Press 90

INDEX

Page numbers in italics refer to illustrations.